ASCENT TO CIVILIZATION

ASCENT TO CIVILIZATION

JOHN GOWLETT

COLLINS
8 GRAFTON STREET LONDON W1
1984

To the memory of my father,
who encouraged my love of the past.

First published in Great Britain by
William Collins Sons & Co Ltd
London · Glasgow · Sydney · Auckland
Toronto · Johannesburg

© 1984 Roxby Archaeology Limited
© Text 1984 J.A.J. Gowlett

British Library Cataloguing in Publication Data
Gowlett, John
Ascent to civilization.
1. Human evolution   2. Fossil man
1. Title
573.2   GN281

ISBN 0-00-217090-6

The book was created and produced by
Roxby Archaeology Limited
Roxby & Lindsey Press
98 Clapham Common Northside
London SW4

Printed and bound in Spain by
Tonsa, San Sebastian

Contents

Chapter I
Mankind in perspective

Civilization, a way of life unique to mankind, has been achieved only after long ages of cultural development through 2 million years of the Stone Age. Civilization cannot be rigorously defined, but it resides in the very nature of our society, in the ways that we interrelate and organize our lives. In a formal sense civilization is associated with urbanism and writing, but even today the great majority of people do not live in cities, and many who are illiterate may have civilized values.

In human society, all this depends upon our handing on ideas and systems of rules for behaviour from generation to generation. How did this pattern – which we name culture – first arise? The needs of the human hunting and gathering adaptation were crucial to the evolution of culture. Hunting and gathering, which our near-relatives, the apes, never needed to achieve, was practised for 2 million years before the appearance of agriculture and cities.

This book emphasizes continuity in man's path towards civilization. It is all too easy for us to imagine an exciting, exotic world of early hominids separated from the cultural peaks of the last 30,000 years by a long period in which not much happens. But in reality those intervening times embrace the most crucial developments in the shaping of mankind. Here, some of the major elements in that perspective are selected to illustrate the human course through the past.

A narrow street in Mohenjo-daro, Pakistan, of c. 2,000 BC, represents civilization on the domestic scale.

The principal avenue at Teotihuacán, Mexico, illustrates the formality of city planning on the grand scale (c. AD 300–650).

The foundations of civilization

The essence of a civilization lies not in bricks and mortar, but in the whole nature of a complex and well-organized society. Human culture is the ultimate foundation of civilization.

For all our many and obvious differences, we human beings are all fundamentally the same, through being members of one species, which is distinct from every other species. The characteristics which we share are not merely physical, but extend to many patterns of thought. If we ask, 'Who am I?' 'What am I doing here?' then we can at least take reassurance from knowing that these questions have been asked many times before, and will be asked many times again.

It is an important characteristic of our species that it seeks to understand what life means, and how it has come about. As far as we know, we are alone in this respect, for even if other advanced mammals such as apes and dolphins have any similar thoughts, they have never learnt to communicate them.

Fortunately, the powerful desire to understand ourselves can be met partly, though not entirely, by all those studies which put us in a wider context – studies of the heavens, of the history of the earth, and of our own evolution. Among these, archaeology is the study which allows us to trace and look at human behaviour in the past, through examining the material remains left by ancient peoples. When we

look at human behaviour and achievements, we see that there is an enormous domain which only archaeology can seek to explain, because no other means of enquiry has access to the crucial evidence.

One of the great achievements of our species is civilization – a way of life known only to mankind, which has been reached through a long process of development. Archaeology offers the best way to investigate its origins, but in the attempt to put civilization in perspective, it helps to look at a more fundamental pattern of human behaviour on which civilization is based: culture itself.

In its broadest sense, culture means all learned information which is transmitted from generation to generation, as opposed to instinctive knowledge. Culture is such an important word that it has acquired too many meanings over the years. As other animals have learned behaviour, not everybody agrees that the term culture should be restricted to man, but for most purposes it is best limited to describing human behaviour. This kind of behaviour is very highly developed in human beings, and we are far more dependent upon cultural

A stele set up by Ur-Nammu, King of Ur, in about 2,100 BC. Its frieze symbolizes the formality inherent in culture and in civilization. The king is represented drawing his authority from the god (seated). The stele originally portrayed other scenes, but it was destroyed and the fragments scattered, when the dynasty of Ur-Nammu eventually fell.

transmission than any other species. The importance of language and communication derives from this, and it is partly because there is so much to learn that growing up to adulthood takes so many years in human society.

Although culture is not easily defined, an important aspect of it involves imposing arbitrary rule systems on the environment. It is arbitrary that we drive on different sides of the road in different countries, but essential that we follow the rule correctly. It is arbitrary, too, that in some societies children take their family names from their father, but in others they take it from their mother.

Civilization represents the culmination of cultural achievement. The term is used in many ways, but essentially it implies a well-organized and ordered way of human existence. Cities and states are obvious embodiments of civilization, but clearly there are many civilized people who live outside cities, and have little to do with the state. As life in rural areas is often as well-organized and rewarding as that in cities, it can be seen that civilization is not restricted to the urban setting.

What, then, is entailed by civilization if it does not reside in bricks and mortar? In an evolutionary scheme devised by the nineteenth-century anthropologist Lewis Henry Morgan, the transition from initial 'savagery' to 'barbarism' was marked by the beginnings of food production, and then the transition from 'barbarism' to 'civilization' by the invention of writing.

Morgan's criteria were purely technological, and are scarcely concerned with social change. His scheme might have been forgotten, except that it was taken up by the weighty figures of Marx and Engels, and related to the economic 'means of production'. In contrast, V. Gordon Childe (1892–1957), an Australian who was one of the most controversial and stimulating archaeological thinkers of his generation, saw that although technology or economy were important in the rise of civilization, the most vital aspect for study was the whole evolution of society. Childe was not prepared like orthodox Marxist thinkers to lay down *a priori* rules of what *must* happen, because in his view it was the aim of archaeology to trace the actual course of events. He was able nonetheless to point out some of the principal features which are normally found in societies regarded as possessing civilization.

As a general rule, urbanism and writing would be present, but there would also occur, for example, specialization of occupations: there would be not only primary producers, such as farmers and fishers, but also professional artisans, such as carpenters and blacksmiths; then, rising up the scale, merchants, officials, priests and rulers. In such societies, social and economic power would be channelled, so that we see institutions and states. Standards would be imposed – laws and codes for the conduct of life, measures of weight, space, and time.

Many other authors have written about the nature of civilization, and we can debate whether even writing and urbanism are essential elements of it, but Childe's views are still useful. The essence of civilization lies not primarily in tangible objects, but in a host of ways of doing things, all of which are interrelated in a living society.

Underlying civilization is our character as a species. More than any other creature we look

forward, we plan, and we organize our lives by systems of rules. None of this could be achieved satisfactorily if we did not have language for communication, or technology for imposing our will on the world.

Is our claim to be civilized a fair one? The criteria mentioned above make no mention of ethics, but for most of us the ideal of civilization includes a humane approach to life. At times this is achieved in

The Ur-Nammu law code, partly preserved on a small clay tablet, is the oldest known list of laws, anticipating that of Hammurabi, which it resembles, by some 300 years. Some of the gaps can be restored tentatively from other law codes. It starts: 'Then did Ur-Nammu, the mighty man, the king of Ur, the king of Sumer and Akkad, by the power of Nanna, the city's king, and by the . . ., establish justice in the land, and by force of arms did he turn back evil and violence.' One law reads: 'If a man has severed with a weapon the . . . bone of another man, he shall pay 1 mina of silver.' The code thus emphasizes kingship, justice, and order established by force – all arbitrarily defined abstract concepts. The code of 'an eye for an eye' did not hold; a more humane compensation was imposed.

societies which are not formally civilized, and at others, sadly, it is lacking in those that are.

How did all this begin? Archaeology, for all its limitations, provides us with the best insights. It allows us to examine human behaviour in the past, even in times before there was written history. In years, prehistory is far longer than history, taking up at least 99.8 per cent of the time for which we have an archaeological record.

Human beings often impose form on the environment in a physical sense, and it is this which offers the basis for archaeology: as we shall see, many results of past actions endure almost indefinitely.

In their work, investigating and analysing the past, archaeologists work alongside many other specialists. The variety embraced by archaeology is astonishing: while the student of early man may work with palaeontologists and geologists, the student of later periods is likely to work with historians and epigraphers. In looking back to this varied past, we can catch the breath of excitement which, even after all his years of study, the American scholar James Henry Breasted (1865–1935) felt about the 'conquest of civilization': that man did this when it had *never before been done*.

The human adaptation

Hunting and gathering was the only way of obtaining food for early man for about 2 million years. Within the last 10,000 years agriculture and stock rearing have largely replaced the earlier way of life.

Human beings, like any other species, must eat in order to live, but they cannot hope to live by obtaining their food at random. In every kind of society, human beings take their food in a systematic way, which fits in with the other wants and needs of the society. In a broad sense this is what is termed an 'economy'.

Today, almost everybody in the world lives on the produce of farming, whether we eat food raw,

of the world, such as North America and Australia.

Hunting and gathering was a successful adaptation for a variety of natural environments. It was the principal economy in the course of human evolution, representing the only means of existence for at least 99 per cent of the archaeological record of over 2 million years. Although hunting and gathering has yielded to agriculture in most parts of the world during the last 10,000 years, it is

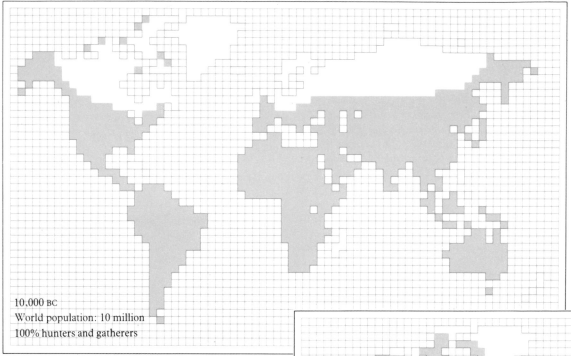

10,000 BC
World population: 10 million
100% hunters and gatherers

Hunters and gatherers occupied most of the world 10,000 years ago, but by AD 1500, they were being rapidly replaced by agriculturalists. Today they are represented by a few widely scattered communities with uncertain futures.

prepare it ourselves, or take it ready to eat from the supermarket shelf. In western civilization, as a result of technological improvement, very few people are actually needed to farm.

It is surprising, then, to find that farming for subsistence – for the immediate and direct food needs of the family – is actually the predominant occupation in the world. In most of Asia outside the USSR, in most of Africa, and much of South and Central America, the great majority of people aim first and foremost to meet their own food needs from land and livestock. Areas where subsistence farming populations are now very dense are likely to have supported this kind of economy for a long time, in our terms; but in the perspective of human evolution, it is a short time, 10,000 years at most. It is clear that subsistence farming is a relatively recent innovation because today there is still widespread evidence of a far earlier way of life: hunting and gathering.

The records of history are only good enough to allow us to look at the past two or three hundred years in many parts of the world, but this is sufficient to show that subsistence farmers have squeezed out hunters and gatherers only very recently across large areas of the world.

Good examples are the forests of Zaire, where Bantu-speaking agriculturalists (crop-growers) have put pressure upon the hunting and gathering pygmies; and southern Africa, where Hottentot pastoralists (herders of livestock) as well as Bantus constantly encroached upon the territories of the bushmen. During the same period, the great European expansion overwhelmed and pushed back the hunting and gathering economies in many parts

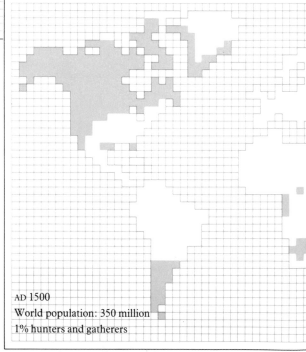

AD 1500
World population: 350 million
1% hunters and gatherers

For most hunters and gatherers, such as these pygmies of the forest of Zaire, plant food provides the bulk of the diet, and the most reliable source of food.

nevertheless the way of life which has shaped the human species.

It is dangerous to generalize about the past from any one hunting and gathering society, since the means of subsistence varies widely from group to group. We must remember too that most of the hunters and gatherers surviving until recently are confined to marginal environments, and that they may be far from typical of the mainstream of the past. We can, however, pick out in their way of life certain fundamental features which help to explain some general characteristics of our species.

First and foremost, hunters and gatherers must be able to survive on what the land offers. It is no good being able to survive ten months in the year, or nine years out of ten. Accordingly, hunters and gatherers exist at a low population density, such as the land can support. Their social structure is flexibly organized so as to allow the concentration and dispersal at different times necessary for the efficient exploitation of food resources. A typical population density for subsistence farmers could be up to hundreds per square kilometre, but for hunters and gatherers, a level of about one per square kilometre would be average.

In spite of this low density, hunters and gatherers do not spend all their time so far dispersed that they cannot operate as a society, for social life is vital for survival of the group. Here we see the key role of an ancient flexibility which we have inherited,

though it applies differently in our society. Food resources often vary from season to season. At times of plenty, the people can congregate, and carry out their social business; during the day, the men tend to go off together and hunt, while the women often stay together as a group, gathering. In each case, the group offers co-operation and protection. At times of lean resources the group must break up and disperse, and here we see the importance of the sexual pair bond and the nuclear family. The usual pattern is for male and female to stay together, and work together, aided by their children.

In practice, hunter and gatherer ways of life varied (and vary) greatly. The Nootka and Kwakiutl people of British Columbia lived mainly by fishing rich waters, and their vast long houses and splendid carvings reflect the wealth of the environment. In contrast, some Australian aborigines lived by exploiting huge areas of arid land, with little more than one or two wood or stone tools in their tool-kit. Although it is useful for archaeologists to examine modern hunter-gatherer societies, they must bear in mind that people in the distant past could have been quite different from any of the modern groups.

The skills of hunting, provide a major source of protein. Much archaeological evidence shows the past importance of hunting in many societies.

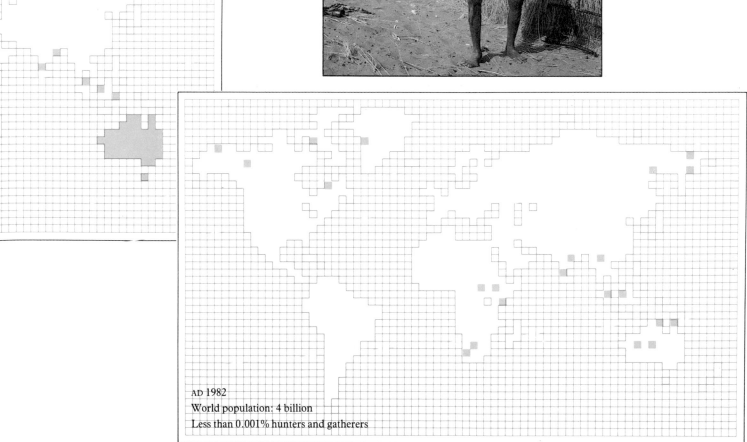

AD 1982
World population: 4 billion
Less than 0.001% hunters and gatherers

Man's place in nature

Man is one of the primates, a group of mammals which has developed during the last 70 million years. This intelligent group includes all monkeys, and the apes, our nearest living relatives.

Chromosomes, which occur in every cell, are made up of DNA and contain the genetic blueprint for an organism. Detailed similarities between particular chromosomes of man and the great apes testify to the very close relationship between the species. Certain bands of the chromosomes fluoresce when chemically stained, making it possible to see changes which have occurred since the species separated.

Where do we, who have these remarkable adaptations of cultural behaviour, belong in the world? Although we are clearly distinct in nature, in countless ways we fit in as one more member of the animal world. Our warm blood, and means of reproduction mark us out as mammals, but other features allow us to be placed much more precisely. In biological terms, man is one of the primates, the major mammalian group (technically an order) which includes monkeys and apes. This is now well known, but it was not so obvious until the relatively recent past.

Early scholars of the Western and Arab worlds came into contact mainly with monkeys, rather than apes which are restricted to fairly small areas of tropical Africa and south-east Asia. The so-called Barbary 'ape' of Gibraltar, is actually a *Cercopithecus* monkey. Thus the Swedish zoologist Carolus Linnaeus (1707–78), who is regarded as the founding father of biological classification, actually had a very poor understanding of the apes, and conjured up fantastic man- (or woman-) like creatures from unreliable reports.

Nonetheless, during the seventeenth and eighteenth centuries, actual apes began to be imported to Europe (though most of them promptly died), and their more genuine anthropoid (man-like) features were appreciated – apes are much more closely related to man than are the monkeys. The English anatomist Thomas Henry Huxley (1825–95), known as Darwin's bulldog for his support of evolutionary theory, clearly set out these shared

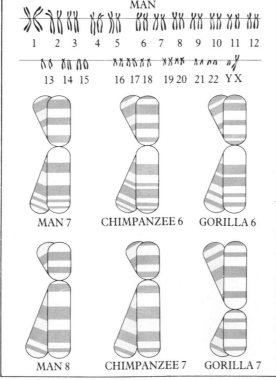

MAN

1 2 3 4 5 6 7 8 9 10 11 12

13 14 15 16 17 18 19 20 21 22 Y X

MAN 7   CHIMPANZEE 6   GORILLA 6

MAN 8   CHIMPANZEE 7   GORILLA 7

characteristics in his book *Man's Place in Nature* (1863). All members of the primates, however, display characteristics which we can see in ourselves too, making their evolutionary history particularly interesting.

Mammals can be recognized in the geological record well over 100 million years ago, but it is in the Tertiary (the last 65 million years) that they have become predominant. Specialized forms of mammals evolved to colonize every ecological niche,

including the sea. The air was also invaded. Bats have a specialized place alongside the birds, while the trees have become home to a host of mammals such as squirrels and the marsupial koalas. Many primates are arboreal – wholly adapted to life in the trees – while many others are well adapted to a foraging life on the ground, only returning to the trees for protection. The success of the primates in the tropics and sub-tropics is shown by the existence of nearly 200 species.

The earliest known fossil primates date back rather more than 70 million years. These are more like present-day lemurs and lorises than monkeys and apes. The lemurs (of Madagascar) and the lorises (of south-east Asia) are prosimians – more primitive forms of primate which have survived through isolation on an island and through specialization for nocturnal life respectively.

Monkeys make up most of the species among the modern higher primates. They are divided into New World and Old World groups which have been separate for over 30 million years and have a whole series of characteristics which reflect their very · successful adaptation to life in the trees. People watching monkeys in the zoo are fascinated to see their 'humanness'; but the features which remind us of ourselves are far older than the human race.

The monkeys' dextrous hands have the same number of digits as our own, with similar nails. As in man, their eyes are positioned close together at the front of the skull. Hand and brain co-ordination is an important aspect of higher primate evolution. The binocular, three-dimensional vision allows a much more precise judgement of distance and is useful for controlling the manipulation of objects. All primates have a relatively poor sense of smell, but this highly developed vision, which doubtless evolved because

The similarities go much beyond the skeleton. Genetic similarities can be traced, at different levels, in the DNA of the chromosomes, and in proteins. Human beings have 46 chromosomes whereas the apes have 48; but many of the individual chromosomes are remarkably similar in arrangement. Equally, it has been found that most human proteins are more than 99 per cent identical in amino-acid sequences with the corresponding protein in a chimpanzee. Blood groups too show remarkable similarities: the ABO system is clearly present in the chimpanzee, even though it includes a somewhat different content.

Now that apes are carefully observed in the wild, it can be seen that there are social similarities too. Orang-utans lead largely solitary lives, but chimpanzees and gorillas live in groups in which social relationships are carefully regulated. In gorilla groups, one large 'silver-backed' male is dominant, and other males usually leave the group as they become adult. Chimpanzee males co-exist more successfully in the group; they may not allow a strange male to join the group, but will commonly accept a female. Chimpanzees often maintain close ties with their mothers for life, and when bereaved may grieve for a long period. None of these characteristics is identical with human behaviour, but they are clearly related to it.

Apes are well able to communicate though they do not speak in a language as we do. Chimpanzee gestures frequently resemble human ones, such as a sympathetic pat on the back. When carefully taught,

Two chimpanzees work together to fish termites from their nests with twigs. Chimpanzees walk on the knuckles of their hands, an adaptation found also in the gorilla.

of the vital need not to make mistakes when moving around fast in trees. Humans and apes have exactly the same number and arrangement of teeth as Old World monkeys, even though shape, size and function are very different.

Although the apes are superficially like larger monkeys, they are much more closely related to human beings. There are only a few species of apes: the agile gibbons and siamangs of south-east Asia, which are furthest from the human line; the orang-utan of Borneo and Sumatra; and finally the African apes – the gorilla, and two closely related species of chimpanzee, the common chimpanzee (*Pan troglodytes*) and the pygmy chimpanzee (*Pan paniscus*). A whole series of shared features help to demonstrate that the apes are more closely related to us than are the monkeys – these can be seen most clearly in the gorilla and chimpanzees which are our nearest relatives of all.

The relationship shows in the skeleton. Like us, apes have lost the tail, and indeed every single bone is shared by human beings and African apes. Only their sizes and shapes have altered. Most monkeys have narrow deep chests, rather like dogs, for this suits their quadrupedal gait. Man and the apes have a flattened chest, with shoulder-blades that have rotated behind the body. This is often taken to suggest that the common ancestor, at some time in the distant past, moved by 'brachiating' – swinging arm over arm in the trees – in much the same way that the modern gibbon still moves. All the larger apes spend part of their time on the ground, and because of their bulk have to go somewhat carefully in the trees; so it seems likely that this shoulder and chest arrangement has also proved especially suitable for the process of climbing from tree to ground and back again.

Some primates are predominantly ground-living, including baboons and the gorilla. But young gorillas, at least, can and do climb trees to obtain desirable food. The human-like form of the shoulders is plainly visible here.

apes can achieve proficiency in sign language, or complex visual codes, showing that in these special circumstances they can employ symbols in their thought processes.

Chimpanzees, in particular, do not only use tools, but make them through simple processes of selection and modification. It has been shown that when fishing for termites with a twig, chimpanzees prefer certain species of plant which are most suitable for this.

How human beings differ from apes

Major evolutionary developments separate mankind from the apes. Adaptation to bipedal walking is the principal structural change, but changes in behaviour, are even more far-reaching.

Although human beings share much with the apes, there are also profound differences. We now know for certain that human ancestors have been separated from the apes for at least 6 million years and quite possibly 12 million years; and that during that time the hominids (the family of man) have followed a quite different course of evolution from the apes. It is true that human ancestors diverged from the stock of the African apes far later than their joint stock diverged from the orang-utan and gibbon ancestors (so from the gorilla's point of view, man is a closer cousin than the orang-utan). But it is the pace of evolution, and the profundity of the structural and behavioural changes which occurred, which serve to separate the hominids as a family.

How then do human beings differ from apes? A long series of features distinguishes us. Human walking is perhaps the most obvious of these. Walking involves fundamental re-engineering of the body into an arrangement different from that seen in any other primate, and hence can have evolved only because it conferred major advantages. Apes are capable of upright walking for short distances, but their anatomy does not permit it to be maintained for long periods. Upright walking and running required lengthening of the legs, a much shortened basin-like pelvis, a curved spine, and development of the arched foot with short toes. All this was a development not just of the bones, but of a whole complex of muscles, all coupled with the necessary inputs and outputs of nervous signals allowing the brain to co-ordinate and regulate a novel system of locomotion.

Human walking has sometimes been seen as a kind of weakness, since we cannot move rapidly enough to escape most predators. It offers major compensations, however, for human beings can move over long distances at a relatively fast pace, wearing down their prey. The upright posture also frees the hands, both for carrying weapons, and for carrying food and other useful objects; by raising the head height it helps to give a greater range of vision.

Human beings have almost entirely lost the coat of hair which most other mammals have. The individual hairs are still there, but they are much shorter and slighter, giving the impression of nakedness. Explanations of this have long been sought. Recent studies show that the larger a primate is, the fewer hairs it has in a given area of skin. Thus when early hominids took to an open country way of life, their coat may have already been too thin to offer full protection against the sun. The answer for an animal with an unusually active life-style was to develop an efficient cooling system not present in any other primates – perspiration from pores over the whole body surface. Loss of most of the remaining body hair would greatly help in this process. Plausible as this is, there may well have been other factors which we do not yet understand.

Although ape hands are like ours in a general way, their thumbs are less versatile, being much shorter. If you consider your own thumb, you will find that you can trace a circle with the end of it, move it to the middle of your palm and touch each separate fingertip. This allows human beings the delicate 'precision grip', such as we employ for holding a pen. Apes are only capable of a much less precise 'power grip', such as we would use when clasping a branch. This dexterity is crucial to our cultural activity and we may be sure that the brain, hand and eye have evolved to match each other.

Although we have exactly the same individual teeth as apes, their shape and chewing pattern have altered considerably. Reduction of the canine teeth is the most obvious single change. As a result we have been able to lose the gaps in the tooth-row (the diastemas) through which, in apes, the canines interlock. These changes are probably partly concerned with diet; the enamel of the chewing teeth is much thicker in man than in the African apes. Another aspect may be increased 'socialization' in man. In apes and monkeys, the canines have an important role in threat displays, and in fighting. Their reduction in man is only possible because of behavioural changes, stemming from changes in the brain and glandular system. In human beings, gestures, including the holding of weapons, have effectively replaced the canines.

Changes of the brain represent the single most important difference between apes and man. The human brain is very largely concerned with manipulating information in symbolic form: this is at the root of culture and language. It is not surprising that in our nearest relatives, the apes, we see rudiments of similar behaviour, but this does nothing to alter the deep chasm between them and us. Apes are best seen as successful apes, not second-rate human beings.

Aborigine hunters in Australia's Northern Territory. Human walking is a distinctive and efficient mode of locomotion which frees the hands for carrying objects, such as weapons.

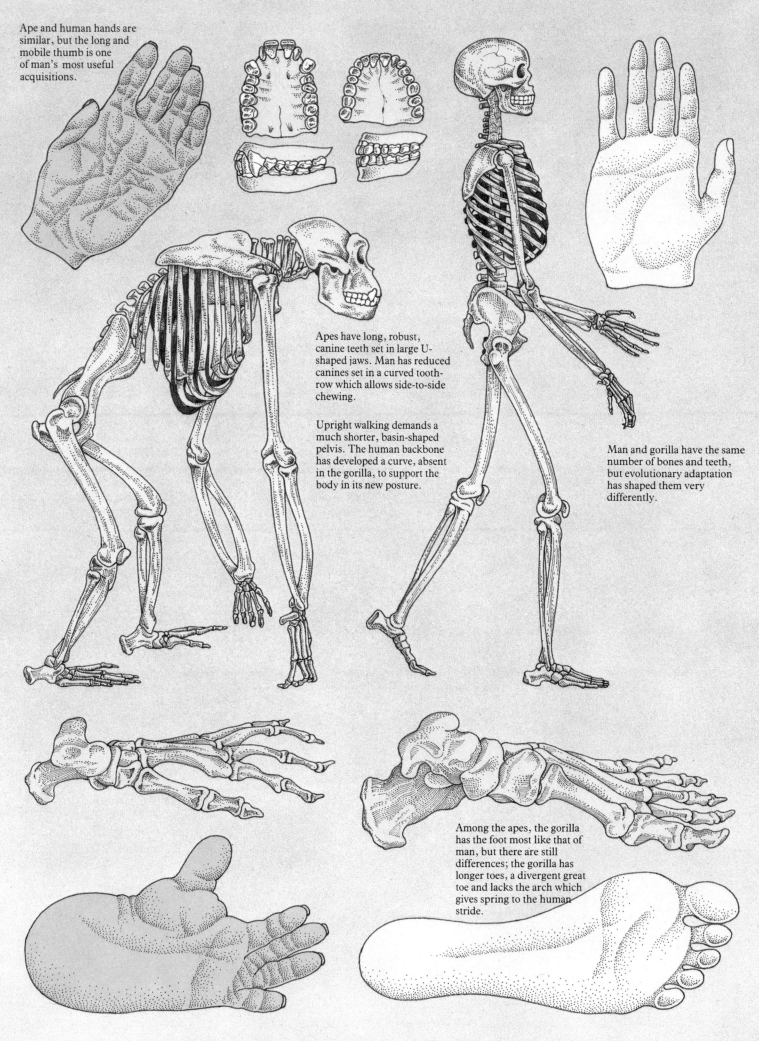

Ape and human hands are similar, but the long and mobile thumb is one of man's most useful acquisitions.

Apes have long, robust, canine teeth set in large U-shaped jaws. Man has reduced canines set in a curved tooth-row which allows side-to-side chewing.

Upright walking demands a much shorter, basin-shaped pelvis. The human backbone has developed a curve, absent in the gorilla, to support the body in its new posture.

Man and gorilla have the same number of bones and teeth, but evolutionary adaptation has shaped them very differently.

Among the apes, the gorilla has the foot most like that of man, but there are still differences; the gorilla has longer toes, a divergent great toe and lacks the arch which gives spring to the human stride.

15

Theories of
human
evolution

Many ideas have been advanced to account for the rapid evolution which has separated man from the apes; these vary from the sensible to the ridiculous. Theories about human social behaviour are important, but the evolution of man's unique ability to plan must also be explained.

In this remarkable photograph by primatologist Dr W.C. McGrew of chimpanzees in the wild, the deliberate and relaxed nature of the food-sharing between the animals is unmistakable.

Why should we have evolved as a species which is so much more intelligent than any other? The chasm dividing man from the apes is real and deep. During the last hundred years many writers have sought to grasp the essence of the remarkable distinctness of human beings.

The simplest explanation, which we inherit from the last century, is that our ancestors split away from the ape line and, under the forces of natural selection, acquired the large and marvellous brain which has made all the other developments possible. The development of language distinguished man, and language, by making rational thought possible, was the key to cultural development. In simplified terms this was the view advanced by Darwin and Huxley from the 1860s onward. If it is somewhat vague, that is hardly surprising, because at the time almost all the fossil evidence for human evolution was still undiscovered.

Many authors have found the generalized idea of natural selection insufficient to account for human evolution. They have searched for particular factors which would account for an apparently sudden move in a different evolutionary direction.

What then could be postulated as the initial 'kick' which set off evolution in the human direction? As far back as 1910 the psychologist Carveth Read produced a theory which seemed highly plausible. Man was the hunting primate, and moreover a social hunter. Hunting required successful co-operation in order to capture the prey; men therefore lived in bands, and had an obvious need for developed communication which gave rise to the development of language.

Variations of this idea have been popular ever since. A more extreme version of the story was popularized by the American writer Robert Ardrey in *The Territorial Imperative* (1960) whose thesis could be summarized as: 'Man is man, and not a chimpanzee, because for millions upon millions of evolving years we killed for a living.'

Superficially the explanation is very convincing, but it has its weaknesses. Recent studies demonstrate just how commonly chimpanzees and baboons capture and eat small animals, usually young primates or baby antelopes. We ourselves, on the other hand, are not exclusively meat-eating. Among hunters and gatherers plant foods make up to 70 per cent or more of the diet. It seems increasingly likely too, that before about 2 million years ago, hominids were too small-bodied to hunt large animals, and probably relied mainly on scavenging carcasses or catching small animals for their meat consumption.

As hominid beginnings lie much further back than any evidence for hunting, there is much scope for other theories. One theory suggests that bipedal walking, one of the most fundamental human adaptations, might be accounted for by a life-style involving a mixture of country living and regular climbing of isolated trees, to gain either food or protection. This might have been coupled with exploitation of a more extended range than that of the chimpanzee or gorilla, resulting in regular travel over substantial distances.

Another interpretation attempts to account for hominid tooth development, particularly the

reduction of the canines and the development of thick enamel. It seems possible that the hominid ancestors might have specialized in eating harder seeds and fruits which were more difficult to open and needed more chewing. These features appear too early to be linked to tool-making and food preparation. They have also evolved in *Theropithecus* baboons, which eat hard seeds.

These are plausible theories, which are put forward to explain the scanty evidence. Another approach altogether is to produce sensational explanations which avoid hard fact. Von Daniken's *Chariot of the Gods* and his subsequent books fall into this category.

Why are his theories so naive as to be ridiculous? According to Von Daniken, about 8,000 years ago our primitive and brute-like ancestors were suddenly enlightened by creatures who arrived in spaceships. This is a ludicrous suggestion for by that date all the foundations of sophisticated human behaviour were already long established. If human behaviour had been influenced from space, why should the whole course of human evolution be so obviously closely related to the rest of nature?

A slightly less far-fetched theory is that championed by Elaine Morgan in *The Aquatic Ape*. Nevertheless, it has no basis in fact. If, as she claims, we had evolved successfully in water (which is supposed to account for our losing most of our hair except on the head) why would we abandon it? Why do we not have flipper-like adaptations, like other aquatic mammals such as seals and walruses?

Social behaviour is of course of great importance in human evolution. The approach advanced by Desmond Morris in *The Naked Ape* plays on our fascination with such behaviour, especially its sexual side. He concentrates on the behaviour which we share with other species, and so tends to leave out technology and linguistic communication – in fact the critically important areas which are most in need of explanation.

Another idea to be taken much more seriously is the social importance of food-sharing. Human beings do not obtain food exclusively for themselves, but share it with others in a formal way: around a camp-fire, around a table, or through processing plants and shops. Professor Glynn Isaac of the University of California has seen this as possibly the most important single step in the differentiation of man from the apes. A weakness, as is the case with so many other arguments in this field, is that somewhat similar behaviour has been observed in chimpanzees.

These social explanations of human evolution cannot account for the complexity of the way in which we arrange our lives. We cannot dismiss culture as being just technology, peripheral to our social lives. Any theory about human evolution must seek to explain our ability to string together long sequences of actions. Social co-operation is the ultimate basis for our communication, but does not explain its refined intricacy.

The simplest general explanation is that throughout the last few million years, human ancestors have lived in demanding environments and that natural selection has constantly favoured the ability to anticipate events and actions.

The diagram on the left illustrates the close relationship of man to the apes, which is shown by biochemical evidence. This evidence does not reflect the rapid structural changes which have occurred in man, and which are probably determined by changes in 'controlling genes' – small numbers of genes which control the developmental effects of many others. The second diagram shows that human evolution has moved in a markedly different direction.

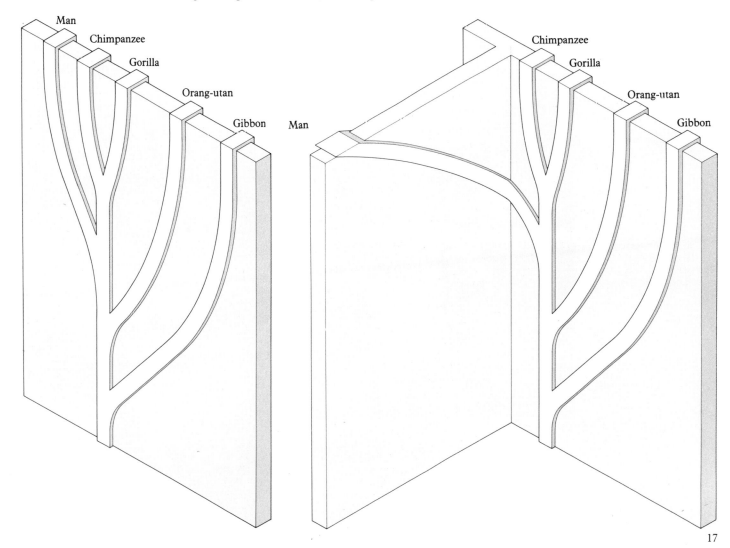

Chapter II
First signs
of humanity

The early history of the apes can be followed from about 30 million years ago, starting with finds in the Fayum area of Egypt. Much is now known about their evolutionary development, but the early stages of human divergence from the ape line are still absent from the record. Remains of *Ramapithecus*, once widely thought to represent a hominid ancestor of about 15 million years ago, are now believed by most specialists to belong to an ape line, possibly related to the orang-utan.

In the last 5 million years, the hominids do become apparent in the fossil record. Finds from the Awash Valley in Ethiopia, recently announced by Professor T. D. White and Professor J. D. Clark, promise to demonstrate that bipedal walking existed at least 4 million years ago. The important early sites of Laetoli in Tanzania and Hadar in Ethiopia have shown that the hominids of 3 million years ago certainly walked upright, and were largely human in body form, even though their brains were small, and culture had hardly begun.

The well-preserved skull of *Proconsul africanus*, a dryopithecine ape of the Miocene from Kenya.

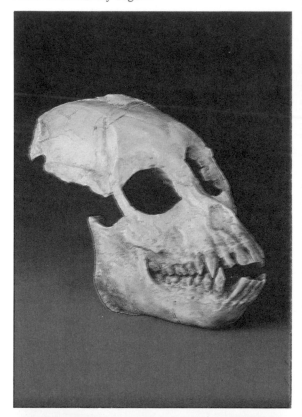

The fragmentary remains of early Miocene apes from Kenya. They include *Ramapithecus*, still regarded as a possible hominid ancestor by some authors.

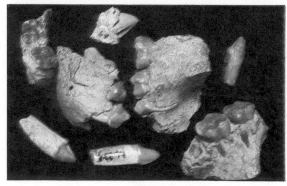

Sediments of the Pliocene sequence at Laetoli, Tanzania, where hominid remains about 3.5 million years old have been found.

Missing links

Recognizable apes first appear in the fossil record about 30 million years ago. We cannot yet tell precisely when our ancestors became separate from the ape line, but it was at least 6 million years ago.

An interpretation of the earlier stages of human evolution, showing the two possible positions of *Ramapithecus*: A, as human ancestors; B, where many anthropologists now believe them to belong as ancestors of other apes. (*Oreopithecus* and *Gigantopithecus* are fossil apes, now extinct.) C indicates the 'missing links' still to be found if B is the correct position for *Ramapithecus*. The uneven outline of the branches emphasizes the limits of our knowledge, but evolution progressed gradually.

An 8 million-year-old mandible from Lufeng, China, which is ascribed to *Ramapithecus*, may be a hominid ancestor. The canines are reduced compared to those of the apes.

There is sometimes talk of searching for the 'missing link', but if we wish to understand the whole course of human evolution, then we are looking for many such links. The living primates give us a very general idea of the course of evolution, but little clue as to the timescale.

Thus we need to look at the fossil record. In barest outline this tells us that creatures more closely resembling apes than Old World monkeys had already evolved at least 25, and perhaps even 30 million years ago. We must attempt to trace the development of these early apes, in order to find, at least approximately, the point at which an ancestral hominid, separated from them. This task is not easy because primates do not commonly become fossils, partly because the forest environments in which they lived are only occasionally preserved in the geological record, and partly because primates are less common and their bones less robust, than some other animals.

We therefore have a series of glimpses of primate evolution and there is a temptation to fill in the story from fragmentary remains according to certain expectations. Recent finds have shown the dangers of this approach because some sections of the story have had to be recast more than once.

Of critical importance in the story, because they are hardly represented elsewhere, are Oligocene sediments (about 30 million years old) preserved in the Fayum depression to the west of the Nile in Egypt. Jaws and teeth preserved here show clearly that primitive apes had begun to emerge by that time.

After the Fayum fossils, there is a gap in the record of several million years, until the next geological period, the Miocene (23–5 million years), when there is evidence of much more developed apes in Africa, Europe and Asia. These species, belonging to a group named the dryopithecines, are very clearly ape-like in their tooth arrangement; they have a characteristic fifth cusp of the molars which is present today in both apes and men – the so-called 'Y-5' pattern.

In the early Miocene in Kenya up to six dryopithecine species are found in the same deposits. This may imply that the apes were more diverse and successful at this period, occupying niches which now belong to Old World monkeys. Specific features of the best preserved specimens strongly suggest that some species of the dryopithecines are the ancestors of the living African apes.

In the earlier Miocene, then, we see real apes, but not yet separate ancestors of our own group, the hominids. But in the middle Miocene jaws and teeth have been found in India, Pakistan, Kenya, Turkey and Greece which belong to another genus, *Ramapithecus*. Unfortunately, little more than these parts of *Ramapithecus* are preserved, (jaws and teeth are the diagnostic parts which survive much the best in the fossil record). Fragmentary though the finds were, various features such as thick enamel on the molars, and relatively small forward teeth, combined to suggest that this was a possible hominid ancestor.

Although this interpretation was widely accepted, in recent years further work in Pakistan and Kenya filled in some of the gaps dramatically, and the new finds cast a different light on relationships. This has led many palaeontologists to believe that *Ramapithecus* is not after all an ancestral hominid, but that its hominid-like characteristics merely reflect evolutionary developments which happened independently a number of times over in the course of anthropoid evolution.

The recent discovery reported by Professor David Pilbeam of Yale University of an ape skull from Pakistan, about 8 million years old, helps to reinforce this suspicion. This find of *Sivapithecus*, which is much more complete than any previously known of that date, combines some features resembling *Ramapithecus* with others which closely link it with the orang-utan, such as very closely spaced eye sockets. From this evidence we may infer a great deal. Although *Sivapithecus* may not be directly ancestral to the orang-utan, it suggests that this group of apes, which included *Ramapithecus*, was already evolving in a different direction.

What then of the African apes and our own ancestry? Genetic and blood group evidence suggest that our ancestors, together with those of the gorilla and chimpanzee, belonged to a common stock for some millions of years after the orang-utan ancestors had diverged. So if it can be shown beyond doubt that *Ramapithecus*, like *Sivapithecus*, is closely related to the orang-utan, it cannot be a human ancestor. Scientists would then still be looking for evidence of the transition from the ape line to that of man, and at present there are very few finds on which to build an alternative story.

The biochemical evidence, particularly resemblances in the proteins, suggests that the hominid ancestor diverged from African ape stock fairly recently, but it is far from a perfect clock. It offers a target zone for looking for the divergence, but this could be anywhere between 6 and 15 million years ago and only the fossil record can provide the answer.

Potentially some of the most important fossils are those which were found in the mid-1970s at Lufeng, China, in deposits about 8 million years old. An almost complete mandible was ascribed to the *Ramapithecus* genus. Recently, several skulls have been found, though these have not yet been described. The mandible is said to have similarities with later hominids, such as those of Hadar in Ethiopia. It is possible that these Chinese finds do actually represent a hominid ancestor, even if the Kenyan and Pakistan *Ramapithecus* finds are on a different branch.

What other clues are there before the first plentiful hominid remains in East Africa, which are about 3.5 million years old? At present there is only a small handful of fragmentary finds including some as yet undescribed, from Kenya, north of Lake Baringo in the Rift Valley.

A piece of lower jaw from Lothagam dated to 5.5 million years indicates that the hominids were already in existence at that date, but little more can be deduced. Most tantalizing of all is a single molar tooth found at Lukeino in the Tugen Hills, aged about 6.5 million years. It has been described as having hominid characteristics, and on the basis of sophisticated statistical analysis, as representing the last common ancestor of man and chimpanzee.

Exciting as this would be, it is not altogether likely, and it has to be admitted that the early hominid story is still unclear and new finds may change the picture yet again.

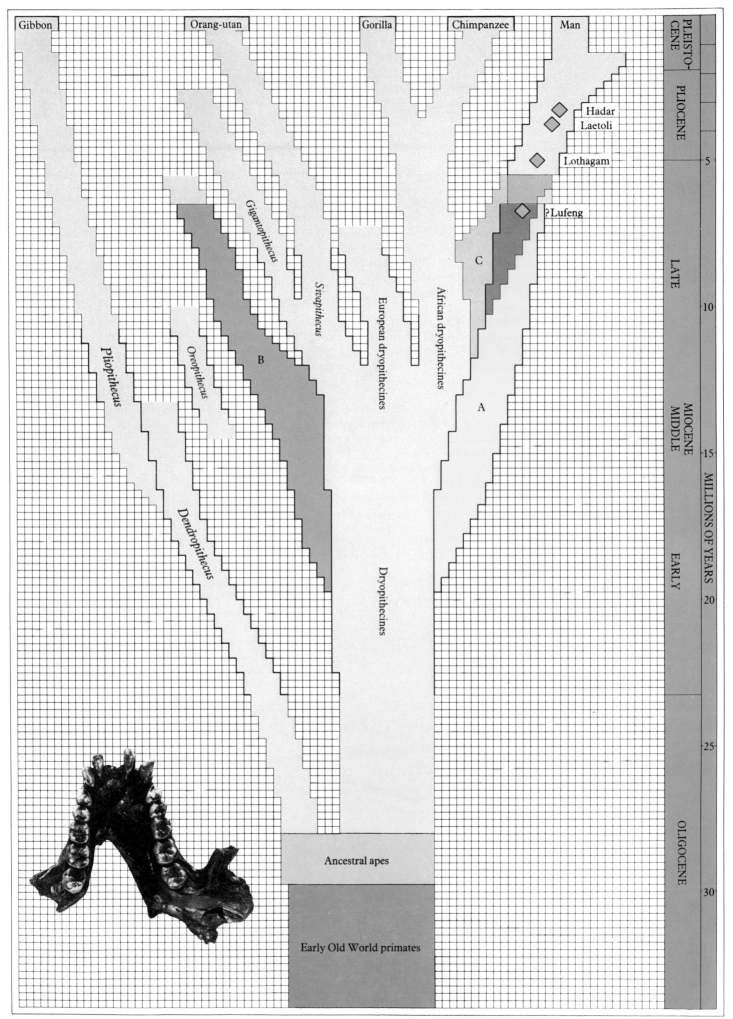

Gibbon · Orang-utan · Gorilla · Chimpanzee · Man

PLEISTO-CENE

PLIOCENE

Hadar
Laetoli
Lothagam
?Lufeng

LATE

MIOCENE

MIDDLE

EARLY

MILLIONS OF YEARS

OLIGOCENE

5

10

15

20

25

30

Gigantopithecus

Sivapithecus

European dryopithecines

African dryopithecines

Pliopithecus

Oreopithecus

Dendropithecus

B

C

A

Dryopithecines

Ancestral apes

Early Old World primates

21

How Rift Valley sites are formed

Only very rarely do circumstances combine to preserve sites for millions of years, and then expose them again by erosion, so that archaeologists can excavate them. The geology of the Rift Valley creates ideal conditions for this to happen.

When digging in your garden, you may find objects of recent date, or even a few centuries old. How deep, then, do archaeologists have to dig to discover remains that are millions of years old? The answer is straightforward: such finds are nearly always made relatively close to the surface. Probably the great majority of early fossils and surviving tools are even now buried far below the surface out of reach of investigation.

The surface of the earth can be divided into those areas where erosion is taking place and those where sediments are building up. Much the greater part of the earth's land surface is being slowly eroded at the rate of perhaps a few centimetres per thousand years. Areas of sedimentation are chiefly low-lying river valleys and estuaries, and lake basins.

Such sediments are not usually preserved indefinitely: sooner or later changes in the drainage pattern allow new streams and rivers to erode them away. The further back we go in time then, the less likely it is that sediments will still be preserved, but there is at least this compensation: some of the rare ancient sediments are being eroded away at this very moment to reveal traces of the past.

Sediments aged a few million years old are therefore accessible only in a very few places, where there have first been conditions of deposition, then long term preservation, then suitable geological changes which have started to re-excavate the sediments naturally. The uplift of huge mountains has allowed this in some areas, such as Pakistan, where many of the Miocene *Ramapithecus* finds have been made. But for the Pliocene and Pleistocene it is the East African Rift Valley which has provided some of the most spectacular circumstances of preservation.

The great Rift system extends through most of the eastern side of Africa, starting as far north as the Jordan valley, running down the Red Sea, and into East Africa. Here it separates into two branches, a western one, marking the western boundary of Uganda and Tanzania, and an eastern one, which passes through Kenya and Tanzania, eventually ending as far south as Malawi.

The Rift system originates in the splitting of the vast tectonic plate of Africa 15–20 million years ago. This splitting never progressed to the point where new plates would be created and drift apart, but where the rifting began, there has been massive faulting, coupled with immense outpourings of volcanic material. The faults are places where rocks have sheared through under stress. The largest Rift Valley faults can be measured in kilometres; the more recent faults have tended to be smaller, but are much more frequent.

The Rift has divided into many local basins, many of which have lakes in their 'sumps'. Streams fed by rain which falls on the flanks of the Rift flow down into the basins carrying sediments, mainly the breakdown products of the local lavas. Boulders and rocks are usually dropped rapidly, but sands, silts and clays each travel progressively farther, so that the finest particles settle in the lakes themselves.

Over thousands of years the sediments have built up thickly, preserving a record of past events. Although their shapes, sizes and levels may have altered through earth movements, today's lakes provide us with a good impression of the ancient environments inhabited by man. The mammal and bird life of Africa had assumed much of its present form several million years ago, though it was more varied and the early hominids had to contend with larger animals.

The margins of the Rift Valley lakes are particularly attractive areas for animal and human life, because they are generally well watered and

The Rift Valley. In the distance is Mount Longonot, a dormant volcano, such as are common along the Rift. The high slopes of the Rift have a greater rainfall than the floor thus making them suitable for agriculture.

support a variety of vegetation. The lakes are sometimes saline, as a result of evaporation, occasionally to the point that they support little life, other than flamingos feeding on algae. Even then, where rivers enter the lakes, fresher water allows the presence of animals including crocodiles, hippopotamus and large antelope (which are all frequently found as fossils). The lower courses of the streams running down to the lakes are generally thickly vegetated.

Volcanic eruptions in the Rift Valley have also contributed to the environment. At times lava flows rolled across the landscape, at others blankets of fine volcanic ash (tuff) descended. Frequently these volcanic deposits are carried down by streams so that great quantities of sediment accumulate rapidly, sometimes to depths of hundreds of metres.

For early man, the lava often provided excellent raw material for making stone tools. For geologists and archaeologists the volcanic materials reinforce the soft sediments, protecting them from erosion, and they also provide a primary means of dating by potassium-argon, which can only be applied to volcanic rocks.

The environment of the Rift was undoubtedly attractive for early man, but there is no reason to think that it is the only area of the tropics which was occupied. For instance, sediments of the Blue Nile, which form a vast fan north-west of the Ethiopian highlands, would probably provide a treasure-house of fossils, if they were near the surface. But they are actually found only in the course of major construction work.

The Rift Valley has been called a natural laboratory for the study of early man. There is much truth in this, for it brings together sediments, exposures, sites and dating evidence in sequences that have scarcely any parallel.

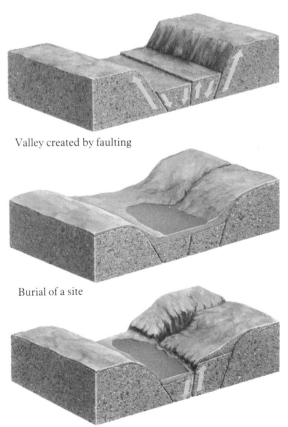

Valley created by faulting

Burial of a site

Site re-exposed by down-cutting

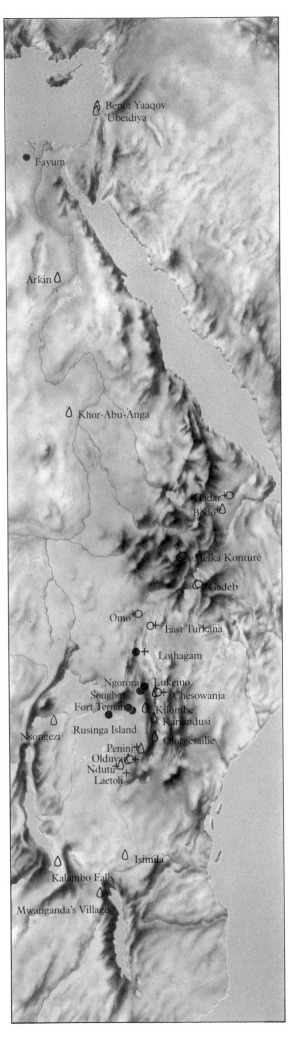

This map shows the major archaeological sites in the Rift Valley from the River Jordan in the north, to the Malawi Rift in the south. The greatest volcanic activity occurred in the areas of the Kenyan and Ethiopian domes, highlands largely consisting of lavas. Lakes are scattered along the length of the valley.

⬓ Acheulean sites

◯ Oldowan and Developed Oldowan sites

✛ Early hominid sites

⬤ Oligocene or Miocene early primate sites

Streams bring sediments down into the Rift Valley, and lakes form as the water cannot drain away. Archaeological sites buried within the sediments are often re-exposed when earth movements alter the landscape, and allow streams to cut down again.

23

Footprints

At Laetoli in Tanzania, human footprints help to show that upright walking was fully developed by 3.5 million years ago. Hominid remains and tracks of many other animals were also found.

One of the most clearly defined of the hominid footprints.

The longest trail of footprints preserved on site G at Laetoli. Along part of the trail, the prints of a second hominid are superimposed on those of the first.

Until about 1970, the twin records of fossil hominids and stone tools could be traced back only about 2 million years. At this point there was a question mark with further hints only coming from very much older finds (see pp 20–21). But during the 1970s new excavations were being carried out in several highly promising regions in east and north-east Africa and it was clear that major breakthroughs were about to be made. These sites included Omo and East Turkana in northern Kenya, Hadar in Ethiopia and Laetoli in Tanzania. Uncertainties in the dating meant that no one could be quite sure which were going to be the oldest sites with the fullest records, but that honour has, for the moment, fallen to Hadar and Laetoli. The main finds from both sites belong to the Pliocene period, which ended about 1.8 million years ago.

The Laetoli Beds are just a few kilometres south-west of the famed Olduvai Gorge, but the sediments are considerably older. Potassium-argon dates show that the fossil hominid and animal remains found there date between about 3.5 and 3.8 million years.

The hominid remains, mainly of mandibles, are somewhat scanty, but there was another discovery which cast an extremely valuable light on the early hominids. This is the famous series of hominid footprints discovered by Dr Mary Leakey's expedition of 1976. They are at least twice as old as any other known human footprints (the next oldest set at East Turkana being 1.5 million years old). The prints have now been fully studied together with the tracks of myriad other animals, which establish the context in which the early hominids lived, more effectively than any fossil bone.

What extraordinary circumstances led to the preservation of these footprints and tracks? Only

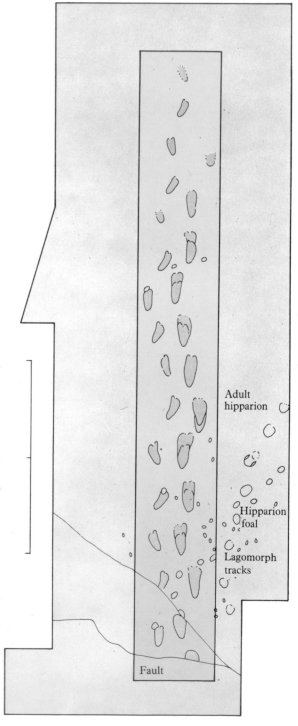

Adult hipparion

Hipparion foal

Lagomorph tracks

Fault

fairly powdery or wet material will retain an impression in the first place. At Laetoli a volcanic eruption provided such material in the form of volcanic ash (tuff) which settled over the landscape in a blanket a few centimetres thick. Dr Mary Leakey and her colleague, the geologist Professor Richard Hay, suggest that chemical processes in the tuff, together with water from rainfall (the impressions of raindrops are preserved in some places) created almost ideal conditions for impressions to be made.

Apparent slight slumping of material at the edges of the prints suggests that the tuff was still slightly powdery when they were made, rather than mud-like. There are many prints, but not many of the tracks are superimposed upon one another, or worn down. This implies that the footprint tuff was covered relatively soon by a new ash fall which sealed in the prints.

The great thrill of the hominid prints is that they do not, like bones, represent the architecture of a whole life, but specific moments from the past. The individuals who left the prints saw the dawn of that day over 1,400 million days ago and we may hope that they arrived safely at its sunset.

The footprints show the tracks of three individuals of rather different sizes (between 1.2 and 1.4 m in height). The longest track amounts to about 30 prints and we can tell that one individual walked in the prints of another, obliterating much of the detail. The tracks are leading in the same direction, and the idea that a small group of hominids walked together is appealing, though not proven.

The Laetoli footprints, together with the evidence of fossil bones from Hadar, have given entirely convincing support to the theory that early human beings already walked upright well over 3 million years ago. The footprints are clearly human in a general sense, for they do not have the diverging great toe of the apes, and show unmistakable signs of the human 'arch'. The stride and pattern of weight transmission are also human. The natural question to ask is just how human are they? There has been some suggestion that the prints show a curious gait with the feet turned out, which might be expected so far back in the history of walking. This view, however, seems to depend on the assumption that the hominids were travelling at a normal pace. Recently one group of researchers has suggested that the irregularities are consistent with human 'strolling' – slow walking such as would be likely on a slightly difficult surface. On this interpretation there is no certain evidence that walking of Laetoli hominids was any more primitive than our own.

Although this bipedal locomotion left their hands as free as ours, there is nothing to show that the Laetoli hominids made stone tools. Extensive searches have failed to locate any such tools, even though the environment would have been suitable for their use. This is negative evidence, but it agrees with the researches at Hadar, and indicates that stone tools were not in use further back than about 3 million years ago.

Nonetheless Laetoli has more information to contribute from the animal tracks which are preserved there and which give a vivid picture of the animal world in which early man lived. Over 3 million years ago the major animal groups of the African savanna had already evolved, but many animals were larger than their modern descendants. Some of the prints are 12 cm across and have been identified as belonging to a *Machairodont*, a large sabre-toothed cat; other predator tracks include those of hyenas. Perhaps equally fearsome were the elephants and rhinoceroses, of which many prints have been found. Horses, giraffes and buffaloes are all represented and even hares and birds. Actual fossil bones recovered from the area allow most of these identifications to be checked.

Although the hominid bones are chiefly mandibles and teeth, we can be reasonably sure that they belong to creatures similar to those which made the footprints, because of the much more complete skeletal remains of corresponding date found at Hadar. Similar finds to these may yet come from Laetoli, for the researches are likely to continue in such a rich area for many years.

These tracks were made by a guinea-fowl and a non-human primate.

An area of the footprint tuff at Laetoli. The track in the centre is of a *Deinotherium* (literally 'terrible animal'), an elephant-like animal. The depression behind may show the place where there was once a small pool of water.

Three million years ago

Unusually complete remains of early hominids were found at Hadar in Ethiopia in the early 1970s. They show that the human form of body had already evolved at least 3 million years ago when the head was still very ape-like.

The eastern Rift Valley continues northwards through the Ethiopian highlands and then plunges down to below sea-level as it approaches the Red Sea, itself another branch of the rift system. This area is called the Afar depression and is now known to contain abundant Pliocene and Pleistocene sediments which make it very important for studies of human evolution. As in so many places along the Rift Valley, sediments deposited along the shores of ancient lakes have re-emerged as a result of earth movements and are being actively eroded (see pp 22–23). At Hadar the deposits amounted to nearly 300 metres in thickness over a period of more than a million years.

The great potential of the area was first suspected by a French geologist, Maurice Taieb, who soon enlisted the support of an American physical anthropologist, Don Johanson, and together they mounted an expedition. The first hominid remains were discovered in 1973 near the end of their first field season, just when they were most needed – for promising finds in the early stages of a new project are vital for attracting financial support. The ideal find might be a hominid skull, but in this case it was a complete knee-joint. It came from a layer dated to over 3 million years and effectively pushed back the history of human walking by more than a million years.

During the next two years, the expedition leaders were rewarded with finds which must have exceeded their highest expectations. Remains of mandibles and a palate confirmed the presence of hominids at a primitive stage of development, and then, of supreme importance, there came the most complete skeleton yet known from any early site, the now world-famous hominid, 'Lucy'. She was named after the Beatles' song *Lucy in the Sky with Diamonds* which was played on a tape back at the camp.

Normally palaeontologists have difficulty in telling whether bones belong together as remains of an individual, except when they are found fully articulated. But with Lucy the consistency in size and shape and the lack of extraneous parts made any other explanation quite unreasonable. Fifty-two major elements are preserved, amounting to over 40 per cent of the skeleton; but since, for many parts, preservation of either right or left example of a bone provides full information about the other side, something like 80 per cent of the Lucy skeleton can be reconstructed.

Other spectacular hominid finds at Hadar come from a single site. Here the remains of at least nine adults or near-adults and four juveniles were found jumbled together. In total there were more than 200 bones.

The first explanation advanced was that a group of hominids travelling together might have fallen victim to a flash flood. In tropical Africa, many of the stream-beds are usually dry, but they may fill with water rapidly and unexpectedly if there is a sudden downpour in mountains upstream.

Although it is difficult to be sure that this is the correct explanation, the circumstances of the finds are certainly curious. There are very few remains of other animals, and no signs of the hominid bones having been chewed by carnivores. Nor are there any signs of deliberate burial. Possibly the hominid group regularly put out their dead in a single place, but the lack of damage by carnivores makes it more

The skeleton of Lucy is over 40 per cent complete, and with the use of information from other Hadar finds, almost all the skeleton can be reconstructed. The cranial vault is the least well-preserved part.

Parts present in Lucy

Parts which can be reconstructed because they are present on the opposite side.
Ribs not indicated
Few of Lucy's hand and foot bones survived, but they are fully represented in other Hadar hominids.

likely that we are viewing the results of a single catastrophe of some kind.

What do these Hadar hominids tell us about this early stage of human evolution? First they make it quite plain that human upright walking had already evolved. The body form of the Hadar hominids is almost entirely human. There are slight differences in the pelvis – Lucy, as a female, demonstrates that the pelvis had not yet had to evolve to allow the birth of a large-brained infant. The hand and foot bones were robust and strongly muscled, and the arms were still relatively long. An overriding impression is that these creatures were small (1.2–1.5 m in height), but for their size very sturdy and strong.

The head, in contrast with the body, is far from human: it is small and has been described as very ape-like. In fact the teeth are largely human in pattern, with much reduced canines; but the upper teeth still show the connection with ape ancestry, for they retain the diastema, the gap between the incisors and canines.

There is general agreement that the Hadar and Laetoli finds represent creatures either on or very close to the ancestral human line. They show that the human form of body had offered a successful adaptation long before a fully human brain had evolved.

Not surprisingly, such important finds have led to some major controversies of dating and interpretation. Initially, it was thought that the Laetoli remains were about half a million years older than those from Hadar; then revisions of the Hadar potassium-argon dates suggested that the two sites were roughly contemporary (3.5–3.8 million years old); most recently it has been shown that one of the volcanic ashes at Hadar is identical with one at East Turkana, suggesting a later date of about 3 million years, but the matter is not yet resolved.

After Hadar, there is a gap in the East African record, bridged mainly by hominid teeth from Omo in Ethiopia. There are, however, other early finds in southern Africa. In the past these have not been given the attention they deserve partly because they were first discovered in the 1920s when there was a reluctance to accept such ape-like creatures as possible human ancestors, and partly because the South African deposits could not be dated by potassium-argon as they were not volcanic. Nevertheless, the genus name *Australopithecus* (meaning 'southern ape') which is given to most of the early hominids, stems from these finds.

Recent comparisons of the fossil mammal remains from east and South Africa suggest that two of the South African sites, Sterkfontein and Makapansgat are about 3 million years old. The hominid remains from these sites are of the so-called gracile australopithecine *Australopithecus africanus*.

If the oldest of these finds are as old as the remains from Hadar, and almost as old as those from Laetoli, then, in the view of South African workers, they merit just as much consideration as possible human ancestors. These specimens of *Australopithecus africanus* share similarities with the Hadar finds, but there are differences in the molar teeth, and perhaps in other features. One suggestion is that *Australopithecus afarensis* from Hadar is just another variety of *africanus*: another view is that some of the Laetoli finds are sufficiently advanced to belong to *Homo*.

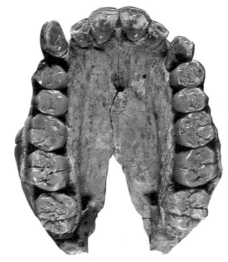

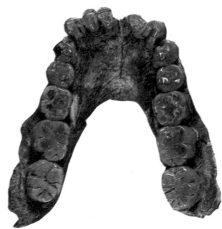

The jaws of *Australopithecus afarensis* show a basically human arrangement of the teeth, but the diastema (the gap between the canines and adjacent teeth, present in the apes) is still very visible in the upper jaw. The U-shape, with the two rows of molars running parallel, also distinguishes the finds from later man.

Working at Hadar involves long hours searching for fossils and studying the ancient sediments of the desolate 'badlands' landscape.

Dating the past

The Pliocene period (5–1.7 million years ago) is followed by the Pleistocene (1.7 million to 10,000 years ago). Recently developed scientific techniques allow increasingly precise dating. Throughout this period there were alternating periods of cold and warm climate. The Ice Age began about 3 million years ago, but glaciers advanced only from time to time, and never reached beyond temperate latitudes.

If one thing is certain, it is that in considering our early ancestors we are dealing with vast extents of time and distance and very few known sites. How then do we begin to order this evidence to make sense of it? First, we need to establish a broad framework of time.

'How old is this site?' is a basic question in archaeology, but knowing the age of a site counts for little as isolated knowledge. Some sites cannot be placed within hundreds of thousands of years, but their place in the overall picture can nonetheless be established because of the framework which has been built up.

In the last 20–30 years dating of all archaeological periods has been revolutionized. Methods provided by physics have produced an absolute framework (in which dates are expressed in calendar years), rather than a relative one (in which phases are placed in a sequence relative to one another). For the later Pliocene and the Pleistocene, the main periods of human evolution, several different dating methods interlock to provide the framework, which can often be extended by one method when another is not applicable.

The single most important absolute dating method for early periods is potassium-argon. When radioactive potassium decays it yields the gas argon at a known rate. Volcanic rocks are the only practicable material for this method; the melting associated with their formation releases the existing argon and any which is subsequently produced is trapped within the rocks. The radiogenic argon can be measured in relation to the potassium and thus an absolute date for the rocks is established.

By a series of fortunate links, the time-scale derived from potassium-argon can be connected with events in the oceans. Over millions of years, the earth's magnetic field has varied and the position of the magnetic poles has wandered. At times, they have even 'flipped' so that the north magnetic pole has moved to the south geographic pole and vice versa. Magnetic particles in rocks and sediments record the direction of the pole at the time they were laid down, so that a history of these changes can be built up. Lavas are particularly suitable materials for recording this. In one or two areas in the world, such as Hawaii, lavas have welled up so continuously that they can be dated by potassium-argon at many successive intervals so yielding the sequence of the ancient magnetic directions. In this way a basic record of magnetic events can be built up with potassium-argon providing the time-scale. As the same magnetic sequence is recognizable in cores taken from the ocean floors, these can be automatically dated to great advantage.

These cores add to our knowledge of the Pleistocene in a very important way because they provide a continuous climatic record. They are taken from the deep ocean floor where little sediment arrives from the land and where disturbance is at a minimum. The slow continuous sedimentation which occurs here consists largely of tiny skeletons of calcareous organisms and other such fine clayey particles as settle through the ocean waters. Throughout the Pleistocene, there have been cycles of climatic change, which are reflected in the cores in two ways. First, oxygen incorporated in the microscopic organisms varies in its isotopic composition (Oxygen-18 relative to Oxygen-16) approximately according to ancient temperatures; second, the proportions of carbonate and of detritus carried out from the land by wind also vary. This

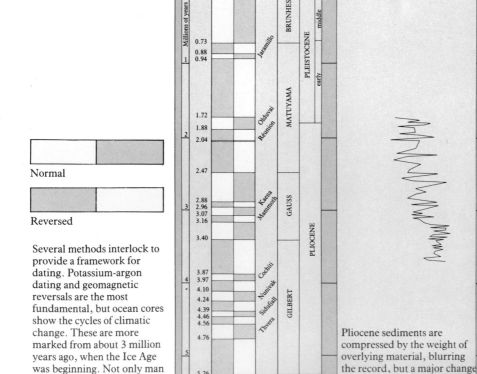

Normal

Reversed

Several methods interlock to provide a framework for dating. Potassium-argon dating and geomagnetic reversals are the most fundamental, but ocean cores show the cycles of climatic change. These are more marked from about 3 million years ago, when the Ice Age was beginning. Not only man was evolving: the successive forms of elephant and pig can help to date the archaeological sites.

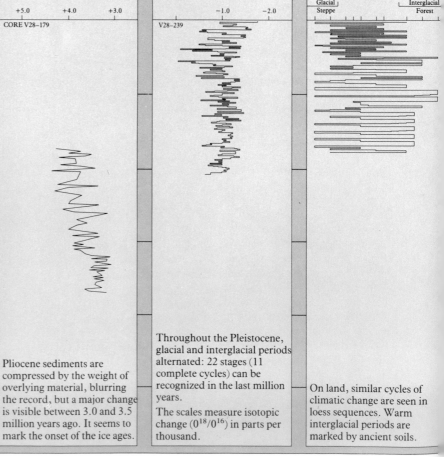

Pliocene sediments are compressed by the weight of overlying material, blurring the record, but a major change is visible between 3.0 and 3.5 million years ago. It seems to mark the onset of the ice ages.

Throughout the Pleistocene, glacial and interglacial periods alternated: 22 stages (11 complete cycles) can be recognized in the last million years.

The scales measure isotopic change (O^{18}/O^{16}) in parts per thousand.

On land, similar cycles of climatic change are seen in loess sequences. Warm interglacial periods are marked by ancient soils.

means that the cores can provide a master record of past ice age cold phases and of periods of increased wind vigour.

One major problem is in correlating dates between sites. Where sedimentation is not continuous from place to place, relative dating by stratigraphy falls down, and absolute dates cannot always be obtained.

Fortunately, several other methods may allow assessments to be made. The most generally used one is faunal dating. Animal species evolve through time, passing through distinct stages. These changes can be charted for many species, using the best dated sites. Then other sites, where absolute dating cannot be applied, can be fitted approximately into the sequence on the basis of the faunal evidence found there. This method has drawbacks for a species thought to be extinct sometimes persists unobserved; it can also be argued that environmental changes and differences may account for changes in fauna. Nonetheless, faunal evolution can pin down sites to something like the nearest quarter million years, which is very useful on the Pleistocene time-scale. The method has been especially valuable in correlating East and South African sites and has helped to highlight absolute dating discrepancies between the East African sequences.

Another valuable way of determining age is provided by studies of changes in the amino-acids in bone and teeth also known as racemization dating. Collagen, the protein which gives bone its structure, is built up in chains of amino-acids. Amino-acids occur in a 'left-handed' form in living organisms. But the arrangement of side chains around a central carbon atom also allows the possibility of right-handed amino-acids. After death, a proportion of the amino-acids converts to the right-handed form, at a measurable rate, which varies according to temperature. If one bone can be dated through association with a potassium-argon date, then the amino-acid ratios can be compared with those in other bones. In this way Professor J.L. Bada of Scripps Institution of Oceanography, California, has correlated various nearby deposits to the sequence at Olduvai Gorge.

The volcanic ashes or tuffs which allow potassium-argon dating also serve as useful marker horizons, for they may run continuously for many kilometres, and the base of a tuff should have exactly the same age everywhere it fell. Sometimes, however, breaks occur: the tuff may disappear because of a fault, or a cover of more recent deposits, or even dense vegetation. When it reappears, how does the geologist know that it is the same tuff, and not a similar one of different age? This has been such a problem that careful chemical studies have been made so that each tuff can be 'fingerprinted' through knowledge of its chemical idiosyncracies.

This technique greatly helped Richard Hay in mapping the beds at Olduvai, and very recently it has allowed precise long-distance correlations between tuffs at Hadar and those at Omo and East Turkana, a distance of over 400 km. In major volcanic eruptions, a blanket of volcanic ash may extend for several hundreds of kilometres, thereby making such correlations possible.

In the last 25 years, the dating of early sites has been revolutionized by the new methods. So far, we are fortunate when we know an age to within 10 per cent of the real value but sometimes greater accuracy and precision can be achieved, especially when several methods can be cross-checked.

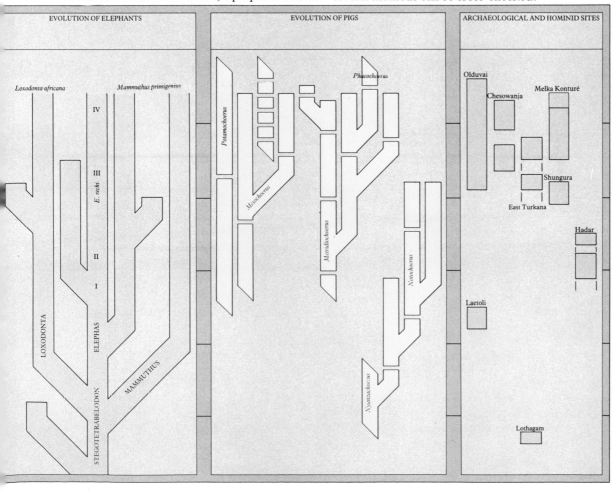

Chapter III
Enter
archaeology

Archaeology begins with the first preserved evidence of cultural activities, about 2.5 million years ago. Throughout the Old Stone Age (99 per cent of the length of the archaeological record) hunting and gathering was the only way of life. Settlements were usually flimsy camps which left flimsier traces. By looking at the camps of modern hunters and gatherers, archaeologists can learn how best to investigate and interpret the evidence of the past.

Once stone tools appear, they act as indelible markers, which guide archaeologists to the scenes of human occupation. In the Rift Valley of East Africa, a series of sites charts the course of human progress in tool-making and other activities. The use of fire now appears to date back to 1.5 million years ago, suggesting an unexpected control of the environment. The large number of archaeological finds in Africa puts an emphasis on this area, but Asia was probably equally important in the early stages of cultural evolution.

A step-trench in the Chesowanja Formation. Such trenches provide an economical way of obtaining clean vertical sections where there is an outcrop of ancient sediments.

The excavation of a site in the Shungura Formation at Omo, north of Lake Turkana. On these sites the stone tools, which are about 2 million years old, were made from tiny pebbles.

The painstaking process of excavation on an early site.

How archaeologists work

Archaeologists work with the material traces left by human activity. The earliest sites are usually found during surveys owing to the presence of stone tools. Stratigraphy is the key to understanding a site's age and how it has been preserved.

Only the later hominids can be studied from external evidence of their behaviour since, for the first time, this includes material culture which has so modified the environment as to leave a permanent record. The appearance of the earliest tools thus represents a great step forward, not just for the hominids, but for the investigation of human evolution.

The task of the archaeologist is to take that evidence and to 'squeeze' it so as to understand past life as much as possible. This is sometimes termed 'reconstructing the past', but this exaggerates what is feasible. We can certainly come to terms with the past, but it is in a simplified way because of the limited evidence and the vast spans of time involved.

Archaeologists, then, take those remaining aspects of human activity, which can be called material culture, and work with these to come to an understanding of past life. Occasionally the picture can be remarkably complete as at the town of Pompeii, Italy, which was buried by a volcanic eruption in AD 79. Almost complete buildings together with their contents are preserved in the most minute detail, and the catastrophe is described in contemporary historical accounts.

For the distant past, the archaeologist has much less to work with. Early people made little direct impression on their environment, often sleeping in the open, protected only by wind-breaks of branches, or at best flimsy huts. Their technology, too, was very simple, and consisted mainly of stone or wooden tools, probably supplemented by the use of animal products such as leather and sinews. Where the original events created such slight traces, even more careful and painstaking work is required to make the most of the surviving evidence.

We can ask what *does* enter the archaeological record? The greater part of human activity goes unrecorded, lost from the moment it happens. Nonetheless, some things are preserved. First, there are actual signs of activity, such as the Laetoli footprints, or even a fingerprint. Then there are objects which people make, ranging from the simplest stone tools to single artefacts as complex as carts or even ships. There is food refuse too, usually consisting of bones, but sometimes even plant remains. Finally, there are the more permanent surroundings which people create for themselves, at the simplest, a row of stones for supporting a wind-break, at the most elaborate, a complete city.

For the archaeologist, the individual object is of limited interest unless it comes from a well-documented archaeological site. Taken out of context, a find loses most of its value for telling us about human behaviour. The site, composed of a whole assemblage of objects in their context, remains much the most important unit of archaeological investigation.

The site is a place where human activity has led to the accumulation of the kinds of evidence mentioned above. Usually sites survive because of the deposition of sediments, as in the Rift Valley, but in some environments tools simply remain on the surface for quite long periods. Occasionally, in more recent times, human activity is responsible for the burial of earlier remains. The classic example of this is the Middle Eastern 'tell' or mound, where houses are built upon the debris of a previous settlement.

The individual site has the limitation of presenting a very local, perhaps idiosyncratic, picture. Archaeologists therefore attempt to deal with numbers of sites, investigating patterns of settlement.

In this way we can attempt to come to a balanced understanding of any period in the past. Excavations cost so much to carry out that we never arrive at a complete picture, but fortunately much information can come from surveys. These are less expensive, cover wider areas, recover more general information, and often indicate which sites can most profitably be excavated.

Patterns of settlement can often be interpreted as a result of a survey, in which a whole area is

A stone tool eroding out of sediments may provide the only sign of a site, but excavation may be necessary for understanding its context.

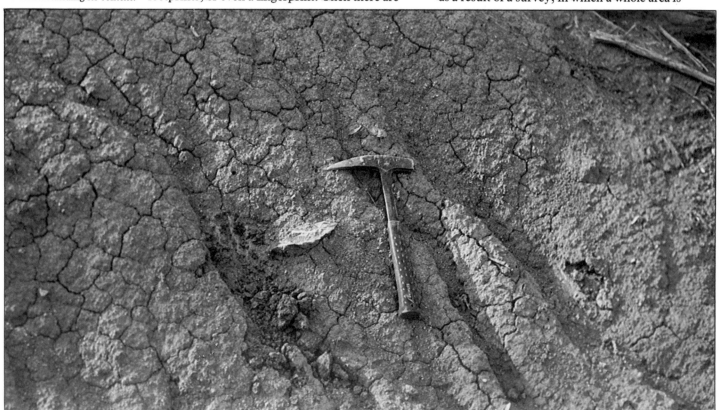

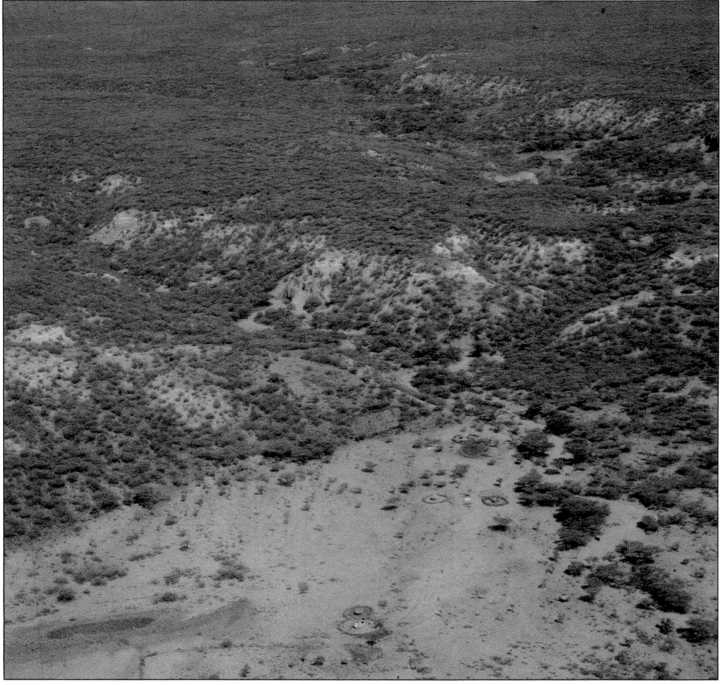

examined systematically. Certain soils may have been favoured or avoided, highlands or lowlands preferred at a certain season, and so on. Maps are fundamental tools in the survey, especially geological maps, and ideally they are used together with aerial photographs.

In early periods, it is very unusual for whole landscapes to be preserved, so there is more emphasis on the individual site; but it has become abundantly clear that one site is not necessarily like another of the same age, so every effort is made to investigate this 'variability' – a very common word in the archaeological vocabulary.

In some areas these wider patterns can also be recovered from off-site archaeology. This method, developed by archaeologists Glynn Isaac and Robert Foley, involves mapping low-density archaeological traces over large areas. This provides a kind of average pattern of those parts – perhaps ecological zones – which were most occupied by early man.

To understand such broad patterns, the archaeologist needs to put the sites in a framework of

time. Here, stratigraphy, a concept borrowed originally from geology, is the most fundamental tool of archaeological interpretation. Sediments, both geological and archaeological, build up in layers, and naturally enough the higher levels are the younger ones. From this evidence we can establish a relative sequence, even when we do not know how old the layers are in an absolute sense.

In geology, sequences may become complex as a result of erosion, tilting, fresh deposition, or volcanic intrusion. In archaeology, it is very often the quirks of human activity – such as the digging of a pit – which make the record complicated, but archaeological and geological stratigraphy are not necessarily separate. In the early parts of the Old Stone Age, archaeological sites are found as fairly minor traces within a series of geological beds, so the stratigraphy is essentially geological. In the last few thousand years, on the other hand, man-made stratigraphy sometimes becomes dominant with, for example, the formation of city mounds which may be many metres thick.

In this aerial photograph of the Rift Valley steep slopes, bare of vegetation, show where Pleistocene sediments are being eroded as rivers cut down. Such exposures are rewarding areas for survey.

The present – a key to the past

'Ethnoarchaeology' can provide insights into the processes – natural and artificial – operating on archaeological sites. When temporary camp-sites are abandoned, they are subject to gradual decay.

Most archaeologists have sufficient knowledge of urban environments to have some success in interpreting their archaeological remains. But when dealing with a hunter-gatherer society, archaeologists have to cope with investigating flimsy traces of an unfamiliar culture. We cannot even be sure that the earliest people were true hunters and gatherers. Scavenging meat from carcases may have been more important than hunting. Nor can we assume that the sites are true camp-sites.

Any direct analogy between modern hunter-gatherers and societies represented in the archaeological evidence would be unwise. Indeed archaeologists are well aware of the danger of comparing like with unlike, but in a general sense they can learn a great deal from any people who do not have the benefits of western technology. Modern hunters and gatherers live in ephemeral camps and like early man they are close to nature. When abandoned, their camps are subject to the same natural forces. Thus we can observe present-day peoples who live in temporary camps, to see both what they do, and what traces their activities leave. The detailed study of recent sites is sometimes called 'ethnoarchaeology'.

Archaeologists have found that it is necessary to make these studies of modern temporary camp-sites themselves, for social anthropologists are principally interested in social behaviour and ethnographic description of material culture is only a secondary aim for them.

Archaeologists who closely observe present-day hunter-gatherers or nomadic pastoralists are often shocked at how little trace of their activities passes into the archaeological record. They notice too how easily the archaeological remains can give a distorted picture of what took place.

In his studies of Turkana pastoralist people in the north of Kenya, the American archaeologist Dr Larry Robbins concentrated on documenting objects – the material culture – and made complete lists of what was in a settlement. Over 60 per cent of the material could be classed as perishable and, even more discouraging for the future archaeologist, nearly everything useful was taken away when the people moved on. In addition, Later Stone Age flints were in the top-soil so the archaeologist who had not witnessed the human activity might be in danger of confusing the two sets of remains.

In a study of modern Australian aborigines at Tikatika in Western Australia the archaeologist Richard Gould made similar points. He describes the daily routine, the tools which the men took with them for hunting and those the women used for digging up roots; then, a lingering dispute on whether a certain marriage should take place. What, if anything, of this kind of information could we expect to pass into the archaeological record? On returning to the site five months later, Gould found far more stone tools visible on the surface than when the people had been present, but this was only a sign of the wind disturbing the stratigraphy. Full reconstruction was out of the question and Gould comments on the futility of attempting it, saying of analogy, 'Here is an idea whose time has *gone*'. Analogy is especially suspect when a practice of one modern people is invoked to explain apparently similar behaviour in the past, for usually there are many other possibilities. The insights provided by ethnoarchaeology help to make archaeologists realistic about interpreting their evidence.

Another useful side of ethnoarchaeology lies in tracing how materials break up. How long do bones lie on the surface before they become fragmented? How long does an abandoned wooden hut take to collapse? What happens to the wood fuel left by a camp-fire when the people move on, for example? In one study two American researchers, Dr Kay Behrensmeyer and Dr Diane Gifford, recorded a small camp-site with a hearth near Lake Turkana which had been used by three Dassenitch men for a period of three days; over several months they were able to record what was preserved, what was washed away and how long it took for the site to be covered.

Where camps are placed and the length of time they remain depends upon the distribution of natural resources and the returns obtained from those resources. There may also be social factors, such as the need to remain together for a marriage, or to disperse because of a quarrel. Vegetable resources may be especially important: once return trips for vegetable food become too long, the camp must be moved. Generally speaking, the more concentrated the resources, the longer the site is maintained, the bigger it is, and the more likely it is that all kinds of activities will be performed there. As archaeologists may sometimes learn most from small sites where a single activity was performed, so it helps to learn from ethnographic studies when and where such activities are carried out.

It may be common sense that seasonal factors will bring a group back regularly to camp in the same place, but that to avoid the litter of previous occasions they will choose a slightly different position for the new camp. Even so, it is helpful to have this demonstrated as fact in modern camps since it is much the most reasonable explanation of some ancient site complexes.

Ethnoarchaeology certainly has lessons for the archaeologist. First and foremost it shows that we should look for sites which have been covered rapidly by fine-grained sediments. Then, we must be content to interpret the record which remains, as fully as we can, without yearning for, or inventing, all the social information which has gone for ever.

Studies of the break-up of an animal carcase help to show how the processes of decay operate in the natural world.

A modern temporary hearth at East Turkana studied by Dr Diane Gifford and Dr Kay Behrensmeyer. After the people who used the hearth had left, the process of alteration and disintegration was recorded.

Huts abandoned by man gradually disintegrate and only a small part of the evidence of the original structure passes into the archaeological record.

Excavating an early site

Each find must be recorded in the slow and painstaking process of excavating an early site. When all the finds are planned and lifted, archaeologists spend months and even years, analysing the data which have been recovered.

A stage in the excavation of a site. The grid of metre squares can be seen. Most finds are made during the course of the excavation, but smaller ones are recovered by sieving any loose earth; this earth is put into a bucket or bowl as soon as possible so that these finds are not lost.

When a site has been located, archaeologists have to decide whether it merits excavation. The decision is sometimes intuitive, but is more often based on a series of clues which suggest that this particular site is worthwhile.

For Old Stone Age sites the most important consideration, which is sometimes overlooked, is the need for a relatively undisturbed site. Only then is there the hope of dating the site accurately, understanding its various phases, and recovering useful information about what went on there.

On the surface the archaeologist will look for artefacts such as stone tools that are in the process of weathering out. If these are sharp and fresh, if there are no signs that tools of different periods have been mixed up, and if the sediments themselves are fine-grained and apparently undisturbed, this may be a good site. Even then, it may not be dug if the position or the surface finds do not suggest that some question of special interest can be answered.

When the decision to excavate has finally been made, and if prolonged work is envisaged, one of the first steps will be the mapping of a general site plan. This is of great help in getting an understanding of the site, and deciding where trenches can best be placed. The site plan can usually be achieved with quite simple surveying equipment, such as stakes, strings and tapes. A plane-table (a map-board mounted on a tripod, used with a sighting instrument) is useful, since it can allow the site to be

plotted from just a small number of base points. The height of the different strata and finds is also important, so a surveyor's level is often used for measuring them, and even contouring the site if necessary. On really large excavations, the accuracy of a theodolite may be desirable, and electronic instruments are beginning to be used for making site planning faster and more accurate.

A common method on Palaeolithic open sites is to begin by placing a series of step-trenches (which run down a slope like a staircase) in promising places. These trenches provide a good clean view of all the layers, for a minimum effort in digging. The next stage might be to open up small excavations in the most interesting areas; it might then be decided to concentrate resources on a large excavation, which may even have to be carried out in a later season.

Large excavations, such as some in Bed I at Olduvai Gorge, provide an incomparably good insight into what is really happening on a site; but it is not often possible to have both one large excavation and many small ones. Most early Palaeolithic localities remain less than 1 per cent investigated in area!

As the excavation proceeds, the archaeologists' aim is to record all important information, both archaeological and geological. Naturally specialist help from geologists and sedimentologists is

Sighting from level

87 No

86 North

85 North

84 North

83 North

Surveyor's

Site Gg Jh 2001

Catalogue	Identification	Unit
FL 392	Flake (phonolite)	△
FL 393	Scraper (quartz)	△
FL 394	Flake (trachyte)	△

CATALOGUE BOOK

Date 23/8

Co-ord E/W	Co-ord N/S	Level	Orientation	O.P
114.48	83.65	99.46	70	20
114.30	83.20	99.49	150	30
113.45	83.40	99.48	200	10

PAGE OF NOTEBOOK
TUESDAY 21 AUGUST
Work continued taking west part of EH down to 97.10 and work started on taking it down to 97.00 Work slow through surveying checks

Rain in afternoon
Artefacts # 320 - 339 were lifted.
Minor irregularities in the weathered surface

FIND CARD
Site Gg Jh 2001
Catalogue #   FL   3 9 4
Class   Stone
Identification   Flake (trachyte)
Excavation Unit   △
Spit   98.50 - 98.45

Co-ordinates

1	E/W	1 1 3 4 5
2	N/S	8 3 4 0

...rain horizon in BH South were drawn in
...made at the south side of the excavation
...ess of the palaeosol and of the
...and to find line to of the underly...
482 N   481.30 N
△ 6
ARTEFACTS

desirable. This information needs to be placed in a framework, which usually takes the form of a three-dimensional grid, usually measured in metres. From the start a trench is laid out in metre squares, and the level is used to measure the corresponding vertical scale. Each metre square can be referred to individually, either by numbers or letters.

An excavator is usually given a small unit to dig, very often a single metre square (which may be dug in subdivisions, say 50 cm × 50 cm). A measured thickness, or 'spit' is then taken off this square, and all the finds are carefully recorded. The spit might be 5 – 10 cm deep, but it is very important to follow the natural stratigraphy; if two distinct layers are recognized within the spit, the finds from them must be kept separate. If this is not done the confusion of finds of different ages could be very misleading.

The tools used for digging are chosen according to the hardness of the sediments. In sands and ordinary soil, small trowels are ideal, but in harder ground a chisel-like tool is required.

Whenever possible, individual finds uncovered in the trenches have their positions plotted precisely, by three co-ordinates. Each find is given a number, which is entered in a catalogue book, and also on the bag in which the find is stored. Duplicate recording is most desirable. The materials used for storage are important, for they must last well and not contaminate the finds. Plastic bags, glass phials and metal labels meet these needs best.

The soil excavated from the site cannot be thrown away immediately, for it still contains information. It must be sieved to isolate small fragments of stone, or the remains of microfauna, such as rodent teeth. Often this can be done only by dry sieving, but water sieving is preferable, since the liquid washes away the sediments more effectively. Some of the soil is retained for other studies such as pollen analysis, sedimentological analysis, or flotation for the retrieval of tiny plant remains.

As the work proceeds, the progress is recorded day by day in the site notebooks. Features and structures are planned and photographed. Eventually, when the trench is as deep as it can go, or the archaeological layers are exhausted, the final stages of the work begin. Sections are drawn, the last finds are lifted. There then follows a period of laboratory analysis which may be much more lengthy than the fieldwork, amounting to years rather than months.

Some large excavations are continued year after year, with the danger that it can take a lifetime for the final report to be completed. Every archaeologist knows to guard against this, but most good archaeology is based on fieldwork.

Archaeologists prefer to have duplicate records – in catalogue books and for find labels. This safeguard is important because accidents can and do happen; during one excavation termites destroyed numbers of record cards during the lunch-hour. The site notebooks contain the most important general observations.

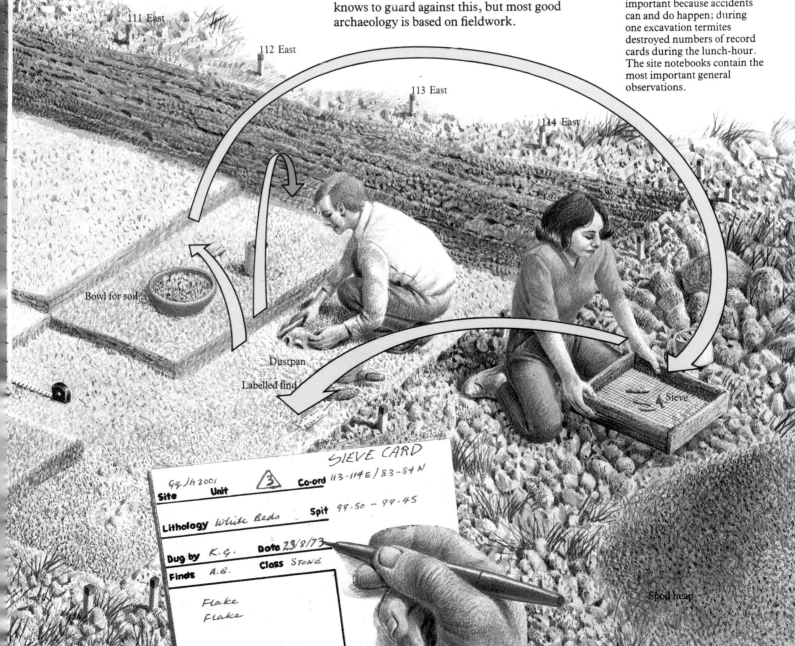

Stone tools: the indelible markers

The most enduring evidence of early man is provided by stone tools, which often indicate the presence of archaeological sites. Even very early tools would have been effective for cutting, hammering and scraping.

The term, the 'Old Stone Age', reflects the great durability of stone tools. No doubt, as the archaeologist Professor Stuart Piggott has pointed out, with different conditions of preservation we might have had an 'Old String Age'; but we have no idea how far back string was in use, because it always rots. Probably the great majority even of stone tools have perished, abraded by physical and chemical weathering – bouncing along in stream-beds, or breaking up through the action of sun, wind and

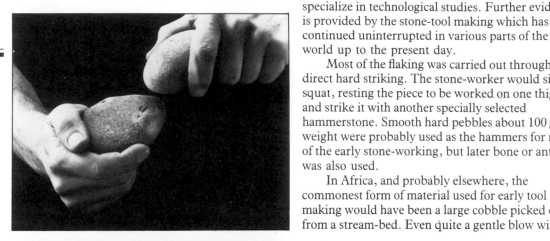

frost. But those stone tools which are rapidly buried in accumulating sediments will survive for millions of years, sometimes as fresh and sharp as when they were made.

Stone tools gave early man an abundance of convenient working edges, suitable for altering other materials, such as wood, meat or bone. The sharp edge of a flint or even a fine-grained lava, can be as keen as the best steel. It lacks flexibility, it is true, and can quite easily be broken, but stone tools can usually be replaced, because most parts of the world abound with rocks suitable for their manufacture.

Flint is often thought of as the best material, for it is sharp and fine-grained, hence relatively easy for the knapper (stone-worker) to control. But it occurs only in some areas; it is rare in Africa where the earliest tools are found, though common in Europe. Other rocks suitable for stone-working, such as fine-grained lavas, volcanic glass (obsidian), quartz, or chert may have been used long before flint.

It is common to read of 'crude chipped stone tools', but for the most part the early stone tools were not 'chipped' and are less crude than might seem at first glance. We know this because the techniques involved can be reproduced by archaeologists who specialize in technological studies. Further evidence is provided by the stone-tool making which has continued uninterrupted in various parts of the world up to the present day.

Most of the flaking was carried out through direct hard striking. The stone-worker would sit or squat, resting the piece to be worked on one thigh and strike it with another specially selected hammerstone. Smooth hard pebbles about 100 g in weight were probably used as the hammers for much of the early stone-working, but later bone or antler was also used.

In Africa, and probably elsewhere, the commonest form of material used for early tool making would have been a large cobble picked out from a stream-bed. Even quite a gentle blow with the hammerstone will strike off a flake, provided that the angles are correct. If the cobble is struck at random nothing much will happen, because the force will be absorbed. A cobble broken in half is a much better starting point, because it offers acute angles, and a piece which projects, however slightly, can be struck off. Provided that the stone-worker selects an angle of the stone which is less than 90°, the force of the blow can be transmitted through and out, and a flake produced.

This process is greatly aided by the property of 'conchoidal fracture' possessed by the stones in common use. Conchoidal means shell-like and is applied because the stone fractures in smooth curves. Hence the experienced stone-worker can

These are the major classes of tool commonly found on Oldowan sites; the tools were probably used for different tasks.

Proto-biface

Discoid

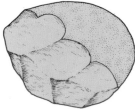

Chopper

Polyhedron

anticipate the shape of a flake with some accuracy.

Stone-working is vitally useful for the archaeologist because it displays a number of characteristic features. The flake is made by striking a particular surface – the platform – and a small area of this is usually detached with the flake, which remains recognizable. The fracture surface of the flake also has distinctive features. At the actual point of impact, there is a 'blip' or swelling, called the bulb or cone of percussion. The force transmitted from here leaves a series of concentric ripples, across the whole surface of the flake. The same features can be observed in negative form on the piece which was originally struck (the core).

Chipping is used when a flake, or core, is modified, not to create a sharp edge (for nothing is sharper than a fresh flake edge), but to have a strong, regular edge. Small flakes are struck, or chipped, from the edge in a process which archaeologists term 'retouching'.

How can human stone-working be distinguished from the effects of nature? Essentially, by the way that the striking on the stone has been effected.

Frost, heat, and collisions between stones in a river-bed can cause flaking, but it occurs at random. In contrast, even the earliest stone tools show a

use for long periods of time over huge areas. The name 'industry' is given to all the tools which are found within a limited area and timespan, and which might have been made by a single group of people. The tools belonging to an industry may have pronounced stylistic features in common – such as a particular form of scraper or point.

New industry names are usually given to each new area investigated, but there are also broader similarities which need to be recognized. Similar industries are conventionally grouped into an 'industrial tradition'. Nearly all the very early industries consist of flakes and rather globular core-forms; these can be grouped into the industrial tradition called the 'Oldowan' after Olduvai Gorge.

A small collection of basalt tools from Hadar appear to be the oldest yet known, if their estimated date of about 2.6 million years is correct. This would make the tools several hundred thousand years older than those from any other early site. A number of the Hadar tools, including choppers, were found by the French archaeologist, Hélène Roche in 1976. Later, further artefacts, mainly flakes, were found in a trench excavated under the direction of Jack Harris. Although these tools are so old, they seem already to have the basic characteristics found in the Oldowan.

systematic purposeful approach to the stone-working. A flake will often have negative impressions of previous flakes taken from the same core; retouch will be concentrated along a single edge; a core will show evidence that many flakes have been detached, often all from the same direction of striking. If a single flaked cobble is produced from a river-bed, there may be doubt about whether it was worked by man, but on an archaeological site there is no doubt.

Stone tools are invaluable markers of human activity and the great majority of early archaeological sites are found through their presence on the surface. Their similarities and differences form the basis for classifying the Old Stone Age. Similar tools were in

Manufacture of an Oldowan chopper from a cobble. In these pictures the tool-maker is left-handed.

1 As the cobble is held in the right hand, the hammerstone is brought down briskly in the left hand.

2 The instant of striking.

3 The blow carries through and a flake is detached.

4 Flakes are taken off progressively to shape the chopper.

5 A finished chopper has a sharp, wavy working edge.

6 A detached flake has characteristic features seen in negative form on the piece which was struck. The bulb of percussion is indicated by the arrow.

| Sub-spheroid | Spheroid | Heavy-duty scraper | Flake scraper | Trimmed flake |

Olduvai

The famous gorge in Tanzania provides an excellent long-term record of the Old Stone Age, from about 1.8 million years ago. It was here that the first discovery of early hominid fossils together with stone tools was made in 1959.

Olduvai Gorge was formed by a river cutting down through ancient lake sediments.

1. Nearly 2 million years ago the early hominids occupied the low-lying ground on the east shore of the lake. Materials for stone tools were brought from the isolated hills, which were sometimes as much as 10 km away.

2. Later (within the last half million years), faulting created a depression to the

east, and a stream began to cut down towards it, eventually forming the Olduvai Gorge.

3. Today the Olduvai Gorge, which cuts through the ancient lake beds and sediments deposited by rivers, is 100 metres deep and many kilometres long. A series of geological faults has displaced the beds along the length of the gorge.

1 Naibor Soit inselberg
2 Bed I lake
3 Lake margin
4 Alluvial fan
5 Volcanic highlands
6 Kelogi inselberg
7 Fault scarps
8 Masek and Ndutu Beds
9 Beds III and IV
10 Bed II
11 Bed I, sedimentary rocks
12 First fault
13 Second fault
14 Third fault
15 Fourth fault
16 Fifth fault
17 Ancient basement rocks
18 Bed I, lavas
19 Olbalbal depression

The world-famous site of Olduvai Gorge in northern Tanzania offers the most complete archaeological sequence of the last 2 million years, even though more recent discoveries have pushed the archaeological record further back in time.

Olduvai lies where volcanic highlands, formed by the tectonic activity which created the Rift Valley, border on the vast Serengeti Plains to the west. It is a gorge in the true sense – a great cleft, over 100 m deep, through Pleistocene sediments – which traverses the plains for over 15 km.

The volcanic mountains had scarcely formed when the nearby Laetoli beds were being laid down over 3 million years ago, but by the time the earliest beds with archaeological finds began to be deposited (1.8 million years ago), towering volcanoes

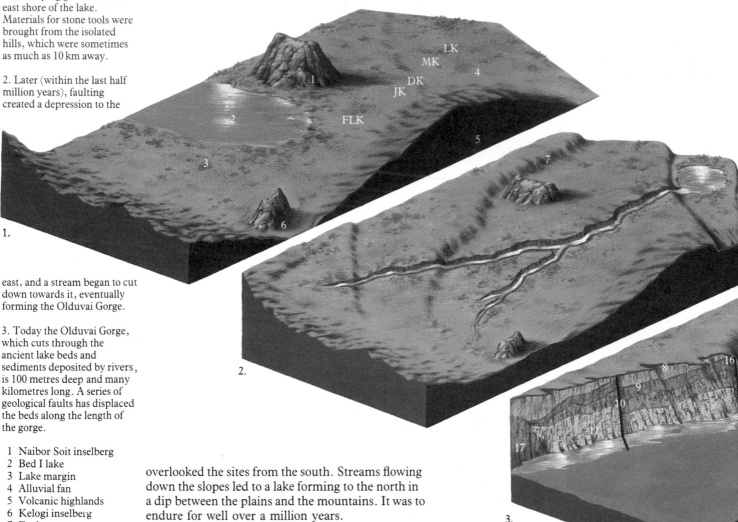

1.

2.

3.

overlooked the sites from the south. Streams flowing down the slopes led to a lake forming to the north in a dip between the plains and the mountains. It was to endure for well over a million years.

During the last 2 million years the lake basin gradually filled with sediments until major earth movements led to a whole section of land to the east dropping by over 100 m to form the Olbalbal depression. This area became the new centre of drainage, and was low enough to give a stream from the west considerable cutting power. Over perhaps 200,000 years, this stream, which runs seasonally, has cut right down through the sediments to form the gorge and is checked at present only by a resistant stratum of lava.

The unparalleled richness of the archaeological finds at Olduvai shows that the lakeside areas exposed in the gorge must have been extremely attractive to early man. Bones found on the sites show that there was an abundant animal population

too. Remains of antelope are especially common in the lower beds, together with those of crocodile and other lakeside animals. The larger antelope came to drink in the fresh streams flowing into the lake, and here they sometimes fell victim to predators. There were also giant buffaloes and sheep, whose horns have been preserved. Elephants, pigs and carnivores all existed in a greater variety than their modern counterparts.

The Olduvai Beds are divided into four main layers (Beds I–IV, from oldest to youngest) and recent geological work by geologist Richard Hay has related other younger beds to the record. The oldest Beds, I and II, alone have yielded about 70 archaeological sites, as well as hominid remains.

Lavas in Bed I have been dated to about 1.8 million years by over 50 potassium-argon dates, making this one of the best dated of all Pleistocene localities. Hay estimates that Bed I and the lower part of Bed II were laid quite rapidly, perhaps in as little as 100,000 years. There follows a significant break, with the upper part of Bed II belonging to about 1.4 million years, and Bed IV coming at about 0.7–0.8 million years.

The importance of the Olduvai sequence was recognized by the German geologist Hans Reck as early as 1913, but it was left to Louis Leakey (1903–1972) to have faith in its archaeological potential. The patience and excavating skills of his wife Dr

Mary Leakey (b.1913) have been indispensable in realizing that potential over the last 30 years.

The site which made Olduvai world-famous is 'FLK' in Bed I, aged about 1.8 million years. Here, in 1959, Dr Mary Leakey found remains of a hominid skull which attracted enormous interest worldwide. It was the first time that very early hominid remains had been discovered with stone tools, and it was also the first important site to be dated by potassium-argon. The date was three times older than many people had expected, and firmly established Africa as the main source of early finds.

The hominid was originally given a new genus name, *Zinjanthropus*, but it is now classified as *Australopithecus boisei* and is quite similar to the robust australopithecines found in South Africa. These creatures were man-like in body, but had strikingly developed teeth (see pp 46–47). In spite of these characteristics, the robusts had brains no larger than those of present-day gorillas or chimpanzees.

Soon after the discovery of *Australopithecus boisei* which had at first been thought to be the tool-maker, another find at a slightly different level cast doubt on the idea that robust australopithecines made stone tools. The new fossils were of a different species which was named *Homo habilis*. The remains were very fragmentary and on the evolutionary borderline between *Australopithecus* and *Homo*, so this designation has frequently been debated. But further finds at Olduvai and elsewhere have

remains of numerous more recent huts, including those from the later Palaeolithic of Europe. It is hardly reasonable to use the argument, as some do, that there are too many stones in the centre which would be objects of potential discomfort, because exactly the same phenomenon is seen in many later huts; it is possible that the stones could have been covered with skins or reeds. Much the most convincing explanation is that this stone circle was indeed the base of a simple hut made of branches. Its excavation must rank as one of the most important of all Stone Age discoveries.

Some of the archaeological sites show that carcases were butchered, such as Site FLK North, where an elephant skeleton and stone tools were found. All the stone tools on the early sites in Bed I and lower Bed II belong to the Oldowan tradition. The core tools include choppers, spheroids, discoids and polyhedrons, and the flake tools include scrapers. Analyses show that the most suitable raw materials tended to be selected for each category of tool. For example, chert which is fine-grained like flint and flakes well, was favoured for small sharp tools, but durable materials like quartz or lava were used for heavy compact ones. The sources of some of the raw materials can be traced accurately, showing that even in these early stages of the Oldowan, stone for tools was transported as much as 10 km. There are also interesting finds from the later beds which extend through to the last few thousand years.

Olduvai has many individual sites of unsurpassed value, but the whole gorge is also historically important. Had major discoveries not been made there in the 1950s, it is doubtful whether work on other East African sites would yet have taken place.

This jaw of *Homo habilis* provided the first certain evidence that *Australopithecus boisei* was not the only hominid type at Olduvai. The teeth of *Homo habilis* are very different in size and shape from those of the australopithecines.

The reconstructed cranium of 'Zinjanthropus' found in 1959 at Olduvai. This specimen was later classified as *Australopithecus boisei* and the photograph shows the characteristic features of this species – the wide cheek-bones, the low cranium and the sagittal crest.

A view across Olduvai Gorge; the plains are in the middle ground with the extinct volcano Lemagrut in the distance. The sequence of Beds I to IV with the more recent beds at the top is visible.

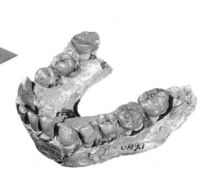

vindicated the idea that one line of hominids was becoming 'human' at this time.

The archaeological discoveries at Olduvai are as informative as the hominid remains. One of the oldest sites, named 'DK', which is at the base of Bed I, demonstrates beyond most reasonable doubts that early men were already building substantial shelters. A circle of stones, about 4 m across, provides the evidence for this conclusion (see pp 50–51). Along one side of the circle are small heaps of stones which suggest places where single branches were supported.

Curiously, much discussion about whether early man had 'home bases' ignores this crucial find. It cannot be dimissed, however, for it is very like the

The early hominids

Controversies about the early hominids often seem confusing, but there is a straightforward interpretation: early *Australopithecus* evolved into *Homo*, which was ancestral to modern man, by about 2 million years ago; a divergent branch, the robust australopithecines, existed alongside *Homo* but eventually became extinct.

The term hominid does not apply only to early man-like creatures but is used to describe all the representatives of the family of man, past and present. We ourselves are hominids. The Hominidae are unusual among biological families in being represented today by just one species (*Homo sapiens*). We thus contrast with most successful evolutionary groups, which are usually able to diversify into a range of different environments by evolving into new species able to compete and survive in each ecological niche. For example, among the primates, the Old World monkeys are represented by almost 60 species.

It would not be surprising, then, if in the past the family tree of man had possessed other branches, but as there is only one species now, we stand a reasonable chance of having had a fairly straightforward history. Equally, as the hominids have come a long evolutionary distance, we would expect some of our earlier relatives to be so different as to merit separate names, not only of species, but of genus. But the story of the first hominids can seem difficult to follow. There are a variety of reasons – the incompleteness of the fossil record, uncertainties in dating and different ideas about classification.

The point at which one species splits can be difficult to recognize precisely in the fossil record, since near the division ancestor and descendants will all be very similar. There is also another problem: in modern human beings, male and female are fairly similar in skeleton, but in the apes there can be marked differences (sexual dimorphism).

A family tree of the hominids, highlighting the period from 4–2 million years ago, where there is most controversy. Alternative interpretations are given for some of the key finds. Some authors believe that more branches existed than are shown here.

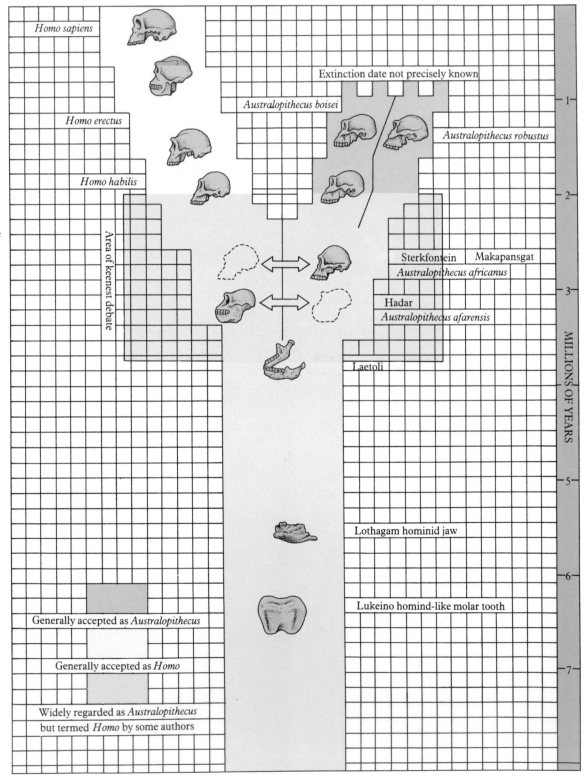

Homo sapiens

Homo erectus

Homo habilis

Extinction date not precisely known

Australopithecus boisei

Australopithecus robustus

Area of keenest debate

Sterkfontein   Makapansgat
Australopithecus africanus

Hadar
Australopithecus afarensis

Laetoli

Lothagam hominid jaw

Lukeino homind-like molar tooth

Generally accepted as *Australopithecus*

Generally accepted as *Homo*

Widely regarded as *Australopithecus* but termed *Homo* by some authors

MILLIONS OF YEARS

—1

—2

—3

—5

—6

—7

Palaeontologists must decide whether they are seeing this sexual dimorphism in their finds, or whether more than one species is represented. In spite of all these obstacles the picture of human evolution does not need to be as complex, or controversial, as is sometimes made out. It is probably a straightforward evolution from early hominid through *Australopithecus* to later *Homo*, with only one or two major side-shoots.

When early man-like remains were first found in southern Africa by Raymond Dart in 1924, he saw them not as men, but as man-like apes and gave them the name *Australopithecus* (southern ape). When such a name is first used, there are, by definition, very few finds. Later when more finds are made and an evolutionary progression becomes

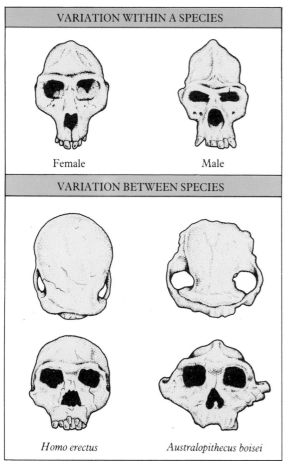

VARIATION WITHIN A SPECIES

Female   Male

VARIATION BETWEEN SPECIES

Homo erectus   *Australopithecus boisei*

apparent, argument is inevitable about where one name should cease to be applied and another start. As these controversies arise mainly from historical accidents of naming, they should not be given undue attention.

The original australopithecine finds define for us how 'unmanlike' a creature must be to merit the name *Australopithecus*. If hominid remains are as primitive (and hence probably as old) as the original South African finds, anthropologists will consider calling them *Australopithecus*.

In following the history of the hominids we are charting a gradual evolution from what is not man to what is man. The point at which we first call it 'man' is simply a matter of definition. Using the archaeology, we could say that the first stone tools show the presence of man; but in a biological definition, the first *Homo* species must be labelled from an actual hominid find.

It would be most economical to look for a single stem theory of human evolution, but, as we have

seen, there has been at least one branching in the case of the robust australopithecines. Without being too self-centered, we can look on ourselves as being the main branch, because we have survived. Where then, along the line did we become *Homo*? This has been hotly debated since the discovery of *Homo habilis* at Olduvai in 1960, which some scientists felt was merely a slightly more evolved form of the southern African *Australopithecus africanus*. Nevertheless, other finds from Olduvai, East Turkana (1470), Sterkfontein and from Modjokerto in Java all indicate a trend towards *Homo* about 2 million years ago.

Today there is the same debate about the Laetoli and Hadar fossils which are more than a million years older. Should they be classed as *Australopithecus* rather than *Homo*? Should they have been given a new species name? In reality, there is no 'should' about this, because biological classification can be changed if it is not flexible enough to deal with the real world.

If we stick to the original definitions, then the Laetoli and Hadar finds are at least as primitive as *Australopithecus* from South Africa, and so would fit into *Australopithecus* rather than *Homo*. Whether they merit a new species name (*afarensis* rather than *africanus*) depends upon very detailed studies of the evidence.

Robust australopithecines found in East and southern Africa have, so far, always belonged to the period of 1–2 million years ago, relatively late in the course of human evolution. When compared with *Homo erectus* from the same levels, it can be seen that the differences are so great that they could not possibly be contained within one species, however variable. The robusts give the impression of being specialized rather than primitive. Once this species had become committed to large teeth and massive jaw muscles, cranial enlargement might have become very difficult, as the whole architecture of the skull would have been against it. The large teeth probably indicate a low-grade diet of large quantities of vegetables and fruit. It is likely that the robust australopithecines and *Homo* had each adapted in order to exploit different ecological niches, even when living in the same general area.

When did the robusts become separated from the line leading to modern man? It was clearly after the development of the human (hominid) body form, for enough skeletal parts remain to show that they were bipedal; but it was obviously before the enlargement of the brain in the *Homo* line, since there is little sign of this in the robusts. In the South African forms there are sufficient similarities between the early *africanus* and the later *robustus* for some authors to think that the one evolved from the other fairly late (2–3 million years ago); but others feel that the separation occurred longer ago.

Whatever the exact date of the branching, it would have required a long period of time and relative isolation for the distinct characteristics of the robust species to have evolved.

On present evidence the likely course of human evolution is a straightforward gradient from *Australopithecus* to *Homo*, with one specialized side-branch of the australopithecines (the robusts) eventually becoming extinct about 1 million years ago. Further discoveries may yet compel us to take a more complex view.

Sexual dimorphism can be seen in gorilla skulls: left, a female gorilla skull and right, the skull of a large male, showing the characteristic bony crest.

The skulls of *Homo erectus*, left, and *Australopithecus boisei*, right. The completely different cranial shapes reflect different evolutionary adaptations, which rule out the possibility that the two skulls belonged to one variable species.

The extents of East Turkana

Lengthy investigations at the remote wildernesses of East Turkana have led to the discovery of large numbers of hominid remains, including the well-known 1470 cranium. Some of the earliest archaeological sites have also been found in this area.

Lake Turkana, also known as the Great Jade Sea, is enormous, more than 300 km long, and as wide as the English Channel. But its basin is larger still – it extends almost from the equator to 9° north, a vast and largely arid stretch of the eastern Rift Valley.

Expeditions in the 1920s suggested the potential of the area, but it was not until 1960 that palaeoanthropologists F. Clark Howell and C. Arambourg mounted the first major research projects to the north of the lake, in association with Louis Leakey and his son, Richard. Over a period of ten years, a major sequence was investigated at the southern end of the Omo valley, but in the meantime Richard Leakey had observed further extensive Pleistocene deposits to the east of the lake, and in 1968 started a new research project in which he was later joined by Professor Glynn Isaac as co-director. This work led to the discovery of a larger number of early hominid remains (from over 150 individuals) than had been found on any other site.

After the exciting years of discovery around Lake Turkana, what are the enduring results? The great extents of the sediments, the thoroughness with which they have been investigated, and the interaction between scientists, specializing in many different fields, have combined to give us a vastly better knowledge of the late Pliocene and early Pleistocene, the period in which the genus *Homo* was emerging.

The hominid finds from Omo bridge the gap in the fossil record from 2–3 million years ago, but they are largely isolated teeth, which can be difficult to interpret. In contrast, the hominid finds from East Turkana are remarkable for the completeness of some of the cranial remains. They demonstrate beyond all reasonable doubt that more than one hominid species existed in the early Pleistocene. Finds from South Africa (see pp 26–27, 66–67) had already suggested that two species of hominid co-existed, but some anthropologists still favoured a single species theory, with considerable variation between the sexes (sexual dimorphism). The 1470 skull, found at East Turkana in 1972, has a relatively large brain and well-rounded cranium. It is evidence of the early presence of *Homo* about 2 million years ago. It thus ranks as one of the most important hominid finds yet discovered. Later in the sequence, at about 1.5 million years, there are remains of more advanced *Homo (Homo erectus)*, and contemporary with it, remains of another type of hominid which could not possibly belong to the same species. This is the robust australopithecine, *Australopithecus boisei*. Richard Leakey and Alan Walker have suggested that in addition to the *Homo* lineage and the robust australopithecines, there was a third line of gracile (more lightly-built) australopithecines.

Lake Turkana runs along the Rift Valley for hundreds of kilometres. The main research areas are to the north and east, but Lothagam is to the south-west.

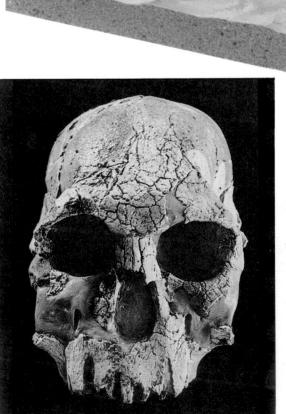

Omo river

Omo archaeological sites

The 2 million-year-old 1470 cranium; its cranial capacity, of about 775 cc, is considerably larger than that of the australopithecines.

Equally important as the hominids are the archaeological results from East Turkana and from the Shungura Formation at Omo. All these sites are at least as old as the earliest sites at Olduvai, and they offer the only available comparisons.

The Shungura Formation sites which date to about 2.0–2.2 million years may be the oldest known, apart from Hadar. On the two sites which have been excavated, tiny splinters of stone were found, associated with animal bones probably indicating a butchery site. Tiny quartz cobbles had been used to provide splinter-like flakes, apparently because no other material was available within many kilometres.

The oldest sites at East Turkana are about the same age as Olduvai Bed I, but they have yielded much smaller quantities of archaeological material – the three best-known sites have provided only 600 stone artefacts between them in contrast with many thousands at Olduvai. This does not make the evidence less valuable, for small sites can contribute very specific information, and there is very little comparative evidence from this time.

At one site, a hippopotamus skeleton was found together with artefacts. The site confirms the evidence from site FLK North at Olduvai that at times early human beings butchered the carcases of large animals, making stone tools on the spot for the purpose. On the 'hippo site' three core tools were recovered, and about 150 flakes and flake fragments. These could have been produced from this very small number of cores, and since a hammerstone and tiny flake splinters have been found, there is every chance that the tools were made at the site. The similarity of the finds with those at Olduvai suggests that this kind of butchery often took place. It is just possible that the tools and carcase could be associated by coincidence, but given the frequency of this pattern throughout the next 2 million years, it is not the most likely explanation.

A series of rather later sites, much richer in archaeological material, has been found in the Okote tuff – levels dated to about 1.5 million years. These sites were excavated under the direction of Glynn Isaac and Jack Harris. In a broad sense, these sites of the Karari Industry fit into the Oldowan, but they have distinctive features. The core tools include heavy-duty scrapers, with a characteristic keeled back. This could not have arisen by chance, but is evidently a specific design feature, although it has no obvious function. A very few hand-axes have been found in the levels of the Karari Industry but on the modern surface, suggesting though not proving a

Excavations at the 'hippo' site, showing how trenches are cut back into the sediments, to follow an archaeological horizon.

link between the Karari tools and the industrial complex which succeeds the Oldowan, the Acheulean (see pp 62–63).

As there are so many sites at East Turkana (more than 16 have been excavated), it has been possible to study variations in the finds in relation to the landscape. The sites are most abundant near to river-channels, where cobbles for raw material were readily available. But other artefacts, generally smaller and lighter in weight are found in flood-plain silts, and near the lake margin, probably far distant from raw materials. This shows that the early human beings were exploiting a range of microenvironments. It is clear that the hominids sometimes travelled considerable distances, but that when they did so, naturally enough, they tended to carry only lightweight tools. On some sites the same location was revisited more than once. This is a pattern that we shall see repeated on later sites.

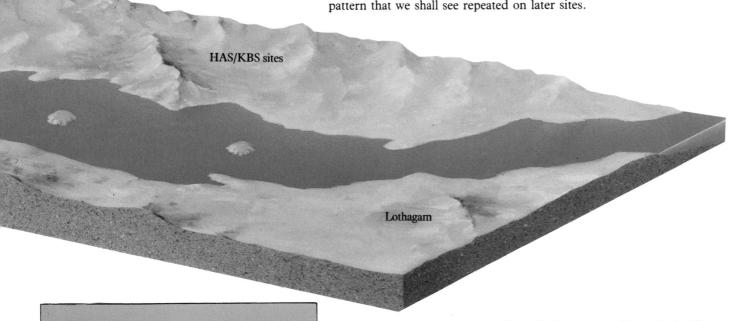

HAS/KBS sites

Lothagam

Another fascinating aspect of East Turkana is that the archaeological sites and hominid remains tend to be found in separate areas. When hominid remains are uncovered within archaeological sites, they are usually mere fragments. The most complete remains are usually in areas where sediments built up quickly and the bones were rapidly covered, so that they were preserved and protected from interference. These conditions favourable to preservation may have occurred more frequently in swampy areas which were unsuitable for human settlement, thus explaining the lack of associated archaeological evidence.

The badlands of East Turkana, created by erosion of sediments.

Chesowanja

Chesowanja complements Olduvai and other major sites, by representing several periods of time ranging from 1.5 million years to a few thousand years ago. A hearth-like feature, found together with baked clay on one site, suggests the very early use of fire.

Chesowanja in the Rift Valley of Kenya is an especially valuable site because it has evidence of at least four major Stone Age periods and is one of the few places where the earliest stone tool tradition, the Oldowan, is known.

Chesowanja is situated on the eastern flank of the Rift Valley, about half-way between Olduvai and East Turkana, which are 500 km apart. The archaeological sites at Chesowanja are in sediments which were deposited around the shores of an ancient lake in the early Pleistocene (approximately 1.8–0.7 million years ago), about 12 km to the east of the present Lake Baringo. As often happens, the sites were first discovered during geological mapping, in this case in the late 1960s. Fossil bones including those of the early hominid *Australopithecus boisei*, were first found in 1969. Then in a later survey carried out in 1973 stone tools were found.

Unlike the majestic steep-sided gorge of Olduvai and the extensive sediments of East Turkana, the Chesowanja site has all the main fossiliferous areas exposed in an area about 1 kilometre square: a mere pocket handkerchief. The ancient lake and sedimentary basin were probably much larger, but the Pleistocene lavas which are so common in the region, and which have protected the sites from erosion, have been eroded away only in small areas.

The earliest beds at Chesowanja are named the Chemoigut Formation. These consist of fine silts and clays, which were deposited around a saline lake, perhaps similar to the modern Lake Nakuru 100 km to the south.

Archaeological sites with stone tools are plentiful in these earliest levels, occurring in most areas where the sediments are exposed. Our early ancestors were probably drawn here nearly 2 million years ago by the presence of water and the variety of plant and animal resources. Most of the sites include stone tools and animal bones. The stone tools are mainly core-tools and flakes which can be included within the Oldowan, because they are similar to those found in the lower beds at Olduvai. The Oldowan finds at Chesowanja are especially interesting because robust australopithecine remains were found nearby and because evidence suggesting the use of fire was found on one of the sites.

Remains of robust australopithecines have been found at two separate places in the Chemoigut Formation, almost 1 km apart. These were of a partial cranium from one area and small fragments from the other, and enough remained to allow a clear identification of *Australopithecus boisei*. Although the instantly recognizable teeth and the heavy bone ridges on the skull which supported the chewing muscles give the name 'robust', the creatures were in fact smaller than most modern human beings, reaching a maximum of about 1.4 m in height. In both cases the remains were close to an archaeological site. From this evidence we might conclude that the australopithecines were the actual tool-makers. But there are arguments against such a conclusion. At some time after these sites were occupied – about a million years ago – the robust australopithecines became extinct, but the stone tool record continues right up to the present. Also, at two other sites, Olduvai Bed I and Swartkrans in southern Africa, early stone tools have been found together with robust australopithecine remains and remains of hominids directly ancestral to man (*Homo*

habilis or *Homo erectus*) which makes the *Homo* line a far stronger candidate to be the tool-maker.

There is another line of evidence which reinforces this view. Dr Alan Walker of Johns Hopkins University, Baltimore, USA, has conducted studies of hominid tooth-wear patterns under the electron microscope. He has observed that robust australopithecine teeth do not have the wear damage which meat-eating would cause (tiny splinters of bone leave characteristic marks). The large chewing surfaces of the teeth also indicate a low-grade diet in which large quantities of fruit or other vegetable matter are consumed. But on most of the Chesowanja sites animal bones and bone fragments are found mixed with the stone tools, suggesting very strongly that the makers of the tools were meat-eaters who butchered animal carcases.

Why then are there no actual remains of the probable tool-maker, *Homo erectus* (known from the same period at East Turkana and elsewhere), and what was the status of the robust australopithecines? The absence of direct evidence of *Homo erectus* is in fact no surprise, because it is only quite rarely that hominid remains are found in the East African archaeological sites. The majority of hominid finds are away from these temporary camp-sites which were probably inhabited for only a few days. So although there is no direct evidence of *Homo* it seems likely from the other evidence that he was there and the presence of the robust australopithecines seems to be more than coincidental association. It is possible that *Homo* hunted the australopithecines; alternatively it could be that the australopithecine remains were scavenged by *Homo*, or even that the two groups interacted socially, as chimpanzees and baboons occasionally do, in a relationship which only eventually faded out.

One of the most exciting discoveries in the Chemoigut Formation at Chesowanja was lumps of burnt clay, which were closely associated with artefacts and animal bones. The largest lumps of clay were found with an arrangement of stones which resemble 'hearths' as found on many later archaeological sites and indeed traces that can be left by a modern camp-fire. Magnetic measurements carried out on the burnt clay indicate a baking temperature in the range 400–600°C, which would be normal for a camp-fire. Chesowanja is the oldest well-dated archaeological site (1.5 million years) with definite signs of burning, which may represent the human control of fire. Who would have made such a fire? *Homo erectus* was responsible for the use of fire at Choukoutien in China (about 500,000 years ago), and it seems likely that much earlier representatives of the same type of hominid left the fire evidence at Chesowanja.

After the earliest levels had been sealed in by flows of basalt, another small lake basin was formed. Sediments began to accumulate over the basalt, rapidly at first, then more slowly as the basin filled and the lake became shallow. There is evidence of continuing human occupation which is preserved for us because of the eruption more than 700,000 years ago of a volcanic ash (tuff) which covered the area in a layer about 1 m thick.

In the top 50 cm of sediment underlying the ash, thousands upon thousands of stone tools are preserved, over an area of many hundreds of square metres. For an early site, these tools are unusual in being consistently small, rarely more than 3 or 4 cm long. It is likely that they were used to carry out one specific activity alongside the lake. The idea that we are seeing evidence of not one single hominid occupation, but of many, is supported by both the very large number of tools, and their distribution throughout 50 cm of deposit. A further indication is provided by one tool which was clearly re-used long after it had originally been made. This particular tool was worn by erosion over a long period and has been sharpened by new flaking; the two stages of use are clearly visible.

As so often, we can only speculate about the actual uses of these 'Losokweta' tools (named after a local river), which may date from as much as 1,400,000 years ago. It is clear that they were made

seemed as if the Losokweta tools included hand-axes, but these were never found in the actual excavations, which suggested that they came from later beds. But then more hand-axes were found on the surface above the tuff which seals in the Losokweta industry, proving that they came from a later phase. This was confirmed when a later stream-channel was found. Here a hand-axe was found *in situ* – crucial evidence for establishing a sequence.

The archaeological sequence at Chesowanja is completed by Later Stone Age finds which belong to the last few thousand years. These are in red silts laid down by the Mukutan River. About 50 years ago, local people diverted the river for irrigation, and the change of direction caused erosion of the sediments, revealing vast factory sites where stone tools had

This excavation in the Chesowanja Formation revealed many hundreds of small tools in a layer immediately underlying a consolidated tuff of volcanic ash (the man holding the surveying staff is standing at the base of this tuff). Laminations in the tuff indicate that it was deposited in still water, suggesting that the site itself was on a lake margin.

small by choice, since there were always plentiful local supplies of lava. It seems unlikely that butchery of animals or processing of hides was their main function, since that would entail early men consistently bringing carcases to the same place, which would be very hard work. Since there are such large numbers of tools, the regular processing of a lakeside vegetable or wood seems the most likely explanation; archaeologists have to be patient about not always knowing the precise use of tools.

The major Acheulean phase (more than 200,000 years old, see pp 62–63) is undoubtedly represented at Chesowanja, in the form of hand-axes which have been found mainly on the surface. Such surface specimens are not much help to the archaeologist, unless their origin can be traced, since they could be of almost any age. At one stage it

been made. As in the earliest times, river cobbles had served as the raw material and thousands of flakes which had been struck from them covered the ground. In among them were animal bones, providing more continuity of Stone Age evidence. New features, however, were pottery and small tools of obsidian, and it is more likely that by this time we are dealing with pastoralists rather than hunters.

Chesowanja does not offer a complete sequence of the past, any more than other sites. However, it does offer a whole series of glimpses of human activity from the earliest periods to the present. Only a tiny percentage of the available area has been excavated so there may be important future discoveries which will answer more questions about the evolution and behaviour of early man during the Stone Age.

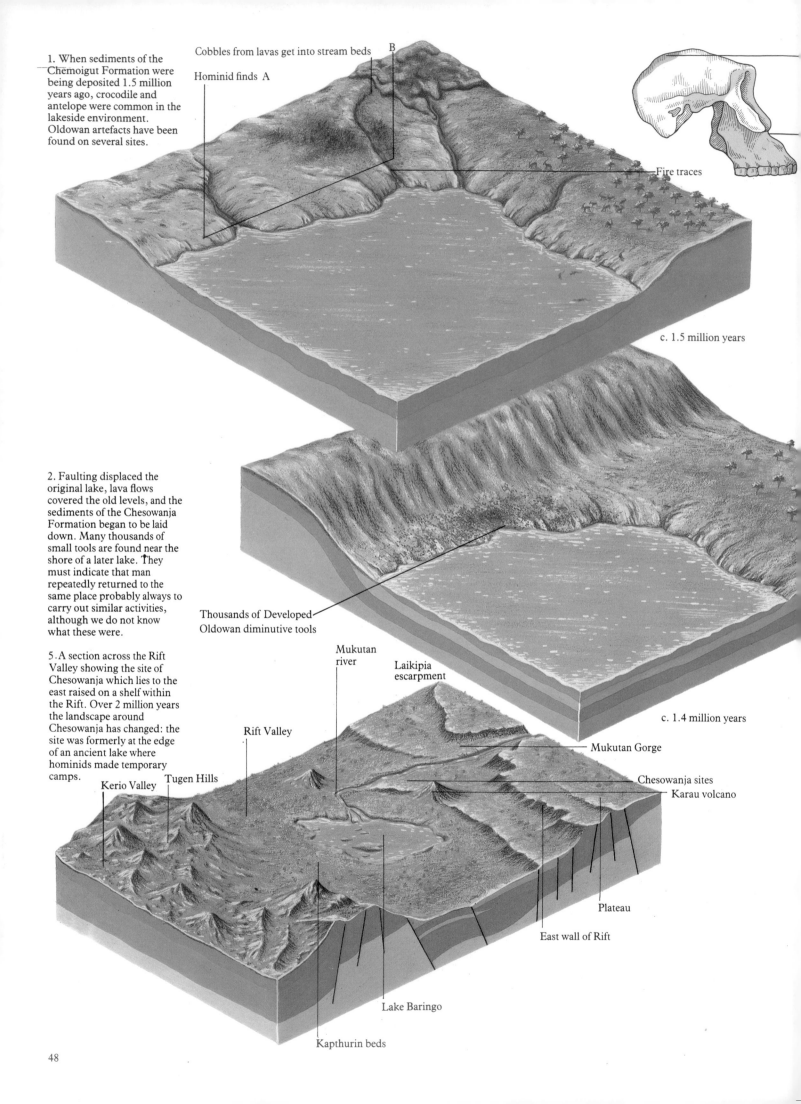

1. When sediments of the Chemoigut Formation were being deposited 1.5 million years ago, crocodile and antelope were common in the lakeside environment. Oldowan artefacts have been found on several sites.

Cobbles from lavas get into stream beds

Hominid finds A

B

Fire traces

c. 1.5 million years

2. Faulting displaced the original lake, lava flows covered the old levels, and the sediments of the Chesowanja Formation began to be laid down. Many thousands of small tools are found near the shore of a later lake. They must indicate that man repeatedly returned to the same place probably always to carry out similar activities, although we do not know what these were.

Thousands of Developed Oldowan diminutive tools

c. 1.4 million years

5. A section across the Rift Valley showing the site of Chesowanja which lies to the east raised on a shelf within the Rift. Over 2 million years the landscape around Chesowanja has changed: the site was formerly at the edge of an ancient lake where hominids made temporary camps.

Mukutan river

Laikipia escarpment

Rift Valley

Kerio Valley

Tugen Hills

Mukutan Gorge

Chesowanja sites

Karau volcano

Plateau

East wall of Rift

Lake Baringo

Kapthurin beds

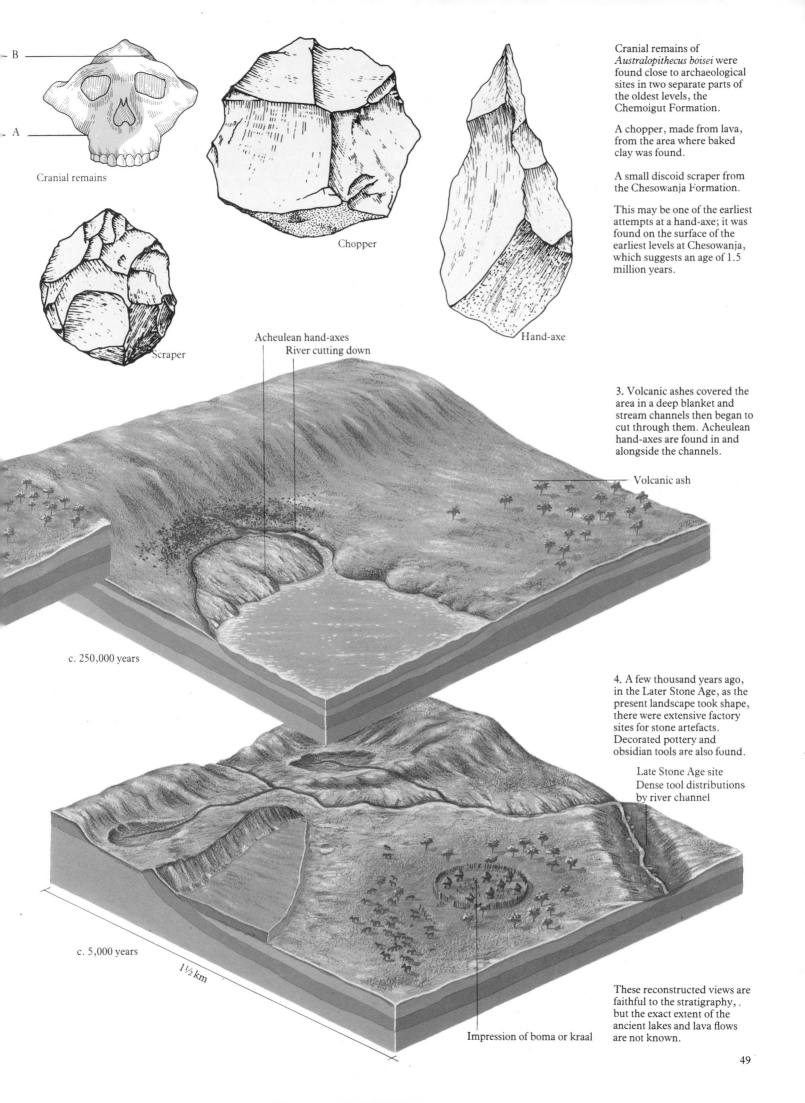

B

A

Cranial remains

Chopper

Scraper

Hand-axe

Cranial remains of *Australopithecus boisei* were found close to archaeological sites in two separate parts of the oldest levels, the Chemoigut Formation.

A chopper, made from lava, from the area where baked clay was found.

A small discoid scraper from the Chesowanja Formation.

This may be one of the earliest attempts at a hand-axe; it was found on the surface of the earliest levels at Chesowanja, which suggests an age of 1.5 million years.

Acheulean hand-axes
River cutting down

3. Volcanic ashes covered the area in a deep blanket and stream channels then began to cut through them. Acheulean hand-axes are found in and alongside the channels.

Volcanic ash

c. 250,000 years

4. A few thousand years ago, in the Later Stone Age, as the present landscape took shape, there were extensive factory sites for stone artefacts. Decorated pottery and obsidian tools are also found.

Late Stone Age site
Dense tool distributions by river channel

c. 5,000 years

1½ km

Impression of boma or kraal

These reconstructed views are faithful to the stratigraphy, , but the exact extent of the ancient lakes and lava flows are not known.

49

Interpreting a site

Archaeological evidence is analysed with care, to ensure that so-called 'sites' have not been created by chance associations of stone tools (moved by water) and animal bones (left by predators).

When a concentration of archaeological material, such as stone tools, is found mixed up with other stones and bones, it seems logical to regard this as evidence of a site and to imagine that, through excavating it, we can begin to 'read' the signs of human activity. Unfortunately, the record is often less simple than it seems.

All the sediments which cover and preserve a site were emplaced by water, or wind, which may have disturbed the remains. The bones may have been chewed by carnivores and the finds may have lain deteriorating on the surface for years before they were finally covered.

Palaeontologists, unlike most archaeologists, frequently study collections of fossilized animal bone which have accumulated naturally so that, when they look at similar material which is mixed up with human artefacts, they legitimately ask: 'how do we know that erosion and water-flow have not brought stones and bones together artificially when originally they were quite separate?'

In some cases there are very good answers to this question. At Mwanganda's Village in Malawi, the carcase of a butchered elephant, excavated by Professor J.D. Clark, is clearly undisturbed since bones of the skeleton are still articulated and the stone tools are neatly clustered around them. Similarly, the stone circle at Olduvai Bed I (see pp 40–41) could not possibly have been created by water-flow because natural forces do not create structural features.

But often the interpretations are much less sure and a branch of study, 'taphonomy', has evolved to investigate the influence of outside forces on abandoned materials. Both archaeologists and palaeontologists regularly apply its techniques in order to gain a better understanding of archaeological and fossil evidence.

How can we tell if a torrent of water has moved the finds on a site? A sensible approach is to experiment by placing objects along the sites of modern streams where they will be disturbed by the water. When stone tools are swept along, larger and smaller pieces tend to separate because smaller pieces are more easily moved and carried further. It is a good first sign that an archaeological site is in 'primary context' (relatively undisturbed) if the smallest waste flakes of less than 1 cm long can be found together with larger tools.

Studies of the weight distribution of finds within a site can also be very helpful for the same reasons. If they are in a 'feature', such as a hearth arrangement, both small and large finds tend to have the same pattern and it is unlikely that water could create this effect.

In another test designed to recognize disturbance by water, the orientation of the pieces is measured. The direction in which long and narrow stone tools or bones lie can be measured by using a compass and the results are then plotted out in 'rose diagrams'. From these, the archaeologist can see if most of the pieces lie in one particular direction. A flow of water insufficient to move the stones and bones bodily may nevertheless realign them, so this test, like most others, can only provide a clue as to what has happened.

The sediments themselves may provide further evidence of disturbance. Coarse gravels are an indication of strong water movement but fine clay particles settle only in very still conditions. Thus, clay sites are the most promising for investigation, but even on these there is the possibility that sudden rushes of water may have left little trace.

The most direct archaeological evidence is provided by the flaking of stones and the breaking

A reconstruction of an early hut at Olduvai. There is no direct evidence for the form of the hut, or the nature of a wind-break, but the evidence on the ground (see pp 40–41) is consistent with this interpretation. The animals are based on the bones found at Olduvai and they include the giant sheep-like creature, *Pelorovis*.

up of bones. If this has happened, the pieces can be reassembled like a jigsaw puzzle and a remarkable reconstruction of activities may ensue. This technique of 'refitting' has been known since the nineteenth century but its great potential has been recognized only recently in work on several later Stone Age sites, such as Pincevent and Meer in Europe, in the Negev Desert in Israel, and at Kapthurin and East Turkana in Africa. It can be applied to Palaeolithic sites of all ages; yet even success with this method does not give a perfect guarantee that a site is in a pristine state, but it does at least provide an effective index of disturbance. If a flake can be rejoined to one found a whole metre deeper down, the archaeologist knows that finds have moved up and down in the sediments and must have been disturbed.

The least-disturbed archaeological horizons from a short-term occupation are only a few centimetres thick, so where the finds are distributed vertically through metres of sediments, it is a reasonable supposition that numbers of different occupations are involved.

Refitting studies sometimes allow the archaeologist to discriminate between different parts of a site. If flakes from within particular areas can be refitted, but it is not possible to match up those from one area with those of another, it suggests that the stone-working was carried out on different occasions.

The technique of refitting is most effective when linked with 'microwear studies'. These are enormously helpful and make it possible to determine the purpose to which the tools were put. Damage is caused to the edges of stone tools by the material on which they are used and by particles of grit on their surfaces. The damage, which often appears as a kind of 'polish', can be studied either under the optical microscope, or at much higher magnification under the electron microscope. Actual fragments of the worked material can sometimes be observed on more recent tools, but often the material which caused the polish cannot be identified. But it is possible to examine the damage made to modern

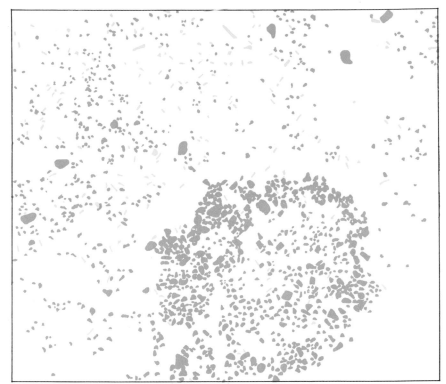

replicated tools when they are used on particular materials such as bone, hides and wood and to compare it with that found on the early tools. This technique enables the uses of individual tools to be identified correctly in about two out of three cases.

Microwear studies have so far achieved their best results on recent sites, such as the Mesolithic Site of Meer in Belgium (9,000 years old), where it was possible to identify the separate areas in which different activities had taken place. On a much older Lower Palaeolithic site at Hoxne in England, Dr Lawrence Keeley was able to show that hand-axes were used for cutting meat. Unfortunately, on very early sites, lava and quartz are unsuitable for this method because of their coarse grain; chemical changes to the rock may also destroy signs of use. Nonetheless, good results from fine-grained rocks like chert seem likely, and it will be a great step forward if the uses of early tools can be determined more exactly as a result.

The stone circle site at Olduvai (DK in Bed I). This is a structure such as has been found on countless later sites. It is the surest evidence supporting the idea that early men had 'home bases' to which they returned at night.

Stones including artefacts

Fossil bones

The potential for refitting is illustrated by this modern replicated hand-axe, seen against the reassembled flakes struck during its manufacture.

Some anthropologists believe that animal bones have far more to tell us about early human behaviour than stone tools. The importance of bones cannot be denied because potentially they can explain which creatures early man preferred to eat, and how the carcases were butchered. But the connection between the bones and the actions of man has to be established beyond doubt. This can be a serious problem because, although association of bones and stone tools is a good indication of human activity, collections of bones can arise naturally. Even where the association strongly suggests a human cause, predators, such as the hyaena, may completely alter the evidence after man has left the site.

The whole subject of bones and their possible uses became controversial when Professor Raymond Dart, discoverer of the first South African australopithecines, postulated his 'osteodontokeratic' culture. The name was based on the ancient Greek words for bones, teeth and horns, and the implication was that the hominids selected and modified these for use as tools before stone tools had been adopted. This idea is a perfectly reasonable one, but it has never been generally accepted for want of convincing evidence. Dart assumed that hominid activity had occurred because, in the bones from Makapansgat, some parts of the skeleton were more common than others. Many of the bones appeared to have been consistently fractured or otherwise modified in exactly the same way. But numbers of studies in recent years show that such selectivity is part of the natural process of bone breakdown. Some bones are generally fragile, and hardly ever preserved, while others contain marrow and will be chewed open by hyaenas and other carnivores. Mandibles and stout limb bones, such as the femur, are much the most commonly preserved. The hominid bones which are represented at East Turkana illustrate just this point.

Dart's argument was that the bones had been used as tools but, more recently, the debate has been extended to another question: were the bones found on archaeological sites abandoned there by man after butchery of animals or are they found on the sites through chance association? How, too, do we know that the stone tools found with bones were actually used for cutting them? A first step in explaining this

A characteristic 'wood polish' appears on the edge of a flint used for wood-working. This is a photomicrograph of the wood polish on a blade used on a Mesolithic site in Northern Ireland (130 times actual size).

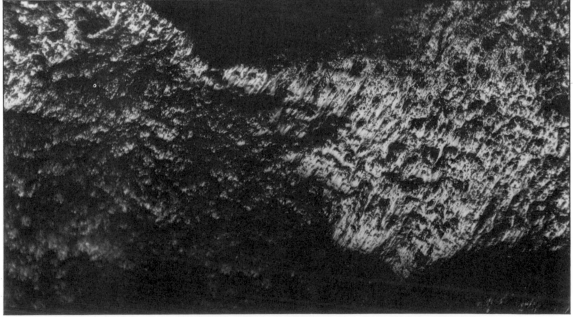

problem is to use one of the techniques of microwear investigation (see pp 50–51).

Although we may be suspicious of ethnographic parallel there is a clear value in observing the activities of people who regularly cut up carcases with simple tools. This is not a haphazard process, for cuts must be made in the right places to remove tendons and disarticulate the bones with the least effort. Observations of Nunamiut (Eskimos) or Bushmen are useful because they are highly skilled in butchery and their methods help us to see whether earlier peoples were likely to possess similar skills.

Under a microscope, marks made by man are distinguishable in various ways from those made by carnivores. Dr Henry Bunn (University of California) observed through an optical microscope at low magnification that stone tools leave V-shaped cuts, which are much narrower than rodent gnawing marks. Where a bone has been hammered with a stone tool, the marks are larger than those caused by carnivore gnawing. Bunn noted also that on bones from East Turkana, the marks occurred in a pattern which indicated expert butchery.

Drs Rick Potts and Pat Shipman, however, feel that on early sites at Olduvai, the marks do not always occur as would result from modern butchering, implying that skilled butchery might not yet have emerged in the earlier Pleistocene. Their work involved use of the electron microscope, at a very high magnification. They found that many bones from Olduvai preserved carnivore gnawing marks, as well as stone tool cut-marks. Very close parallel striations were indisputable evidence of the stone tools, for no edge of a flake is perfectly straight, and each protruding sharp piece leaves its mark.

Such cut-marks were not restricted to bones which would yield a substantial quantity of meat. This interesting finding suggests that other uses of animal products were already known to early man. It seems probable, from the position of some marks, that tendons were being severed to detach sinews which could be used for cord. Skins too were probably cut up and used for bags, rugs and perhaps even clothing.

Each year the range of techniques employed in interpreting sites increases. Microscopic fossils can tell us about the local environment and preserved pollen can explain the vegetation. Studies of the sediments can determine the rocks of their origin and the way in which they were deposited. Yet, it will still be many years before the full potential of such methods is reached.

Stone tools are as effective as steel for cutting meat. Modern experiments show that early man could have butchered animal carcases very efficiently.

Mental abilities

Human beings are able to perform complex tasks which are the sum of many smaller operations. Abilities of this kind are seen even in early archaeological evidence, showing that the human brain and mind evolved gradually over a long period.

How human were the early hominids in their abilities? The study of cranial remains gives some indication of the direction which hominid evolution had taken, but otherwise we have to draw what inferences we can from the archaeological traces of human activities.

One important way in which we differ from other animals is the extent to which we look ahead to the future, making plans and carrying out long sequences of related actions. We can therefore use the archaeological record to look for signs of this kind of behaviour in the past.

The stone tools of the Oldowan provide the first opportunity for us to do this. They allow us to examine the way in which early men solved past problems, both in making the tools and in taking them to their place of use.

A persistent feature noted by archaeologists on the early sites is that some stone tools had been carried considerable distances. This was not done haphazardly for, as we have seen, stones carried over some distance were those which were the most suitable for particular kinds of tool (see pp 40–41).

Thus, when tools were carried for 10 or 15 km, as happened quite regularly during the course of the Oldowan well over 1 million years ago, this tells us about both the distances over which the early hominids travelled and how far they planned ahead. By the time of the Acheulean, we find transport distances of up to 40 km, which suggests that plans were sometimes conceived more than one day ahead of their execution.

If the early human groups knew that a particular rock was suitable for one kind of tool, and that an outcrop of a different rock several kilometres away was suitable for another type, then they must have had a remarkably detailed knowledge of their environment. A very great familiarity with rocks, plants, animals and general topography is characteristic of modern hunters and gatherers. The archaeological evidence suggests that it is a fundamental part of the human adaptation which was already developing millions of years ago.

For modern man to become expert in any particular field, the mind has to build up a vast internally cross-referenced system of information.

Human beings anticipate events and actions much further ahead than other animals. They formulate suitable plans for achieving their aims and then execute these as a chain or sequence of related actions. The results of these actions are evaluated in relation to the ultimate goal.

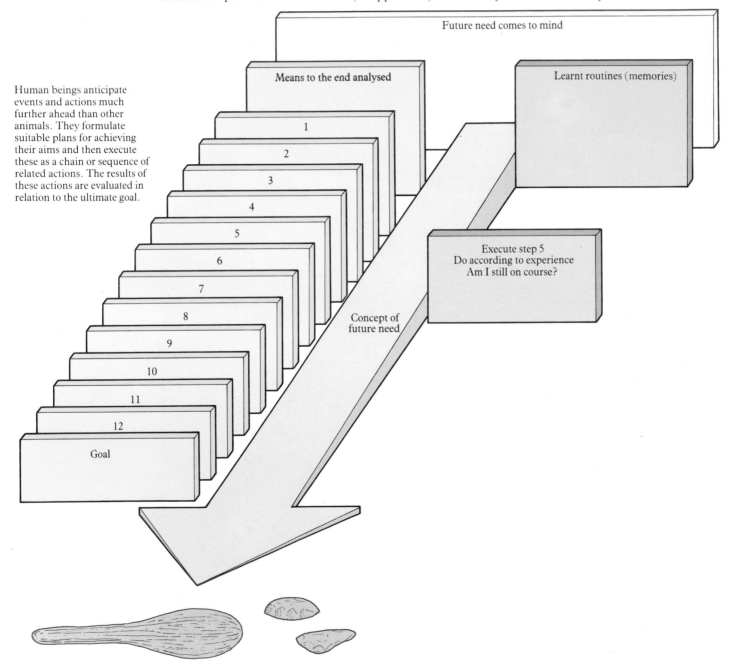

Future need comes to mind

Means to the end analysed

Learnt routines (memories)

1
2
3
4
5
6
7
8
9
10
11
12

Goal

Concept of future need

Execute step 5
Do according to experience
Am I still on course?

These mental abilities must have long evolutionary histories, for the human mind is clearly uniquely complex and could not have appeared in its present form overnight.

The stone tools tell us a great deal about early mental abilities because they preserve an accurate, blow-by-blow account of how they were made. Even a fairly straightforward core tool like a chopper or discoid can only be made by striking flakes in an ordered sequence. Each individual flake which was struck represents a problem solved by the tool-maker; in addition each flake had to be an integral part of the overall flaking process which was used to manufacture the desired tool. It is a feature of this 'operational chain' in modern or ancient stone-working, that the individual flake struck is subordinate to the ultimate aim – the production of a successful tool.

Choppers and discoids have set shapes, which were not rediscovered every time a new core was worked. The stone-workers knew what was possible, and this implies that they had the whole routine for the tool-making process stored in their heads,

somewhat like a computer programme. Computer programmes are, however, generally rigid, whereas early man could modify the routine to solve this or that problem, just as we can.

Studies aimed at creating artificial intelligence have begun to result in more sophisticated computer programming, in which concepts such as planning and flexible responses are arranged. These have much more in common with the human thought processes which were used for making early stone tools. Advances in artificial intelligence studies may therefore provide us with more means of evaluating early human abilities.

Many of the activities of early man which have left traces were co-operative, social ones. Does this then imply the use of language from the time of early tool-making? There is no direct evidence for this, but the sequences of operations involved in tool-making have parallels in structure with those of producing sentences. Language would have been of great assistance, especially for conveying cultural skills, but its possible presence and nature can only be postulated among the Oldowan tool-makers.

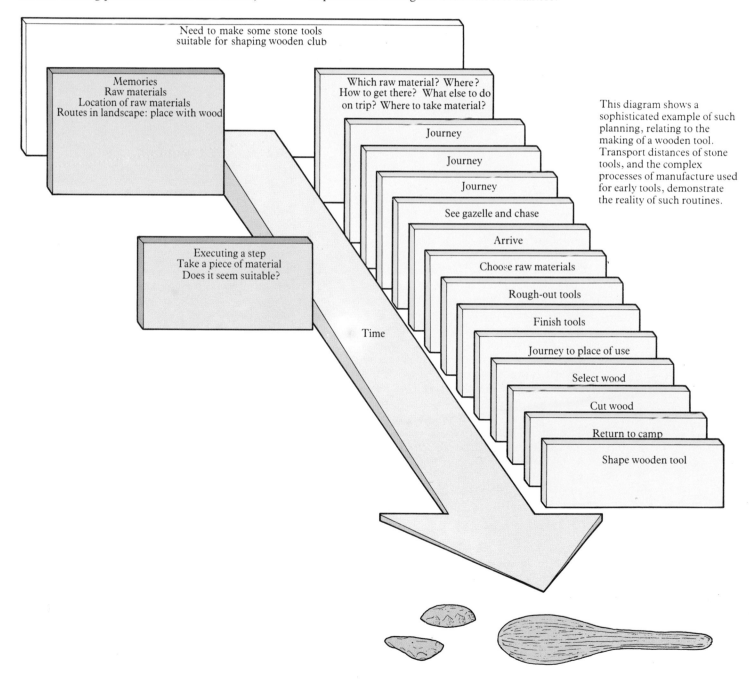

This diagram shows a sophisticated example of such planning, relating to the making of a wooden tool. Transport distances of stone tools, and the complex processes of manufacture used for early tools, demonstrate the reality of such routines.

Origins of fire

The control of fire was a major step in man's mastery of the environment. Accumulating evidence suggests that this skill developed as much as 1.5 million years ago, but the early record is controversial.

Sites with certain or possible fire evidence are shown on this chart: dating evidence as well as the small number of sites limits our interpretation.
1. Olorgesailie
2. Gadeb
3. Karari
4. Chesowanja
5. Choukoutien
6. Yuanmou
7. L'Escale
8. Terra Amata
9. Vértesszöllös

The Kalahari Bushmen retain skills in fire-making: practice is necessary to convert the heat of the drill into a successful fire, through the use of tinder, consisting of carefully selected dry vegetation.

Sparks are regularly struck unintentionally in the course of stone-working: they may have been recognized as fire by early man, but it is unlikely that this method was used for kindling because the sparks die so rapidly.

The control of fire is of critical importance to humanity; it provides warmth, protection and a means of cooking. For early man it was also a technological catalyst – with the aid of fire numerous processes became easier – wooden objects could be shaped and flint could be heated so that it flaked more easily. Fire is so rooted in culture that it has a symbolic significance; religion has its fire-gods and innumerable habits and rites connected with fire have been recorded, revealing its deep spiritual importance. The ability to control and use fire sets man apart from the rest of the natural world. Therefore questions about how the use of fire began, how widespread its use was in the past and how it has shaped the evolution of the species are vital ones.

From explorers' accounts of the last few centuries it seems that knowledge of fire was universal among all primitive peoples, however limited their technology. Eskimos, South Sea islanders and the aboriginal inhabitants of Tierra del Fuego all had the use of fire. It is less certain that all peoples knew how to kindle fire, for some kept a small fire burning continuously, watched over by

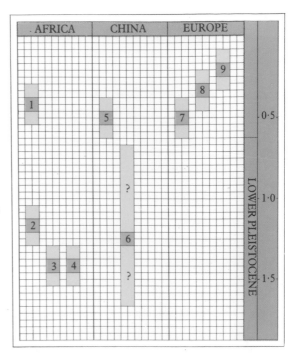

one person whose duty was to maintain it.

When we observe what happens in nature, we see that the unique association of fire with mankind may be less than clear-cut. Bush fires in Africa and probably elsewhere are used by intelligent predators as a means of trapping prey. Animals such as the cheetah will position themselves so as to pounce on animals fleeing from the flames, and hawks will do the same. Fire-using behaviour is less well attested among primates, but the Victorian anthropologist, Edward Tylor, records the travellers' story that 'pongos' (apes, probably gorillas) would settle around an abandoned fire, warming themselves until the fire burned down, but not having the wisdom to add new fuel. All this could suggest that fire-use evolved gradually in interaction with nature.

Fire is not an easy subject for the archaeologist to investigate, because of the nature of the evidence. It can be said that there is a two-step process: first to discover certain evidence of burning, then to link it with human activity. If you light a small camp-fire, different traces will be left after it has burnt down; ashes and charcoal from the wood, or other fuel; perhaps a ring of stones which you might have set up to contain the fire; perhaps soil baked by the heat of the fire; and any objects or food remains – such as bottle tops and animal bones – which you might

discard. If all these were preserved, there would not be much doubt that there had been a fire, but usually only a fraction, if any, of this evidence passes into the archaeological record. Fine wood ash is easily removed by wind and rain, wood rots, bone breaks up and stones may be moved.

This means that the chances of finding direct evidence of fire in archaeological excavations are quite low, especially in the case of open sites. Throughout the last half million years, fire traces are frequently absent on open sites, even though contemporary caves testify to fire use. Consequently, when very early evidence suggesting fire use is found, such as that on the 1.5 million year-old open site at Chesowanja, East Africa, it comes as a surprise. But a near absence of fire evidence on open sites over 500,000 years old does not prove lack of knowledge of fire: it is merely negative evidence.

On the later Palaeolithic sites of the last 200,000–300,000 years evidence of fire is seen much more often. Though many sites do not have fire evidence, there are a number of hearths of this period, such as those at Terra Amata in France, Vértesszöllös in Hungary and Dolní Věstonice in Czechoslovakia. Some of these are just spreads of charcoal, but others have definite structures of hearth-stones. On occasion baked soil or clay is

Rubbing pieces of wood together to create friction was probably the oldest method of kindling fire. The drill method has been refined in the last few thousand years, by the use of a bow and string, so that fire can be kindled efficiently in less than a minute.

found alongside the charcoal.

In the protected environment of caves fire is more likely to be found because, as the sediments accumulate, ashes and charcoal are incorporated directly, sheltered from wind and rain. In the caves at Choukoutien, near Peking, China, which were inhabited by *Homo erectus*, layer after layer of ashes, baked sediments and charred animal bone were found. Although matted vegetation can sometimes catch fire naturally through the build-up of heat from decay, as with haystacks, it is most unlikely that this happened repeatedly at Choukoutien to leave the layers of ash and charred bone. This evidence, therefore, links fire with *Homo erectus* at a period of about 500,000 years ago. There are two other examples of fire remains of around this time, which are both preserved in French cave sites. At L'Escale, which is thought to be 700,000 years old, traces of fire have been found beside a subterranean lake; and at Pêch de l'Aze there is fire evidence in a cave inhabited as much as 300,000 years ago.

In spite of a steady accumulation of convincing evidence, the question of the early use of fire as much as 1.5 million years ago remains highly controversial. There must have been regular bush or forest fires caused by lightning or lava flows. It can be reasonably argued that these account for some of the occurrences of burnt material found with early archaeological remains. But it is unlikely that these natural causes would occur repeatedly in just the place of human occupation, and neither lightning, nor lava flow, can build a hearth arrangement. Why then is there hostility to the idea of early fire among some archaeologists? One view is that fire use represents a considerable mental advance over stone tool manufacture, and that it must therefore be expected at a later stage. Holders of this opinion are unwilling to postulate the use of fire at any time earlier than is actually proven. But it seems likely that early human beings who were skilled in stone tool manufacture and use, would have a similar familiarity with wood (although it is never preserved). If we look at the operation of fire-making and the thought processes and practical skills involved, we can see that it involves essentially similar steps to those used in making stone tools; the necessary materials have to be chosen and collected, with the intention of carrying out a future activity, such as cooking a meal or butchering a carcase.

If the use of fire really goes back to the Early Pleistocene (almost 2 million years ago), as now seems likely, then we can argue that to all intents and purposes our ancestors at that time were already human in their basic character.

Distribution of early man

Africa is often regarded as the 'cradle of mankind', but early finds have also been made in the Far East, implying that the hominids may have evolved across a broad band of the tropics and subtropics.

The map indicates the area which seems to have been occupied more than 1 million years ago.

It is easy to jump to the conclusion that the distribution of early man must have been limited to eastern Africa, since the Rift Valley is so rich in early finds. This is not the case however, for early hominids and archaeological sites have been found in other areas, such as southern Africa and China; unfortunately the volcanic rocks which would allow potassium-argon dating are often absent, so that the chronology of these sites is much harder to establish.

Human evolution is likely to have taken place across a continuous band of the tropics and subtropics, extending from Africa in the west, through Arabia and India to China and South-East Asia. All these areas may have been occupied continuously during the last few million years, but our only certain evidence comes from a thin scattering of early archaeological sites and human remains. These testify directly to the early occupation of large areas, including southern Africa and the Far East, from 2 or 3 million years ago. Heavily forested areas, the natural habitat of our cousins the apes, were probably colonized much later, perhaps within the last 100,000 years.

In southern Africa, the most important finds come from ancient caves in the limestone of the Transvaal region where, in 1924, Raymond Dart discovered the very first remains of *Australopithecus*. The oldest sites appear to be Makapansgat and Sterkfontein which are certainly over 2 million years old, and very likely to be as old as 3 million. There are no stone tools, but there are remains of a small and lightly-built (gracile) australopithecine named *Australopithecus africanus*.

A later level at Sterkfontein, aged about 1.5 million years, is also of great interest since it has yielded remains of early *Homo*, together with stone tools of the Acheulean type. These *Homo* finds are somewhat like early *Homo* (*Homo habilis*) from Olduvai Gorge. This is therefore further confirmation that the early australopithecines were small-brained and did not use stone tools but that, by more than 1.5 million years ago, *Homo* had emerged as the stone-tool making lineage.

Two other South African sites, Swartkrans and Kromdraai, have yielded many remains of robust australopithecines which are fairly similar and approximately contemporary to those found in East Africa (see pp 42–43).

The total number of archaeological sites over 1 million years old is very small but a few potentially early ones have been found in North Africa including those at Sidi Abderrahman near Casablanca, and Ternifine in Algeria. They probably represent industries at the Oldowan stage of development but none of the sites has yet been excavated by modern techniques.

Ethiopia has a major share of early sites for, in addition to Hadar, there are other important sequences at Melka Konturé, and Gadeb. Melka Konturé has a number of different levels ranging from Developed Oldowan through to Late Acheulean. On one site, aged about 1.5 million years, there are indications of a cleared area, probably lying within a wind-break, and the excavator, Jean Chavaillon, suspects that fire was in use. At Gadeb, Professor J. D. Clark and colleagues

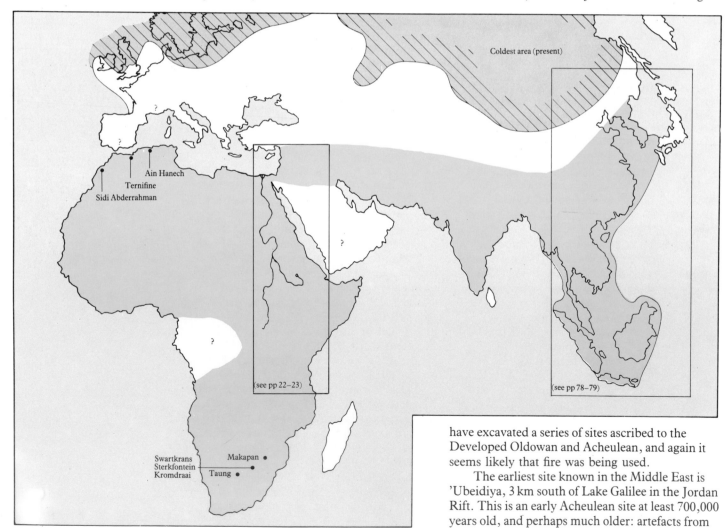

have excavated a series of sites ascribed to the Developed Oldowan and Acheulean, and again it seems likely that fire was being used.

The earliest site known in the Middle East is 'Ubeidiya, 3 km south of Lake Galilee in the Jordan Rift. This is an early Acheulean site at least 700,000 years old, and perhaps much older: artefacts from some layers resemble the Developed Oldowan of Olduvai.

Further east, in Iran, Pakistan and India, there are only hints of very early industries, and no reliable absolute dates whatever. But the early presence of man in the Far East as well as Africa makes it highly likely that occupation was always geographically continuous across southern Asia.

The full importance of the Far East, and especially China, in the story of human evolution cannot yet be appreciated because extensive fieldwork is only just beginning, but there is enough evidence to show the great potential of the area. Although it is sometimes suggested that human occupation of the East only started with the migration of *Homo* from Africa at the beginning of

In China, at least three important early Pleistocene sites have been found in recent years. The Hsihoutu site in Shangsi province, investigated by Drs Chia Lan-po and Wang Chien, is believed to be as much as 1.8 million years old on the basis of palaeomagnetic evidence; this would make the site approximately contemporary with Olduvai Bed I. Stone tools were found in cross-bedded sands and gravels fully 60 m below the present surface. Thirty core tools and flakes made of quartzite, quartz and lava were found, which were apparently similar to the Oldowan in technology. Animal bones, horse teeth, and deer antlers were found; some of the antlers apparently had cut-marks, others had been burned. There is thus a strong possibility that the site represents very early use of fire, but

A view of the ancient cave deposits at Sterkfontein in southern Africa. The consolidated cave filling appears on the left, part of the old roof to the right.

the Pleistocene, this seems unlikely. Some of the very first fossil hominid remains ever found are those of *Homo erectus* from Java, which can hardly have been the first stop on a migration route. In addition to these historic finds made by Eugène Dubois in 1891 near the Solo River, other more primitive specimens have since been discovered in the older Djetis beds. All the indications suggest an evolutionary development from very early *Homo* (the Modjokerto skull) to a developed form of *Homo erectus*, and a similar story can be discerned in China. Indeed the American anthropologist, William Howells, has written that 'On the basis of the fossils found before World War II . . . *Homo erectus* would have appeared to be a population of the Far East.'

unfortunately it was not possible to obtain a radiometric date to confirm the early age.

At Yuanmou in Yunnan province, human remains were found in the form of two incisors. Excavations in the area yielded charcoal and several quartz artefacts, all of them scrapers. In Yang Yuan county, Hepei province, a rich archaeological site was discovered which has yielded over 800 stone tools. The age of the site is uncertain, but it probably belongs to the Lower Pleistocene.

Other finds in China which are likely to belong to the Lower Pleistocene include the early *Homo erectus* mandible and skull from Lantien and a skull found in 1980 in Anhwei Province. There is every reason to suppose that further important finds are still to be made.

Chapter IV
Progress or
standstill?

From about 1.5 million years ago, we can safely talk of true men, as represented by the finds of *Homo erectus*. But we can wonder just how human they were in detail, and look for clues in the archaeological finds. By the time that *Homo erectus* had appeared, a new tool form had been perfected – the hand-axe. It was due to stay in favour for over a million years, often prompting the view that this was a period of primitive standstill – but that is far from the case. The tools themselves tell us much about the human minds from which they stem – a long axis, a symmetrical form, a carefully shaped edge – all this was created in stone. True, change was slow, but men of these times appear to have been competent hunters dealing with fearsome animals, sometimes larger than those of the present day. During the Middle Pleistocene (700,000–125,000 years ago), sites became plentiful and human beings spread across Europe and northwards into Asia.

Excavations on a Developed Oldowan site at Gadeb in Ethiopia. Tools are spread densely on an ancient surface. The site is estimated to be over 1.2 million years old.

The *Homo erectus* specimen 3733 from East Turkana, Kenya. It is one of the most complete crania of *Homo erectus* to be preserved, and it is aged 1.5 million years, a million years older than the specimens from Choukoutien.

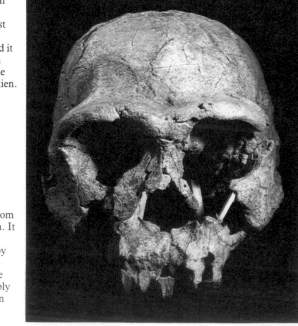

An Acheulean hand-axe from the deserts of North Africa. It is made from a silicified sandstone, now polished by the abrasive effect of sand-carrying desert winds. The missing corner was probably softer rock, which has been eroded.

Hand-axes

More sophisticated tools named bifaces or hand-axes began to be made about 1.5 million years ago. Eventually this Acheulean tradition occurred across most of the inhabited areas of the Old World, except in the Far East. The hand-axes continued in use for over a million years.

The map shows the greatest extent of the hand-axe industries and major finds of *Homo erectus* or *erectus* like fossils.

Hand-axe industries common

Hand-axe distribution sparse or not yet substantiated

All our ideas stem ultimately from our experience of the world. Although there was nothing to indicate to early man the full potential of stone-working, except everyday experience, we can see that gradually new ideas were incorporated, without being sure how they originated or when they were first practised.

One and a half million years ago people regularly made large stone tools of the kind which we call hand-axes, or bifaces. These hand-axes were to endure for over a million years, and thus must represent a useful and efficient tool.

What are the essentials of a hand-axe? First, it has a long axis like a boat. Second, it is symmetrical about that axis, also like a boat. Third, it has two opposed convex faces, rather like the two halves of a walnut shell. The edge bounding the two faces is continuous, and sharply worked. The hand-axe is a major cultural achievement, for it integrates several different ideas in its simplicity.

The idea of working two opposed faces of a stone can be traced right back to the early Oldowan at Olduvai, where it is seen in 'discoids'. A stone-worker has every incentive to discover this form, for flakes can only be taken off a core at an acute angle and the best way to do this is to work right round the circumference of a cobble from both sides. At some time the concept of a long axis became linked in with this method. There are several possible sources for the idea of the long axis: it may have been transferred from wooden tools, in which nature was the inspiration, since trunks and branches are long and thin; it may have arisen from the observation that flakes are nearly always longer in one dimension.

Once this combination of ideas was established the hand-axe was refined, with careful working of the point and edge. An allied form, the cleaver, which has an axe-like edge, was also used, especially in Africa.

It has been suggested that the hand-axe could only develop when early man had learnt how to strike special long flakes, which would serve as 'blanks' to be fashioned into the finished article. This need not be the case, for many hand-axes are quite small (8–10 cm long), and could satisfactorily be made from cobbles. Nevertheless, large flakes are a very good starting point for making the hand-axe, and on many African sites it is evident that they were specially struck for this purpose. These flakes were frequently 15–20 cm long, much longer than any previous stone tool.

The hand-axes became a regular part of the tool-kit, and the name 'Acheulean' is given to industries where they are present. The name is derived from the site of St Acheul in northern France, a region where stone tools were collected by a customs official, Boucher de Perthes before 1847. Modern dating reveals that some of the African sites where Acheulean tools are found are three times as ancient as St Acheul (less than half a million years old), so the use of the name does not imply that the people were the same in culture or adaptation, only that their stone-working had these ideas in common.

Important as the hand-axes are, they were not the only tools which were made; in some areas they may have been unsuitable, or perhaps there was a cultural preference for other tools. The older forms of core-tools, flakes and scrapers continue throughout the Acheulean, and on some sites they greatly outnumber the hand-axes. Sometimes a few flake tools are found, but no hand-axes, so the name Acheulean is not applied. But the archaeologist cannot assume that the early tool-makers did not make and use hand-axes somewhere else nearby.

The Acheulean is sometimes called the 'great hand-axe tradition', because it lasted so long, and spread so far. Exactly when it ended is not certain, but it probably endured into the last 200,000 years. Acheulean hand-axe industries are known throughout the length and breadth of Africa, in the

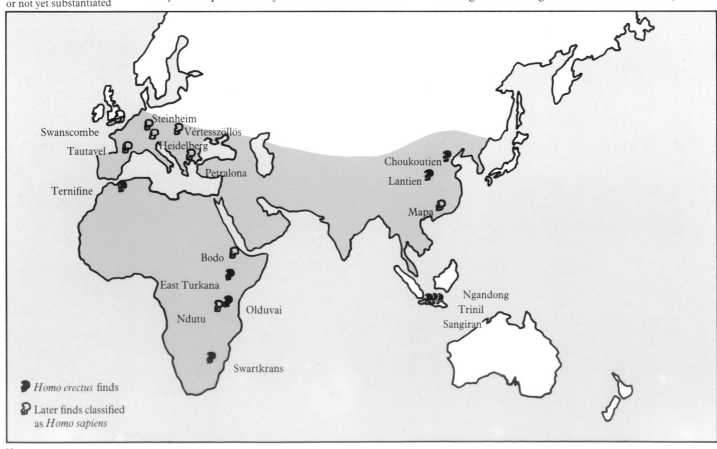

Swanscombe
Steinheim
Vértesszöllös
Heidelberg
Tautavel
Petralona
Ternifine
Choukoutien
Lantien
Mapa
Bodo
East Turkana
Olduvai
Ndutu
Swartkrans
Ngandong
Trinil
Sangiran

🦴 *Homo erectus* finds

🦴 Later finds classified as *Homo sapiens*

Middle East, and in most of Europe and in the Indian sub-continent. Recently they have been found in the mountain chains of Asia, but no further north. They were not believed to have been used in eastern Asia, but recent finds make it plain that there was an Acheulean in Mongolia, and even in Korea.

There used also to be much speculation about who made the hand-axes. The original *Homo erectus* specimens came from Asia, and were not connected with the Acheulean. The widespread hand-axes were not associated with hominid remains, with the possible exception of a skullcap found in Bed II at Olduvai in 1960. As this was not actually found in direct contact with hand-axes, the question was said to remain open, but that state of affairs is now long past. *Homo erectus* remains have been found with the Acheulean at Ndutu near Olduvai, and in Bed IV at Olduvai. One form or another of *Homo erectus* must have made most of the hand-axes, but it is worth remembering that the association of names is the result of our modern naming. The tools were made by early people whether or not we call them hand-axes and *Homo erectus*. Probably *Homo erectus*, as we define it, emerged before the hand-axes, and more certainly the latest hand-axe makers fall within our definition of *Homo sapiens*.

1.

2.

3.

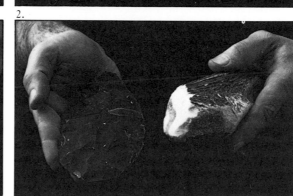

4.

Making a hand-axe:
1. A large flake is struck, or a cobble selected, to serve as the blank. A stone hammer is used at this stage.
2. Trimming the large flake begins on one face. Quite large flakes are detached in the early stages. Often the stone-worker will use an antler or bone hammer to gain better control over the flaking.
3. A regular edge is created by flaking from both sides.
4. In the later stages the flakes which are trimmed off are quite small. This one has been fitted back to illustrate its shape and position.
5. The finished specimen is elongated and approximately symmetrical bilaterally.

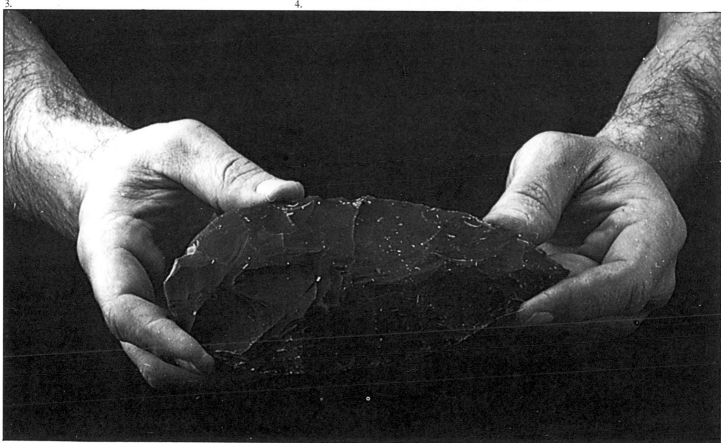

5.

The pattern of hunting and gathering

Modern hunters and gatherers use their immense knowledge of their environment to obtain food efficiently. The foundations for this systematic exploitation of natural resources were probably laid far back in the Pleistocene.

By the time of the Acheulean, it seems reasonable to assume that the pattern of hunting and gathering had become established. The popular image of hunters and gatherers is of people who are completely unsettled, wandering far and wide, living a catch-as-catch-can existence. In the real world, hunters and gatherers can only survive by having a systematic approach to exploiting their environment. They operate within a quite closely defined territory, and have a remarkably detailed knowledge of their surroundings which they exploit in a pattern which will extract the maximum of resources at a given time for the greatest economy of effort – the so-called 'optimal foraging strategy'. In his encounters with bushmen of southern Africa, Laurens van der Post realized that they could read the natural world like a book, while he himself hardly recognized a single word on the pages.

Quite probably hunters and gatherers of the Early and Middle Pleistocene operated with less efficiency, but in observing later hunters and gatherers we may gain some insight into the basic elements of the pattern and the demands which it puts upon the human species.

It is noticeable that hunters and gatherers live in small groups, that their social organization allows them to respond flexibly to seasonal changes in resources and that their population levels are controlled in accordance with those resources.

Compared with subsistence farmers, hunters and gatherers usually need to do less work each day to obtain their food. Normally, therefore, they have much time to spend in social activity.

alters within quite a short period of time. Only close relatives and people who particularly get on stay together for long periods. This flexibility is helpful for meeting variations in resources.

There is however a larger group size of hunters and gatherers which we can term the 'maximum band'. In Australia such a large group is often termed the 'dialectal tribe' (the word tribe being acceptable in this context). This is the largest group which speaks a common dialect. Language is a complicated and essential part of culture which cannot be maintained in identical form across indefinite areas. Hence, it seems that a group speaking a common dialect cannot reach great size. According to the Australian evidence, aborigine tribes of over 1,000 are rare. This makes sense when most individuals do not travel far, and when the different environments demand different descriptive terms for places, plants, animals and technology. Language must be learned, and it therefore has an inbuilt propensity towards change.

Evidently hunters and gatherers have a sense of identity as a people, indicated by the way that they often recognize related peoples by name. According to Dr Paul Wobst of the University of

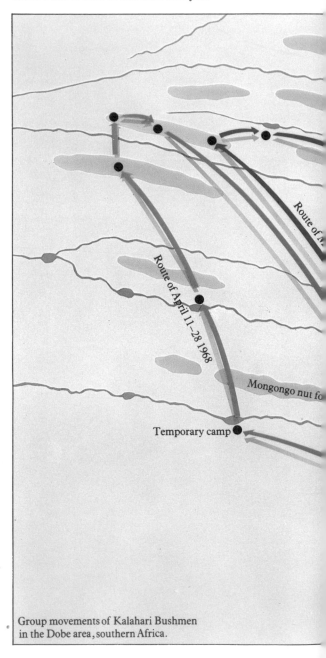

Group movements of Kalahari Bushmen in the Dobe area, southern Africa.

A theoretical structure of a hunter-gatherer population. The band, consisting of about 25–30 people is part of a larger group, the 'maximum band', the size of which varies.

One band — 25–30

175

475

Maximum band

The trips made by hunters and gatherers can be observed today. Kalahari Bushmen sally forth from the 'core areas' around water-holes when abundance of particular resources justifies this. Adjacent bands have territories of exploitation which slightly overlap.

How then is this pattern of life organized? Anthropologists try to avoid using the word 'tribe' which is imprecise, but nevertheless, all peoples are organized in groups. It is very common for hunters and gatherers to operate in bands of about 30 people. This provides a large enough number for social co-operation both in hunting and gathering.

Some authors feel that a rigid concept of the band has been overstressed. It has been shown that, among the Hadza of Tanzania, band composition

Massachusetts, a maximum band (dialectal group) represents the highest level of social integration amongst hunter gatherers - that is, the largest social group with which an individual identifies. Among hunters and gatherers most marriages take place within quite short geographic distances, and Wobst attributes special significance to the maximum band as being a group which marries within itself. His computer simulations, based on smaller bands of 25, suggest that maximum band sizes should vary between about 175 and 475. In Australia figures range overall from about 200 to occasionally as much as 2,000, but about 500 is a typical number.

The closeness of adaptation to resources can also be seen in demographic studies of Australian aborigines. Rainfall varies very much from area to area, and although band size remains quite constant, population density varies according to the average rainfall. In areas with high rainfall and high population density, tribal areas are correspondingly smaller.

How do the hunters and gatherers control their population levels, when we find it so difficult? Since the landscape often seems much emptier of people than is strictly necessary, the mechanisms which operate must be subtle. Population is kept down to what the land can support at the worst times. Probably cultural knowledge about the likelihood of droughts and other disasters helps people to anticipate how many children they can raise: long gaps between pregnancies, and infanticide when necessary, play a part in checking the population.

The actual population figures can be very low indeed. Professor Richard Lee estimates about 16 persons per 100 sq km for bushmen, noting that they spend most of their time within 10 km of water points, thus defining 'core areas' of occupation. The general average for Australia was much lower, about 3 per 100 sq km.

How much does all this help us to interpret the earlier parts of the Pleistocene? It seems reasonable to believe that the pattern was already being formed but, as we have seen, it can be difficult to prove. Stone tool distributions do tend to suggest that people spent most of their time fairly close to water. The distances over which stones were carried are also what might be expected. One difference is that most modern hunters and gatherers have been squeezed into difficult habitats, whereas early man also had the richest ones. This may explain the great size of some early sites, and the wealth of finds.

Plant foods were and are important to most hunters and gatherers. Many of the plants are also food to other primates with which the hominids successfully competed. The diagram shows the percentages of 461 plant genera eaten by humans, chimpanzees and baboons areas of Africa where they in co-exist.

H human
C chimpanzee
B baboon

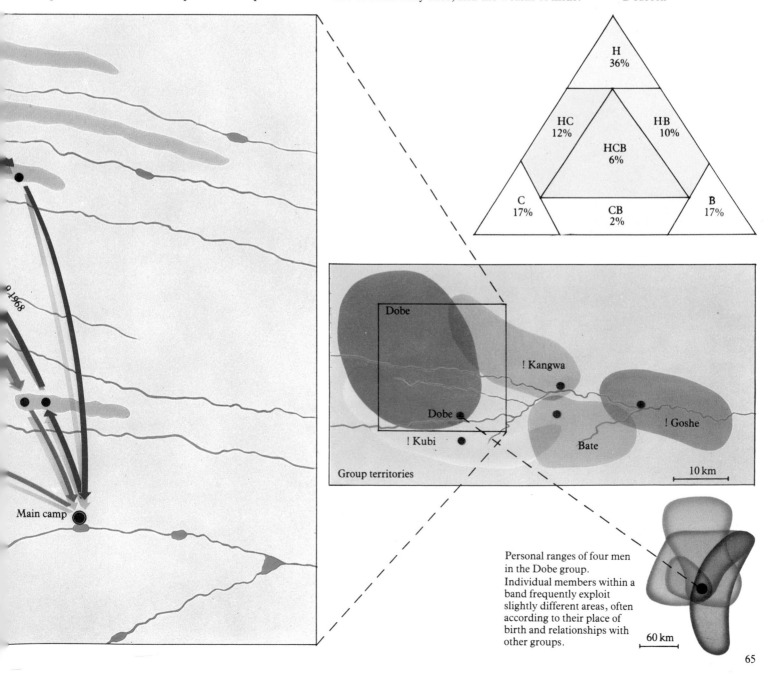

Group territories

10 km

Personal ranges of four men in the Dobe group. Individual members within a band frequently exploit slightly different areas, often according to their place of birth and relationships with other groups.

60 km

When did Homo become the last hominid?

At an unknown date, perhaps a million years ago, the robust australopithecines died out, leaving *Homo* as the last hominid. Human success may have deprived other hominids of their ecological niches. Acheulean and Developed Oldowan tools found on contemporary sites at Olduvai and elsewhere are more likely to represent a variety of activities practised by one group, than the tool-kits of two species.

This hominid facial fragment (SK 847) from Swartkrans is the only substantial specimen of *Homo* from the site.

The tool-kits of the Acheulean and Developed Oldowan are distinguished more by percentages than by tool types. Each tool drawn here represents 10 per cent of the shaped tools in a typical assemblage.

Hand-axes

Small hand-axes

Cleavers

Choppers
Polyhedrons
Sub-spheroids

Scrapers

At some time during the Pleistocene, the *Homo* line became the only representative of the hominids, for the robust australopithecines became extinct. When and how this happened we can only infer from tenuous evidence. Robust australopithecine remains are found as late as about 1.5 million years ago at Chesowanja, Olduvai and Swartkrans, and perhaps somewhat later at Kromdraai, but never on any of the later sites.

Extinction is not an uncommon event, for huge numbers of mammalian species became extinct during the Pleistocene, and in the long term only a few lines have survived to evolve into new forms.

If we take the hominoids (Hominoidea is the superfamily which includes both apes and men) as a group, the signs of real evolutionary success are very restricted. There are fewer ape species today than there were in the Miocene, and their distribution is more limited. The hominids as a family did no better, for we can pick out only a few species at most, and some of these seem to have been confined to Africa. The *Homo* line has been the exception in its outstanding 'success'.

This raises intriguing questions: did the other hominoid species fade out, or become restricted, because of human success, or because of their general incapacity to compete with other forces in the environment?

In the forest, the Old World monkeys seem to be the chief culprits, for they have occupied niches probably formerly held by apes, whereas man entered the forests as a competitor perhaps only quite recently. Possibly, however, hominids played some role in limiting the ape distribution, by occupying similar niches in the open country which separated forest zones.

The robust australopithecines were therefore open-country, or at least savanna, groups which were not in the long term successful enough. If they ate leaves and fruit, and perhaps roots, they would have been in competition with a wide range of successful mammals, many of which had been expanding their niches over a long period. Baboons, including the giant *Theropithecus*, would have been eating similar food; and there would have been overlap, too, with pigs and antelopes.

As direct evidence, we can only trace the demise of individuals, not of a species. At Olduvai,

Chesowanja and Swartkrans stone tools were present in the same neighbourhood as the australopithecine remains and in two cases there was direct evidence of *Homo*. The presence of robust australopithecines on the sites needs some explanation, because of the tooth-wear evidence suggesting that they did not eat the meat from the animal bones so closely associated with stone tools. Although this evidence is suggestive, it cannot be proved that *Homo* was systematically hunting robust australopithecines. After all, we are dealing with individual *Homo* specimens on most of these sites, and their presence only shows that *Homo*, too, was just as likely to die in the same place. Nevertheless, the existence of robust australopithecines on archaeological sites with many animal bones is suspicious, in view of the likelihood that they were not meat-eaters.

At Swartkrans, the tally is different: 1 *Homo* to 60 robusts. Dr Bob Brain, a South African scientist

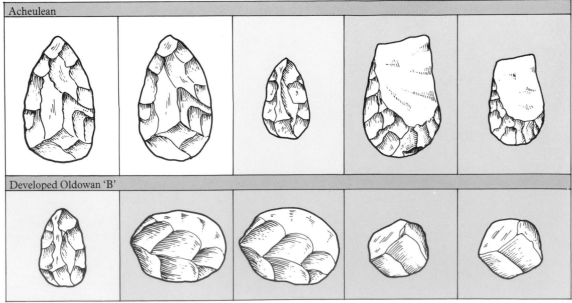

Acheulean

Developed Oldowan 'B'

who has studied these remains, believes that leopards are much more likely to account for the presence of so many fossils, rather than hunting by other hominids. If so, does not the very count of *robustus* indicate that they were very much more vulnerable to such predation than was *Homo*? As leopards habitually do their hunting by night, we must envisage the possibility that the robusts, unlike *Homo*, lacked effective weapons, and even the use of fire to protect themselves.

Extinction, however, probably arises from a combination of circumstances. The action of one kind of predator would not usually be enough to bring it about, for predators usually exist in much smaller numbers than their prey, and cull only a small proportion of it.

Very possibly the developing hunting and gathering pattern of *Homo* involved exploiting a variety of ecological niches, rather than just one, and this range came to include the natural habitat of robust australopithecines. The pressures then created may have made the robusts more vulnerable both to predators, and to the competition with other species.

An important question, given the similarities of cranial organization shown by endocasts (casts made from the inside of the skull), is whether the robust

australopithecines, like *Homo*, could have been cultural animals, making stone tools. They did have very reduced canines, and hands made free by bipedal walking. This idea that more than one hominid species may have made stone tools was strengthened by Dr Mary Leakey's discovery that Developed Oldowan and Acheulean sites existed side by side in contemporary levels of Olduvai Bed II. Some of the tool assemblages were dominated by core tools of the Oldowan kind, accompanied by just a very few small and crude bifaces; other sites had large numbers of well-made Acheulean hand-axes. Mary Leakey's suggestion was that *Homo habilis* made the Developed Oldowan, and *Homo erectus*, initially an intruder to the area, made the Acheulean. Those who feel that *Homo erectus* evolved from *Homo habilis* clearly would not agree with this view, and would point to the variability found on other sites, Acheulean and later, as an indicator that people of the same species, and the same group, could have a variety of different tool-kits for different tasks.

Truth can, however, be stranger than the rigorous interpretation of archaeological facts usually allows. If most of history was represented only by an archaeological record, many strange events which actually happened would be rejected.

How then can we be sure that the robusts, or a second species of *Homo*, did not make some of the tools? Variation similar to that seen between separate sites at Olduvai seems to occur within single sites at Kilombe, and perhaps elsewhere. In these circumstances where all the tools are mixed together, it is much more difficult to believe that more than one species was involved. Then, too, similar kinds of variability in the tools occur on later Acheulean sites, such as Isimila and Olorgesailie, long after we believe the robust australopithecines became extinct and more than a million years after the last signs of *Homo habilis*. All this tallies with the tooth-wear evidence suggesting that the robusts may not have eaten meat. There is also perhaps a feeling that complex tool-using comes from a very specialized kind of mind, which is unlikely to have evolved more than once.

For the moment, however, we do not have sufficient evidence to blame our ancestors for the demise of our nearest relative, and we are free to enjoy our loneliness on the cultural pedestal.

SK48 from Swartkrans is one of the best-preserved robust australopithecine crania from southern Africa. These hominids generally resembled the robusts of East Africa, but are different in detail.

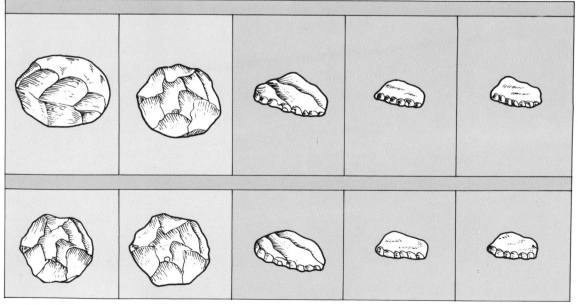

Success

Large Acheulean sites, such as Kilombe in Kenya, show that people returned to the same place repeatedly because they had achieved a successful way of life there. Some of these sites extend over several hectares.

If hunters and gatherers lived only in small groups and habitually stayed a short time in one place before moving on, we would not expect to find any large archaeological sites. Yet, as research continues, it becomes increasingly obvious that our early ancestors were capable of bringing together vast quantities of material so that the stone tools on a site can sometimes total many tons in weight.

What does this mean? Above all, it must mean success. The same activity goes on in the same place time and again, only when the results pay a dividend. For early man, this meant that directly or indirectly the energy expended was recouped in terms of food obtained.

Kilombe is a massive Acheulean site in Kenya. Artefacts on the site were first noticed in 1972 by geologist Dr W.B. Jones as an extensive scatter on the surface, evidently weathering out from nearby Pleistocene beds. Excavations have shown that hundreds upon hundreds of hand-axes and cleavers lie together on a single surface which was later sealed by a covering of volcanic ash. Sometimes as many as a dozen are found in a square metre, and at an average weight of 0.5 kg, the tools can weigh up to 100–200 kg per 100 square metres.

The explanation might be that this is a factory site, where there was a suitable outcrop of lava. This does not seem to be the case, however, for there are scarcely any of the large cores from which the hand-axes were struck, and most of the flakes are small trimming flakes. As there are not nearly enough of these to account for the shaping of the hand-axes, they are probably the result of re-sharpening tools.

It seems plain, then, that the hand-axes were brought onto the site, even though they were mostly made of local lava and therefore not brought very far. But why are there so many of them? Many theories have been suggested, such as *Homo erectus* was too dull-witted to realize that the old tools could be reused, or that the hand-axes were made and used for throwing at predators.

The explanations are probably more straightforward. The great number of pieces suggests that there was a guaranteed return for the

trouble of making a hand-axe and carrying it to the site. The 'cost' of making a hand-axe was not high, provided that the raw material was near. A few minutes' work at most suffices to shape a hand-axe, and in some cases a few minutes' use is enough to blunt the edges, so that a new tool seems preferable. If such a tool was abandoned on a clayey surface, like that at Kilombe, and perhaps covered by water for part of the year, it would soon become unattractive for use and new tools would be brought to the site.

None of the evidence explains what was actually happening, and it is perhaps the most frustrating aspect of studying the Old Stone Age, that archaeologists can so rarely determine the precise

20 km

nature of what has taken place. One reason for this difficulty in interpretation is that microwear studies (of edge damage to the tools), which might otherwise provide an answer, are not possible on sites with coarse-grained or weathered lava tools.

Thus we have to interpret from the whole pattern of archaeological evidence, and from the nature of the ancient environment. The regularity of the pattern at Kilombe is confirmed by remarkable similarities in the size and shape of hand-axes from different parts of the site. As it is hardly possible that so many tools were all made at the same time, it seems more likely they were made and left by small groups of people who returned to the site regularly. This too suggests that there were reliable resources in the site area.

On some sites, hand-axes were probably used for butchering animals (see pp 72–73), but there are few instances in Africa where they are definitely associated with a carcase. All except the lightest animals were probably butchered where they fell, so it is unlikely that they were all brought together at one place, even though Kilombe, like most Acheulean sites, has a 'mixed bag' of animal remains. The few preserved bones are of elephant, gazelle, buffalo and pigs. These may be the result of occasional nearby kills.

The most likely explanation for the concentrations of tools is that a particular kind of working of plant material took place. With the bifaces there are a roughly equal number of cobbles, some of which, when pressed into the ground, may have offered small work surfaces. Was just one specialized activity going on? Is it possible, that by a trick of nature, most of our Acheulean evidence relates to something trivial? On balance, this seems unlikely. Large sites represent a large input of energy, and are thus places where people tended to come together and where a variety of tasks was performed. This seems borne out by the variety of tool-kits that are found in large Acheulean sites, not only at Kilombe, but also at Kariandusi and Olorgesailie in Kenya, at Isimila in Tanzania and on many other sites.

At Kilombe, the main level containing the hand-axes is fairly stable in composition, but nearby there are quite different sites dominated by heavy-duty choppers, or by light-duty flakes, and in one place there is a curious paving of heavier stones, associated with a gentle hollow.

If people did come back time and again, the local resources must have been able to support this repeated habitation. Even after almost a million years of landscape change, it is clear that Kilombe was in an especially favourable position. The site nestles at the foot of the wooded mountains of Kilombe and Londiani and was near the shores of a lake, whose waters rose and fell seasonally.

It may be that wood-working or some other secondary task was carried on at Kilombe, but perhaps the most reasonable explanation for the archaeological evidence is that the preparation of a plant food was the main activity, supplemented by a variety of other tasks, including butchery.

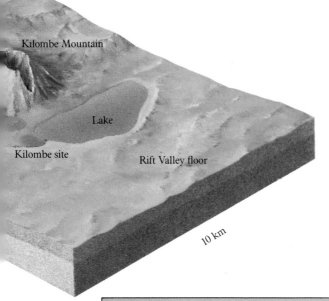

Kilombe, an Acheulean site dating to about 700,000 years ago, has an ideal position at the foot of mountains, on a gentle spur overlooking the Rift Valley. It had access to several different microenvironments in the hills and plains. Some stone tools were probably brought from over the hills to the north-west, a journey of perhaps 15 kilometres. The size of the lake is hypothetical.

Phonolite lava, found abundantly near the site and used for over 90 per cent of tools.

Trachyte lavas from Kilombe Mountain, at least 4 km away, and used for 5–7 per cent of tools.

Olivine basalt, 10–15 km from site, apparently used for occasional tools.

The main horizon at Kilombe is preserved along a length of hundreds of metres. Bifaces and other tools occur on an ancient ground surface at the foot of a volcanic ash, which washed in to cover the site.

A matter of form

Human beings regularly impose form on their environment. The shapes of stone tools are amongst the earliest evidence for this ability, which underlies all modern design.

Where there are large numbers of tools on a site, as at Kilombe, they can be used to study the underlying ideas of the stone-workers who made them. With modern mass-produced implements, such as table-forks of the same make, there is no point in studying more than one, because all are identical. In contrast, each hand-made tool represents different circumstances of manufacture. They vary according to the purpose for which they were intended, the size of the stone-workers' hands and the kind of raw material that was available. Individual, isolated tools are too idiosyncratic to inform us about the design plans. Thus it is very helpful to be able to study a large series of tools of the same age, for from these a picture of the makers' ideas may emerge.

It has long been appreciated that the bifaces of the Acheulean show some sort of aesthetic sense. They are much better made than is strictly

In the excavations, groups of hand-axes lie together. The central specimen is a fine example in trachyte, different in appearance from the others of local phonolite.

This carefully selected flattened pebble was used as a hammerstone at Kilombe. The distribution of wear marks around the circumference is evidence of the precision with which it was used.

necessary, but perhaps this was not just a luxury: the tool-makers needed to be able to cope with difficult, as well as good raw materials, and when these hard-won abilities were applied to the better materials, unusually fine results sometimes appeared. For example, the obsidian (volcanic glass) bifaces from Kariandusi, Kenya, are particularly fine for tools made a million years ago, partly because obsidian is a material which flakes very well, but also because the tool-makers had acquired the abilities to exploit its potential. This is not to say that no pleasure was taken in making the pieces. This is quite possible but there was perhaps a more fundamental advantage: having standard methods, such as those used in making bifaces, can provide a more efficient approach towards managing life. Problems do not have to be solved each time they are encountered and information can be transmitted from person to person more easily. The abilities which allowed some tasks, such as the making of hand-axes, to be executed better than function alone demanded, probably paid off handsomely when employed in planning or carrying out other tasks which presented greater problems.

Kilombe offers an especially good opportunity for studying hand-axes in large numbers, since they all come from the same horizon. Probably all were made by the same group of people over a relatively short period of time (but this could have been as long as 100 years).

Most of the hand-axes were made on 'blanks' which were large flakes. There is no doubt about this, because many of these large flakes were only gently retrimmed in the final shaping and the original form is quite apparent. It is also plain that these large tools were struck to fairly constant sizes

and proportions. This regularity is not likely to be accidental because a large flake 15 or 20 cm long can only be struck with care and attention, and as all the tools have similar proportions, a particular technique must have been employed, and a careful selection made from the results.

This observation is borne out by a study of the relationship between length and breadth in the hand-axes from Kilombe. The two dimensions are highly

correlated, so that as length increases, breadth increases proportionately. In sites where there are collections of flakes not intended for hand-axes, the correlation is not high, but at Kilombe it is very marked, normally achieving over 80 on a scale where 100 indicates a perfect correlation.

This correlation allows us to test whether the biface-makers had a sense of proportion in a geometric sense – that is, did very small bifaces have the same relationships between length and breadth as very large ones? A line which represents the 'best fit' of length and breadth can be fitted to the plotted tools by a simple mathematical technique. The actual bifaces were made only in lengths between about 8 and 24 cm, but on paper the line can be extended back, and passes very close to the origin of the two axes. This demonstrates fairly conclusively that as much as a million years ago *Homo erectus* already possessed important abilities which are preconditions for the later skills of art and mathematics.

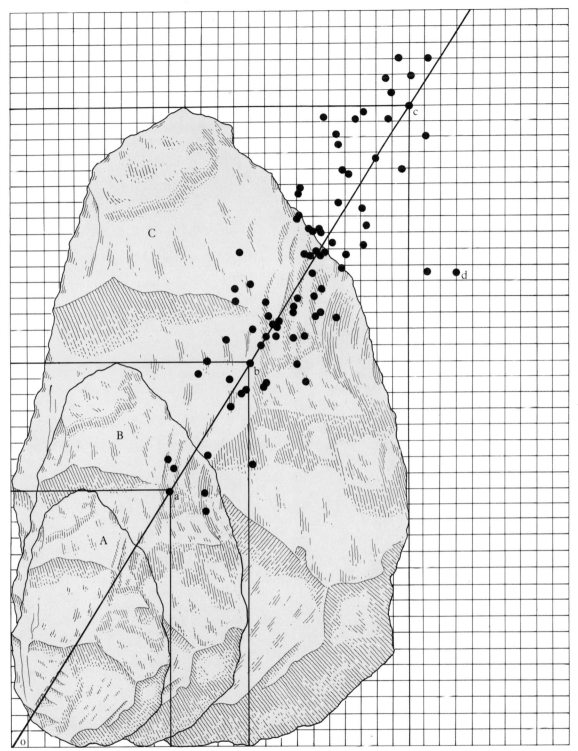

In this diagram the diagonal line represents a perfect correlation between length and breadth of a hand-axe or cleaver. The dots furthest away from the line denote the most irregular specimens. All these bifaces came from one area of the Kilombe site and the great majority were made in proportion so that small and large specimens are the same shape.

o Origin of axes
a Hand-axe A
b Hand-axe B
c Hand-axe C
d Most irregular hand-axe

The essence of these abilities can be summarized: other animals can be taught to recognize a symbol, but what they cannot do, is to recreate that form externally. For example, ducks and chimpanzees can be trained to recognize a plastic triangle, and they can certainly recognize it as the same symbol whether it is shown large or small. But the human ability is much greater, because man can not only retain the idea of a form in the mind but can recreate it as a tool in the external world.

The Kilombe hand-axes together with hand-axes from many other sites, show that early man could employ the same 'template' in making tools of different sizes. In other words, the mental apparatus already existed for making basic mathematical transformations without the benefit of pen, paper or ruler. Making hand-axes in the same proportions at different sizes provides the earliest practical demonstration of principles treated hundreds of thousands of years later in Euclid's *Elements of Geometry*. Similar abilities are fundamental to the practice of visual art, (see pp 128–129).

Could such templates be passed from person to person, from mind to mind, by visual copying alone? All our present experience of using such skills suggests that language would be required. If we accept the probability of the early use of language this ties in with the evidence about planning abilities and with the knowledge we have about the organization of the brain.

Hunting: a case study

Many remains of extinct giant baboons were found on an Acheulean site at Olorgesailie in Kenya. Recent research strengthens the view that they were hunted by early man.

Animal bones are much better preserved at Olorgesailie than on most other major Acheulean sites in Africa. Hand-axes were found weathering out on the surface by Louis and Mary Leakey in the 1940s, and it soon became evident that this was one of the major Middle Pleistocene localities of East Africa. The sites lie in the floor of the Rift Valley, about 60 km south-west of Nairobi, in sandy and tuffaceous deposits which were laid at the margins of a former lake, now completely disappeared.

Several archaeologists have investigated at Olorgesailie, but excavations directed by Professor Glynn Isaac have yielded some of the richest and most remarkable occurrences. On one site, DE/89, in the floor and at the edges of an ancient sandy channel, over 400 hand-axes were found, together with a large quantity of animal bones and teeth. Prominent among these were remains of one particular species of baboon, now extinct, called *Theropithecus*, an animal about the size of a female gorilla.

Such a concentration of primate bones is most unusual and Isaac formed the opinion that the baboons had been hunted by man, perhaps having been herded together and dispatched in a single ferocious episode. He viewed the matter with some caution, however, because of a suspicion that many of the Olorgesailie sites were somewhat disturbed. In the semi-arid regions of Africa, stream-channels are mainly dry on the surface but, after rain in nearby upland areas, they may flow strongly for a few hours or even a few days. There was a considerable chance that such stream activity had brought the fossils together, and this seemed strengthened by a second finding: the archaeological sites with many small-sized finds had very few large ones, and vice versa. This could suggest either that the water flow was separating the finds by weight, or that man was using different tool-kits on different occasions.

An explanation seemed available from local ethnographic analogy. A people nearby in Tanzania would from time to time set out to hunt baboons.

The 'cat-walk' site at Olorgesailie with Mount Olorgesailie in the background. Hundreds of hand-axes and cleavers were found on the surface here, and they have been preserved as an open-air museum display. Many of the raw materials for stone tools were brought from the mountain.

Bones of the baboons were preserved in a highly selective fashion – long bones were frequently found broken in a similar way.
Right, damage caused to these baboon femurs is not characteristic of carnivore activity; the most likely cause is that the tendons were severed with a hand-axe.

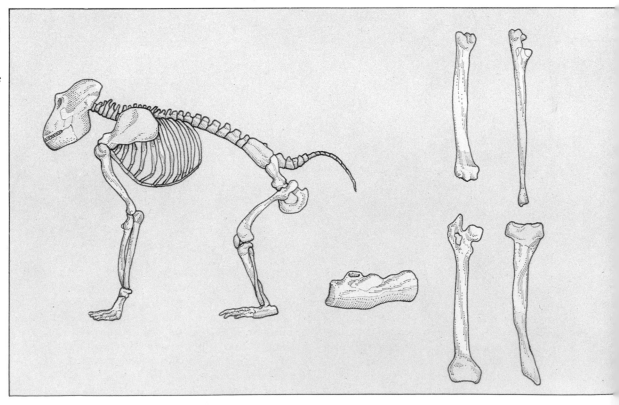

The best time to attempt this was not during the day, when the baboons were foraging widely, but at night, when they might be gathered together in a tree for safety from other predators such as leopards. In the early evening or before dawn, the people would surround the trees where the baboons were roosting and frighten them with firebrands and shouting. The fleeing animals would then be attacked and killed with clubs and other weapons.

This idea could be tested by more detailed study of the bones, which was undertaken by a group of American researchers. On several grounds they concluded that human activity was responsible for the deaths of the baboons, although they rejected the idea that all the baboons died on one occasion. Some of the bones were more heavily weathered and cracked than others, suggesting that the remains were deposited over a period of time.

Human activity is thought likely because the baboons are of varied ages, with a preponderance of juveniles, and because all skeletal parts, including very small bones, are preserved – implying a lack of water action to separate bones of different weight. Also, there are pronounced patterns in the way that parts of some bones are preserved, implying a systematic way of exploiting the baboon carcases for

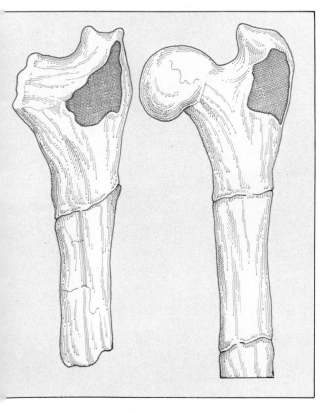

meat. Finally, there are traces of cut-marks and of battering.

Although this combination of features is very convincing to experienced palaeontologists such as Dr Kay Behrensmeyer, the hunting theory is still disputed by the American archaeologist and anthropologist Professor Lewis Binford. The individual elements of the pattern above *can* occur naturally. Yet how likely would they be to occur together? T.H. Huxley considered the man who might dispute that fossil shells are derived from ancient shellfish, and wondered how that man would prove that mussel shells in his dustbin were the result of a meal eaten the night before. If we demand proof that the Olorgesailie baboons were hunted and butchered, perhaps we should first wonder how to prove that we had carved yesterday's joint. Certain proof is often elusive when dealing with evidence from sites such as these, but it does seem likely that the baboons died at *Homo*'s hands.

The Olorgesailie sites are important for many other reasons than the hunting evidence. The sites occur not as one extensive horizon, like Kilombe (see pp 68–71), but as a set of small ones, scattered here and there in the area. Often, the exact stratigraphic relationships between the sites cannot be established because small faults make it difficult to follow the layers horizontally.

The archaeology of the sites is varied. Some of them are dominated by hand-axes, others by small tools, particularly scrapers. When testing the results of measuring large series of the stone tools by statistical means, Glynn Isaac noticed two major points: first, that there were greater differences of size and shape, between the hand-axes on separate sites than would be expected to have occurred naturally; second, that there were sites where hand-axes were predominant, and those where there were more small tools, but few intermediate sites. Perhaps, then, the hand-axes were used for one activity, such as butchering baboons – and the small scrapers were used for something else, such as scraping hides.

The size and shape differences of the hand-axes may be partly explained by the possibility that the separate Olorgesailie sites differ in age, by perhaps hundreds of years. At Kilombe, where the concentration of finds on a single surface may have taken place over a shorter period of time, all the hand-axe samples are very similar. Glynn Isaac has suggested that, although the basic ideas of hand-axe manufacture were strictly controlled, there was some latitude for change, and the variations at Olorgesailie represent a random drift in cultural 'norms' (localized preferred styles). Such changes in preference may have developed over the course of a few lifetimes.

Each major site complex, such as Olorgesailie, Kilombe, Isimila or Kalambo Falls, presents a slightly different view of the Acheulean. Olorgesailie and Isimila show us how varied the tool-kits of early man could be. The baboon bones at Olorgesailie keep alive the possibility that hand-axes were primarily butchering tools, even though elsewhere, for example at Kilombe, they may have had more general uses. Archaeologists have learnt to expect only gradual progress through painstaking studies, but the archaeology of these Middle Pleistocene times can be very exciting.

Stone tools, including hand-axes, exposed in one of the excavations. The sites are believed to be about 400,000 years old on the basis of potassium-argon dates.

Language, brain and performance

Studies of the brain can lead to greater understanding of the nature of human distinctiveness because behaviour is regulated by the brain. Information from even the distant past can be recovered from cranial casts. Early hominid brains had a human-like organization, which may imply the early development of language.

We have seen that some mental abilities can be deduced from the archaeological record – but how can we learn more about the brain, and language, the most vital element in human communication?

In addition to the archaeological evidence, it is possible to look at actual human remains. With care, an internal cast can be taken of a human skull, using a thin latex mould. The cast from this mould then gives an outline of the brain in the form of an endocast. Since, in life, the outer surface of the brain is encased in a membrane which lies against the skull, most of the surface detail is lost in the cast, but the brain's overall shape and its major component parts can be seen clearly.

The most visible part of the brain in higher primates is the cerebrum. In evolutionary history it developed later than the underlying parts, such as the cerebellum and the brain stem, and is concerned with most of the advanced faculties of behaviour.

In the course of evolution, the human brain has become much larger than that of the apes, and the surface of the cerebrum, if the wrinkles were straightened out, would amount to the area of a small tablecloth. The human brain is on average 1,300–1,500 cc in volume, compared with 400–500 cc in the chimpanzee. The early australopithecines had small brains, no larger than those of the great apes, but in making comparisons, we must take into account that their bodies were also much smaller than ours and those of the African apes. Thus, relative to body size, hominid cranial enlargement had begun even at the australopithecine stage.

As there is great variation in modern human brain size, without a corresponding variation in intelligence, it is clear that the organization of the brain is important, as well as the size. Professor Ralph Holloway of Columbia University, New York, who has assembled over 40 endocasts of fossil hominids, has been able to show that even the earlier hominids had brains more on the human than on the ape pattern. Although there is little surface detail on the endocasts, it can be seen from the fold of the lambdoidal suture that in australopithecines, including the robust variety, the occipital lobe (the back area) is much reduced compared with that of the chimpanzee, and therefore similar to modern man. The parietal (side) region of the brain is also much deeper and fuller in its contours than that of the chimpanzee. These features are yet more marked in specimens of *Homo erectus*, with greater expansion of the frontal and temporal lobes.

Whether language was in use is a particularly critical question. It has sometimes been suggested that it developed during the last 100,000 years, together with the modern cranial form, but its presence must be suspected very much earlier, because of the large amounts of cultural information which were successfully transmitted.

Although apes have the capacity to handle symbols, they seem to lack the ability to string them together in elaborate syntax, just as their operational chains of practical activity are more limited than human ones. Human vocalization would also be difficult for apes, because of the organization of the

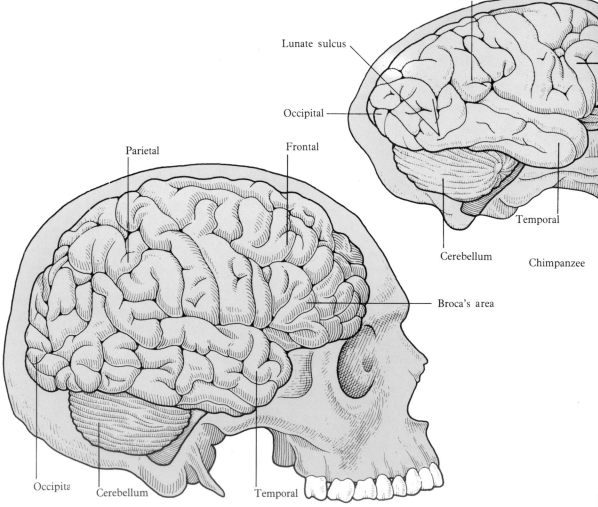

In modern animals, the full detail of the brain can be studied. Compared with man, the chimpanzee has a much smaller brain with a larger occipital lobe, but smaller and less developed frontal and temporal lobes. The cerebral cortex is less convoluted and thus has a much smaller surface area.

Homo sapiens sapiens (modern man)

throat, but it would be unrealistic to think that this is the main obstacle preventing them from speaking, or indeed that different throat organization in earlier hominids would have limited their speech.

In modern man, it is well known that there is a 'lateralization' of the brain organization which is partly concerned with language. For a right-handed person it is usual for the left half of the brain to control language, and for the right side to be superior in conceptual skills, such as visio-spatial abilities. The position with left-handedness is more complicated, for it does not necessarily entail a complete reversal of functions, but seems to vary from individual to individual. Language is closely connected with a part of the brain called 'Brocas's area' which occurs on the lower part of the relevant frontal lobe.

Why should lateralization have developed, and what part in language does Brocas's area play? It seems that the very precise sequencing of words used in language is best controlled from a single zone of the brain, and that interference, sometimes leading to stammering, results if both hemispheres are involved. Similar lateralization has evolved in some songbirds, supporting the idea that a single area of the brain is involved with the sequencing of language.

Endocasts do not allow detailed study of a zone such as Brocas's area. Recent work by Holloway and his colleague De La Coste-Lareymondie has however begun to show positive evidence of a human pattern of brain asymmetry even in the early hominids. The starting point was to have a large series of modern human and ape endocasts, and to study the patterns of asymmetry in petalias – localized 'plates' discernible on the surface of the casts. *Homo erectus* shows a similar pattern of petalias as modern man: left occipital/right frontal. A similar human-like pattern seems to be present in australopithecines, though the number of specimens available for study is much smaller. In modern human beings, the relationship between petalias and left- or right-handedness is not always absolute, but it is clear that patterns of petalias give a very good measure of brain asymmetry. The pattern probably relates both to linguistic organization, and the organization of complex tasks.

All this evidence supports the idea that the evolution of the human brain and mind has been a prolonged, gradual process, in which the main foundations had been laid by the time of *Homo erectus* and the Acheulean tradition of tool-making.

Although there is a great deal that we do not understand, the brain seems in some way unitary in its organization, for all complex tasks, whether organizational, practical or verbal seem to have an underlying common pattern in the way in which they are carried out. The brain has to be able to organize or 'overview' the general scheme, long before the detailed sequence fits into place. This is so whether we are embarking on a sentence, a stone tool, or a new development in technology. The technology of *Homo erectus* leaves no doubt that the essentials of human performance were already present in Acheulean times.

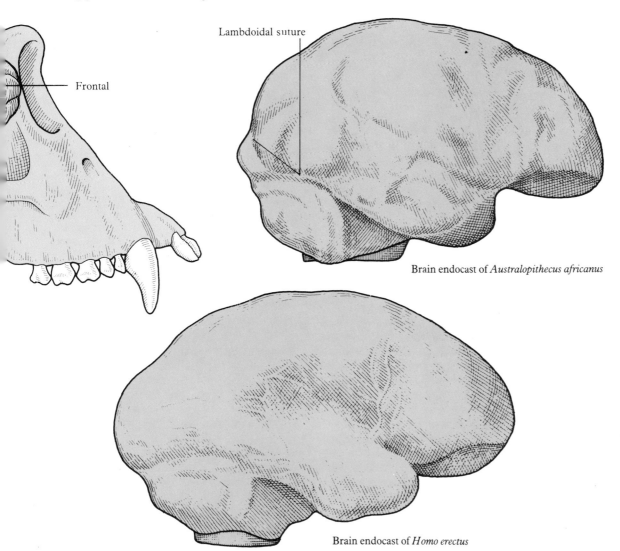

Frontal

Lambdoidal suture

Brain endocast of *Australopithecus africanus*

Brain endocast of *Homo erectus*

Casts of early hominid brains lack the surface detail, but preserve the general outline of the brain structures. Both the australopithecine (above) and *Homo erectus* (below) are distinctly human-like rather than ape-like in the pattern of organization.

75

Early occupation of Europe

The time of the first human occupation of Europe is not known for certain, but it was certainly as early as 700,000 years ago. A definite site of this age has been found in Italy, but other sites in Spain and southern France may be as old or older.

When was Europe first occupied by man? This keenly debated question may never be answered precisely, for the circumstances of preservation are not nearly as favourable as in Africa, but nonetheless there are enough sites to give us useful clues.

Although Europe was the area which was most researched by early prehistorians, it has become plain that it was quite peripheral – almost a backwater – throughout the greater part of the Pleistocene. Most of the Pleistocene was colder than it is now, and from certainly 1.5 million years ago, glaciers advanced time and again from the north, reaching at their furthest limits into southern Britain and the north of Germany. They also spread out from separate centres in the Alps and Pyrenees. At such times, Europe would have been a cold peninsula, unfavourable for human settlement, except in the south-west and south-east. But the rigours of the Ice Age should not be exaggerated unduly: for more than half the time, the climate was cooler than today, but would have allowed settlement in Europe up to about 50° north, roughly on the same latitude as Amsterdam. There is ample evidence that in these interstadial times, large mammals, including elephants, rhinoceros and bison, and also deer, were abundant in Europe.

For only about 10 per cent of the time was it as warm or a few degrees warmer than it is now. Such warm interglacial times, coming perhaps once in every 100,000 years, seem to have been rich in human settlement.

There is at least a chance that evidence of very early hominid occupation of Europe could be found because we know that the range of dryopithecine apes extended this far north. As volcanic activity is rare in Europe, there are few opportunities for potassium-argon dating, except in late Tertiary deposits of the Massif Central in France. These have rich mammal assemblages dating from about 3 million years ago, but although primates are represented, there are no traces of hominids. This is negative evidence, but for the moment it is safest to assume that the first occupation of Europe would have been by tool-making men in the earlier Pleistocene. Many archaeologists believe that man could have moved north into temperate Europe only through having the use of fire, which would imply a date about 1.5 million years ago or later.

The oldest possible sites are controversial because they have yielded only a few tools, in uncertainly dated positions. The best known is the cave at Le Vallonnet in southern France, where there are remains of the beach left by a very high sea-level, some time early in the Pleistocene. Between 2 and 1 million years ago, there are signs that the sea-level was regularly much higher than at present – as much as 100 or 200 metres though it fell to lower levels during glacial periods when water would be locked up in the ice.

Four flakes and five pebble choppers were found at Le Vallonnet in the cold-period sediments which overlie the beach. As they are 'primitive' and Oldowan-like in character, and the underlying beach is undoubtedly ancient, we might be tempted to see this as the earliest evidence for man in Europe. Unfortunately, however, the case is far from proven, for the tools could be much younger than the beach, and beach pebbles have commonly been made into tools at much later dates.

Similar doubts exist about Stranská Skála, a site in loess deposits in Czechoslovakia. Loess is sediment created mainly in glacial times, and traceable to the actions of glaciers. Rocks and soil pulverized by the weight and movement of the ice are carried forward and deposited by streams as ice melts in the spring and summer. Winds – which were probably stronger in glacial times – pick up the sediments and transport them for hundreds of kilometres. Such loess forms a thick blanket in much of central Europe, and in parts of China. In Czechoslovakia, loess deposits can be traced back through at least 700,000 years, and they frequently preserve archaeological sites. Chips of stone at Stranská Skála are quite possibly the result of human stone-working, but this is not universally accepted.

Fortunately, a site that is definitely older than 700,000 years (and hence belongs to the Early Pleistocene) has recently been found in central Italy near Rome. This is the one part of Europe where Pleistocene volcanic activity allows a potassium-argon record. The site, Isernia, can be dated by potassium-argon from volcanic ash immediately overlying the archaeological horizon to 0.73 million years. This date is completely consistent with the reversed magnetic direction of the sediments, which suggests an age of over 700,000 years. Isernia has been investigated very recently by an international team from Italy, the Netherlands and the USA. These researches show that it was a site by a lake in the hills where animals regularly came to water.

Finds on the site at Isernia, Italy. The stone tools do not include hand-axes.

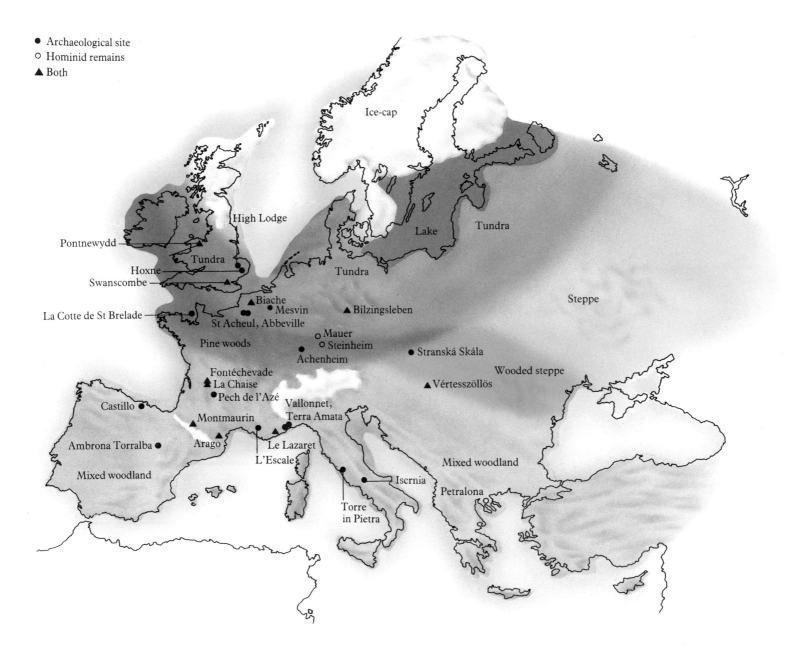

- ● Archaeological site
- ○ Hominid remains
- ▲ Both

Ice-cap

High Lodge

Pontnewydd

Tundra

Hoxne
Swanscombe

La Cotte de St Brelade

Biache
Mesvin
St Acheul, Abbeville

Bilzingsleben

Lake

Tundra

Tundra

Steppe

Mauer
Steinheim
Achenheim

Stranská Skála

Wooded steppe

Pine woods

Fontéchevade
La Chaise
Pech de l'Azé

Vértesszöllös

Castillo

Vallonnet,
Terra Amata

Montmaurin

Ambrona Torralba

Arago

Le Lazaret
L'Escale

Mixed woodland

Mixed woodland

Iscrnia

Petralona

Torre
in Pietra

Both the stone tools and animal remains discovered at Isernia tell an interesting and unusual story. The tools do not recall the Acheulean, predominant in contemporary African sites, for they consist largely of limestone choppers and smaller flint flakes. The limestone was suitable for large tools because of its abundance and the size of the available pieces. Flint was preferred for small tools because of its superior sharpness. Scrapers and retouched points are found among the small tools.

These tools occur in their thousands and among them are many bones of large animals, in particular elephants and bison. It is surprising to learn that some of these species were in existence at such an early date, for they were thought to belong to the Middle Pleistocene. There are none of the deer remains which are so abundant on later European sites. The investigators believe that climatic conditions of a short wet season and long dry season created steppe-like conditions more suitable for larger mammals.

What of the Acheulean, the great hand-axe tradition? We will see that there are other early sites in Europe, as well as Isernia, where pebble choppers and flake tools remind us of the Oldowan rather than

the Acheulean. This has led to the suggestion that human beings with Oldowan technology entered Europe at an early stage and only later were 'swamped' by an Acheulean second wave. This seems unlikely because even the oldest sites in Europe are much younger than the earliest Acheulean in Africa. More probably, the early inhabitants of Europe adapted their technology to the raw materials readily available. Even in Africa, hand-axes were not always made, and are not found on all sites.

The Acheulean does appear in Europe, especially in the west, but the sites are nearly all more recent than Isernia. A question remains: how had human beings reached the Italian peninsula? The obvious route is from Turkey, via the Balkans, but at periods of low sea-level two other routes may have been used. It may have been possible to cross from Tunis to Sicily and the number of sites in Spain, including some possible early ones, suggests strongly that the straits of Gibraltar were crossed. The discovery in 1982 of early human cranial remains, possibly of Early Pleistocene age, from Orce, near Granada, strengthens the evidence for early occupation of Spain.

An impression of Pleistocene Europe. During the ice ages, cold and warm periods succeeded one another, and sea-levels rose and fell. But most of the time, conditions were intermediate: colder than today, but not fully glacial. At such times, sea-level was generally somewhat lower than today. This map represents such a phase (not a specific one), and shows some of the major sites over 150,000 years old (see also pp 88–93).

In the East

Most finds of *Homo erectus* come from the Far East, where the early archaeological record is potentially as important as in Africa. As yet there are no long well-dated sequences, but at Choukoutien in China, *Homo erectus* and stone artefacts occur together in a site of exceptional significance.

Human occupation of the Far East probably extended throughout the whole Pleistocene, but at only a few of the sites can we observe evidence of Middle Pleistocene man.

The most famous of these is Choukoutien near Peking. In the 1920s early human remains were discovered in a cave, together with large quantities of stone tools. The human finds, at first ascribed to a new genus – *Sinanthropus* – were later seen to be similar to the *Homo erectus* finds from Java discovered in 1891.

Choukoutien is not a single site but a complex of caves at different levels formed by the erosion of limestone hills. The largest number of human remains, including 14 crania, came from the Lower Cave, Locality 1. Unfortunately these finds were all lost mysteriously at the beginning of the Second World War; they were packed into boxes and loaded onto an evacuation train heading for the docks and were never seen again. This is less of a tragedy than it might have been because the original finds had been excellently cast and described, and also because new finds have been made in recent years.

General view of excavations at Choukoutien. Excavation of the site originally began in the 1920s and was resumed in the post-war period.

Excavations at Choukoutien. Some of the sediments are so consolidated that pneumatic tools are needed for their excavation. Horizons with finds are excavated by hand.

Although the Choukoutien caves preserve more information about *Homo erectus* than any other early site in the East, they leave us with a number of puzzles. The first is the age of the sites. They are widely accepted to belong to the Middle Pleistocene, but dating estimates range from 0.7–0.3 million years ago. Although older estimates (0.7–0.5 million years) seem more reasonable, the basis for this is mainly the character of the stone tools and comparisons with more developed late *Homo erectus*/early *Homo sapiens*. All these dating arguments are dangerously circular.

The stone tools are most certainly not Acheulean. Over 100,000 artefacts have been found, including vast numbers of flakes, some scrapers and choppers. In Europe or Africa, Acheulean bifaces would have been expected, and the discrepancy at Choukoutien and on other Far Eastern sites led the American archaeologist Professor Hallam Movius to postulate a chopper/chopping tool complex east of the 'Acheulean World'. The Choukoutien finds are actually similar in technology to the Developed Oldowan, and could reasonably be described as such except for their later date and far-separated location.

Very recent work, however, suggests that the Acheulean did after all appear at some time in the Far East. A site in Mongolia, described by the Russian archaeologist A.P. Okladnikov, and the site of Chongokni in Korea, excavated by Dr Wha Chung, are the prime evidence for this. Nonetheless, most of the Far Eastern assemblages plainly do not have hand-axes.

There are several possibilities which might account for the kind of assemblage found at Choukoutien. Perhaps the biface idea originated in the West and had not percolated through; perhaps the raw materials – mainly vein quartz – did not exist in suitable form; perhaps hand-axes were used, but do not appear in the caves.

Such a bias is possible, for as we have seen, caves do not contain a random selection of finds. At Choukoutien skulls survived surprisingly often in relation to the rest of the skeleton. This pattern contrasts with that at other sites which have many hominid remains, such as East Turkana. At Choukoutien the crania, which are relatively delicate, are well-preserved, whereas not even the ends (the toughest parts) of long bones, such as the femur and humerus, survive. But the bases of the skulls are broken open and it has been suggested that they were the trophies of head-hunters, separately brought into the cave where the brains were eaten.

Alongside the human remains were bones of many animals, mainly a species of deer with large horns, but also large carnivores, elephant, horse, water buffalo and others. It was originally assumed that these were the food of *Homo erectus*, but it has to be recognized that many of them could have been introduced into the caves by natural means, for example, being dragged in by carnivores. Taking an extreme view, we could dispense with the activity of man altogether and see the cave as a vast rubbish dump in which the bones of animals collected and were chewed over by carnivores. This interpretation is given the lie, however, by the huge numbers of stone tools and, above all, by the constant evidence of fire: Davidson Black, the original excavator, describes layer upon layer where the sediments were baked, bones were charred and ashes preserved.

There is no doubt that man was regularly in the cave and shaped the course of events there. Quite possibly, too, his activities included the killing and eating of human beings. Whether there was an element of ritual in this early form of cannibalism we can only guess, but the recent discovery that the skull from Bodo in Ethiopia had been scalped shows that such possibilities are real.

The more general course of events in the Far East, the evolution from *Homo erectus* to *Homo sapiens*, can only be followed with difficulty, since there are hardly any reliable absolute dates. But the overall impression is that in this part of the world, as elsewhere, *Homo sapiens* emerged gradually from *Homo erectus*, and that stone technology gradually became more sophisticated during the same period.

Several localities at Choukoutien appear to be more recent than the main *Homo erectus* sites. Locality 15, only 100 m further south, has technologically superior stone tools, which are classed as Middle Palaeolithic. The striking platforms of flakes were carefully prepared before they were struck, as is commonly the case when

Levallois technique is practised (see pp 80–81). The scrapers and points were also well finished. At the Hsintung (New Cave) site nearby, a human tooth was found together with a few stone tools.

More complete human remains come from the sites of Tingtsun and Mapa. These cranial pieces suggest parallels with the Java *Homo erectus* finds, and all are generally regarded as early *Homo sapiens*.

As research continues, the number of sites in east and south-east Asia steadily increases. Crudeness of manufacture is not a sure sign that stone tools are ancient, for on some sites of the Hoabinhien tradition of South-East Asia the tools have been shown to belong to the last 10,000 years. Many early sites have been reported in Japan, but by no means all Japanese archaeologists accept their antiquity on the basis of the present evidence. Until stratified sites are found and carefully excavated, there will be no definite answer. New discoveries of early sites in Korea, however, including Chongokni which is described as an Acheulean site, strengthen the possibility that Japan, too, was occupied, since the islands were at times linked to the mainland.

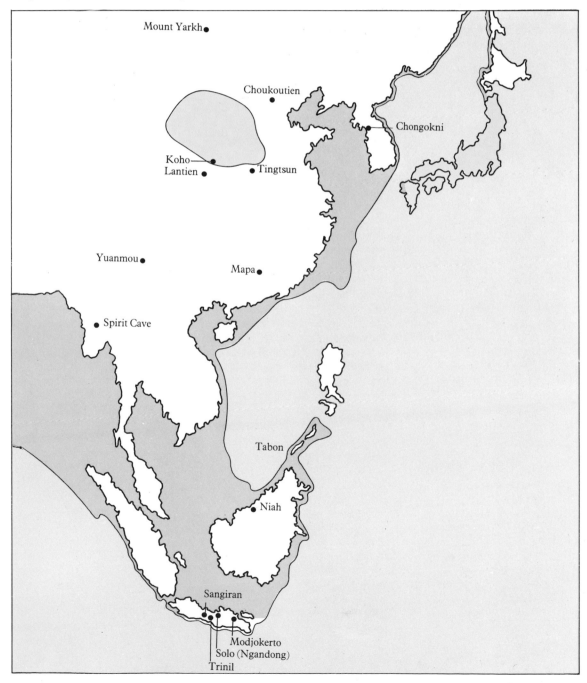

Important Stone Age sites and hominid remains in the Far East. The densest distribution of Lower Palaeolithic sites is in northern China. The oldest known archaeological sites in Indonesia, Borneo and the Philippines are less than 100,000 years old, but far older hominid remains come from Java, including the original finds of *Homo erectus*.

Dense distribution

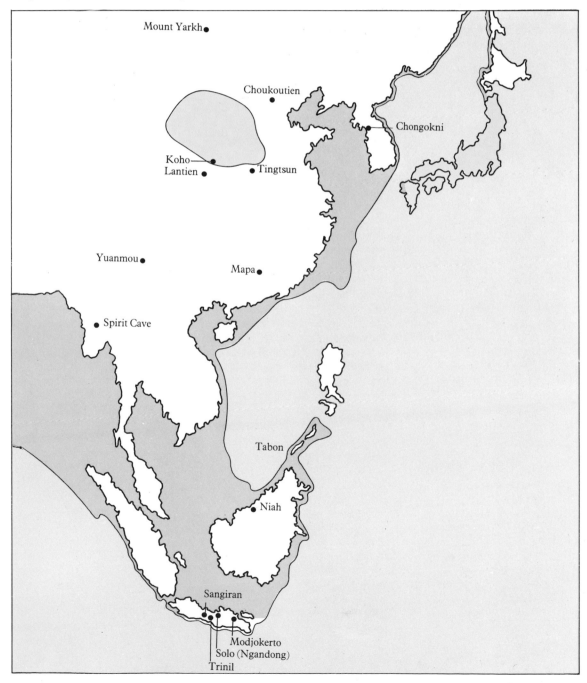

A hidden transformation

The Acheulean period is sometimes regarded as a million years without any noticeable developments. But during this time *Homo sapiens* was evolving; and late Acheulean sites near Lake Baringo, Kenya, and elsewhere demonstrate the technological skills which had developed.

Pre-shaping of tools on the core – the Levallois technique – can be accomplished by modern flint-knappers. Such tools may have been regarded as particularly useful as they have robust, but sharp, edges around most of the circumference.

The most remarkable feature of the Acheulean tradition is that it went on for so long. The first hand-axes were made 1.5 million years ago, and they were still in common use 200,000 years ago. No wonder that the Acheulean is often looked upon as a long standstill, associated with a slightly dim-witted *Homo erectus*. Yet this would be a hasty judgement. There are many grounds for thinking we are seeing just the tip of the iceberg, and that significant changes were in fact taking place during this long period.

Towards the end of the Acheulean, in the last quarter of a million years, the development of spectacular skills can be seen in the manufacture of the hand-axes themselves. Spectacular is the right word, for techniques came into use which demanded such skill that they can be emulated by very few modern stone-workers.

The good raw materials, which encouraged the manufacture of hand-axes, often occurred in such large blocks that the best way to get material was to strike off a large flake, perhaps to serve as a blank for making a hand-axe. When early men were striking a series of such big flakes, it would always be easier to strike the next one from a place on the core where a crest had been left between two previous flake scars. They would thus be preparing the way for the next flake as they went along. This simple procedure is visible from the evidence of early sites such as Kilombe and Kariandusi, but over the next few hundred thousand years it developed in a remarkable way. In later Acheulean times before a hand-axe blank was struck, many flakes, perhaps 30 or more, would be taken off the face of the core to give it precisely the right shape. Then the platform would be carefully shaped by taking off more small flakes, until eventually all was ready. Finally, with a single carefully-placed blow, the completed hand-axe was detached. The result would be success or disaster, according to the skill of the stone-worker.

This technique became widespread in areas where there was good raw material, such as fine-grained lava or quartzite. In Africa it was commonly used for making hand-axes and called Victoria West technique after a site in South Africa. In Europe a

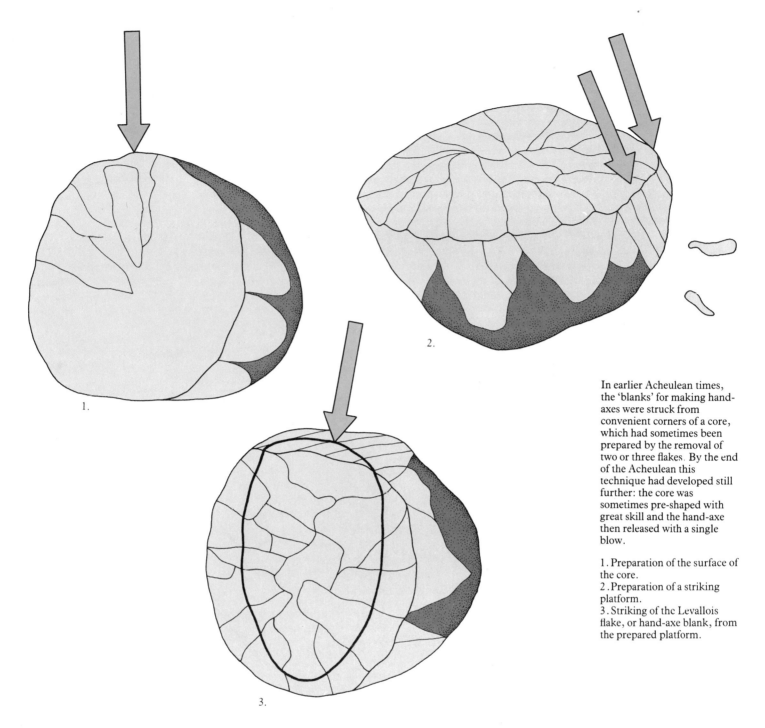

In earlier Acheulean times, the 'blanks' for making hand-axes were struck from convenient corners of a core, which had sometimes been prepared by the removal of two or three flakes. By the end of the Acheulean this technique had developed still further: the core was sometimes pre-shaped with great skill and the hand-axe then released with a single blow.

1. Preparation of the surface of the core.
2. Preparation of a striking platform.
3. Striking of the Levallois flake, or hand-axe blank, from the prepared platform.

similar technique became used for making smaller flint hand-axes and many flake tools which required careful shaping. It is then generally known as the Levallois technique, after a site in France.

A curious and fascinating aspect of the technique is that this extra care does not appear to have been necessary. Two common explanations advanced for the extra work which Levallois technique entailed are that it allowed tools to be made with a special form, and that it made the best use of raw material where these were scarce. Neither interpretation is altogether convincing. Many of the large Levallois flakes were later trimmed into hand-axes and just the same form could be obtained by using the older techniques. The method creates many small waste flakes for each successful end product and so it was most used in places where there was abundant raw material. People probably developed and used this technique because it allowed them to produce exactly the result which they wanted.

When did this technique appear, which tells us about the development of higher skills? It was during a period which is difficult to date (see pp 86–87), but we can make a general estimate: the technique is not yet evident in the major Acheulean sites of Isimila or Olorgesailie, which are over 400,000 years old, nor at Kalambo Falls (about 200,000 years), but it does appear in outstanding form at Kapthurin, near Lake Baringo, on a site apparently aged about 230,000 years. It also occurs in very early Middle Stone Age sites in Ethiopia, aged about 180,000 years. In Europe, it seems to be absent in sites over 300,000 years old, but is certainly present by 200,000.

The Levallois technique seems to indicate that gradually people came to take a pleasure in technology for its own sake. In the course of these developments, the hand-axe itself was eventually abandoned and forgotten, but the Levallois method remained common for flake tool manufacture and in some places continued into the last 30,000 years.

Chapter V
Out of
Homo erectus,
Homo sapiens

A series of key finds shows us that *Homo sapiens* emerged gradually from *Homo erectus*, a process of change so gentle that many finds are on the borderline. We can estimate that this was happening about 300,000 to 400,000 years ago, but it is very difficult to measure the rate of evolutionary development. At this time we begin to see life in more detail – wooden tools are preserved, including spears which give proof of hunting. Advance into Europe and Russia meant a serious encounter with the rigours of the Ice Age. Slowly, human beings aided by control of fire – and almost certainly by clothes – extended their colonization northwards.

Part of a cranium from the cave of Arago at Tautavel in southern France. It is over 300,000 years old and is important because it preserves facial bones.

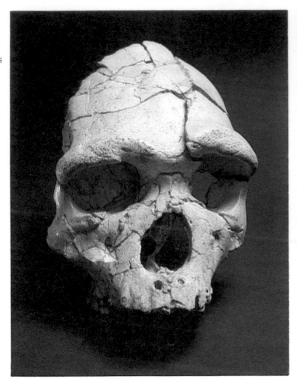

The rugged coast of Jersey. The sea has returned to much the same level many times, which has resulted in the extensive wave-cut platform of eroded rocks. The cliffs formed by previous high sea-levels are still partly masked by sediments, including raised beaches of the last interglacial. They appear as red colouring in the distant cove. The photograph was taken close to the archaeological site of La Cotte de St Brelade.

The earliest finds of Homo sapiens

Homo sapiens evolved gradually from *Homo erectus*, so the borderline between the species is arbitrary. Early finds which can be assigned to *Homo sapiens* come from several areas of the Old World.

During the million or more years of the Acheulean in which mankind had been making tools, what changes had taken place in the human form? Here we have solid evidence, in the shape of human remains, though they are often only small fragments and sometimes hard to date in relation to each other.

Homo erectus was already human in body form, and to a large extent human in the cranium. Brain size was smaller, however, and this is reflected in the shape of the lower cranial vault. In addition the teeth were much larger than our own. We can be reasonably sure that *Homo sapiens*, our species, gradually evolved out of *Homo erectus*. The best evidence for this lies in the number of finds which have transitional characteristics, and in a lack of reasonable alternative theories. At the beginning of the Middle Pleistocene, 700,000 years ago, we find only *Homo erectus*, but by 200,000 years ago, we find only *Homo sapiens*.

There is a continuing debate among anthropologists about which of the transitional specimens are *erectus* and which *sapiens*. The finders of new fossils are sometimes tempted to classify a find as *erectus* so that it will be seen as more archaic and therefore more interesting. The exact labelling of a find is, however, less important than the fact that the overall trend towards a larger, rounder skull is clear, despite the small number of well-preserved, well-dated specimens.

One of the oldest finds whose shape shows some of the characteristics of *sapiens* is the Bodo cranium from Ethiopia. This rugged specimen, to which no precise age can be attached, was found with Acheulean tools close to Hadar, and is remarkable for the cut-marks which it bears. The marks, almost certainly made by a stone tool, resemble the marks on modern skulls which have been scalped, and the American anthropologists Timothy White and Lewis Binford agree in concluding that this is much the

most likely interpretation. It is pointed out that the scalp offers little that is worth eating, and that consequently its removal probably has symbolic significance. Should we really picture the scalping of a dead enemy (or even a friend) for the purpose of keeping a trophy or memento? However unlikely this might seem, it is consistent with the other 'advanced' human characteristics which we have already encountered.

Elsewhere in Africa, other significant finds can be placed in early *Homo sapiens*, including cranial remains from Saldanha in South Africa (about 200,000 years old). Most other African finds are probably rather later in date (see pp 118–119).

For this period, Europe now provides a series of finds showing similar development from *erectus* to *sapiens*. A mandible found at Mauer in Germany is probably the oldest hominid find from Europe, and may be more than half a million years old. Other early remains come from the site of Bilzingsleben in East Germany, 70 km west of Leipzig, where freshwater limestone or tufa has helped to preserve finds. On the basis of pollen evidence and faunal remains, the site is probably at least half a million years old. The shape of the cranial fragments found suggests *Homo erectus*: they can be quite satisfactorily fitted into the cast of a *Homo erectus* skullcap from Olduvai Bed II (1.4 million years old), evidence which accords with the probable early date. At Vértesszöllös in Hungary (see p 89), a later site with similar tufa deposits, only the rear region of

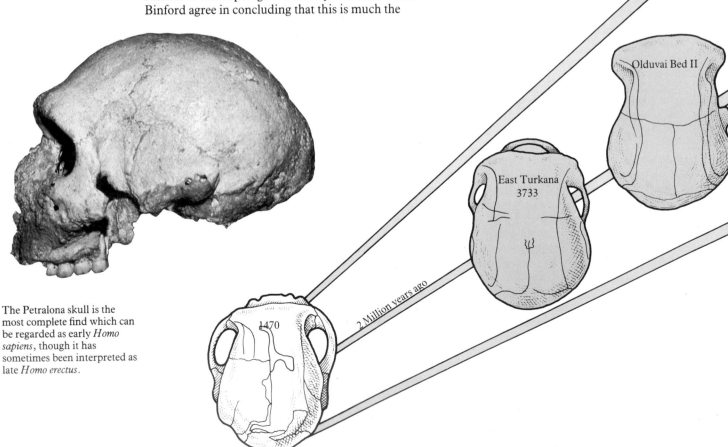

The Petralona skull is the most complete find which can be regarded as early *Homo sapiens*, though it has sometimes been interpreted as late *Homo erectus*.

1470

2 Million years ago

East Turkana 3733

Olduvai Bed II

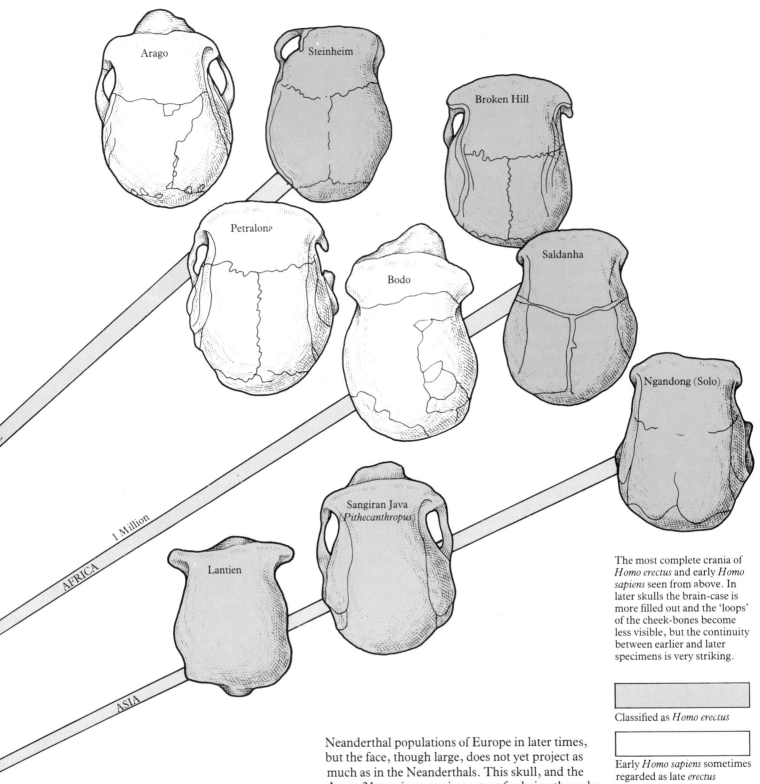

The most complete crania of *Homo erectus* and early *Homo sapiens* seen from above. In later skulls the brain-case is more filled out and the 'loops' of the cheek-bones become less visible, but the continuity between earlier and later specimens is very striking.

Classified as *Homo erectus*

Early *Homo sapiens* sometimes regarded as late *erectus*

Classified as *Homo sapiens*

the skull was preserved; it can be seen as early *Homo sapiens* or as a transitional form.

Several other European finds, probably from a later period than Bilzingsleben, are better classed as *Homo sapiens*. This series is represented by finds from Tautavel (Arago) in southern France, Steinheim in Germany, Swanscombe in Britain, and Biache in northern France. All these finds are more rounded, or 'filled out', in the skull than the classic *Homo erectus* specimens such as those discovered at Choukoutien.

The remarkably complete skull from Petralona in Greece retains much of the size and shape of earlier *Homo erectus*, but has a larger cranial vault. It can be seen as an early *Homo sapiens* ancestor to the Neanderthal populations of Europe in later times, but the face, though large, does not yet project as much as in the Neanderthals. This skull, and the Arago 21 cranium, are important for being the only specimens of this age range preserving the face. The Arago 21 cranium belongs with *Homo sapiens*, and like Petralona it shows sufficient resemblances to the Neanderthals to suggest that their distinctive characteristics evolved gradually from *Homo erectus* within Europe and probably western Asia. The Swanscombe and Steinheim finds also have some characteristics which are suggestive of the Neanderthals.

In Asia, this period of man's development is much less well recorded, but there are enough similarities between *Homo erectus* of Java and China, and later *Homo sapiens* of the last 100,000 years, to suggest once again that evolution was continuous and gradual.

The dating gap

The middle part of the Pleistocene (c. 700,000–125,000 years) is notoriously difficult to date. Several methods developed by physicists now offer better hope for dating archaeological sites from this period.

It would be quite natural to think that the closer we come to the present day, the easier it is to date finds, but this is not always so.

In the Early Pleistocene, the potassium-argon (K-Ar) and palaeomagnetic methods interact powerfully to help build a time-scale, but within the last million years, both become much less serviceable. As well as being limited to dating volcanic material, potassium-argon can only be used reliably on rocks over a certain age, since radiogenic argon forms very slowly, and sufficient must have formed to be measurable. Some potassium-argon dates are on material as young as 200,000 years, but there are few satisfactory ones younger than 0.5 million years. Palaeomagnetism too becomes less useful as an aid in dating, because for the last 700,000 years polarity has been normal (as today), except for one or two very brief excursions.

The well-known radiocarbon dating method will never be effective on material more than 100,000 years old, because carbon-14 decays quite rapidly. This means that there is a dating gap of almost half a million years which scientists and archaeologists are working to bridge.

An overall framework for the Middle Pleistocene period is given by the deep-sea cores, because they are continuous, and can be dated by radiocarbon for more recent times and by the last major geomagnetic reversal (730,000 years) earlier on. They show that during this period, there were about nine major cycles of climatic change, reflected in colder and warmer ocean temperatures.

Several dating methods have great promise for filling out this framework, but at the moment their uses are still being developed. Most of the methods depend in some way on the radioactive element uranium. As in radiocarbon and potassium-argon dating, use is made of the fact that radioactive elements break down at a known rate, which cannot be affected by any chemical change. This breakdown can thus supply an entirely reliable clock, provided that suitable radioactive elements can be trapped or isolated in some way. Then, only the relevant breakdown products – those formed since the event to be dated – will be measured.

The most precise of the methods which contribute towards filling the dating gap is uranium series dating, although it can only be applied in certain circumstances. Uranium, the heaviest naturally occurring element, is soluble in water, in which it is present as a tiny fraction of parts per million. But the principal elements into which uranium breaks down, thorium and protactinium, are not soluble in water, and hence are not found in it. Consequently, any calcareous organisms such as shells, which form from carbonates dissolved in

water, trap uranium, but not the daughter elements. As the trapped uranium breaks down long after the organism has died, it yields protactinium and thorium, and their ratios give us a measure of how long the process has been going on.

Since the daughter products of uranium themselves break down, their build-up eventually stops, giving the method a maximum limit of about 350,000 years. The chief hazard of uranium series dating is that new material may have contaminated the specimen under study in the intervening period affecting the concentration of the elements, but there are various ways of checking whether contamination is a problem.

In marine deposits uranium series dating is most successfully applied to ancient corals. This means that where there are coasts with coral reefs, traces of the old high sea-levels left by warm periods or interglacials can be dated. This method has shown that there were high sea-levels about 120,000, 220,000 and 330,000 years ago. Dates older than these cannot be obtained directly, but they can sometimes be calculated by relating such dates to other measurable and fairly constant changes, such as the geological uplift of land. Drs J. Chappell and H. H. Veeh have been able to take advantage of the steady uplift of Timor and Atauro islands in Indonesia to calculate periods of high sea-level. Although in this case only the most recent high level (about 120,000) could be dated directly, ages for other raised beaches could be dated on the assumption that uplift of land was constant over a much longer period. Very similar results have been obtained from New Guinea and Barbados.

Another promising application of the uranium series method is in the dating of stalactites and stalagmites which form in caves, and layers of travertine (freshwater limestone) which form around springs. Again, the daughter elements of uranium are trapped in the newly formed carbonates. Among the results are dates of between 185,000 and 106,000 years ago for occupation of the cave La Chaise in France, where there are human remains. Another date of about 150,000 years ago for an evolved Acheulean industry at Zuttiyeh Cave near Galilee is especially useful in showing that hand-axes were still being made at this time.

The radioactivity of uranium and its daughter elements is also the key to the other methods which

Thermoluminescence (TL) is light released when a crystal structure which has been irradiated is heated. The glow, given off by striped fluoride and calcite spectacularly here, must normally be measured in carefully controlled conditions.

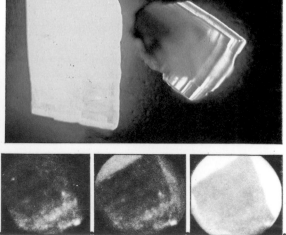

When a natural calcite specimen is heated in an enclosed oven, the amount of TL emitted varies according to the temperature of heating, yielding the TL 'glow curve'. The photograph shows the TL emitted as a sample is heated in steps. The calcite is visibly inhomogeneous in its TL, a factor which has made dating more difficult.

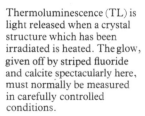

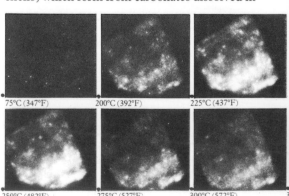

75°C (347°F) 200°C (392°F) 225°C (437°F)

250°C (482°F) 275°C (527°F) 300°C (572°F) 325°C (617°F) 350°C (662°F) 375°C (707°F) 400°C (752°F)

can be used to fill the dating gap. These are thermoluminescence (TL) and electron spin resonance (ESR). They are feasible because uranium exists at low density in most materials. As the uranium trapped in quartz or calcite breaks down, some of the emitted particles cause electrons to become 'lodged' in the crystal lattice, and their accumulation can be measured and an age calculated.

With TL, the measurement is achieved by heating the sample, and measuring the light (trapped energy) emitted. The rate at which the sample would accumulate such energy is then assessed by giving it an artificial exposure to a known dose of radiation. This method must be applied very carefully since it is necessary to take into account the dose of radiation received from all sources, not just from breakdowns within the sample itself.

TL was originally best known as a method for dating pottery, developed by Dr M. J. Aitken and colleagues at the Research Laboratory for Archaeology, Oxford. It has been extended to the dating of burnt flint, calcite and sediments, and although most of these applications are at an experimental stage, some dates have been published.

ESR attempts to measure the same stored energy in a non-destructive way through registering the 'resonance' of the electrons involved, but it has as yet yielded few reliable dating results.

Petralona, in northern Greece, is probably the most controversial of Middle Pleistocene sites which scientists have yet attempted to date. The finds were first uncovered, not by archaeologists, but by local people who kept no records. Some accounts speak of a skeleton as well as the skull, but no evidence of this has ever been produced. Even the exact stratigraphic position of the skull has been debated. The archaeologist most closely associated with the work, S. Poulianos, has claimed a very great age for the find, as much as 700,000 years, because of the allegedly primitive nature of the cranium itself.

Some early dates obtained at the site, for instance by uranium series, may be correct, but nevertheless relate to deposits which are much older than the actual human remains. Most recent results by ESR and uranium series suggest that the real age is between 200,000 and 300,000 years, which would agree well with the general form of the skull. But expectation provides a highly dangerous means of dating, and the debate over Petralona underlines the importance of having well stratified finds, so that dating methods can give useful results.

Much support will be found among archaeologists for further development of the most promising methods, because there is a vital need to understand better the rates of evolutionary and cultural change during the Middle Pleistocene.

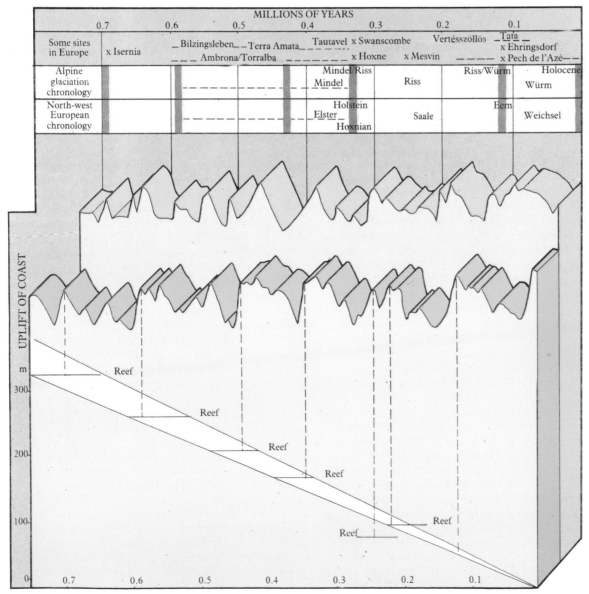

Cores taken from deep-sea deposits provide continuous records throughout the Middle Pleistocene. The variations in the ratio $0^{18}/0^{16}$ provide an index of ice volume, and hence of sea-level variations. Recent work provides very precise dating of these glacial/interglacial cycles (see p 199). Estimated dates for high reefs at Atauro correlate well with interglacial periods in the cores. Higher proportions of coarse sediment measured in one core show that wind strengths were much higher in glacial times.

Glacial

Interglacial

Wind rigour measured from coarseness of transported sediments in ocean cores

Sea-level variations measured from ocean cores

Early sapiens in Europe and Western Asia

In the last half million years, sites become plentiful across Europe and in the Middle East. Some are in caves, but there are also open sites, preserved in loess, or in freshwater limestone in river valleys. The earliest sites in central Asia are about 250,000 years old. Human occupation probably advanced during the interglacials, and retreated in glacial times.

From about 3 or 400,000 years ago, the traces of man become abundant across Europe. Many of the sites belong to the warm periods, the interglacials, but there was certainly some occupation during cooler times also. Europe provides a much more detailed record of this period, when our species *Homo sapiens* was taking shape, than any other part of the world. By picking out some of the most informative sites, especially those where human remains are preserved, we can trace in outline man's development during this later part of the Middle Pleistocene period.

Because of the dating uncertainties which we have just encountered, our time framework for looking at these sites has to be very provisional. It helps to mention a chronological system which was in use long before radiometric dating methods were made possible by advances in physics. The system originated when geologists noted that in the Alps, and elsewhere in Europe, there were traces of several distinct glacial periods. Apart from changes in the shape of valleys and hills caused by the passage of ice, the key evidence for this is provided by the moraines – deposits of earth and rocks gouged up and left as banks on either side of the glaciers. At the maximum extent of the glaciers, end-moraines, raised like dykes, would be left as evidence after the ice had retreated. Ground-up material also formed a blanket under the glaciers, and this till, or boulder clay, covers large areas of Europe and North America.

The geologists Albrecht Penck and Eduard Bruckner calculated, in a classic work published in 1909, that there had been four major glaciations, which they named from oldest to youngest the Gunz, Mindel, Riss and Würm, after Alpine rivers. From the sum of modern knowledge, including the geomagnetic record, we can now be fairly sure that the last three of these glaciations belong within the last 700,000 years, but when we consult the deep-sea cores for the same period, we find there are about nine major cycles of climatic change. It is clear that only a few of these cycles are represented in the classic glacial record on land. These may be the most major phases, but it is also possible that we often combine into one phase deposits which are actually of different ages. Recognizing the complexity of the picture, archaeologists and geologists now prefer to name local phases, rather than state definite relationships with the Alpine sequence. But some correlation is necessary here, to obtain a perspective on the archaeology.

A major time line is given by the Holstein interglacial of north-west Europe, recognized in many exposures. It can be linked with a sea-level about 25 metres higher than the present day, and can be correlated with well-studied warm period deposits ascribed to the Hoxnian phase, named after the key site of Hoxne in eastern England.

Some uranium series dates from England suggest that the Hoxnian is about 250,000 years old, but these are probably underestimates of the real age, being based on bone, and in any case near to the limits of the method. Dr N. J. Shackleton of Cambridge University who has examined deep-sea cores suggests that there are only two phases within the last half million years warm enough to have produced the high sea-level associated with the Hoxnian/Holstein interglacial: these are at about 330,000 and 420,000 years. If we provisionally accept a correlation with 330,000, we can relate to this age many sites which are contemporary with the Hoxnian/Holstein or are definitely earlier or later.

Across Western Europe, there is a thin scattering of sites which may be older than the Hoxnian. The Somme valley in northern France provides a good starting place. Though better known for its tragic history in the First World War, it was frequented by early man hundreds of thousands of years ago, and helped nineteenth-century prehistorians to build their relative chronological framework before the advent of absolute dating methods. In major river valleys such as the Somme, when the sea-level was high, the valley would choke with sediment, but when the sea-level dropped, the river cut down and carried away most of this material so that the remnants formed terraces. It is now recognized, however, that such sequences of terraces are usually too complex to allow a certain chronology.

Some of the oldest Somme sites are at Abbeville, where on one site 2 or 3,000 bifaces are said to have been found. Remains of the early zebrine horse, *Equus stenonis*, which later became extinct in Europe, help to demonstrate the antiquity of the sites. Other sites at Abbeville are of about the same age as the Hoxnian warm period, as probably are the sites of St Acheul itself – the type site, containing hand-axes, after which all the Acheulean is named.

There is a possibility that some finds from Britain are older than the Hoxnian: for example the high terrace finds from Fordwich and from Kent's Cavern near Torquay. The importance of such finds lies in the demonstration that perhaps as much as 500,000 years ago, man was able at least for a time to colonize Europe out to its extremities. At Westbury-sub-Mendip, in south-west England, remains of extinct animals associated with very few stone tools suggest contemporaneity with the Cromerian phase, estimated at c. 0.7–0.5 million years, and named after beds in eastern England, where there are faunal remains but no archaeological traces. Fauna of this phase is also represented at La Belle Roche in Belgium, an important site still under investigation, and exciting because much further work is possible.

Later on, in the time of the Hoxnian interglacial itself, there was abundant occupation at many sites in south-east England. They have produced many thousands of Acheulean hand-axes, but at a few sites, judged to be early in the Hoxnian, the tool-kit consists only of large 'chopper-cores' and flake tools. This is the Clactonian industry, named after Clacton, on the east coast of England. Recent studies show that the Clactonian is truly different from the Acheulean in its stone-working, but they do not tell us conclusively whether it represents a separate cultural tradition belonging to a people who did not make hand-axes. The Clactonian appears to have been a localized phenomenon, restricted to the opening phases of the interglacial.

Hand-axes are so plentiful in later phases of the Hoxnian that we can be sure they were just as useful in the local temperate woodland environment of Britain as in the African savanna. They have been found at Hoxne itself, and many other sites including Swanscombe on the south side of the Thames estuary, where parts of a cranium of early *Homo sapiens* were found in terrace gravels of the ancient river. Clactonian tools were found in the lower layers, but Acheulean were found in higher levels, including those contemporary with the skull. Most writers accept that Swanscombe is broadly contemporary with the Hoxne site.

At Hoxne an excellent pollen record was recovered which shows the development of mixed woodland during the interglacial. Both at Hoxne and at Swanscombe, a species of fallow deer (*Dama clactoniana*) was found in the fauna. Alterations in the pollen spectrum at Hoxne, and traces of charcoal on the site, have suggested that man was creating bush fires, but a natural explanation is also possible. Hoxne is, however, one of the few sites where we have a definite indication about the use of Palaeolithic tools: microwear studies carried out by Dr Lawrence Keeley on tools from Hoxne show that the hand-axes were used for cutting meat.

Important finds, which may be considerably older than those at Hoxne, were made at La Caverne de l'Arago at Tautavel in the eastern Pyrenees. This site, one of the most famous in Europe, has been known since 1838, but the richness of its remains has only recently been shown in work organized by Professor Henri de Lumley since 1964. Most of the sediments at this site belong to cold periods, which are probably older than the Hoxnian or Holstein interglacial. Various dating techniques have suggested ages of between 350 and 400,000 for the layers which have yielded human remains, though some workers would argue for a younger, or even an older, age.

The Arago site is a deep, narrow cave, facing eastwards. The cave preserves a number of human fossils, including a parietal (side region) of a skull, which belongs to the same individual as the face and frontal bone (Arago 21). The stone industry consists mainly of flakes, with a very few hand-axes. Larger stones in the cultural layers may represent traces of shelters put up within the cave, since they are absent in the layers that do not show human habitation.

Another site in southern France, Terra Amata, where excavations were also directed by Henri de Lumley, preserves what may be the oldest evidence yet found in Europe of man's use of fire, except possibly Ambrona and Torralba. At Terra Amata hearths have been found with charcoal and surrounds of stones. Acheulean bifaces were found in old beach deposits. Most were made from beach cobbles, which were also used to produce flakes. The site is probably much the same age as those at Hoxne and Swanscombe.

The long cold period which followed the Hoxnian/Holstein interglacial, known as the Saale glaciation in northern Europe and as the Riss in the Alps, lasted from about 300,000 to 125,000 years ago. It seems to have had one or two more temperate intervals (interstadials), especially in the south and west of Europe, where sites are common. In northern Europe finds become much rarer, but a few sites probably do belong to this general period, such as Pontnewydd in Wales (where a fragment of a human jaw has been found), High Lodge in the east of England, Buhlen in Germany and Mesvin near Mons in Belgium. Alluvial deposits at Mesvin belong to an early part of the Saale glaciation, and uranium series dates of 300–250,000 years exactly bear this out.

At Mesvin there are no signs of the classic Acheulean, but the old technique of bifacial stone-working is still in use for a variety of scrapers and knives. Thus the site offers an intermediate form between the Acheulean and the later Mousterian flake industries which became prevalent in Europe from perhaps 150,000 years ago. Most interestingly, there was preserved what may be a worked bone point. It would be one of the oldest found anywhere, but the investigator, Dr D. Cahen, now suspects that it may have been produced naturally, through the polishing effects of freezing and thawing soil.

Vértesszöllös in Hungary was once thought to be one of the oldest sites in Europe, but uranium series dates now suggest that it is about 200,000 years old. Vértesszöllös lies about 50 km west of Budapest, on a terrace of the Atelier, a tributary of the Danube. As at the much earlier site of Bilzingsleben in East Germany, the remains are preserved in deposits of tufa or freshwater limestone. Such deposits form only in areas where water contains dissolved calcium carbonate, which can be precipitated in the area of a spring. This happens normally only in warm conditions, so we can be fairly sure that the sites belong to a warm interglacial or interstadial period, as is demonstrated by the animal remains.

Tufa, or travertine, is suitable for use as building stone, and this site was discovered by chance in a quarry. In addition to cranial remains of early *Homo sapiens* found in one area, molluscs and the fractured and partly burned remains of large animals were found in a cultural layer. The thousands of stone tools were made from small pebbles, probably because this was the only raw material available. Their average length is only 2.4 cm, but many chips only 2–3 mm long show plainly that this is the actual place where the stone-working was done. Such tiny tools appear to be common on early sites in eastern Europe, where suitable flint for making hand-axes and large flakes was rare. At Bilzingsleben, too, the artefacts are remarkably small, on average 3 cm.

The site also provides further early evidence of the use of fire in Europe. No charcoal was preserved, but there was a concentration of fragments of burnt bone. The excavator, M. Kretzoi, has suggested that they may have been used to raise the temperature of the fire, or to keep it going. Charles Darwin noted the value of old cow bones used for fuelling fires when he was visiting the Falklands in the 1830s.

A major site, where occupation probably began during the early Saale glaciation, and where we can trace the development of human hunting and butchering, is La Cotte de St Brelade, a sea cave in impressive cliffs on the south coast of Jersey in the English Channel. It was excavated under the direction of Professor Charles McBurney over many seasons. The sediments on the site provide a long and continuous record of cold intervals, perhaps as far back as 250,000 years ago. During glacial times, wind-blown loess was deposited in the cave, blanketing the remains.

At present the island of Jersey is separated from the Normandy coast of France by 25 km of water, but the whole context of the site makes immeasurably more sense if we imagine it as it was in times of low sea-level. Then it would have been part of the mainland, and the cave would have provided fine views across low-lying plains on which large animals would have grazed. At two levels of La Cotte, there were remarkable concentrations of large

Bilzingsleben in East Germany is probably at least 500,000 years old, one of the oldest archaeological sites in Europe. Animal remains are richly represented among the finds.

A hearth at Terra Amata, Nice, in a depression surrounded by stones. This is one of the earliest sites in Europe with fire evidence, and one of the oldest preserved hearth arrangements.

A view of the excavations at the late Lower Palaeolithic site of High Lodge in Suffolk, England. Two flake industries were found near the edge of lake sediments, stratified between two glacial tills. They are probably over 200,000 years old.

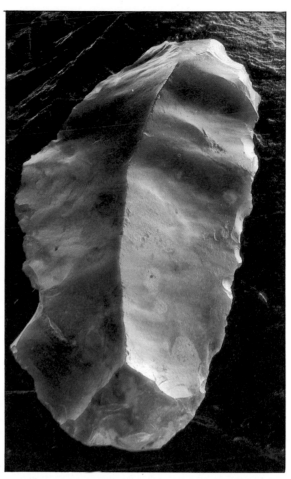

If this piece of bone from Mesvin, Belgium, is a shaped point, it would be the earliest known; but the excavator believes that it was probably shaped naturally by the effects of freezing and thawing soil.

A fine flake tool from Purfleet in southern England, typical of those made where good flint was available. The colouring is due to surface alteration of the flint, named patina.

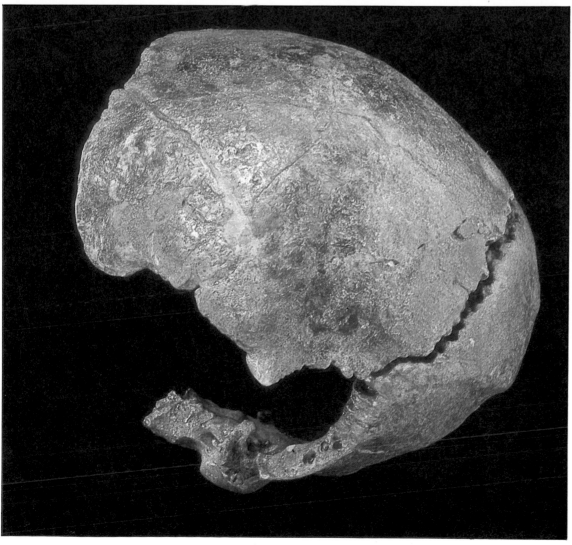

The three remaining bones of the Swanscombe skull were found on separate occasions in 1935, 1936 and 1955. Unfortunately the face is missing, but the remains represent an early form of *Homo sapiens*.

animal bones, exclusively of mammoth and rhinoceros. Such animals could never have crossed to an island, let alone have found sufficient food.

The heaps of bone consist mainly of skulls and shoulder-blades. The bones are far too massive to have been moved by predators, and their presence can only be attributed to man – in one case several shoulder-blades were stacked in a pile. Kate Scott of the University of Cambridge, who has studied the finds, thinks that they are most likely to represent the remains of two spectacular hunting episodes, when herds of mammoth and rhinoceros were stampeded over the cliff edge, to fall to their deaths

been found recently on the Acheulean site of Mitzpeh Yiron in Israel.

Other Acheulean sites in the Middle East demonstrate that in general hand-axes became smaller towards the end of Acheulean times. Gradually they became very specialized and, in the latest industries, they are halfway to being small points, and are accompanied by numbers of specialized angular scrapers. This phase is called Acheulio-Jabrudian after Jabrud rock-shelter in Syria, and uranium series dates suggest that it began about 150,000 years ago. The transition from Acheulean to the succeeding flake industries can be

The steep cliffs at La Cotte de St Brelade, Jersey, were once far inland from the sea. On at least two occasions hunters appear to have driven herds of rhinoceros and mammoth to their destruction over the precipitous crags.

50 metres below. The remaining bones are ones which do not carry much meat, or from which the meat can easily be cut. Quite possibly these stacks of preserved bones are the waste from butchery, moved to be out of the way as the carcases were dismembered. Hunters do not often move large animal carcases, but in this case they may have carried limbs and meat a short distance to camp.

We can also see from La Cotte that here, at any rate, Mousterian stone industries based on flakes had replaced the Acheulean at least 150,000 years ago, evidence which tallies with a pattern of change also seen in Africa and the Middle East. These industries, though based on small pieces of raw material, achieve a standardization and sophistication not previously seen in flake tools. Ordinary flakes were selected and converted by retouching into a variety of small neat side scrapers which form the predominant tool of the Mousterian.

At the east end of the Mediterranean, human occupation was fairly continuous, for glacials and interglacials had less effect. Acheulean sites are known, among them Latamne in Syria, excavated by Professor J. D. Clark. Here too, as in the sites in southern France, there are traces of shelters in the form of arcs of limestone boulders, which must once have supported wind-breaks or huts. At Latamne the tools, including elegant hand-axes, are mainly of fine local flint. Artificial arrangements of stone have also

traced in several caves, including et Tabun on Mount Carmel.

In a very general sense, then, events in the Middle East parallel those of Western Europe: after a period in which Acheulean hand-axes were very common, from 200,000 to 100,000 years ago the hand-axes of Acheulean type become much rarer, and there is much more emphasis on smaller, more refined points and scrapers.

It used to be thought that the steppes of central Asia were not inhabited by man until the last 100,000 years, but there is now evidence that inhabitation began about a quarter of a million years ago. This fits in with the earlier presence of the Acheulean industries both in the Caucasus and the Indian subcontinent. In glacial periods, conditions in central Asia must have been atrocious, with severe cold in the winters. It was dry, however, probably with less winter snow than at present, but loess would have blown incessantly, especially after each spring thaw, steadily building up on the ground. In interglacial times, steppe soils developed on the loess, and grass and sometimes wooded vegetation would have appeared. Deep sections of the loess in Soviet Central Asia reveal sequences similar to those found in Czechoslovakia: a series of nine major cycles of soil formation since the Brunhes/Matuyama geomagnetic transition dated to 700,000 years ago.

Two central Asian sites give us a glimpse of

human adaptation to life in these open plains. They are Karatan and Lakhuti 1. Their position among the periods of soil formation would suggest an age of c. 250,000 years, which seems to be borne out by thermoluminescence dating of the quartz grains in the loess. At Lakhuti, remains of some animal bones were found with stone tools on the site. The bones are of deer and gazelle, which may be open country animals, but they could also imply the presence of some wooded vegetation.

All the sites found so far have been in weathering horizons or soils, which only formed during the warmer periods, rather than in unaltered loess. This carries a strong implication that human beings were able to advance northwards in interglacial conditions, but that inhabitation could not survive the renewed onset of each successive glacial. The same may be true for much of Europe, but at the moment we have very few ideas as to how fast human groups could expand into new territory in times of favourable conditions. Interglacial periods lasted from about 10–30,000 years. We shall see that such a length of time may be sufficient for hunters and gatherers to extend far across a continent, as seems to be the case in Australia and the Americas in more recent times.

Excavation of a buried soil at Karatau, southern Tadzhikistan. This level has been dated by a thermoluminescence technique to at least 200,000 years ago. A stone tool industry consisting mainly of flakes and tools made from pebbles was found in this horizon.

The first evidence for the use of wood

Wood was probably one of the first materials used by man. Spears and clubs are among the oldest surviving wooden artefacts.

Wood is one of the most important natural resources in the world today, and it is likely to have been of importance to man from the earliest times.

It is possible that branches of thorn trees were the first defence used by early man against predators. The Dutch ethologist, Dr Adrian Kortlandt, has shown that a chimpanzee will pick up a branch to ward off a predator, such as a leopard. Other experiments show how even lions are deterred by thorns, failing to get meat placed underneath them. The Masai of East Africa frequently use thorn bushes to block access to water-holes, which they have dug in dry stream-channels, so as to keep away unwelcome animals. From the earliest times, hominids could have manipulated such materials to their advantage, perhaps using them as protective surrounds to their encampments. This may be speculation, but it is probably significant that most of the simple tools used by chimpanzees are drawn from the plant world – for example, plant stems for fishing out termites, or leaf sponges for getting water. We have no means of knowing whether such behaviour has evolved independently in the chimpanzee, or whether it is part of a pattern which goes back earlier than the hominid divergence.

People may have used wood even before they used stone, but stone tools are likely to be preserved, whereas the chances of wood surviving are almost nil. The cellulose of wood is broken down by many agencies such as fungi and bacteria. A permanently waterlogged environment does, however, inhibit the action of bacteria, and wood may survive in such conditions. But because of climatic fluctuations, such sites are exceedingly rare.

The oldest wooden implement yet known is a spear tip found preserved in peaty deposits at Clacton in eastern England in 1911. This find, which has recently been re-studied carefully, comes from sediments of an early phase of the Hoxnian interglacial, and so is probably more than 300,000 years old. The wood is identified as yew by Dr Peter Andrews, of the Natural History Museum, London, which fits in well with the prominence of this tree among the fossil pollen from the site.

The implement was made from a branch about 4 cm in diameter, and a length of about 35 cm survives including a tapered point. This point was achieved by cutting, as seems well demonstrated both by X-ray photographs and a study of microscopic wear traces. The scratches on the wood appear consistent with those that would be made by a flint implement.

What was the Clacton 'spear' used for? Professor J.D. Clark has considered various possible uses, and made comparisons with ethnographic material. It seems possible that game traps, in which

sharpened stakes were placed in concealed pits, may already have been in use at this stage. Many African peoples used to prepare such traps on game trails, sometimes for trapping animals as large as elephants. But the Clacton spear tip is rather slender for such a use. Another use that seems to be ruled out is that of a digging-stick. Most modern examples of these tools, which are widely used for digging up roots, or in simple agriculture, acquire a polish on the surface caused by abrasion in digging, and they generally have a broadened tip.

This leaves the possibility of use as some kind of spear. Modern spears can generally be divided into thrusting or throwing types, according to their weight and centre of gravity. Throwing spears are usually more slender and light than the Clacton specimen evidently was, and Professor Clark's conclusion is that this was probably a kind of thrusting spear.

Another ancient spear, from Lehringen in Germany, also seems to have been a thrusting type, though it is less robust than the Clacton one. This spear, which belongs to the last interglacial period, about 120,000 years ago, was actually found piercing through the ribs of an elephant skeleton. As this was in swamp deposits, we may imagine the wounded animal tiring there and collapsing. The hunters did however catch their prey, for flint flakes were also found with it. Presumably, the spear was so damaged that it was not worth retrieving.

Vital evidence for much wider use of wood in the Acheulean comes from Professor Clark's excavations at Kalambo Falls on the border between Zambia and Tanzania. This site was once estimated to be as late as 60,000 years old, but racemization dates (see pp28–29) suggest it to be about 200,000 years old. It is an exceptional site because a large quantity of organic material was preserved, permanently waterlogged.

The wood finds include charred tree trunks, and a number of indisputable artefacts. Apart from sharpened, pointed sticks possibly used for digging, the most important single find is a carefully shaped wooden club. But as none of the Acheulean hand-axes found with the objects had any trace of wooden hafts, it confirms for us that they must have been hand-held.

Few though these sites are, they alert our minds to a whole lost world of wooden artefacts that must once have existed. Microwear studies of stone tools too, prove their use in working wood, but they do not tell us what kind of tools were being made.

In a dangerous world, long wooden spears may have been the most reliable weapon of both defence and attack, against large animals, and other human beings. Some human remains, such as those of

The Clacton spear, which is probably more than 300,000 years old. The cut-marks from the original trimming of the wood are visible.

Trimming wood with a flint flake. Stone tools were highly effective for fashioning wooden implements.

Tabun in Israel are said to show evidence of wounds ascribed to spear thrusts.

Although no traces remain, we may suspect that wood had many other uses, apart from weapons. Wooden containers, and even wood canoes were almost certainly used long ago. Small water-craft probably provided the means for crossing the straits of Gibraltar hundreds of thousands of years ago, and were certainly a prerequisite for the colonization of Australia, perhaps 60,000 years ago.

The last interglacial

Just over 120,000 years ago, for a period of about 10,000 years, the climate was very similar to that of today. Raised beaches in many parts of the world show that sea-level was 5–8 metres higher than at present. Traces of man's presence are widespread.

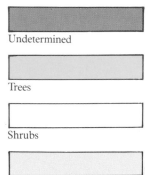

Undetermined

Trees

Shrubs

Herbs, Dwarf shrubs

This pollen diagram is derived from sediments preserved in a Norwegian fjord near Bergen. It shows that the last interglacial, known as the Eem in Europe, had vegetation similar to that of the Holocene. Early in the interglacial, coniferous trees were predominant, but later mixed deciduous woodland became established.

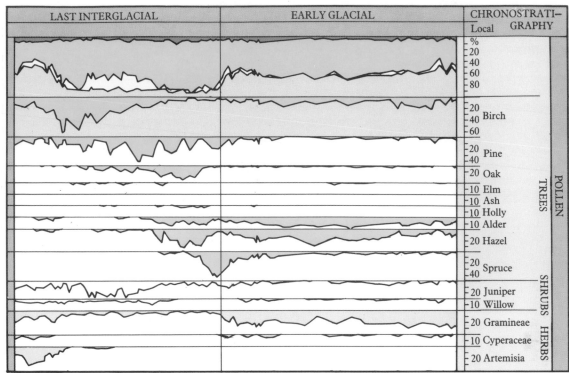

During the last interglacial the climate was approximately as warm as it is today, and the world was similar to its present form in the shape of land and sea, and in vegetation. In that favourable period, man probably spread out further than ever before. But the course of events was quite different from that of the last 10,000 years. There was no sudden development towards civilization, no agriculture, no higher technology. Although the environment of 120,000 years ago offered mankind opportunities very similar to those of the present interglacial, they were not taken in the same way. The last interglacial does, however, stand out as a very well-dated and well-defined period, so we can use it to take stock of human progress.

This period, known as the Riss-Würm in the Alpine scheme, and as the Eem in the Netherlands and Germany, began very similarly to our Holocene, with a retreat of the ice sheets, accompanied by a marked rise in sea-level, and the gradual recolonization of northerly and southerly latitudes by temperate zone plants, animals and man.

In many parts of the world, there are remnants of old shorelines – raised beaches – which show that sea-level was about 5–8 m higher than at present, for a period of a few thousand years, about 130,000–120,000 years ago. Uranium series dates from widely separated areas, such as Barbados, the English Channel, the Mediterranean and New Guinea, consistently mark out this time as being the interglacial maximum.

A possible interpretation of the high sea-level is that more of the polar ice had melted than in the present, and hence that temperatures were slightly warmer than they are now. Today's lower sea-levels could also be explained by the principle of ocean-floor spreading (see p 154), a process which has continued throughout the Pleistocene. Studies of vegetation support the idea that temperatures in the last interglacial were generally very similar to those of the present, but at times 2–3° warmer. In western Europe, the climate may have been more 'continental' with hotter, drier summers.

There is very good evidence, for example from Norway, that the pollen sequence characteristic of the warmest part of the interglacial is contemporary with the high sea-level. Near to Bergen, interglacial deposits were preserved in the floor of a fjord, where they escaped destruction by glaciers in the subsequent cold period.

In Europe, the large mammals were exotic in comparison with today's animals. Hippopotamus was plentiful in Britain (though it had not been found in the earlier Hoxnian). Rhinoceros, elephant, hyena and lion were also common. Although these species are now found only in tropical areas, this need not imply that temperatures were higher then than now, because both minor differences in land connections, and human competition, are likely to have affected distribution of these species within the last few thousand years.

The warmest period of the Riss-Würm or Eem lasted for about 10–11,000 years, raising at least the possibility that our own interglacial will not last much longer! But full glacial conditions did not return immediately, and a series of relatively warm periods lasted until about 80,000 years ago, interspersed with short, sharply colder spells.

The interglacial period is well represented in archaeological open sites, but less so in caves. In warm times, loess is not deposited, and less material falls from the cave roof and walls through frost action. As archaeological traces are not covered by sediments, they have little chance of preservation. Chemical weathering and soil formation are much more active, so older layers may even be destroyed.

In some cases, the last interglacial is represented in caves by the weathering of older levels (as at Combe-Grenal: see pp 112–113), or by peat formation (as at La Cotte de St Brelade), but this is geological rather than archaeological evidence. Recently a number of uranium series dates have been obtained on interglacial stalagmite, for example at Pech de l'Azé in France, and Tata in Hungary.

Crayford is a British site which can be dated to the last interglacial, known in Britain as the

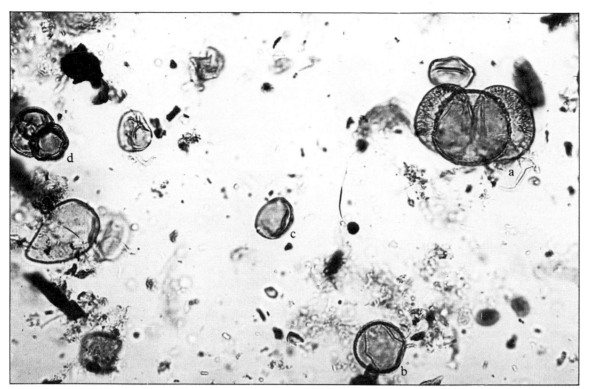

Fossil pollen grains extracted from interglacial lake sediments. Pollen of a) pine, b) oak, c) hazel and d) heather show very different forms and surface features and can easily be distinguished.

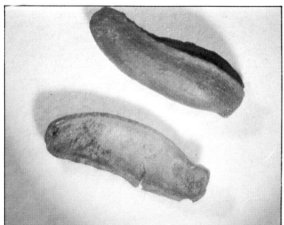

Ipswichian. Here, on the south bank of the Thames, 10 km west of Swanscombe, loams (known as brickearths) were built up by the river, probably as water-levels in the estuary rose because of a rise in sea-level. The mammalian fauna of the site is very rich, and exceptionally fine flint artefacts are found with the bones. The Levallois technique was much used for creating elongated flakes known as flake-blades. Preferences for similar tools made by the Levallois technique were widespread in Africa, the

Middle East, and other parts of Europe, during this time but they were not universal.

A contrast is provided by Ehringsdorf, Taubach and Weimar in East Germany. These sites occur in the valley of the Ilm (a tributary of the Saale), where there was a lake in the last interglacial, resulting in the deposition of considerable layers of travertine (freshwater limestone). Animal bones of a variety of species, including elephant (*Elephas antiquus*), were found at another site, Rabutz, 50 km to the north-east. All four sites are characterized by relatively small flake tools, among which points and scrapers are the most common. This does not necessarily mean that these people perform quite different tasks from those practised at Crayford. It seems more likely that the available raw materials encouraged different traditions of tool-making.

During this general period, the long-favoured hand-axe was finally losing its importance. Although the Mousterian industry is best known as the tool-kit of Neanderthal man during the subsequent ice age, it is now evident that similar tool-kits based on flakes were in use much earlier, perhaps as much as 200,000 years ago (see p 89). Some Acheulean techniques did survive in the flake industries of this period, and small specialized hand-axes are often found, even in Mousterian industries.

It is possible that during this period, from about 200,000 to 100,000 years ago, more sophisticated ways of hafting stone tools were being developed. There is virtually no concrete evidence for this, but it seems likely that the general purpose, weighty hand-axe and the long wooden spear were replaced by improved composite tools. The technical ideas underlying the hand-axe were conserved, but used for smaller points, which might have been fitted to spears. During the same period, we see that flake scrapers became much more standardized. Possibly these were fitted into wood or resin handles.

The last interglacial was probably not a period of dramatic cultural change, but it was a favourable time for man. When much colder times returned, they would present very different challenges.

Fossil fruits from interglacial sediments in East Anglia. Top: during the last interglacial the Montpellier maple (*Acer monspessulanum*), now restricted to southern Europe, extended its range to Britain. The right-hand specimen is fossil – the typical 'wings' of maple and sycamore fruits do not survive fossilization. The left-hand specimen is a modern one for comparison. Bottom: the floating waterweed, water-soldier (*Stratiotes aloides*) is uncommon in Britain. It never sets seed under present climatic conditions and spreads by vegetative reproduction. Fossil seeds from deposits of the last interglacial suggest warmer summer temperatures than those of today.

Chapter VI
Into the last 100,000 years

In the last interglacial, 125,000 years ago, it was at least as warm as in the present day, but from then on a series of climatic deteriorations led into the last ice age. All the signs suggest that mankind adapted to the worsening conditions with considerable success. Across Europe and Asia, Neanderthal people inhabited caves and rock-shelters, and where these were not available built huts and shelters. Almost everywhere in the Old World tool-kits of stone scrapers and points prove that people were there. In the tropics, the finds show that the equatorial forests had been penetrated for the first time, another sign of human success. An abundance of evidence from archaeological excavations shows us ways of life in finer detail than ever before. In Africa more generalized forms of *Homo sapiens* seem to have existed alongside the northerly Neanderthals, offering the possibility that this is where modern man, *Homo sapiens sapiens*, arose, but this question which has been of interest for so long, remains open.

A small plaque of mammoth ivory from Tata, Hungary, which is about 100,000 years old. It was possibly used as a charm and is one of the oldest objects, apart from stone tools, which demonstrates the early human aesthetic sense.

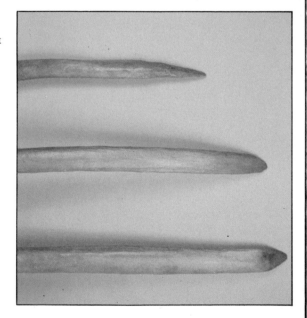

Three bone points from the Middle Palaeolithic site of Salzgitter–Lebenstedt, West Germany, which are fashioned from the ribs of large mammals.

The cave at Shanidar in Iraq in which several Neanderthal remains were found.

Searching for the human mainline

Homo sapiens of 100,000 years ago already possessed the brain size of today, but the characteristic modern skull shape had not yet evolved: brow ridges were still large and the forehead retreating.

Maps showing the distribution of human finds from the period in which Neanderthals lived. The majority of the finds come from Europe and western Asia, the areas which Neanderthals inhabited. This helps to explain why such archaeological emphasis has been placed on these populations which were neither universal, nor typical of people of the time.

As we enter the last hundred thousand years, we are coming down the home straight of human evolution. *Homo sapiens* in a broad sense had already been in existence then for a longer time than has passed since. But because we can see the last hundred thousand years in more detail, or perhaps because events were moving faster and became more complicated, the picture becomes less straightforward and more fascinating.

Although the last interglacial has yielded few human remains in comparison with the succeeding cold period, the fragments that have been found allow us to take our bearings in relation to the development of *Homo sapiens* during this time.

Two of the most complete human finds are the skulls of Ngaloba at Laetoli, Tanzania, and of Broken Hill in Zambia. These probably fall in the time range 120,000 to 100,000 years ago.

The Ngaloba skull, which was found in 1976 on one of Dr Mary Leakey's expeditions, is important because of its completeness, including the facial structure. In spite of its age, it is quite modern anatomically in many ways, according to Professor Michael Day of St Thomas' Hospital, London, who has described it. The cranial capacity is estimated at about 1,200 cc, greater than most specimens of *Homo erectus*, and within the range of modern man. The vault of the skull is well filled out in comparison with earlier hominids, but the forehead still slopes back dramatically. It does not, however, have the massive brow ridges characteristic of *Homo erectus*, or as seen in some European Neanderthals. Further studies of the Ngaloba skull will probably tell us more about its relationship with other African finds.

The skull from Broken Hill has a similar overall appearance, but larger brow ridges. It preserves evidence of painful dental problems including caries and a major abscess, all the more noticeable because in most fossil hominids the teeth are heavily worn but show few signs of decay.

These remains show us that the brain size of modern man had been reached by the time of the last interglacial, that the skull was filling out, but that there were still primitive features remaining. A similar story can be read from broadly contemporary finds in Europe, such as Ehringsdorf, Saccopastore and Krapina, in all of which Neanderthal characteristics are evident, and in the various remains from Solo in Java.

The remains of skeletons, as opposed to crania, from the Middle and early Upper Pleistocene are approximately modern, but generally very robust. As the cranial size in adults was already about as large as in modern man, the birth canal of the female pelvis had probably evolved to allow the birth of a large-brained infant. This arrangement has disadvantages as well as advantages – the altered shape of the pelvis somewhat impedes efficiency in running, and the large head of the infant leads to risks in birth – so it demonstrates once more the premium on intelligence in human evolution.

We possess no direct evidence whatever about the colour of human skin, hair or eyes in the distant past, and nothing to tell us whether earlier people were more or less hairy than ourselves. But we can be quite sure that by the time of the last interglacial, when man had already occupied large areas of the Old World for long periods, some adaptations to

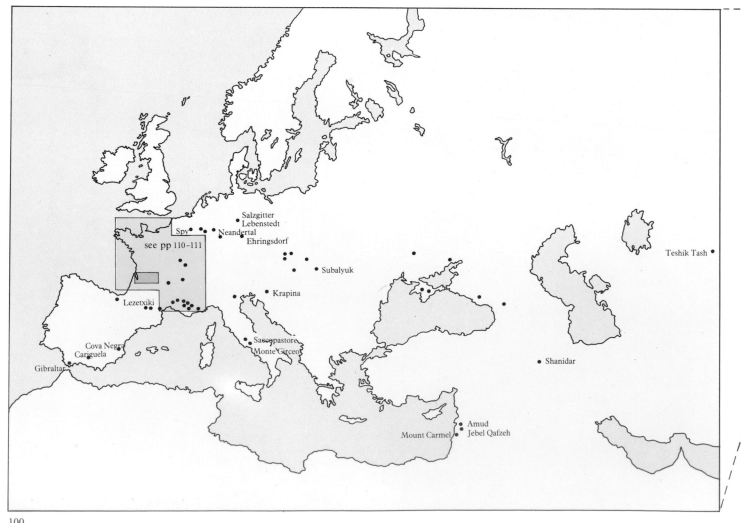

local environments would have taken place. Such adaptation is the basis of racial differences in modern human populations.

The pigmentation in dark skin is produced by melanin, which offers substantial protection against the sun. Populations living in the tropics would almost certainly have been dark-skinned, so quite possibly brown was the original human colour. Further north, this protection was not necessary, and indeed a light skin has the advantage that it allows more synthesis of vitamin D from the small available amounts of sunshine. Light-coloured eyes and hair probably also evolved in northern latitudes.

We cannot be sure that the present-day variety of skin colours had evolved by the Middle Pleistocene but it does seem likely that such adaptation happens relatively quickly. For example, New World Indians of the tropics, who are descended from people who entered America via the polar regions, have developed darker skins over a period of 30,000 years.

Should we attempt to look for a human mainline – to relate the fossil remains of 100,000 years ago to modern populations in the same areas? In detail, this would be unwise, but some of the features which distinguish modern human groups may already have begun to emerge. It is quite impossible for us to unravel the evolutionary significance of minor differences in teeth, or cranial form, but distinctive characteristics sometimes endure for long periods. For example, a distinctive curvature (the so-called 'shovel shape') at the edges of the incisor teeth, found in the Far East today, is also found in fossil man in China. Such characteristics reflect small

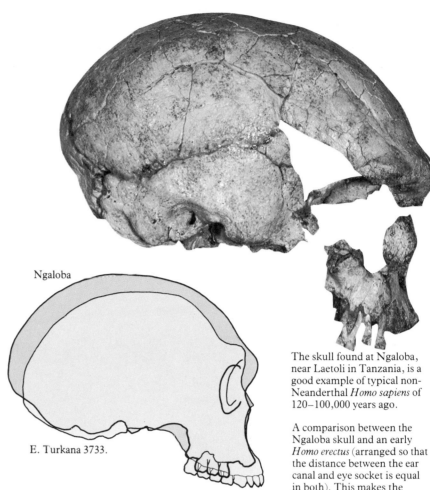

Ngaloba

E. Turkana 3733.

The skull found at Ngaloba, near Laetoli in Tanzania, is a good example of typical non-Neanderthal *Homo sapiens* of 120–100,000 years ago.

A comparison between the Ngaloba skull and an early *Homo erectus* (arranged so that the distance between the ear canal and eye socket is equal in both). This makes the 'filling out' of the skull very apparent.

genetic differences in populations, which may have been advantageous in some respect.

Since the people of the last interglacial, about 5,000 generations have passed. It seems likely that useful local adaptations have survived through that time, but there has also been time for evolutionary

changes of major benefit to take place in all human groups, notably changes in the form of the skull. Some groups, such as the Neanderthals, appear to have contributed less than others to modern populations, but it seems unlikely that their genes, which were well suited to the northern climes, disappeared altogether. It is probable that all the ancient groups have contributed something to the genetic stock of modern man. All the populations of 100,000 years ago can therefore be considered as our ancestors, and all are equally relevant to anthropological studies.

The last ice age

The last ice age, known as the Würm in Europe, lasted from about 80,000 to 10,000 years ago, broken by some warmer interstadial phases. In the coldest times, about 60,000 and 20,000 years ago, glaciers advanced over great areas in Europe, Asia, Canada and the Andes.

A modern glacier in north-east Greenland showing terminal moraines (foreground). These indicate that the glacier was formerly more extensive. They were possibly formed in the 'Little Ice Age', a period in the Middle Ages when temperatures were lower than today. Similar moraines are common in formerly glaciated areas of the world.

The last ice age covers most of the last 100,000 years, except for the last 10,000 years, which form our own epoch, the Holocene. The prolonged cold period was not the first of its kind, but it is the one nearest to us which we can see in most detail, and it is the one to which man adapted most effectively, as is shown by the extent of occupation in cold areas.

Climatic deterioration set in about 115,000 years ago, after the peak of the last interglacial, but there was no immediate return to full glacial conditions. We can say this with real confidence, because the framework of this Late Pleistocene period has become remarkably clear in the last ten years. Not only do we have temperature curves from ocean cores, but for the first time we have pollen records

which extend back continuously from the present day. On land, these records usually come from small enclosed basins, where sediments built up without a break in damp conditions which are favourable to the preservation of pollen, as at Grande Pile in eastern France.

Parallel pollen records come from ocean cores taken close to the continental margins. In these can be found traces of pollen which was swept up by winds and carried out to sea. Such records are generalized, for they include pollen from many different areas of a great continental land mass. Two key examples, one from the Arabian ocean, and the other from the north-east Pacific, are illustrated. From these we can see what common sense would in

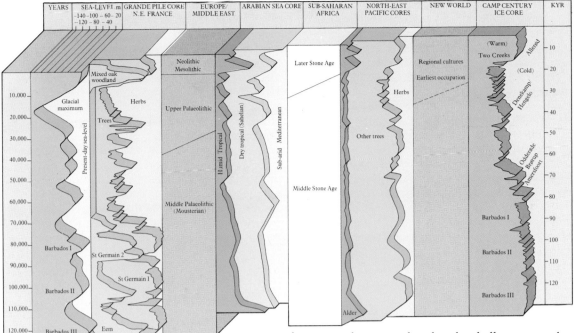

The chronological framework of the last glaciation (the Würm in Europe, the Wisconsin in North America) is becoming very well known, because of the records preserved by deep-sea cores, lake cores and ice cores. Preserved pollen tells us much about vegetational history. Fitting archaeological sites into the sequence is more difficult, but progress is steadily being made.

any case suggest, that changes of climate have different effects in different areas.

From the various curves of temperature and pollen, we can see that the worst times of the new ice age were not reached immediately, nor did they continue without abatement. A cool wet period in Europe lasted from about 115,000 to 80,000 years ago, broken by several short cold intervals. In much of this period, it would not have seemed much cooler than in the present day.

Even in the following colder periods, there were occasional temperate intervals, named interstadials. In the coldest periods, tree-lines in Europe would have been pushed far south, even to the Pyrenees and the Alps, but during the Chelford interstadial in Britain, which is probably equivalent to the Brørup phase in northern Europe, woodland is known to have returned. Some of the warmer intervals were too short for woodland to recolonize the landscape, but fossil remains of warmth-loving beetles help to demonstrate the higher temperatures.

Just how much the temperature dropped in the coldest periods is debatable, but estimates of 8–11°C (14–20°F) are common. As the temperature dropped ice sheets spread out in both the northern and the southern hemispheres, and major changes took place in the wind systems worldwide. Dr N. J. Shackleton and Dr D. W. Parkin have shown that ocean cores from the Atlantic near to North Africa incorporate more Saharan sand in glacial periods than in interglacials. This indicates that more sand was blown out to sea, hence that winds were more vigorous in glacial times.

It is known that the Sahara has been well-watered at times in the past, but during the glacial maximum, it was almost certainly even more arid than today, extending further south. Fossil sand dunes in the Sahel zone of north central Africa testify to this. They can be traced from the Sudan to northern Nigeria. They are truly sleeping deserts, for if another change of climate suppressed rain and vegetation, they would begin to move again.

How did human populations adapt to these climatic changes? The short answer is, with success,

but we need to remember that the challenges posed were very different in different areas. In the tropics, the lowered temperature and altered patterns of rainfall led mainly to a readjustment of climatic and vegetational zones, which migrated horizontally, sometimes by hundreds of kilometres, and vertically by many hundreds of metres. In areas which became too arid, people would probably have had to move out – there are gaps in occupation in some desert areas – but in southern Africa, the coldest part of the continent, occupation of numbers of caves seems to be continuous through the colder periods.

Habitation in Europe, Russia and China was probably less continuous, and in the north restricted to the warmer phases, most particularly the period following the last interglacial up to 80,000 years ago. After this, conditions appear to have been too severe to sustain permanent settlement north of the Alps, except in some milder phases.

Although many sites across Europe and Asia are found preserved in loess, which is deposited mainly during cold glacial periods, archaeologists have a general impression that such habitation was not actually contemporary with the loess. At times of deposition, conditions may have been too unpleasant for both man and animals, with intense cold and continual high winds carrying dust and grit.

South of the ice sheets, we must remember that conditions were not exactly like those of modern tundra, which is mainly treeless and vegetated only with lichens and herbs. Air temperatures were much lower than today, and winds much stronger, but the hours of sunlight, and the angle of the sun, would have been as today. In the summer months, temperatures in the sun might sometimes have been as high as in modern times. Although it was probably drier than at present, checking tree growth in most areas, in sheltered places there would have been more trees than in present-day northern-latitude tundras.

These conditions led to a great wealth of animal life, if not of vegetation, in the areas bordering the ice sheets, so it is not surprising that man came too. But in the worst times, conditions were exceptionally severe, threatening all life, and challenging man to adapt or perish.

The Neanderthals

The Neanderthals inhabited Europe and much of Asia during the last glaciation. They represent a distinctive population of *Homo sapiens*, which had evolved gradually, but was destined to disappear suddenly about 30,000 years ago. Neanderthal remains have often been found with Mousterian stone tools.

The Shanidar I skull. A recent study indicates that the peculiar shape of the back part of the skull is the result of deliberate cranial deformation, which was perhaps achieved by strapping with a board or bandages during childhood.

The Neanderthal skull from Forbes' Quarry, Gibraltar, found in 1848. In 1926, excavations at a nearby site uncovered fragments of a child's skull, associated with Mousterian implements.

In 1857, at a small cave in the Neander Valley near Dusseldorf in Germany, a partial human cranium was found. It was one of the first specimens of fossil man to be recovered, and its status, and that of many other finds similar to it, has been debated ever since. Neanderthal man is named from this find, though it was not actually the first discovery of its kind. A more complete cranium had been found at Forbes' Quarry in Gibraltar in 1848, but its importance was not fully recognized at the time.

Neanderthal people were different from modern man, but not as much as is often supposed. Neanderthal man is now generally classed as a subspecies of *Homo sapiens*: the full names for modern and Neanderthal man are *Homo sapiens sapiens* and *Homo sapiens neanderthalensis*.

The Neanderthal population lived from about 150,000–35,000 years ago. The 'Neanderthal problem' has played a major role in studies of the period for many years, since it became apparent that Neanderthals were replaced in a shorter time in western Europe than the period in which they had evolved, by men who were anatomically fully modern. This raised the question of whether the Neanderthals were direct ancestors of modern man, or whether they were an evolutionary sideshoot, possibly exterminated by modern man.

The Neanderthals were characterized by heavy brow ridges, long low skulls, and large teeth, but so were other early men, such as those from Ngaloba and Broken Hill. Neanderthal crania are, however, particularly long and low from front to rear.

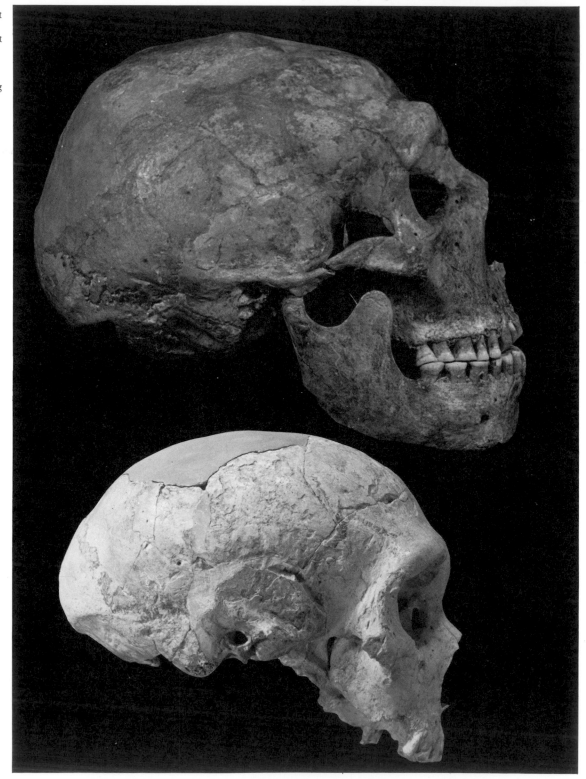

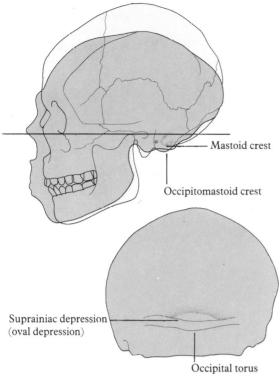

Mastoid crest

Occipitomastoid crest

Suprainiac depression
(oval depression)

Occipital torus

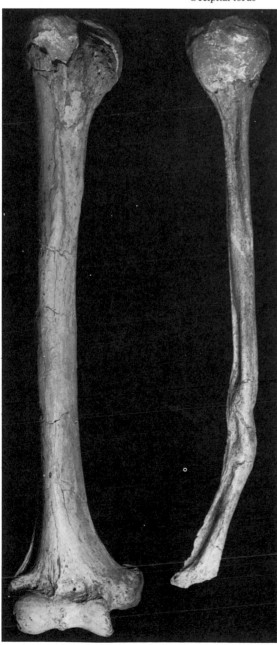

More peculiarly characteristic of the Neanderthals is a very large forward-thrusting middle face. The mid-line, from top to bottom of the nose (or where the nose would be), is particularly forward-placed, whereas the cheekbones slope much further back than in modern man. Other particular diagnostic features have been found by A. R. Santa Luca in all the best-known Neanderthal fossils, but not in contemporary man in other regions, nor in earlier or later remains. Neanderthals have an enlarged mastoid process, an occipitomastoid crest, and also, on the rear of the skull, just above where the neck muscles would be attached, a distinctive ovoid depression. These are found in the classic Neanderthal finds of the last century, such as those from La Chapelle-aux-Saints, and La Ferrassie in France. Dr Erik Trinkaus of the Department of Anthropology, Harvard University, has pointed out other minor differences from modern man, for example in the shoulder-blade.

Another Neanderthal characteristic is the robust, stocky skeleton. This is apparent in the stout, sometimes bowed, limb bones, and in the size of the rib cage. The body proportions are similar to those of modern populations, such as Eskimos, who endure cold – stocky and compact to minimize loss of body heat. Neanderthal bones in general preserve evidence of a hard life, showing that their sturdiness was necessary. Traces of lesions, and even of healed fractures, are common.

These characteristics appear to mark out the Neanderthals as a distinct breed or race of human beings, rather than a general stage through which all mankind passed. Some of the features can be traced in older European finds, such as Swanscombe and Steinheim, suggesting that peculiarly Neanderthal characteristics evolved gradually.

How primitive were the Neanderthals? Their image suffered greatly at the time when few early and truly primitive human remains had been found. There was a tendency to adjust the Neanderthals downwards, to fit them midway between man and ape. This supposed primitiveness was unfortunately exaggerated by the palaeontologist Marcellin Boule (1861–1942) in his study of the skeleton of an old man from La Chapelle-aux-Saints, whose bones were partially distorted by severe osteoarthritis. The Neanderthal brain size, skeleton and posture were in fact essentially modern.

Among the best known Neanderthal finds are those from Shanidar Cave in Iraq. One forearm of the skeleton of an old man had been so severely damaged that it would have been almost useless. He would not have been able to hunt, but he had been helped to survive, perhaps through an early sense of humanity, or because his knowledge was valuable. His eventual demise was caused by a chance rock fall, under which his bones were found.

Detailed studies of two crania from Shanidar have led Dr Trinkaus to the conclusion that they were artificially deformed, since their unusual shape seems to leave no alternative explanation. Such deformation is known from various parts of the world in modern times. It is achieved by strapping hard pads to the head throughout childhood, and may be intended to match up to a concept of beauty. If, as it seems, Neanderthal people practised skull deformation over 50,000 years ago, this casts a remarkable light upon their cultural activities.

Neanderthals are distinguished from modern man by the long low cranial vault, prominent brow ridges and forward thrusting face; but some of these characteristics are shared with other early men (see pp 100–101). The features shown in the diagram – an ovoid depression on the back of the skull and the enlarged mastoid crest – are unique to Neanderthals and distinguish them from both modern and other ancient populations.

Modern man

Neanderthal

The two humeri (upper arm bones) of an elderly Neanderthal man found at Shanidar. One of the bones is completely withered, showing that the whole arm was crippled. The bone is evidence that a handicapped individual was able to survive because others in the group helped him.

Burials

The rite of burial is the first clear sign of religious feeling which appears in the archaeological record. Over 20 burials have been found from Middle Palaeolithic times, in far separated parts of Europe and Asia. Some of them were accompanied by grave offerings, such as food, for the after life.

The rock-shelter of La Ferrassie was used as a cemetery in Middle Palaeolithic times. Adults were buried in graves, infants under low mounds. The photograph shows the end section of La Ferrassie after H. Delporte's recent excavation.

Human beings are unique in having religious feelings, and in knowing that their time is limited – that one day they will die. Thus the care which is shown for the dead can be taken as some measure of humanity, a mark of understanding of the nature and value of human life.

For the earlier periods of human existence, there is nothing to show that the dead were treated with any great respect. Usually, on living sites, we do not find complete skeletons, but small parts of them. In some cases there is even evidence that the bones may have been opened up and the contents eaten by other human beings. The cranial base region of some of the Choukoutien skulls was broken away, to give access to the brains. Some recent peoples have regarded the human brain as a delicacy and it has also sometimes been eaten ritually, since it was alleged to impart the qualities of the deceased person. These habits may also have occurred in the ancient past for there are other known instances of specific attention being paid to the skull, for example the scalping of the Bodo cranium.

Such apparently bizarre practices survived into the last 100,000 years, when for the first time we can be quite sure that they had a ritual character. One of the most curious later finds involving a skull was made by a farmer in a cave at Monte Circeo on the west coast of Italy. A beach had formed in the cave during a former high sea-level, but later it had been suddenly closed by a rock fall, and when rediscovered it was entirely undisturbed. Inside was a scatter of bones and stone tools, and in the centre of the chamber, a human skull of Neanderthal type sitting among a circle of stones. Here, too, the cranial base region had been broken away to give access to the brain. We may interpret this find as an example of an ancestor cult, or of religious feeling, but perhaps most of all it tells us that the surviving evidence allows us only to scratch the surface of the ancient culture and beliefs of 50,000 years ago.

Signs of deliberate and careful burial of whole bodies appear only within the last 100,000 years. La Ferrassie in the Dordogne region of France is of the greatest importance, because it is the oldest known cemetery, preserving not just one skeleton, but a whole group. The site is a rock-shelter, in a quiet side valley. The plan obtained by Denis Peyrony in his original excavations in 1908, and added to in recent work by Dr Henri Delporte, shows plainly that several bodies were interred on the same orientation, from east to west. Further out from the shelter wall, similar pits were found in which there were no bodies. It is possible, though unlikely, that the bones had entirely decayed, but disturbance by carnivores or man is also a possibility. In addition to the grave trenches, a series of low mounds was found. Most of these yielded no human remains, but one contained the remains of a baby, of about 23 months. It seems very likely that all the mounds represent infant burials, but for some reason the bones near to the back face of the rock-shelter were better preserved.

Some of the Neanderthal remains found at the cave of Shanidar in Iraq were probably victims of a rock fall, but in other cases the interment seems to have been intentional. Pollen from soil by the head

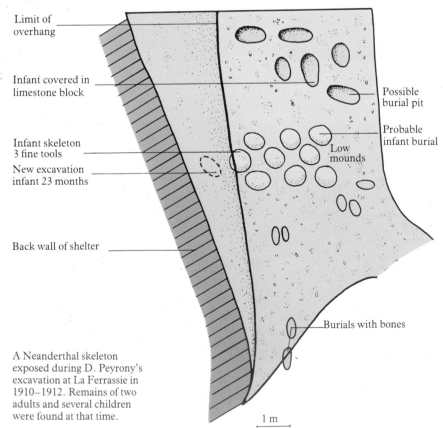

Limit of overhang

Infant covered in limestone block

Infant skeleton 3 fine tools

New excavation infant 23 months

Back wall of shelter

Possible burial pit

Probable infant burial

Low mounds

Burials with bones

1 m

A Neanderthal skeleton exposed during D. Peyrony's excavation at La Ferrassie in 1910–1912. Remains of two adults and several children were found at that time.

of one skeleton suggests that wild flowers adorned the head. Decoration and offerings are known from other early burials. Sometimes red ochre was scattered on the body, in a rite of unknown significance. Perhaps it was body paint, and the red colour may have represented life symbolically.

The burial of a Neanderthal boy in the cave of Teshik Tash in Russia is a further example of a carefully buried body. The cave faces south, towards the river Oxus (Amu Darya) which today marks the Afghan border, only 80 km away. Several pairs of mountain goat horns were arranged around the body. A hearth nearby may be connected with the burial, possibly being the place where the goats were consumed: there may well have been a funeral feast. Later, as further layers of sediments accumulated, several other fires were lit from time to time, and stone tools were left in the cave. But there was no great intensity of occupation; they were probably short visits, and the burial represents a tragic event which occurred during one of them.

All the burials more than 30,000 years old which have been found so far are Neanderthals of Europe and Asia, and all are in caves, with the exception of a recently announced Middle Palaeolithic skeleton from Egypt, buried flexed in a pit, and an infant burial from Border Cave in southern Africa. The total sample comes from only a handful of sites, mainly in south-west France and the north of Israel. Nevertheless, we may suspect that the custom of burial was already widespread, simply because evidence has been found in places so far apart. At La Ferrassie, it seems that the rock-shelter was reserved for burials, implying that the people actually lived in another cave, or in the open air. Very probably the majority of burials were in the open, but we have much less chance of finding them.

We cannot suppose that all bodies were treated with respect, for in the cave of Hortus in France, Neanderthal remains are fragmentary and dispersed, much as in earlier sites. But each careful burial

testifies to a sense of loss, a knowledge that an individual has gone, an idea that he may have another journey before him. The persistence of these feelings is shown by the large number of burials and grave goods in all later periods, from the Upper Palaeolithic onwards.

A Neanderthal burial from Shanidar Cave, Iraq. Pollen analysis has suggested that wild flowers were laid by the head of the corpse.

The burial of a boy at Teshik Tash, USSR. Pairs of goat horns were arranged around the body.

Advances in dating

New techniques of radiocarbon dating promise to extend the range of the method. Few sites over 30,000 years old have been dated, because large quantities of organic material were necessary, but radiocarbon-accelerators now allow small samples to be dated as far back as 70,000 years ago.

The main components of an accelerator dating system. A beam of carbon ions (charged particles) is accelerated to high energy, so that carbon-14 can be separated from all other molecules, and measured.

The radiocarbon accelerator installation at the Research Laboratory for Archaeology, Oxford. The photograph shows the accelerator (centre left) and the ion source where the samples are inserted (foreground).

The best known of all dating techniques is radiocarbon dating, but it has played no part in any of the archaeology discussed so far, because for most purposes it has until now been limited to dating the last 30,000 years. Radioactive carbon decays quite rapidly, halving in quantity approximately every 5,730 years. Thus, by the time a sample is 37,000 years old, less than one per cent of the original radioactive carbon is left; in another 37,000 years, less than one per cent of one per cent remains. In these very small quantities, it becomes very difficult to measure.

How does radiocarbon dating work? Carbon, one of the more common elements in nature, is a basic building block of life, occurring for example in every amino-acid which helps to make up a protein molecule. The carbon occurs in three forms, of different masses or weights, carbon -12(C^{12}), carbon-13 (C^{13}), and carbon-14(C^{14}). Almost 99 per cent of carbon is C^{12}, C^{13} comprises one per cent, and C^{14} occurs as just one atom in a million million. Yet the presence of these C^{14} atoms was recognized, because they are radioactive, breaking down at a known rate and emitting particles which can be detected. This means that the age of a sample can be calculated by finding out what proportion of C^{14} it still contains.

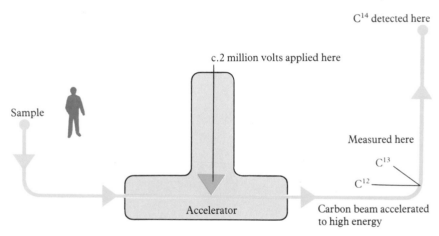

Sample

c.2 million volts applied here

Accelerator

Carbon beam accelerated to high energy

C^{12}

C^{13}

Measured here

C^{14} detected here

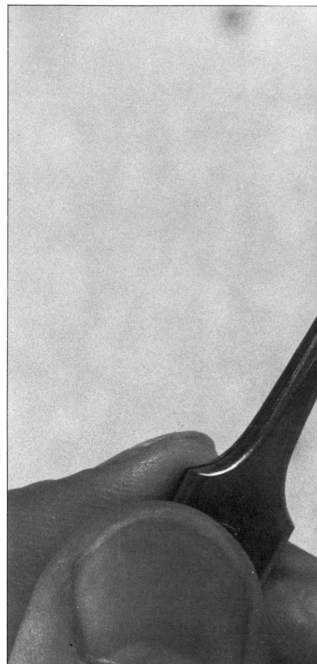

As C^{14} decays quite rapidly, and the earth is thousands of millions of years old, we might wonder why any of it is left. The reason is that the C^{14} is replenished, at a quite constant rate, through new production by cosmic rays which bombard the upper atmosphere. This has gone on for a long time, and the rate of production very much matches the rate of decay. New C^{14} atoms rapidly combine with oxygen in the atmosphere to form carbon dioxide, which fairly quickly mixes with the carbon dioxide already present, so that radiocarbon levels are quite constant, and every living organism takes up a proportion of the radioactive carbon.

When a radiocarbon date of 40,000 years is produced, it is assumed that the proportion of C^{14} taken up 40,000 years ago would be the same as that taken up by a modern organism. Our reference point, however, is 1950, for the levels of radiocarbon have been greatly increased since then through discharge by nuclear bomb tests.

How effective is radiocarbon dating? The best answer lies in the 50,000 dates which have been produced in the last 30 years, and the great

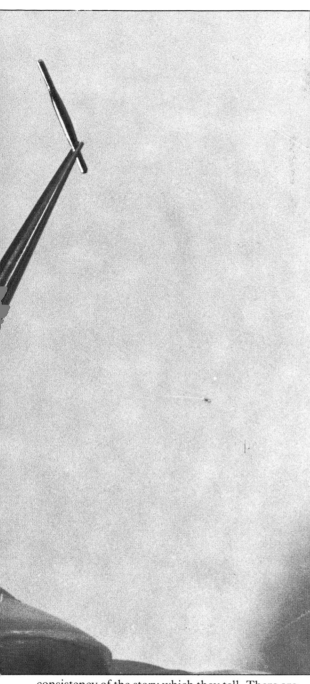

achieved with anything like the same precision – an estimate usually allows a margin of doubt of at least 20,000 years.

Radiocarbon accelerators offer a totally new approach to radiocarbon dating, which helps to overcome some of the problems of dealing with very old samples. With conventional dating, the radioactive signal becomes very weak in an old sample. For example, 200 g of bone can easily be dated if it is 5,000 years old, but at 50,000 years, the signal can only be detected by special measures to avoid interference by other radiation, and a very long counting time.

Accelerators provide a useful alternative because they can be used to detect the C^{14} not by its radioactivity, but by its mass, which is greater than that of C^{12}, since the nucleus contains extra neutrons. This is a very considerable feat, for a charge of 2 million volts is necessary to give the particles sufficient energy, and as the proportion of C^{14} atoms is so tiny, many operations are necessary to screen out other unwanted particles, and to let through only those which must be measured. Radiocarbon accelerators have now been developed to a stage where they can produce dates certainly as accurately as the conventional method from about 10,000 years backward.

Radiocarbon accelerators have the enormous advantage that the sample which they require is over 1,000 times smaller than in the conventional method. Not only is less required, but the smaller quantities are much easier to purify chemically. One-hundredth of a gram of wood or charcoal is sufficient for a date. It is possible, too, to date a single seed. Equally useful is the fact that the quantities of bone required are much smaller. Bone is 80 per cent inorganic in weight, but the protein collagen, which makes up most of the rest, is well suited for dating. Where this collagen has not decayed, accelerator dates can be obtained from about 1 g of bone. A great realm of opportunities has therefore opened up for the direct dating of early human remains, and the dating of Mousterian sites from bones included within them will become very much easier. These are just a few among the possibilities offered by the new method.

The prepared radiocarbon sample consists of graphite coating a tantalum wire, no more than 1 cm long.

The accelerator control console. Measurements made by the machine are fed into a computer for analysis.

consistency of the story which they tell. There are, however, slight fluctuations in the production of C^{14}, caused at least partly by changes in the earth's magnetic field. Thus, although the actual breakdown of C^{14} is at a constant rate, applying it to dating is like having a clock which runs sometimes a little fast and sometimes a little slow (see pp 198–199).

Up to now, the main limitation of radiocarbon dating has been that only one or two laboratories have been able to produce dates of over 50,000 years. With such old material, there is the constant problem that the tiniest contamination by newer carbon would greatly add to the radioactive signal, and thus make the date too young. Very stringent chemical purification methods are used to guard against this.

Now a new generation of exciting techniques is beginning to make radiocarbon dating much more feasible far back into the last glaciation. This would be extremely useful, for as we have seen, the framework for the period is remarkably well established, but the dating of individual archaeological sites, or human remains, cannot be

Mousterian cave sites in France

Caves often provide archaeologists with long undisturbed sequences from many successive occupations. In south-west France there are many Mousterian sites belonging to the early and middle parts of the last glaciation.

The Dordogne Valley, seen from close to Combe-Grenal. The limestone cliffs in the distance are typical of those which form rock-shelters.

The best known image of the Old Stone Age is that of the caveman. Why were caves so important? They have a number of features which made them particularly desirable for early man. An obvious first one is shelter and warmth. Caves may seem damp and wet, but they are not intensely cold, and can be heated. Then, a cave or rock-shelter provides a natural defence to the rear and often overlooks valleys, so many caves are naturally good vantage points for surveying game animals. In the Epirus region of Greece, archaeologists have found that the most-occupied cave sites are those which are south-facing, and overlooking small plains. South-facing sites catch more sunlight, and the heat absorbed by the rock during the day is radiated out again during the evening.

As rock fragments flake off from a cave roof, and wind-blown sediments accumulate from outside, material gradually builds up, filling the cave, and incorporating any traces of human activity left there. These traces amount to a tiny percentage only of the deposits, which are mainly geological. Many archaeological sites are strictly speaking rock-shelters, rather than caves, since they are not fully enclosed, but the picture is essentially the same. Archaeologists may unearth a record of 50,000 or 100,000 years, preserved in successively accumulated layers, with luck containing stone tools, animal bones, and other evidence, such as charcoal for radiocarbon dating.

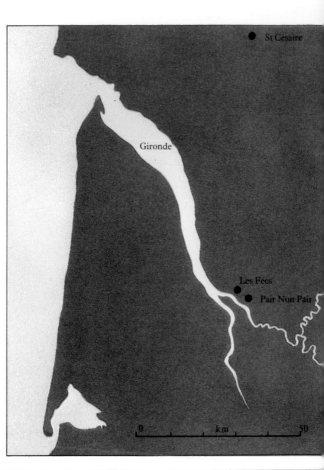

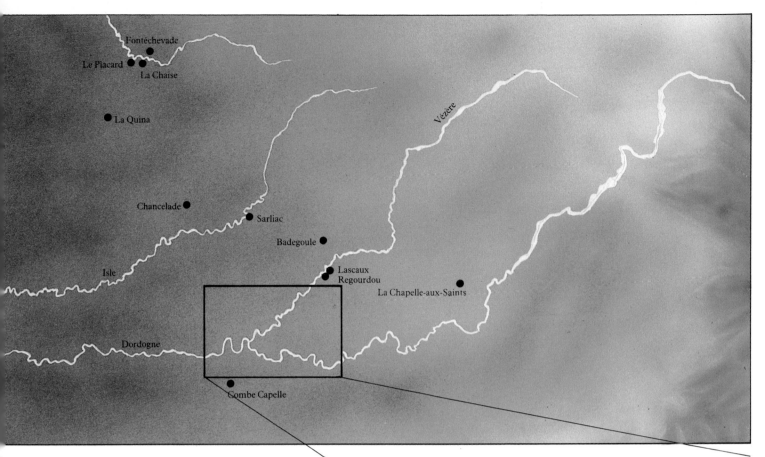

Fontéchevade
Le Placard
La Chaise
La Quina
Chancelade
Sarliac
Badegoule
Isle
Lascaux
Regourdou
Dordogne
La Chapelle-aux-Saints
Vézère
Combe Capelle

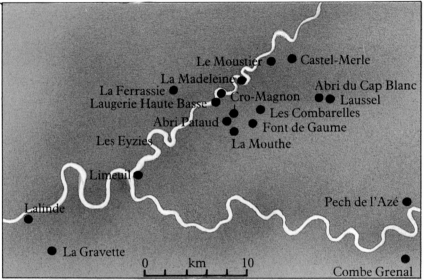

Le Moustier
Castel-Merle
La Madeleine
Abri du Cap Blanc
La Ferrassie
Cro-Magnon
Laussel
Laugerie Haute Basse
Les Combarelles
Abri Pataud
Font de Gaume
Les Eyzies
La Mouthe
Limeuil
Pech de l'Azé
Lalinde
La Gravette
Combe Grenal
0   km   10

The valleys of the Dordogne
and neighbouring rivers are
especially rich in
archaeological sites.

The distribution of
Neanderthal remains in
France.

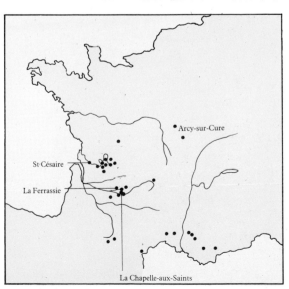

Arcy-sur-Cure
St-Césaire
La Ferrassie
La Chapelle-aux-Saints

Only a few very old cave sequences are accessible. The great majority of cave sites which can be easily investigated belong to the last 100,000 years. In Europe, such sites are common in limestone areas, for example in the Upper Danube region of south Germany. The best known concentrations are those of the Pyrenees and the Dordogne region in southern France. In the Dordogne, impressive limestone cliffs flank river valleys, and there are many caves and rock-shelters at their base.

Some of the Dordogne caves show that there was human occupation throughout most of the early phases of the last glaciation. Variations in the sediments, and in fossil pollen, testify to the many minor climatic changes. During these times, the inhabitants were undoubtedly Neanderthals.

At times, the temperature was at least 8°C (14°F) lower than now and the Dordogne had a cold, dry, steppe environment. In these phases, pine is the only tree which is represented in pollen preserved within the cave sediments, and it probably survived only in sheltered places. At other times, the climate was warmer, and the remains of red-deer, roe-deer and horse indicate the richness of the fauna. The flint industry found in these levels of the French caves belongs to the Mousterian, traditionally regarded as the tool-kit of Neanderthal man, since the remains of Neanderthals have often been found in Mousterian layers. The tradition is named after the rock-shelter of Le Moustier in the Vézère valley, a few miles from its confluence with the Dordogne. In Europe, archaeologists apply the name Mousterian to the remains from almost all sites dating from about 120,000 years (the last interglacial) down to about 35,000 years ago.

The Mousterian tool-kit is based chiefly on the use of flint flakes about 4–7 cm long. These are shaped into specialized tools by the process of retouch. The most common tools are side scrapers, made by detaching minute flakes along the working edge of the piece, so as to create a regular, sharp edge. The Mousterian point, originally thought to be the most characteristic tool, is less common, and does not occur on all sites.

Many caves in the Dordogne were first excavated in the nineteenth century when modern recording techniques had not yet been developed.

Two modern excavations of Mousterian sites which stand out for their scientific precision are at Combe-Grenal and Pech de l'Azé. They were dug by Professor François Bordes in the 1950s and 1960s, with the assistance of a team including specialist workers on sediments, pollen, and animal remains. The sites are close to the Dordogne river, a few kilometres to the south-east of the well-known caves of the Les Eyzies area and they offer an unusually good record of the activities of man during the cold periods of the last 100,000 years.

Combe-Grenal, 2 km east of Domme, at the edge of a dry valley tributary of the Dordogne river, is a rock-shelter with a complex history of geological development. At various times the overhanging rock has broken off and tumbled down, as the back wall of the shelter has retreated up-slope through erosion; most of the deposits are now down-slope from the overhang. From the lowest 'step' of limestone, they pass up through 64 archaeological horizons (distinct levels), amounting to a depth of 13 m in total, and extending for 30 m from front to back.

These archaeological layers are ranged in three groups. The oldest, furthest out from the rock face, consists of the bottom eight layers, which all belong to the Acheulean, and contain well-shaped hand-axes. A zone of weathering on top is believed to represent the last interglacial warm phase, strongly suggesting that these layers are over 125,000 years old. The two later groups seem to belong to earlier phases of the last glaciation: sediments, animal remains and pollen combine to show that deposition took place in a cold climate. Large limestone blocks which sealed in the deposits at one level indicate that the overhanging roof collapsed at some time. Periods of soil formation cap both the middle and upper groups of layers, apparently indicating warmer periods within the glacial period. All the tools in these levels belong to one phase or another of the Mousterian.

The Pech de l'Azé sites present a similar and complementary picture. Altogether there are four sites, but the important Mousterian sites are Pech de l'Azé I and II, both sizeable caves, which interconnect through a gallery; the deposits occupy the large cave mouths at both ends. Pech de l'Azé II has a suite of deposits in five formations, the lower three being Acheulean, again older than the last interglacial, as is confirmed by a uranium series date of 120,000 years on calcite. The fourth set of deposits lacks all archaeological evidence and consists of shattered limestone fragments deposited during a very cold period. The fifth belongs to the last glaciation, and has a sequence of Mousterian levels, characterized by smaller tools than is usual. Pech I is less complicated, with a single series of 12 levels, 6 m thick. These too were deposited in a cold phase, but the excavators think that they cannot be contemporary with the upper levels of Pech II, since the tools are different, and it is perhaps unlikely that both shelters would be in use at the same time.

What does this record of tools on the two sites – which may cover a period of 120,000 years – tell the archaeologist? In any later period, we might expect to see a clear trend of technological and cultural progress, but this is not easily apparent.

Even a brief study of the layers in the caves shows that different tools predominate at different levels. The explanation for this has long been a topic

The characteristic tools of the Mousterian: a side scraper and a Mousterian point (both are shown about actual size).

of debate among archaeologists. François Bordes divided the total spectrum of tools into about 60 different recurring types, his 'typology'. Particular groups within these types are more or less common in different levels on the Dordogne sites, and everywhere else that the Mousterian is found. Bordes felt that he could discern certain characteristic groupings, or variants, which he regarded as the tool-kits of particular Mousterian tribes. In addition to the Typical Mousterian, and a variant which includes hand-axes, there are the Quina and Ferrassie types which are noted for particular sorts of scrapers, and the Denticulate Mousterian with its 'saw-edged' tools.

Other archaeologists feel that it is unlikely that several separate tribes would co-exist in the same area for many thousands of years without influencing one another. This view seems to be borne out by the fact that different Mousterian variants frequently succeed one another almost at random in an excavation. Another view, advanced by the American archaeologist Lewis Binford, is that the different tool-kits were used for distinctly different activities: for example, one set might be used for scraping hides, another for butchering meat, and so on. The weakness of this theory is that many of the horizons represent long-term occupations, and very probably many activities took place. Bordes responded to Binford's idea with a cartoon in which these special activities were going on under large signs on different parts of a site; he was emphasizing that this was an artificial expectation.

A third view is supported by the British archaeologist Dr Paul Mellars. He believes that one major evolutionary trend accounts for much of the Mousterian variation in south-west France, and that the variants often occur in a progression.

So far, it has not been possible to apply radiocarbon dating to the critical phases, so it is difficult to be sure whose interpretation is nearest to reality. Very probably each is at least partly correct: different functions do demand different tools, different people do use different tools, and through time there is always some evolution.

Although Mousterian industries were first recognised in south-west France, they extend across Europe in a wide arc, from Spain into Russia. By using the one name, Mousterian, archaeologists imply a basic similarity in the stone tools, not that all the people who made them would have had exactly the same language, tools, or economy. Local differences in the tools help to show this variety: alongside the scrapers which are so common in the west, there are far more carefully shaped bifacial tools found on sites in the east. Bifacial points are found north of the Alps on German sites, which mainly belong to the mild period following the true interglacial. In the more severe climatic conditions which followed, occupation was pushed further south. In eastern Europe, along the course of the Danube river, sites are found with remarkable laurel leaf points.

All these tools can be fitted within the Mousterian, because it suits archaeologists to use the same name, but what we are really seeing is that local groups had their own preferences in styles of tools, particularly in the form of the points which they probably used to tip spears.

The cave site of Pech de l'Azé is at the foot of the cliff; it commanded a good view along a tributary valley of the Dordogne. The cave has a second opening, behind the cliff to the left.

Africa: Middle Palaeolithic and Middle Stone Age

Excavations in major caves in Africa span most of the last 100,000 years. Regional adaptations to diverse environments are reflected in the variety of tool-kits found.

Excavations in the Haua Fteah, in the early 1950s. The trench is entirely contained within the huge cave, whose wall can be seen in the distance.

The drawn sections of the Haua Fteah show the many layers which were encountered. The size of the trench was diminished at low levels, for reasons of safety and convenience.

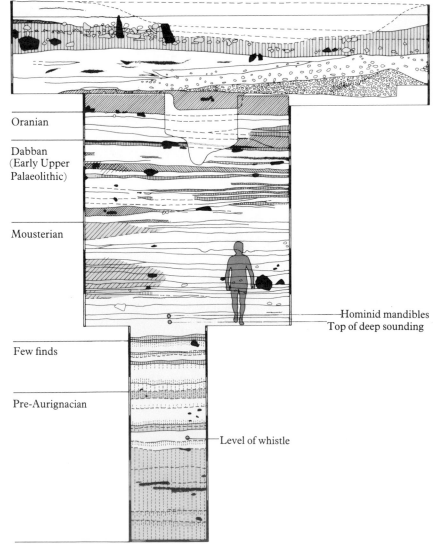

Oranian

Dabban (Early Upper Palaeolithic)

Mousterian

Hominid mandibles
Top of deep sounding

Few finds

Pre-Aurignacian

Level of whistle

Although Mousterian sites occur in a few areas of North Africa, most of the contemporary industries in Africa are so different that they need their own local names. It would be helpful if at least the major divisions which archaeologists use in classifying the Old Stone Age were the same in all areas, but this is not the case, for historical reasons. In the 1920s, scholars who were pioneers in unravelling the prehistory of Africa felt that the main phases of the Old Stone Age there might be so different from Europe as to need a quite different approach. Thus they were named Early, Middle and Late Stone Ages, and with some modifications this scheme still survives. Some outside terms such as 'Acheulean' have encroached, and in northern Africa the Lower/Middle/Upper Palaeolithic scheme is generally used.

Middle Stone Age industries, like the Middle Palaeolithic, emerged out of the local late Acheulean more than 100,000 years ago, but some Middle Stone Age industries are found as late as 15,000 years ago. In contrast along the coast of North Africa, as in Europe, the Upper Palaeolithic replaced the Middle Palaeolithic more than 30,000 years ago.

Both Middle Palaeolithic and Middle Stone Age tool-kits are based mainly on the use of medium-sized flakes, converted into shaped tools by retouch. But the side scraper, the favourite tool of the Mousterian, was not much used in Africa, where lightly trimmed Levallois flakes were more common.

Caves are rare across much of Africa, but in some parts suitable geological formations have made them abundant, and sea caves fringe the coast. Those which have been excavated are invaluable for the framework of events which they provide for the last 100,000 years. Along the Mediterranean coast, several caves have been investigated, in Morocco, Algeria and Libya. The most impressive of these sites is the Haua Fteah, in Cyrenaica, Libya.

The great mouth of this cave, which is about ¾ km from the sea, is 20 m high and 60 m wide. It probably had a depth of many hundreds of metres, but it is almost entirely filled with sediments. Excavations directed by Professor Charles McBurney in the 1950s recovered a long and continuous sequence. The site was dug to a depth of 13 m, providing a record which has been dated by radiocarbon back to about 45,000 years, but which extends much further, to a warm period which was probably at the end of the last interglacial.

The oldest finds are extraordinary large blade tools, which anticipate the forms used in the Upper Palaeolithic (see pp 122–123). But probably these tools were associated with hand-axes in a very late Acheulean; similar early blade tools have been found on several sites in Africa and the Middle East. On this site they are named 'Pre-Aurignacian', following the use of the term at Jabrud in Syria.

The most remarkable find from these levels is part of a bone whistle. This is undoubtedly the oldest known musical instrument. Others are known from the Palaeolithic, but only within the last 30,000 years in Europe, and this find is more than twice as old. It may have been played for pleasure, but it is also possible that it was used for imitating the calls of birds or animals, to assist in decoying them.

The Pre-Aurignacian at the Haua Fteah is succeeded by Mousterian levels, very like those of Europe and the Middle East. But this is unusual in North Africa, and is found in only a very few sites along the coast. The great majority of North African sites of this period belong instead to a distinctive local tradition named the Aterian, after Bir el Ater in Algeria. The makers of the Aterian possessed ideas of stone-working not yet known elsewhere. They made beautifully shaped 'pressure-flaked' points, which sometimes have tangs, showing beyond doubt that they were hafted, probably as spearheads.

The Aterian is found across wide areas of the Sahara which are now uninhabited desert, implying that rainfall was once much higher. On some sites the tanged points are plentiful, but on others they hardly occur. In recent years radiocarbon dates have been obtained which suggest that the Aterian started about 40,000 years ago, lasting until perhaps 24,000 years ago. This means that it was contemporary with a quite different tradition found on the coast, the Upper Palaeolithic Dabban, which follows the Mousterian at the Haua Fteah. The implication is that the coastal region and the interior were inhabited by two very different human groups.

In eastern Africa, the Middle Stone Age industries are sometimes characterized by a different form of projectile point which was classically lance-shaped (the Stillbay point). In Kenya, at sites such as Lukenya Hill and Prospect Farm, obsidian was commonly used.

There are few dates for the early Middle Stone Age in eastern Africa, but potassium-argon dates from Gademotta in Ethiopia suggest that it began over 150,000 years ago. Racemization dates on bones from the Ndutu beds at Olduvai place it there at about 56,000 years ago. In the Nubian area of the Nile Valley, and throughout East Africa, some Middle Stone Age occupations are less than 30 or even 20,000 years old.

In some areas, particularly forested regions, heavy-duty stone tools were retained. At Kalambo

Falls, many radiocarbon dates place the Sangoan, which includes heavy Acheulean-like core tools (core-axes), at 45–30,000 years ago. It is succeeded about 29,000 years ago by a more conventional Middle Stone Age industry, the Lupemban, also found in Zaire and Angola, in which heavy-duty picks and double-ended stone picks also occur.

A number of major cave sites have been excavated around the South African coast, and in the hinterland. Part of the importance of these South African cave sites is that they demonstrate the early emergence of advanced technologies, which were

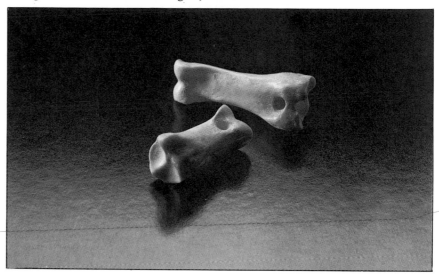

thought to have originated very much later.

The 'Howieson's Poort' industry, which is found at Klasies River Mouth, Nelson Bay Cave, and Border Cave, is characterized by many small tools, often described as 'microliths'. It is thought that these were fitted to wooden shafts, such as spears, to serve as composite tools. Until a few years ago, such tools were believed to have been restricted to the last 10 or 20,000 years, but in this particular area of southern Africa, it can now be seen that they appeared about 90,000 years ago. But the new tradition did not last without a break – by about 50,000 years ago, an ordinary Middle Stone Age tool-kit had reappeared on some sites.

Such sequences emphasize that human progress is not always linear, or unbroken. Perhaps the 'advanced' tools conferred no outstanding advantages, and were only preferred by some groups. Nonetheless, it seems likely that the ideas involved in microlith manufacture were retained by some groups, rather than re-invented later, when they became very widespread in the Old World (see pp144–145).

The site of Klasies River Mouth, in the south of Cape Province, is of particular interest as it preserves the earliest known record of human exploitation of marine resources. Shells were found in all the layers, showing that the sea was still reasonably accessible, even when it lay at a lower level (at times it was depressed by 120 m). As the shells come from many successive layers, their record could be studied by oxygen isotope methods. The result was a curve of values which corresponds remarkably well with the record of the ocean cores through the last glacial period. At times when the sea was close, bones of large sea mammals – especially seals – appear among other animal bones, a sign that marine foods were already fully exploited.

Part of a bone whistle was found deep down in the Haua Fteah. The only parallels are later Palaeolithic whistles made from reindeer phalanges: the modern replicas shown here produce a shrill note.

The Middle Palaeolithic east of the Balkans

Middle Palaeolithic tool-kits, broadly similar to the Mousterian of western Europe, are also widely distributed in eastern Europe and western Asia.

People made tools resembling the Mousterian over such a large area, and for such a long period, that we can only pick out a few of the more interesting features and sites.

In the Middle East, the Mousterian emerged out of the late Acheulean, sometimes by way of local

has already been noted in the Middle East and parts of Africa. At Asprochaliko, the succeeding phase is quite different, with the use of very small flakes for scrapers, which occur in their thousands. The bifacial tools which are so widely distributed further north in Europe are not to be seen at all. The sudden change of preference at Asprochaliko is disconcertingly like that seen between two industries

Teeth of mammoth, rhinoceros or horse

Mammoth tusks

Stones

Bones

Flint artefacts

0　　　Metres　　1　　　　2

In a curious structure found in excavations on the Mousterian open site of Ripiceni-Izvor in Romania, mammoth tusks and teeth were found together with large stones, and numbers of stone tools.

variants such as the Jabrudian and Amudian, and it endured through much of the last glacial period. It is found on Neanderthal sites such as Et Tabun, Amud and Shanidar, but is also found associated with more modern-looking men at Es Skhul and Djebel Qafzeh. According to dates from Nahal Zin, in the Negev Desert, the Mousterian was evolving into Upper Palaeolithic type industries by about 45,000 years ago.

In south-east Europe, recognized Mousterian sites are not yet plentiful, but they are known to exist. Asprochaliko, in north-west Greece, provides a typical example of a major rock-shelter site. It has a splendid view overlooking the Louros gorge, and was certainly ideal for monitoring the progress of migrating game, which would have been restricted to following the river valley.

At this site, the stone tools occur in definite phases, with a distinctly local pattern. The early levels consist of a Mousterian industry with large blade-like tools. As these levels may date back to the later stages of the last interglacial, perhaps 80,000 years ago, it is possible that they represent northerly limits of an early fashion for blade-like tools, such as

at Chesowanja, as much as a million years earlier. At Asprochaliko too, it seems unlikely that the sources of available raw material suddenly changed, or that people's basic activities suddenly became different.

The principal lesson to draw from this pattern is that archaeological variability is to be expected. We cannot always tell whether a new group of people suddenly took over, or whether an existing group, almost by chance, evolved a new way of doing things. The record of the last 100,000 years does, however, make it plain that there were choices not wholly concerned with efficiency, and hence there was a hint of style in our modern sense.

Although the Mousterian is better known from caves than open sites, the latter must have been as important. They probably formed the great majority of all sites, since there is no reason for occupation to be limited by the distribution of caves. In Greece, red earthy sediments found in many areas and deposited at least in part during the last glacial period commonly contain Mousterian tools.

Further north, Mousterian sites are most likely to be preserved by burial in loess, as in many places in the north of France, the important site of Solvieux in south-west France or on the open sites of Romania and Russia. At Ripiceni-Izvor in Romania, Mousterian levels were found near the base of a succession of sites from later periods, demonstrating that the same place had remained favourable to occupation over a long period. The most important find at Ripiceni is a curious oval structure, partly constructed from mammoth tusks, partly from large stones. The excavators thought that it was unsuitable for a hut structure, and concluded that it may have had a ritual significance. In this period, that is quite possible, since there are other signs of the emergence of religious feeling; but such a structure could have had a function which we cannot interpret.

That huts were being built – as in far earlier times – need not be doubted: at Molodova in Russia,

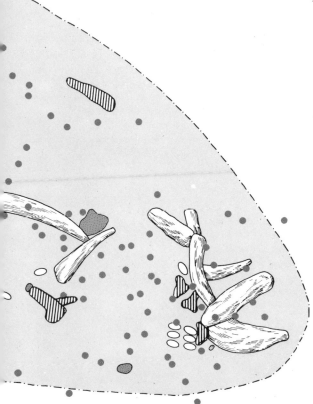

an excellent example is preserved, with evidence of numerous hearths inside it. The boundary is marked by mammoth skulls and other large bones.

Middle Palaeolithic artefacts somewhat resembling the Mousterian have been found on sites far to the east of European Russia, including Teshik Tash. Whether they are actually named 'Mousterian' is largely a matter of definition. In the Middle East, the characteristic Mousterian features of side scrapers and points are still common, so the name can be used. But even in Europe, some industries do not fit the mould: for example, those of Hungary, where leaf points of the Szeletian are far more common than Mousterian points. In Russia too, the bifacial 'Pradnik' knives are different from the classic Mousterian.

The contemporary industries of India and Pakistan have been little studied until recently, and are generally classified merely as 'Middle Stone Age'. Those of China too are little known from formal study, but it is evident that they cannot be classed as Mousterian.

As far east as Afghanistan, sites are found which are sufficiently similar to the classic Mousterian to be embraced within the name. This similarity of technology does not, however, imply any close cultural relationship with the Mousterian groups of France, or any other area.

Afghanistan is a wild country of high mountains, which must have been even more inaccessible in the past. But even here, man penetrated. Several Upper Palaeolithic sites were already known when Professor Charles McBurney discovered a Mousterian site in an unlikely place.

On the north side of the Hindu Kushm, at Kishm, a deep valley – which was probably filled with ice in glacial times – is overlooked by steep foothills, with lofty mountains beyond. High up on one hillside is a small cave, hardly a suitable place for a major site. But just outside the cave, sufficient sediment remained to allow an excavation, and traces of Mousterian occupation were revealed, represented by 20 or 30 stone tools. One of them was a typical Mousterian point, such as might be found in Europe.

At Kishm in northern Afghanistan, a small Mousterian site was found in a rock-shelter perched high up on a hillside, commanding dramatic views across the valley.

When, and why, would people have chosen to go to such a high and inaccessible spot? It could only have been usable in a warm period, perhaps the last interglacial. Hunters would need at times to bivouac in an out-of-the-way, but sheltered place, where they could survey animals in the plains, perhaps many kilometres away.

Towards modern man

It is not known for certain where anatomically modern man first evolved. The oldest finds are from South Africa, but similar developments in south-west Asia and the Far East were probably broadly contemporary. These developments took place while Neanderthal men still survived in Europe.

The Skhul V skull is the best preserved among the remains of ten individuals found in the Es Skhul Cave between 1929 and 1934. These 'Mount Carmel people' represent an early variety of modern man (*Homo sapiens sapiens*), characterized by very robust brow ridges.

Anatomically modern man is a distinctly strange-looking creature in comparison with the earlier hominids; the transformation of the skull within the last 100,000 years has been a remarkable one.

The essentials of the transformation are that the cranial vault has become heightened, the forehead almost vertical, and the face reduced and tucked in. This is a complex of characteristics, probably all related. We do not know what was cause and what effect. Perhaps a considerable reduction in tooth size during the preceding period was the major cause of change. Professor Loring Brace of Michigan University has noted that tooth size remained approximately constant throughout the Middle Pleistocene, but then became reduced by as much as 40 per cent between 100,000 and 40,000 years ago. This diminution would allow the face to recede, together with the complex of chewing muscles, and would incidentally alter the balance of the head on the spinal column. It is tempting to see our high forehead as representing a major intellectual advance over the Neanderthals and their contemporaries, but there is little evidence that the frontal lobes expanded during this time. It was rather that a different spatial relationship developed between the face and the cranial vault, so that our faces sit much

more under the brain. This said, we do have enormous evidence for cultural advance during the last 100,000 years, and acceleration within the last 40,000 years. It seems more than likely, then, that natural selection has operated to increase intelligence even within this quite limited period.

Archaeology and physical anthropology can tell us something about the actual emergence of modern man, *Homo sapiens sapiens*, although we lack many details. The earliest specimens appear to come from Africa and the Middle East. In South Africa, a modern-looking cranium at Border Cave is estimated to be at least 39,000 years old and may be much older; Australia was populated by modern man at least 40,000 years ago, implying the earlier existence of similar populations in South-East Asia. Only considerably later, by about 30,000 years ago, do we find burials of modern man in western Europe, where they are strongly represented in south-west France, as at Cro-Magnon. In detail, most of these specimens of *Homo sapiens sapiens* are, not surprisingly, not quite fully modern. Some burials in Australia have archaic features, and so do some of the first remains of modern man from Europe.

Radiocarbon dates tell us that in Europe Neanderthal populations survived distinctly later

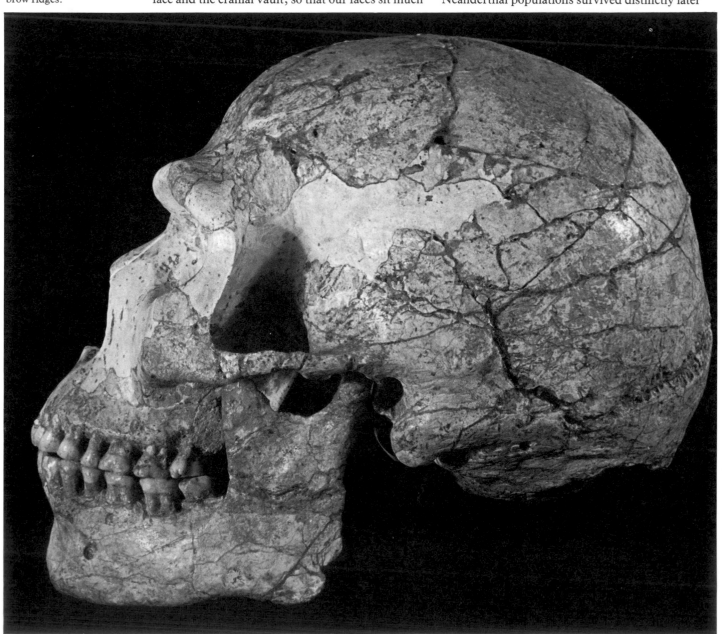

than the first appearance of modern man in the Middle East and Africa. A find in 1981 at St Césaire in south-west France shows that Neanderthals still existed there as late as about 30,000 years ago.

The dates make it plain that modern man did not evolve indigenously in western Europe, where new tool-kits of Upper Palaeolithic type, and many other features such as decorative art, appear suddenly. It would seem a reasonable surmise that these advances were brought in by a new kind of man. On occasion, a dramatic 'replacement' hypothesis has been put forward: a superior race of men swept in, and the Neanderthals were exterminated, or could not compete. This theory accounts for the actual result: that the Neanderthals, who had been the only kind of man in the area for perhaps 100,000 years, disappeared within probably 2 or 3,000 years. On the other hand, we have no evidence whatever to support visions of genocide.

One possibility which has been suggested is that for quite a long time there was space for Neanderthals and Cro-Magnons to come and go without encroaching upon one another. To some archaeologists this seems a more likely explanation than the idea that waves of invaders exterminated the previous inhabitants. A great deal can happen within 1,000 years, as we know, but 30,000 years ago, a millennium is the shortest time interval that we can generally recognize. In other words, we lack the resolution to pick out rapid series of events, such as have occurred within historical periods. Perhaps over the course of 1,000 years or more, contacts led to considerable interbreeding and the Neanderthal genes disappeared, simply because the new physical developments, which were the expression of new genes, were more advantageous.

Archaeologists and anthropologists have learnt to beware of over-simple explanations, but history serves to tell us that sometimes these are right. There are many cases of one people being displaced by another, and quietly perishing, so we should not disregard this possibility.

In the Middle East, there are certain specimens which used to be interpreted as transitional between Neanderthal and anatomically modern man, but recent interpretations do not support this view. These specimens, from the sites of Mount Carmel (Es Skhul cave) and Djebel Qafzeh, are early representatives of *Homo sapiens sapiens*, with an essentially modern skull form, but still preserving robust brow ridges. The finds – over 40,000 years old – probably represent a late stage of a continuous evolutionary gradient from people similar to those of Broken Hill and Ngaloba towards modern man.

In parts of Europe and western Asia the replacement of the Neanderthals was probably the most important event of the period from 35,000 to 30,000 years ago, but on the broader scale of human evolution, it was a sideshow. Throughout Africa, in much of the Middle East, south Asia and the Far East, there seems in contrast to have been continuity of physical evolution, in which the early emergence of *Homo sapiens sapiens* was accompanied by major cultural development.

The cave of Kara Kamar (literally 'Black Belly') in Afghanistan was first excavated by Carleton S. Coon in 1954. A further sounding was dug by Professor Charles McBurney in 1971. The site is remarkable for yielding an early Upper Palaeolithic industry, associated with a radiocarbon date of about 34,000 years ago.

A skull of 'modern man' from the Cro-Magnon rock-shelter contrasts markedly with one of the Neanderthals from La Ferrassie (left).

Chapter VII
The heights of Palaeolithic achievement

About 40,000 years ago, we have the first positive evidence of fully modern man in Africa and the Middle East and then soon afterwards in Europe. At about the same time, in an explosive surge, mankind swept into Australia and the New World for the first time, with a rapidity which reflects the great cultural changes which were under way.

The archaeological record, now within the range of radiocarbon dating, shows us again and again the specialization that was the route to success: specialized stone blade tools, bone harpoons and even spear-throwers; hunting of selected animals – reindeer in western Europe, mammoth in the east. Visual art appears for the first time in the form of superb cave paintings and fine bone carvings.

A small carved ivory head from Brassempouy, France.

One of the finest Solutrean blades which was shaped into laurel-leaf form by delicately controlled flaking over the entire surface. It is about 28 cm long.

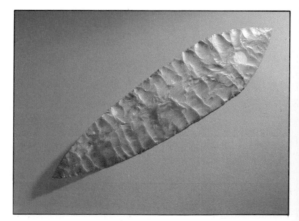

A curious scene from the cave at Lascaux. It is very rare for human figures to be portrayed, or for the paintings to represent a scene. But here a man lies dead in front of the bison which has killed him. We can only guess at the significance of this painting.

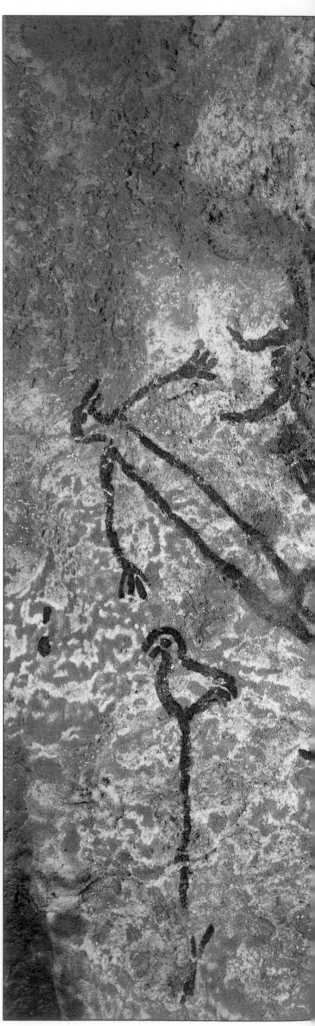

Sophisticated stone and bone technology

In Europe, the Upper Palaeolithic heralds new peaks of achievement, in stone-working and the use of bone. The new traditions appeared about 34,000 years ago in western Europe, and are often associated with the remains of modern man. Similar stone-working seems to start at an earlier date, as much as 40,000 years ago, in eastern Europe, the Middle East and North Africa.

Blades of Upper Palaeolithic type are struck here with an antler hammer. They are characteristically long and narrow.

The core tends to become cylindrical, as the process of detaching blades continues.

The Upper Palaeolithic era is well known as representing the peaks of Old Stone Age achievement in large parts of the Old World. From about 40,000 years ago a new stone technology, characterized by blade tools, took over in the Middle East, North Africa and eastern Europe. New stone and bone tools were used which were more sophisticated and standardized in their forms, and for the very first time visual art appeared. By about 34–33,000 years ago the new technology had also spread into western Europe.

This tradition is strongly associated in Europe with anatomically modern people, the so-called 'Cro-Magnon race'. We know that in detail the relationships are more complicated. For example, some of the first Upper Palaeolithic traces from western Europe may be associated with Neanderthals and elsewhere some of the earliest industries of this type may have emerged before a fully modern form of man.

The main innovation in tool-making during this period was the practice of using long, narrow blades as the basis for nearly all the tools in common use. These blades came in all sizes and shapes: the largest were over 30 cm long, but the more usual size was 8–10 cm, and many projectile points were made on smaller blades or bladelets. A special technique was necessary for producing such blades consistently. The fine results which were achieved stemmed from the degree of preparation of the stone-core, and the skill of touch of the stone-worker. Long narrow blades can be produced in a sequence, and if the core is prepared so that the first one can be detached successfully, the others can be made to follow along the same lines. As blades are struck in sequence from a single platform, the core may begin to look like a cylinder or prism. Sometimes the stone-worker would use a bone punch so as to gain extra precision in striking the blade, hitting the punch itself with a harder hammer.

The blades were converted into tools in a number of ways, usually by retouch. Endscrapers provide a typical example. Steep retouch along one edge of a blade was used to give it a penknife form, useful for a cutting tool, or perhaps for a spear point.

Another technique involved invasive flaking of both faces of a blade so that retouch extended across the entire surfaces, and a beautifully shaped leaf point, or a similar form, could be produced. Such tools are characteristic of the Solutrean phase in France (19,000 years ago), but also appear at other times and in other places: for example in the last few thousand years in North and South America, or in late predynastic Egypt.

122

Results of this kind are commonly achieved by 'pressure-flaking' in which the invasive flakes are released by pressing down from the edge of the blade with a hard stone or bone point and controlling the release of the flake on the underside with the fingers. The technique demands great skill and probably more examples were broken during manufacture than completed to satisfaction.

A specialized tool found in various forms in the Upper Palaeolithic is the burin, or graver. It has a sharp angle produced usually by striking a tiny flake or spall from the corner of a blade. Burins were often used for shaping and carving bone and antler and such tools show a new increased interest in the working of these materials.

Where did the Upper Palaeolithic begin? How far did it extend and what advantages did the new technology bring? All these questions have long been argued over. There is no definite reason why blades should be more effective than ordinary flakes, nor why they could be made by only anatomically modern man. Indeed, blade technologies first appeared at least 100,000 years ago (see pp 114–115) in parts of the Middle East and Africa, but they were never the sole tools in an industry, nor were they made by the most developed techniques of the Upper Palaeolithic; and above all they did not evolve in a single coherent popular tradition.

Although the Upper Palaeolithic blade-using cultures were totally dominant in Europe, the Middle East and much of Asia, the use of these tools was never favoured to the same extent in sub-Saharan Africa. In the Far East too, other older techniques were conserved.

In most of Africa blade tools were known, but simple Levallois-type flakes remained the most popular 'blank' for tool-making. Tool-kits of this kind in Africa or Asia are conventionally put into the 'Middle Stone Age', which actually began many thousands of years before the Upper Palaeolithic. In spite of its great importance, therefore, the Upper Palaeolithic cannot be described as a worldwide Stone Age phase.

Where the Upper Palaeolithic, in the strict sense, first evolved, may never be known – it was possibly quite a gradual development which happened in a number of places. In Hungary, for example, at the site of Istállóskö, there may be a gradual transition from Szelethian leaf-point Mousterian industries into forms of the Aurignacian, the first major Upper Palaeolithic tradition.

At the Haua Fteah (see pp 114–115), the first Upper Palaeolithic industry, named the Dabban, appears suddenly 40,000 years ago, and therefore may indicate the intrusion of a new group of people perhaps from the eastern end of the Mediterranean. It has long been thought that somewhere in south-west Asia, the Upper Palaeolithic may have been conceived in relative isolation, and then brought forth in a fully developed form. Its real origin seems

mysterious, but we may be making our interpretations too complicated.

Most of the Neanderthal finds are associated with Mousterian tools, whereas the burials found with the Upper Palaeolithic are exclusively those of modern man, except for one: the recent find from St Césaire in France. Here a very late Neanderthal is associated with an early Upper Palaeolithic phase, the Châtelperronian. The association seems to demonstrate that the Upper Palaeolithic technology could indeed be mastered by Neanderthals. It does not alter the fact that the time of modern man had come, and that the Upper Palaeolithic which spread so rapidly accompanied the new way of life.

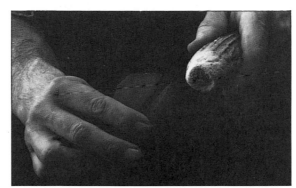

A burin, or engraving tool, can be made by the striking of a small flake, or spall, from the side of a blade. This produces a sharp chisel-like angle, especially useful for working bone and antler.

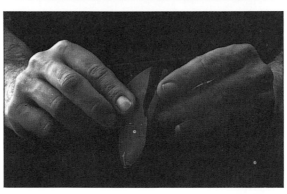

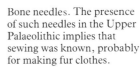

Bone needles. The presence of such needles in the Upper Palaeolithic implies that sewing was known, probably for making fur clothes.

Bone points of early Upper Palaeolithic type found at Istállóskö in Hungary. The split base of one of the points is characteristic of early Aurignacian bone-work. A radiocarbon date of over 40,000 years at Istállóskö suggests that the Aurignacian first began in eastern Europe, several thousand years before it reached the west, but a single date is insufficient to settle the question.

Palaeolithic economy

The excellent preservation of bone on many sites allows us to investigate what animals were important to Palaeolithic man. Exploitation patterns can be assessed by studying sites in relation to their natural surroundings.

The ability to reap food from nature successfully lies at the heart of the hunting and gathering way of life. The improvements in technology which took place during the Upper Palaeolithic must have occurred because they enabled the acquisition of food to become more sure and certain. The gathering of plants does not present great difficulties, so it was surely the challenges of hunting which offered the main incentive for advances to be made. By looking at the stone and bone tools of the Upper Palaeolithic (wood is rarely preserved even by then) we begin to see details of the excellence of human adaptation to the environment during this period. From this evidence alone we might surmise that there was a keen sense of economy.

Animal bones are plentiful from both Middle and Upper Palaeolithic sites; from studies of the bones it is possible to determine which animals were hunted, at what age they were killed and sometimes even at what season. An estimate, usually a minimum value, can be made of the numbers of animals found on a site. Most of the remains come from cave sites, so the problems of determining who ate what are still present, but to a lesser degree than on some open sites (see pp 72–73).

We can see from many modern examples the needs which impel hunters and gatherers to move, usually seasonally. Within the last 50,000 years, for the first time in the archaeological record, the evidence becomes full enough to examine wider patterns of exploitation, to see what governed the movements of human groups, where they went, and the natural resources that they followed.

Comparisons have been made between the animal economies of the Mousterian in Europe, and the succeeding Upper Palaeolithic. The great majority of Mousterian sites from the west of Europe to the Urals yield a mixed bag of fauna. A single species predominates only where the environment especially favoured its occurrence in large numbers: for example, reindeer at Salzgitter-Lebenstedt or mammoth at Ripiceni-Izvor, but even on these sites other species are represented. The remains of bison, deer and wild ass are all commonly found, as well as cave bear in cave areas, and in general the mixed pattern of animal remains is very consistent.

In contrast, Upper Palaeolithic people often specialized in hunting only one or two species, almost to the exclusion of all others. At Le Roc Solutré in eastern France, remains of over 100,000 horses were found outside the rock-shelter, many of them charred from cooking. These remains can only be the results of persistent selective hunting over a long period of time. Elsewhere there is evidence showing that hunting efforts were concentrated against reindeer, and even mammoth at different times in different areas. Such specialization implies very close knowledge of the animals concerned and the best methods of hunting them. Naturally enough, the positions of the sites chosen for habitation reflect the needs of the hunters.

A desire to understand the economic organization of such Upper Palaeolithic peoples led to the development of an archaeological approach called 'site catchment analysis'. Although vegetation has changed greatly in the last 10,000 years, very

The Mousterian 'mixed-bag' – the proportions of animal remains of various species found on some important Mousterian sites in central and eastern Europe. Animals common in a particular area were extensively hunted, but others are also found.

Rhinoceros

Cave bear

Deer

Mammoth

Bison, bos

Reindeer

Horse

Ibex

Others

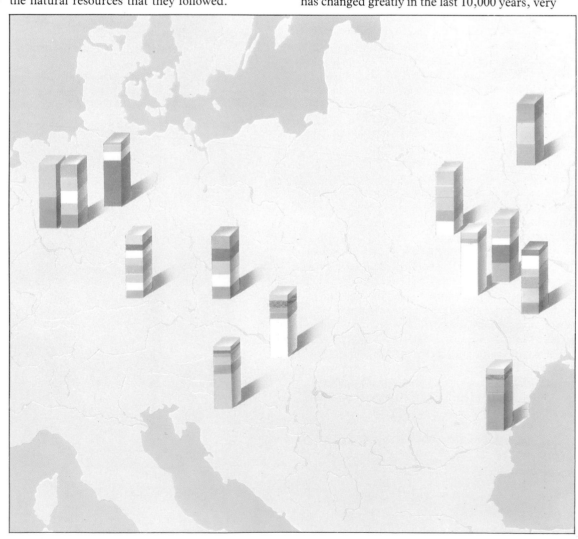

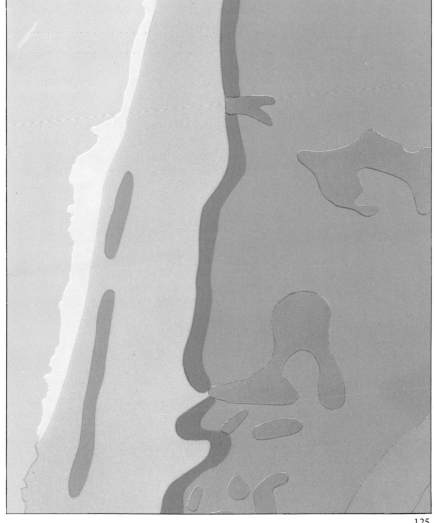

A painting of a horse from Lascaux. Some of the surrounding marks may represent spears and harpoons. Horse was a favoured food in Upper Palaeolithic times.

The principle of site catchment analysis – a Middle Eastern example. The Mount Carmel caves in Wadi El Mughara lie close to the boundary between very different environments, which could have been exploited at different seasons of the year in Palaeolithic times.

Arable

Rough grazing

Grazing/potentially arable

Seasonal marsh

Sand dunes

often the actual landscape has not. Knowing that certain sites were important, the archaeologist can hope to work out from their position which areas of the surrounding landscape were exploited, and how. This approach is linked, too, with the knowledge that animals often move seasonally, and that people would need to follow them. In exceptional circumstances, the archaeologist could hope to find the winter and summer camps of people belonging to the same cultural tradition in separate places. This is not a vain expectation because the time of year at which some sites were used can be pinpointed from the animal or plant remains. The stage of development of deer antlers, or the presence of particular seeds, sometimes defines the season of occupation to the nearest month.

The idea underlying site catchment studies is that people, who are known to us only from the archaeological record, would have acted much like later hunters and gatherers and generally not have moved further from the camp than was economically necessary. Two hours' walk out from the camp and back again would define a circle of about 10 km around the site. The effort expanded in walking this far, or further, would need to be repaid in food that they gained.

Site catchment studies can often provide us with a greater understanding of early patterns of habitation, but there are serious difficulties for the archaeologist in using this approach to reconstruct ancient patterns of life. The sites studied are often not the only major ones in the area, and they are often close to others which might have had almost identical exploitation territories. The concept of a fixed exploitation territory is also suspect, insofar as modern hunters and gatherers are not daunted by distance, and may travel great distances when it suits them, provided that they have a reasonable chance of obtaining adequate food and drink at some point along the way.

The economic approaches of archaeology are no less fallible than any other area of archaeological enquiry, but they do provide an insight into the strategies required by Palaeolithic man.

A classic sequence

Upper Palaeolithic sites are widely distributed, but the classic sequence remains that of the Dordogne area in south-west France. Here, caves and rock-shelters have been investigated from the nineteenth century onwards, so that the succession of cultural traditions is particularly well known.

The earliest Upper Palaeolithic of Europe appears in the east, but the area where the age was first studied and where the classic sequence was recognized, is in south-west France.

In the Dordogne area, where the great cliffs of white limestone are so conspicuous, the pioneering archaeologists, Edouard Lartet and Henry Christy, began to explore cave sites in the 1860s. This was at just the time when the publication of Charles Darwin's evolutionary theories had provided such a strong stimulus for such studies. The simultaneous construction of railways in the area increased the chance of accidental discoveries. Most of the Upper Palaeolithic skeletons from the Dordogne, including those from Cro-Magnon, were found at this period.

Why had the area been so attractive? In a period of severe cold, it enjoyed the mildest maritime climate of Europe, which was perhaps ameliorated by the Gulf Stream. Steep-sided valleys provided many south-facing places where trees could grow and shelter could be found, both for animals and men. Further downstream along the rivers known today as the Dordogne and the Lot, instead of the Gironde estuary, there were continuing plains, extending to the sea. Here, and on other grassy areas were herds of bison, mammoth, horse and reindeer.

In the Upper Palaeolithic a series of changes can be recognized much more like those of recent times than any we have seen so far. Unlike the Mousterian, which changes so little, successive phases of the Upper Palaeolithic show us that there were far-reaching changes of culture and technological preference within just a few thousand years.

Although hundreds of sites have been investigated, only a few provide really long-term sequences from which the order of these cultural phases can be worked out. The most useful of these sites are those where many radiocarbon dates have been obtained. The most important in this sense are the rock-shelters of La Ferrassie, Abri Pataud, Laugerie-Haute, and La Madeleine. A comparable sequence has also been obtained at the caves of Arcy-sur-Cure much further north in France.

The first Upper Palaeolithic phase in the sequence is called the Châtelperronian by English-speaking archaeologists, but French archaeologists term it the Lower Perigordian. It is known from only a few sites, which are all in France. The most characteristic tool is the Châtelperronian knife, a penknife-like blade. One view is that the Châtelperronian developed directly from the underlying Mousterian, another is that it is intrusive and was brought in by a new group of people from the east. The recent find of a Neanderthal skull in

Châtelperronian layers at St Césaire raises many more questions than it answers! It does, however, make this explanation worth considering: that Mousterian industries were manufactured by Neanderthal groups in this area, until there came a 'wind of change' – news of new technologies may have led to their adoption, in locally adapted forms. Very soon afterwards, the people who had introduced the new technology expanded westward until they finally reached the Atlantic coast.

That the Aurignacian was brought in by newcomers seems most likely, since similar tool-kits have earlier radiocarbon dates a thousand kilometres further east. The Aurignacian tools have a distinctive character, in the forms of the blades and scrapers. Long blades retouched around the entire margin were sometimes also narrower ('strangulated') in the central part. More common than endscrapers were steep-sided scrapers, sometimes called 'carinate scrapers'. There were also finely shaped bone points, some of which were split at the base, presumably for easier hafting onto a wooden shaft.

There are some signs that the early Aurignacian and the Châtelperronian were contemporary, for on one or two sites such as Roc de Combe, Châtelperronian layers appear on top of or between the Aurignacian levels. This may indicate both that the density of population was low, and that different groups could come and go at different times, perhaps scarcely encountering one another. Such a peaceful explanation may appeal to our modern ideals, but many later events of prehistory and history make it naive to imagine that all transitions were achieved without bloodshed.

The Aurignacian, in which the first signs of representational art appear, lasted from about 34,000 to 30,000 years ago. The wealth of sites indicates that these people lived at least partly in one of the warmer times of the last glaciation. The Aurignacian was succeeded by another major phase, the Gravettian, which again extended eastwards as far as the Russian plains, but we cannot tell where it originated. (In France it is known as the Upper Perigordian, implying a link with the Châtelperronian, Lower Perigordian). Radiocarbon dates allow us to place the Gravettian at about 27,000 BC on sites in Czechoslovakia and it seems to have appeared at about the same time in France. Although the Aurignacian might have evolved gradually into the Gravettian, it seems more likely that the Gravettian was a separate cultural tradition, since the whole aspect of the tool-kit changed, not just one individual kind of tool. Backed blades and narrow penknife-like projectile tips are very numerous from now on. These Gravettian backed blades are considerably narrower than the Châtelperronian knives which may have had a different function. With them are found endscrapers, rather than the steep-sided scrapers of the Aurignacian. In the Perigord region of France very specific styles of tools become predominant at certain periods. It is fair to say that we now encounter style in something like the modern sense. In one phase, tanged points (the 'Font Robert' points) were favoured and also, for a short interval, burins of a type called 'Noailles'.

But these phases passed and, at about 19,000 BC, there gradually appeared a new development in the form of exquisitely worked laurel-leaf points belonging to the Solutrean. Cruder

The great cliffs at Laugerie, south-west France. Laugerie-Haute and Laugerie-Basse are two separate rock-shelters nestling under the same line of cliffs.

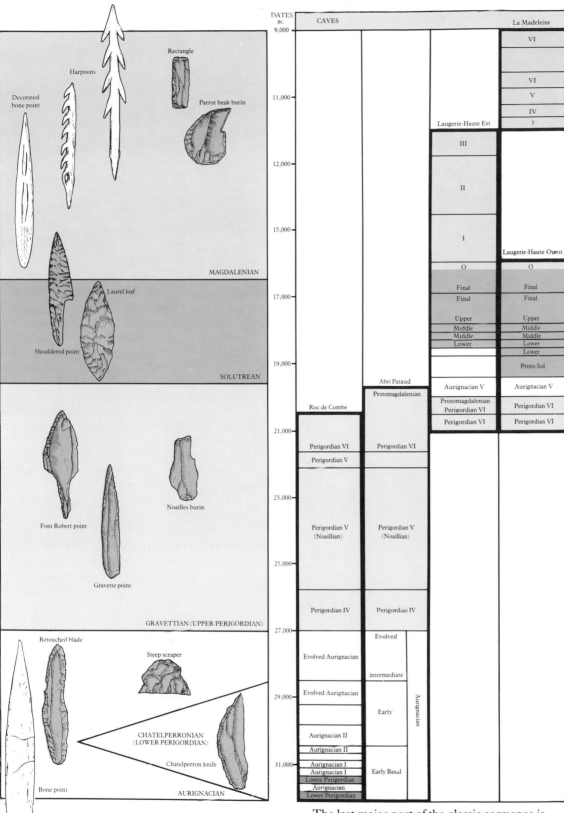

The main phases of the classic Upper Palaeolithic sequence in south-west France are shown here, together with the phases recognized in four particular sequences. Key styles of stone and bone artefacts are indicated: these may, however, form only a small percentage of the tools in any level.

varieties of these had existed in the Mousterian of central and eastern Europe, but we cannot tell whether these new Solutrean forms were an entirely fresh tradition, or an old idea conserved. The Solutrean technology was a local development found only in France, and in Spain on such sites as Parpallo. The whole phase lasted only 1 or 2,000 years and then the Solutrean groups either died out or changed their habits. We cannot tell, but their finely-worked laurel-leaf points represent outstanding skill and aesthetic sense.

The last major part of the classic sequence is represented by the Magdalenian, named after the site of La Madeleine. Early sites of this period are rare, but later ones are very widespread not only in France, but in Belgium, Germany, Switzerland and parts of Spain. The stone tools of the early phases are surprisingly idiosyncratic and crude, and the later stone tools resemble those of the earlier Gravettian, from which the tradition may be directly descended. But this phase is chiefly distinguished by its very fine bone work in bone, ivory and antler. The early development of this superb work can best be traced in south-west France, on sites such as Laugerie-Haute and Le Placard.

Palaeolithic art

The earliest known representational art is about 30,000 years old. Cave painting, rock engravings and decorated objects begin to appear at this time in Europe. Some of the finest Palaeolithic representations are engraved on small slates or slabs. Those of the late Magdalenian include stylized female figures and beautiful naturalistic animals and birds.

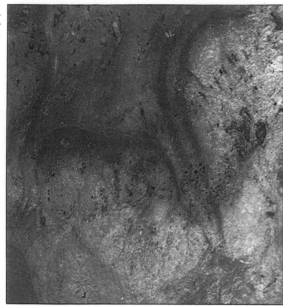

A large reindeer from Font de Gaume has long antlers, which are depicted impressionistically, sweeping upwards.

A large bison with red horns at Font de Gaume. Some of the paintings in the cave are now badly faded. Bison is an especially common subject.

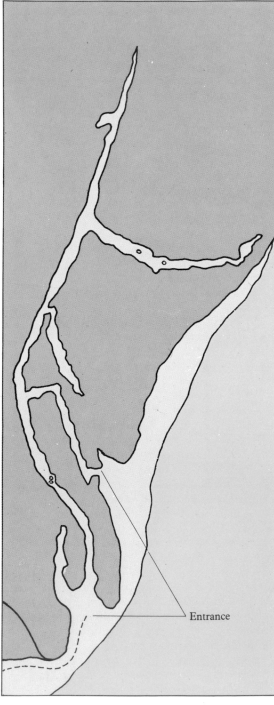

Entrance

The cave of Font de Gaume in south-west France opens off a large cliff face. The cave is over 120 m long, and has three branches. Apart from the entrance zones, most lengths of wall are decorated with paintings.

Representational art – painting and sculpture – first appears in the Upper Palaeolithic, about 30,000 years ago. If it has any earlier history, we do not know of it.

The discovery of Palaeolithic art in the last century caused great excitement, and many different explanations have been put forward of its meaning and purpose. But perhaps its most fascinating aspect is that it gives us the chance to see the world of many thousands of years ago through the eyes of people who actually lived in those days. From their accurate observation, we know that the mammoth was woolly, as has also been shown by the recovery of many frozen remains in Siberia.

Concepts of what art is vary greatly in the modern world. However we interpret it, there is no doubt that the presence of ancient artistic representation tells us a great deal about the development of human abilities. What does the creation of visual art involve? First, the artist has to be able to observe the outside world, to analyse it, and to hold this information in the mind's eye. Then he has to use his materials to recreate this image in the external world, starting from a first touch, and working to the complete form. In doing this, the artist depends greatly on memory, but also on making large numbers of mental transformations of the kind which we first find in early tool-making (see pp 70–71). When the Palaeolithic artist painted a bison on a wall, the image he created depended on many past sightings of bison, probably many

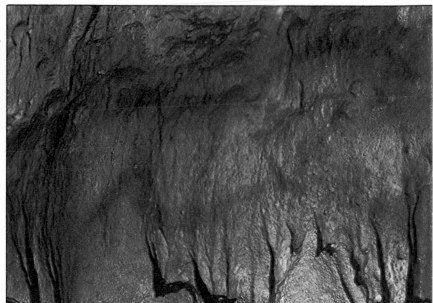

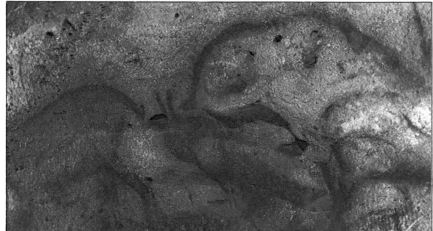

impressions of other painters' attempts, and finally on a specific plan for his own particular painting of the animal.

As well as providing information about these abilities of early man, Palaeolithic art has a vast potential for telling us about the early artists' eye for detail, and their use of symbolism. We can also speculate about their beliefs and values from the subjects they chose to paint, among all that was available to them.

Some of the earliest Palaeolithic art known is that seen in the Aurignacian levels of La Ferrassie. Animal representations, and symbols, including female genitalia, were engraved or painted on flat pieces of limestone. In the Aurignacian, and even more so in the Gravettian, there are many specimens of so-called mobiliary art – movable pieces, chiefly small statuettes. At Pavlov in Czechoslovakia these were modelled out of clay and then baked. But most of the female figures were carved from ivory or bone, in a variety of proportions, but usually with exaggerated breasts and buttocks. It has been suggested that these 'Venus' figurines were connected with fertility rites, but this is no more than a reasonable speculation, although fertility rites have been important in many more recent societies.

Most of the cave paintings which have been preserved belong to the later part of the Upper Palaeolithic, from 20,000 years ago onwards. By definition they can only occur in regions where caves form, but even so, they occur in much greater density in south-west France and northern Spain than in other areas where there are caves.

Different techniques were used in the cave drawings. Sometimes, as at Les Combarelles, the drawings are formed by engraved lines, which may originally have been filled in with colour. Many others are actually paintings, as at Lascaux in France, and at Altamira in Spain. There are very few compositional arrangements: often paintings or engravings have been carried out one on top of another many times over, without regard for the earlier work.

Animals form the chief subject matter, especially the large game animals – mammoth and bison. Reindeer are less commonly shown, even though they were much hunted. A much larger variety of animals, including carnivores like the lion and wolf, occurs on occasion. In addition to animals there are also representations of various abstract shapes (one appears above the head of a horse at Lascaux, see p125). It is notable that, other than in the Venus figurines, human figures are represented in just a very few instances, and nearly all of them are female. We do not know why this is, but it has been suggested that representing the human form or features in painting was thought to bring bad luck.

The cave of Font de Gaume, not now so well known as Lascaux or Altamira, provides one of the finest series of cave paintings. Font de Gaume is in the heart of the densest group of cave painting sites, very close to Les Eyzies, and just a few kilometres

In this painting of a leaping horse at Font de Gaume, the form of the stalactites has been skilfully used to enhance the modelling of the body.

Arrangements of animals are sometimes found in Palaeolithic cave art, but specialists disagree as to whether the positions of the animals relative to one another had special significance. At Font de Gaume there is a reindeer painted without a head (left) and bison (right).

The Gönnersdorf sketch of a
crow is astonishingly lively,
captured with a skill which
would rival that of any
modern cartoonist.

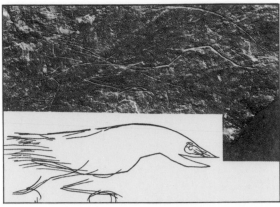

south-west of Lascaux. Palaeolithic art was first
discovered at Altamira in 1875, but La Mouthe was
the first site to be recognized in the Dordogne, in
1895. The initial excitement had not yet died down
when in 1901 Denis Peyrony recognized the
antiquity of the paintings at Font de Gaume, just
three days after the discovery of the engravings at
Les Combarelles. Peyrony, together with the
archaeologist Professor Capitan and the Abbé
Breuil, later published a classic study of the cave of
Font de Gaume.

The main cave passage at Font de Gaume is
about 120 m long, usually 2–3 m wide, and a few
metres in height. In three places there are side
galleries, and at times the passage becomes so
narrow that it is difficult to pass. The paintings do
not begin near the narrow entrance, but deep within
the cave. Lamps were indispensable for working in
dark caves, and these have been found at Lascaux
and elsewhere. They were simple carved stone
bowls, in which animal fats would have been burnt
with a wick.

The outlines of almost all the figures were drawn
in with a fine scratched line, and this was then
accentuated with black pigment. In one or two cases,
the whole form is painted black, like a silhouette, but
usually only the hooves, in addition to the outline,
were painted in this way. Generally, the whole body
of the animal was coloured in with red ochre. Where
the undulations of the rock surface allowed it, the
artist would sometimes place the figure so that the
shape of the rock accentuated its form. If there were
any doubts about the authenticity of the paintings,
these could easily be dispelled by the coat of
transparent stalagmite which has formed over some
of the figures, deposited by the trickle of water
during the course of thousands of years.

The two main pigments used at Font de Gaume
were studied by Professor Henri Moisson, the
distinguished chemist, who was the first to

undertake such work. He found that they were made
of ground-up rock, insoluble in water and without
any organic material. The black powder consisted
mainly of a manganese oxide, the red ochre mainly
of iron sesquioxide. The powder was probably
moistened for application; possibly fat was added as
a binder. Though brushes were probably used, we
have no evidence for them. We know that on some
sites organic materials such as charcoal were used,
raising the exciting possibility that some paintings
might be dated by radiocarbon, now that new
techniques allow the use of very small samples.

Is there a pattern in the paintings which might
help us to understand their 'meaning'? Any
interpretation depends on whether all of them
belong to one period: both the Abbé Breuil and
Professor André Leroi-Gourhan agree that the bulk
of the paintings are Magdalenian, but that some
belong to an earlier phase, Solutrean or older.

An explanation often put forward for
Palaeolithic cave art is that of 'sympathetic magic'.
The representation of the animals within the caves –
perhaps regarded as 'special' places – would assist in
hunting them. More recently, André Leroi-Gourhan
has stressed the importance of symbolism. He
ascribes special significance to the positions within
the caves of certain species, and of the symbols
which he interprets as representing males and
females. These interpretations stress the importance
of sexuality, and of association: the main groupings
are those of man-horse-spear and woman-bison-
wound.

It is also possible that many of the paintings
refer to myths which had special importance to the
people concerned. Even if we assume that any of
these ideas is correct, there is no guarantee that the
explanation valid for one site is appropriate to
another. Any close analogy with modern 'primitive'
art is unwise, but it helps to be aware of the variety of
motives underlying more recent representations.

The great majority of the paintings at Font de
Gaume are of bison and horse, and however we
interpret them, we cannot doubt the economic, and
perhaps therefore the symbolic importance of these
animals. Among the signs painted on the cave walls
are 'tectiforms', so-called because of their roof-like
shape. Some of them are superimposed on a bison,
for no known reason, but the surmise that they
represent the open-country dwellings or tents of the
people seems a plausible one, since we know that
such huts were built at this time.

The majority of settlements were no doubt in
the open rather than in caves, and we know that art
played a part there too. At Limeuil, where a steep
hillside overlooks the confluence of the Dordogne

At the late Magdalenian site of
Feldkirchen-Gönnersdorf,
overlooking the Rhine near
Koblenz, many engraved
slates were found, illustrating
widely varying subjects.
Stylized female
representations were
common. In this example they
are arranged in a pair.

At Limeuil, where the Dordogne and Vézère rivers come together, Palaeolithic hunters would have been able to watch animals fording the rivers.

and Vézère rivers, many small plaques of stone were found with reindeer engraved on them. From this vantage point the hunters could probably watch the reindeer herds fording the rivers and observe them in detail. Such outdoor sketching almost certainly took place, executed on these small 'slates'. It seems likely that the expertise used in painting the large images in the caves was acquired by practice on this smaller scale.

Similar plaquettes are now known much further afield, for example from the Magdalenian site of Feldkirchen-Gönnersdorf, in the lower stretch of the Rhine gorge in Germany. The site is on the east bank of the river, raised on the flank of a small side basin, so that it has fine views across the river and to the north and south. The central features of the site, which was excavated by Professor G. Bosinski in the late 1960s, were hut foundations, made up of many slabs and blocks of a local slate. These probably helped to support staves which held up the roofs of skin tents, very much like those indicated by the signs at Font de Gaume.

As the slates were cleaned, it became apparent that many of them were engraved with representations of animals, every bit as fine as those in cave paintings. The engravings include mammoth, horse, and a number of less common animals, all depicted with great realism. The shading, effected with many small lines, gives a fine impression of the coat of the mammoth and the woolly rhinoceros. A crow is caricatured with all the zest and skill of a modern cartoonist. Even its eyes are represented with techniques which have recurred ever since. Other birds which we know were hunted, like the ptarmigan, were also engraved.

Stylishly executed representations of women found at Gönnersdorf have parallels on other Magdalenian sites: this is a tradition which seems to have lasted for many thousands of years. The forms are more attractive to modern eyes than those of the earlier Venus figurines, but no attempt is made to portray the head and face, and it seems certain that these are symbolic representations, again perhaps charms to enhance fertility.

Other objects found on the site were almost certainly amulets. One is made up from an arc of reindeer teeth, cut from the lower jaw. Another is composed of the foot of an arctic fox, with the bones still articulated. There were also schematic female figurines made of bone, and small shale objects

which include 'rondelles', discs with holes bored through them. They appear on other sites, usually made of bone. Whether they were primarily decorative or functional is unknown: they could have been sewn to the edges of a skin tent flap to keep it down in the wind.

The implications of Palaeolithic art have been considered by scholars for many years. There is no necessity that all the art was produced for the same reason. In the case of a finely carved spear-thrower, for instance, there are many possible explanations which do not rule one another out. Pleasure in carving is one of these. We do not know whether specialists carried out these carvings, or whether most people were capable of them. Pride of ownership, and the status of having a fine object, may have been as important then as now. Religion, magic and superstition, so often invoked to account for the art, cannot be dismissed: there are enough hints of these elements to show that they undoubtedly played an important part.

Many species appear on the limestone plaques which were engraved at Limeuil, but reindeer are the most common. If the animals used to migrate along both valleys, they would have been forced to cross at least one of the rivers near this point.

A horse's head from Gönnersdorf is portrayed with a sensitive line, and shading of the mane and hairy cheeks.

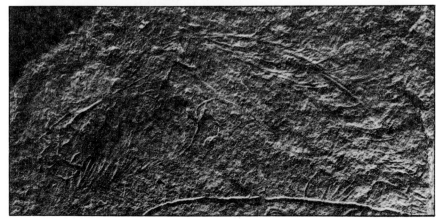

Increasing skills

The variety of skills practised in the Upper Palaeolithic is most apparent when bone is well-preserved. In the later stages of the Magdalenian in Europe, bone and antler carving were used to create objects of practical use which were often of great beauty.

The skills so apparent in Palaeolithic art had evolved mainly for dealing with the more practical side of life. Human beings became increasingly able to influence their environment with more specialized technology and the variety of bone-work found during Magdalenian times in Europe (from about 16,000–9,000 BC) shows clear evidence of these developing skills.

By the late Magdalenian, antler harpoon points had improved considerably and had one or two rows of barbs down the sides. This pattern of the barbs was so effective that it can be seen again and again in later cultures, such as those of North Africa a few thousand years ago and, more recently, in those of the Arctic. Some of the harpoons have a hole drilled near the base, or an expanded boss, indicating that, in the same manner as modern Eskimos, Upper Palaeolithic men might have attached a line to the harpoons in order to recover them.

A new device, the spear-thrower, appears for the first time during this period and was probably used with hafted harpoons. This was a carefully shaped instrument made of bone or antler, which was about the length of a human forearm. Normally, the amount of thrust available in throwing a spear is limited by the length of the thrower's arm; but the spear-thrower, into which the spear is fitted, has the effect of giving the arm an extra segment. Most of the spear-throwers were probably made of wood but we are fortunate that some were made from bone or antler and so have survived.

Many have been decorated with the most remarkable carving of animals: often one or more horses, or sometimes a faun. In some examples, a curious scene is shown which portrays a faun excreting and a bird pecking at the droppings. This curious scene may relate to a story told among the Magdalenians. It is interesting that the same scene is portrayed on a number of throwers, but it is unlikely that all were sculpted by the same craftsmen. The same ideas often recur in Palaeolithic art – for example the stylized form of the female figure appears in places far removed from each other.

These sculptures in antler and bone show us mastery of carving in the round, a skill which was sometimes applied to larger sculptures, such as the bas-relief female figures on the site of Angles-sur-l'Anglin in western France.

Such skills depend on very complete knowledge of the materials to be worked. Stone tools were as specialized as modern metal tools: burins and awls are common on later Upper Palaeolithic sites. Much of the Magdalenian carving used reindeer antler which is especially suitable in texture and durability. Preserved remains from some sites reveal that long strips were cut from the antlers, following the natural curve, and that the craftsman had the skill to straighten these out so that the pieces could be used for making harpoons and other tools.

The repertoire of bone tools includes needles and awls for sewing. Given the evidence that tents were in use, and indications from Russia that beads were sewn to tunics, the possession of tools such as these is scarcely surprising.

There are some which have defied all modern attempts at explanation. Among these are the *bâtons de commandement* which were made from a stout shaft of antler, with a hole bored at one end. These tools occur from Spain to Russia and are frequently

A late Magdalenian spear-thrower, carved in the form of a horse.

A late Magdalenian harpoon with twin rows of decorated barbs, and an expanded neck around which a line was probably tied.

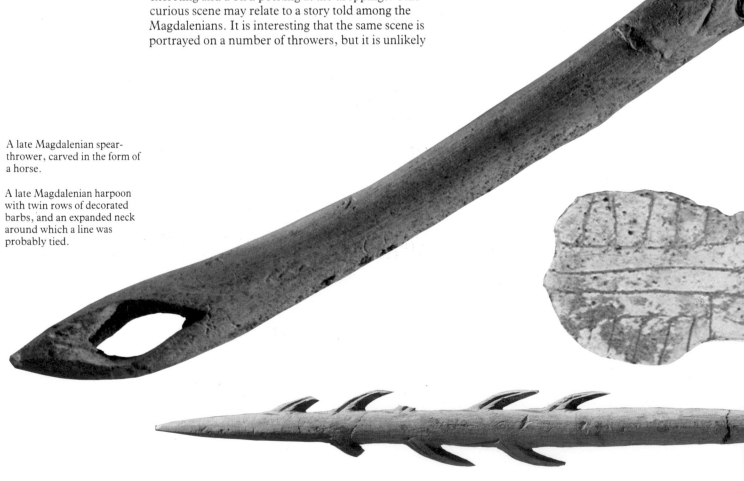

carved with elaborate designs. Many theories have been conceived about their use, but none proven. Were they used in the hunt, in the home, or did they have a more symbolic significance? We do not know, but would we have guessed the use of spear-throwers had there not been modern peoples who still use similar tools?

Among the bone tools are some with notches cut into them which do not appear to be decorative. They give the impression that somebody was keeping a tally and this seems especially likely when there is a row of nicks along the edge of a piece which have clearly been made by different stone tools on separate occasions. A special study of such objects has been made which suggests that quite complex computational systems were in use over 10,000 years ago. But we are unlikely to find any one correct explanation for the patterns of nicks and lines on bone-work. Present-day peoples, after all, have numerous reasons for the patterns they create on objects and there is enough evidence to show us that Upper Paleolithic people also lived in a similarly complex world of habit and belief.

An eskimo uses a spear-thrower to launch a harpoon from his kayak. A cord attached to the harpoon head allows its recovery. Archaeological finds show that similar harpoons were used over 10,000 years ago.

(©1981 Time-Life Books B.V. From 'Peoples of the Wild' Series.)

An engraved bone found at the cave of Remouchamps in Belgium in 1970. The lines have been interpreted as representing numbers, and it has been suggested that the object was used in a game of chance.

Mammoth-hunters

Mammoth ranged freely on the plains of eastern Europe and Russia, though they were rare in western Europe. They were exploited to the full by man, and in Czechoslovakia and Russia their bones were used even for houses. Mammoth bones were sometimes carved, and the animal itself was often represented in art.

The most splendid of the large Pleistocene mammals were the woolly mammoth and the woolly rhinoceros. We know what these animals looked like, not only from the cave paintings and engravings, but from the evidence of their bones which remains. A few completely preserved mammoths have been found in the ice of Siberia, too, testifying to the accuracy of the drawings.

The ice-age plains were probably drier than present-day steppe, and therefore had less snow, but they would still have been chillingly cold. This combination of conditions would have ruled out the growth of trees and restricted vegetation to grasses and herbs.

The mammoths offered great quantities of meat which, in the cold phases, would not rapidly go bad. Yet in western Europe, the horse and reindeer were more plentiful and less dangerous to hunt. We know, however, that resourceful use was made of mammoth remains, and can infer that in the areas where they were common, mammoths were frequently and successfully hunted.

In a number of cases in eastern Europe and in European Russia, remains of huts have been found which were actually built almost entirely from mammoth bones, some of which were as much as 2 m long. At the eastern Gravettian site of Mezhirich in Russia the bones were arranged with great skill and regularity in order to use every piece to the maximum advantage. The chinks between the bones were probably filled with a packing consisting of moss and herbs.

At Mezhirich also, a complete mammoth skull has been found, on which there are painted decorations. Similar decorations occur on bones of the Gravettian period much further west in Europe. The presence of a pattern of small dents on the mammoth skull has led to the suspicion that it may have been used as a drum, and that the hut where it was found had possibly been built specially to house it, perhaps for use in ceremonies.

The sheer quantity of mammoth remains on some sites is amazing. At Předmost in Czechoslovakia, the remains of 8 or 900 mammoths have been discovered, together with a variety of other animals. Here too, mammoth bones were used, in a variety of forms. Ribs were often decorated with series of geometric incisions: but whether these artefacts had a practical function is not known. Some other items can only have been made as toys, or objects of religious significance; for example a baked clay figure of a glutton (or wolverine) at Předmost, or mammoth and rhinoceros figurines at Pavlov, another famous Slovakian site.

These Czechoslovakian sites belong to later phases of the eastern Gravettian, and date to a little over 20,000 years ago. Features of the stone tool-kit, such as the numerous backed blades, and of the art, are often similar to those found in contemporary western Europe.

An astounding find made at Předmost in the nineteenth century was of a pit, measuring 2.5 by 40 m, which was flanked with stones and contained about 20 human skeletons, the majority of which were undisturbed. The heads were orientated

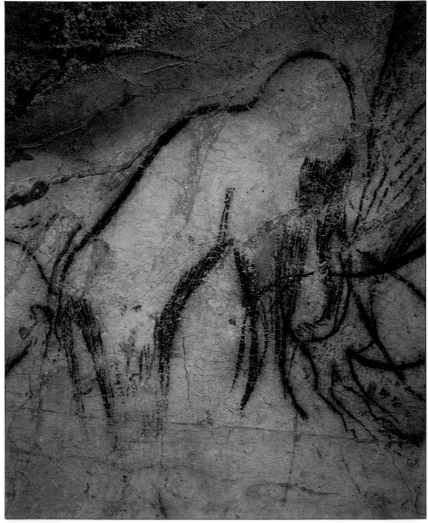

A painting of a mammoth in the cave of Pech Merle in south-west France; mammoth bones are rare on French sites, but the animals clearly made a strong impression on Palaeolithic artists.

towards the north, and all was covered with flat stones and mammoth shoulder-blades. The remains were of individuals of different ages and sex, but what event resulted in this mass burial we shall never know because, unfortunately, the finds were destroyed in the Second World War before the techniques of modern scientific study could be applied to them.

We can learn a great deal from such graves where the evidence is still complete. For example in three Palaeolithic burials from Sunghir in Russia, the pattern of numerous beads and other objects indicates the former presence of fur clothes, including hats. This shows that the Upper Palaeolithic clothing in those areas was quite similar to that worn by modern Lapps (see p 150) in its general aspect.

Did the way of life of these people continue unchanged for thousands of years? At Předmost, there are several archaeological layers, but only the one with massive deposits of bone. Camps were probably made here in a slightly warmer phase, when there was a pause in the deposition of loess. There is much less sign of occupation during the coldest phase of the last glaciation (the glacial maximum) which began about 20,000 years ago. At this time, even the most well-adapted animals and human groups may have been driven south.

A resurgence of similar occupations in the late glacial stages shows that any slight amelioration of climatic conditions allowed a northward advance. But the mammoth (*Mammuthus primigenius*), a species which had existed for hundreds of thousands of years, suddenly disappeared. It is still to be seen on the Gönnersdorf engravings of 10,000 years ago, but it must have died out very rapidly after that date. The same general period saw the demise of many other species, such as the woolly rhinoceros.

Many reasons for the disappearance of these animals have been suggested. The most convincing explanations are sudden climatic change to which the animals could not adapt; or alternatively extermination by man. There had been many comparable climatic changes in the previous million years, but perhaps this particular one had more severe effects for reasons which we cannot appreciate. Some mammoths have been found with their stomach contents preserved; it is therefore known that their diet consisted of herbs which still exist today in Siberia suggesting that environmental changes do not explain the disappearance.

In studies of similar threats of extinction to modern elephants and rhinoceros, ecologist Dr Malcolm Coe points out their inherent vulnerability caused by their slow rate of reproduction. Animals like these, which have only one offspring every few years, are extraordinarily at risk to prolonged pressures which hinder their breeding. If human beings concentrated on hunting young animals, at a time when environmental conditions were in any case difficult, this might help to account for some of the extinctions. But the only certain facts are that human skills were steadily increasing during the later stages of the last glacial period, allowing easier capture of even the largest animals, and that at the same time many species disappeared.

A reconstruction of the hut constructed of mammoth bones, found at Mezhirich in Russia. It was probably covered over with moss and grass when the framework was completed. The painted mammoth skull may have been used as a drum. The clothes in the drawing are based on the patterns of beads found in some burials.

135

Australia – colonization of the island continent

Human occupation of Australia and New Guinea appears to have begun at least 50,000 years ago. By 30–20,000 years ago, even the south of the continent had inhabitants. The first people must have arrived by boat, at times when sea-level was low and land areas much greater; but even so the distances crossed by sea were over 100 km.

The aboriginal inhabitants of Australia never built cities but their prehistory deserves full mention, not least because the crossing to the continent ranks as one of the great achievements of early *Homo sapiens*.

Today Australia is an island continent as large as the United States. It was never directly accessible by land-bridge even at times of lowered sea-level during the Pleistocene; but in those times it was joined to New Guinea and Tasmania to make an even larger land area, known as Sahul. At least 100 km of open sea separated Sahul from mainland Asia, a distance which only man could cross. Asian placental

The fact that these waters were crossed, shows beyond doubt that small boats were already in existence. None have been preserved, so their nature can only be guessed at. They were probably not simple dugout canoes made from a single log, as the fire technology necessary for hollowing these out appears to be relatively recent, but were more probably constructed from logs lashed together. Long voyages in such small craft are hazardous since the boats are primarily designed for inshore use, and once the coast is a few kilometres away, the risks increase dramatically. It is not likely therefore that

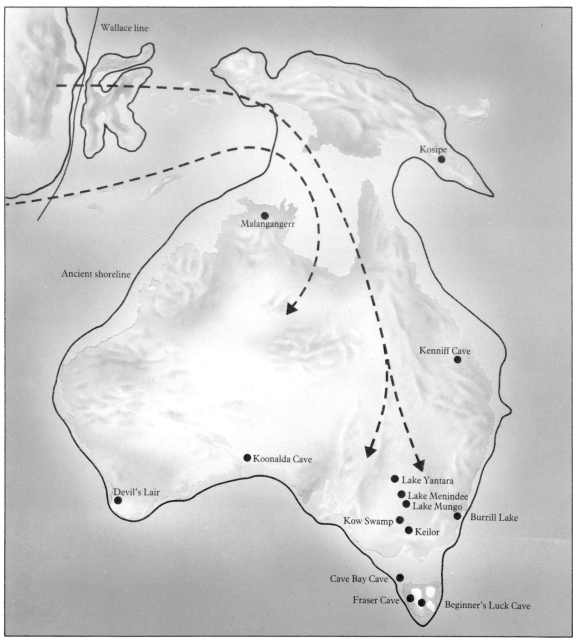

The relationship of South-East Asia and Sahul at times of low sea-level; the arrows indicate two probable entry routes into Australia by 'island-hopping' and possible routes of dispersal through the continent. All the named sites have radiocarbon dates of c. 20,000 years or older.

mammals could not move further south than the outlying islands of Indonesia because of the deep waters marked by the 'Wallace line' (named after the nineteenth-century evolutionary biologist A. R. Wallace); Australian marsupial mammals were therefore kept free from competition by placentals.

Exactly when man did first cross to Australia is no easier to elucidate than any other major problem of prehistory, but Australian archaeologists have found and excavated sites over 30,000 years old in the southern part of the continent, which suggests that the original crossing was made at a considerably earlier date, possibly 50,000 or 60,000 years ago.

long voyages into the unknown were planned deliberately. From time to time, however, such little craft might be caught up by squalls and swept away, yet by good luck survive to come ashore on an unknown land.

We know that somehow a complete breeding population arrived in Sahul. This may have been as little as one couple, but a somewhat larger group would have been much more viable. The descent of Australian aborigines from people of South-East Asian stock seems plain from their present-day characteristics, including genetic evidence, as well as from similarities in early human remains.

One of the cremations at Lake Mungo, just after discovery.

A view of the area at Lake Mungo known as the 'Walls of China', where the sediments are in the course of erosion.

Australian archaeologists have been remarkably successful in recovering evidence of the early prehistory, including human remains. Though much more awaits discovery, the sample of later Pleistocene human remains is already as good as that from the whole of Europe.

The oldest sites yet known are concentrated in the south-east of the country. The true antiquity of the habitation of Australia was scarcely expected until the first radiocarbon dates were achieved from deep sequences. Kenniff Cave in Queensland, excavated by Professor D. J. Mulvaney (Australian National University) in 1960, was the first site to produce a date approaching 20,000 years. By 1973, Dr Rhys Jones (ANU) was able to list over 20 such dates from more than a dozen sites.

The oldest thoroughly investigated sites with indisputable dates are at Lake Mungo in western New South Wales. Here there was a series of lakes, the Willandra system, which have now dried up. At times in the past, when rainfall was higher, and the lakes were fed by a river, fish and shellfish would have been plentiful. It was this ready source of food and fresh water which made the site so attractive.

The oldest finds from Lake Mungo include hearths and a clay oven dated by radiocarbon to

The excavations at Kenniff Cave Queensland, in 1962, showing the fine horizontal layering of the sediments.

Engravings of kangaroo and emu tracks on a limestone horizontal surface at Scott River, Western Australia. These are practically the only naturalistic engravings known in the south-west.

Stencils of hands and of a child's foot at Kenniff Cave. Similar forms are known in Palaeolithic art in Europe, but this does not imply any relationship.

about 32,000 years ago, a result confirmed by thermoluminescence dating. Three human skulls have also been found here; these are the oldest yet known from Australia. One, of a female, dated at about 25,000 years ago is as gracile and modern as the skulls of present-day aborigines. The remains of this female are also remarkable in that they show that the body was cremated; this is perhaps the oldest-known evidence of a cremation anywhere in the world.

Another very early site, which Australian archaeologists have interpreted less unanimously, is Keilor in Victoria, where river terraces have yielded flake tools. Some of the finds may be natural, rather than human creations, but it is agreed that certain flakes are man-made and that they are at least 30,000 years old.

During the last few years, the extent of occupation of Sahul prior to 20,000 years ago has become fully apparent. Evidence of early occupation in New Guinea was to be expected, since it was joined to Australia until 7 or 8,000 years ago. This was confirmed by excavations at Kosipe in the east of the island, where a date of about 26,000 years ago was obtained from charcoal. Flaked axe adzes were already in use here. Adzes, common in Australia and elsewhere in the last few thousand years, are axe-like tools, used for shaping wood.

Sites which are almost equally early have been found in the far west of Australia, and in the extreme south. The cave of Devil's Lair, near the coast in the south-west, was occupied at least 24,000 years ago.

At this time, Tasmania and the surrounding islands were part of the mainland. A series of sites investigated in recent years shows that this whole area was occupied over 20,000 years ago. The first site to be found was on Hunter Island, to the north-west of Tasmania. Here, in Cave Bay Cave, Dr Sandra Bowdler found a bone point and two pieces of flaked quartz in a layer dated to about 18,500 years ago. Subsequently, discoveries of several other sites, including Fraser Cave and Deena Reena Cave, in Tasmania, have confirmed the early human occupation of this area, which was partly glaciated 18,000 years ago.

Who were the early inhabitants, and how do they relate to modern aborigines? Human remains similar to those from Lake Mungo have also been found at Keilor (15,000 years ago) and Green Gully, Victoria (8,000 years ago), and all these finds are within the range of the variation of modern aborigines. But Kow Swamp, in northern Victoria, has yielded remains of very different people. At this site more than 40 skeletons have been excavated, providing one of the best collections of Late Pleistocene human remains known in the world.

The skeletons had been buried in various positions and some were accompanied by grave goods, including ochre, shells and teeth. They belong to the final stages of the last glacial period, as is shown by several radiocarbon dates of between 9,000 and 10,000 years ago.

These remains are extraordinary in preserving a series of truly archaic features at such a late date. The forehead region of the skull is reminiscent of *Homo erectus*, with marked brow ridges. The forehead slopes back, and the skull is narrowed behind the eyes, as in earlier hominids. Dr Alan Thorne (ANU) points out that all the Kow Swamp jaws are too large to fit the Broken Hill cranium from Zambia, which may be 100,000 years older.

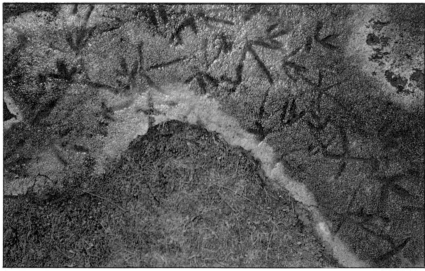

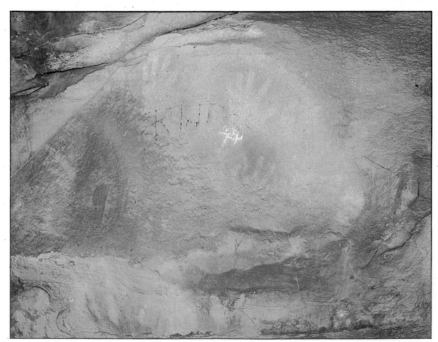

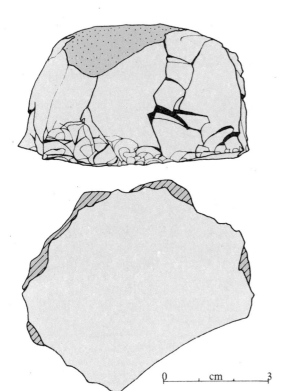

It is remarkable that such a population should have existed at least 15,000 years later than very modern people such as those from Lake Mungo. This may, however, be explained by the pattern of early colonization of Sahul.

The early dates for Mungo and Keilor, which are in the south, imply a much earlier entry to the continent. The times of lowest sea-level occurred about 18,000 years ago, in the glacial maximum and before that on several occasions between 40 and 80,000 years ago. It is most probable that human groups crossed over on more than one occasion, but Australian archaeologists are divided as to whether the evidence indicates two, or possibly three or more such colonizations. Possibly one group, with affinities to South-East Asian *Homo erectus*, crossed over as early as 60 or 70,000 years ago. Another, rather more modern-looking population may have arrived perhaps 40,000 years ago. In a land area the size of Australia, the two might have existed side by side for many thousands of years. But this is speculation, for the remains from Lake Mungo are very variable in their form, and it may be that the original inhabitants were equally variable. Primitive features may be accentuated in the Kow Swamp group, because they were strongly expressed in a very small ancestral group which split off from other ancient Australians.

It seems sure that there have been further incursions into Australia within the last few thousand years. For example, the dingo, the only animal which was domesticated by the aborigines, probably came across by boat from South-East Asia within the last 6 or 7,000 years. Archaeological and genetic evidence suggests that the peoples of New Guinea have had contact with the north, but this is less clearcut, since the two areas were probably similar before the ocean waters rose at the end of the last ice age.

The two major changes which occurred in the environment of Sahul are this last rise in sea-level and the extinction of larger marsupial mammals, the 'megafauna'. Bones of these animals, including the giant kangaroo, have been found in some of the cave sequences, but not in great quantities, so the date of their extinction has been difficult to establish. Did they become extinct before man arrived in Australia, or only subsequently, perhaps as a result of excessive hunting? The site of Lancefield Swamp in Victoria has yielded plentiful remains of the megafauna at a date of about 26,000 years ago, several thousand years later than the earliest known archaeological sites. The presence of these animal remains in levels where stone artefacts have also been found suggests human involvement in the extinction of the megafauna, but it also shows that these animals survived alongside man for a considerable period, and were not exterminated in one great burst of hunting activity. There are signs that the megafauna gradually died out over a long period, but whether this was primarily a result of climatic change, or human actions, or a combination of both, remains unresolved.

Gradually, the study of Australian prehistory has shattered the myth that aborigines were the most primitive of peoples, unable to influence their environment. Polishing and grinding of stone tools seems to date further back in New Guinea and Australia than anywhere else in the world. Grinding stones appear very early at about 15,000 years ago, showing an emphasis on exploitation of seeds. Cremation as a burial practice also appears at a very early date. Cave paintings are widespread and some are of great antiquity; for example, those at Koonalda Cave, South Australia, are as much as 20,000 years old. Not much of Australia was a suitable environment for the early domestication of plants, but in the northern parts, as in New Guinea, there are indications that horticulture, for example, the management of root crops, has a history of thousands of years.

Australian aborigines reveal to us the fine levels of adaptation possible for hunters and gatherers, even in the harshest of environments. Peoples so well adapted to such a vast country were not under pressure to evolve civilization as we know it, but the social wealth of their existence is very evident from their complex kinship systems and religious concepts.

A core scraper from Kenniff Cave, of the type which is widespread on early Australian sites.

The main excavation at Devil's Lair Cave, Western Australia, directed by Dr Charlie Dortch. The photograph illustrates the importance of lighting and safety precautions in a deep cave excavation.

Occupation of the New World

The date of the first human entry to the Americas has been debated for many years, but there is agreement that people crossed the Bering land-bridge from Siberia at times of low sea-level. A date of about 30,000 years ago seems most likely, but earlier and later estimates are strongly championed.

Within the later Pleistocene – the last 125,000 years – North and South America have become colonized by man. The descendants of these people are known as 'Indians' as a result of Columbus' mistaken belief that he had reached India. In origin, however, they are clearly of Asian stock. The distribution of blood groups in present-day American Indians suggests that only a fairly small population originally entered the New World: in the ABO system, group B is entirely absent except in Alaska, and group A is absent south of the Canadian/United States border, so that in most of the Americas, only group O is represented.

The peopling of the New World is a more controversial topic than the colonization of Australia. A few American archaeologists argue for very early dates – over 100,000 years ago – whereas others are unwilling to believe that there was any occupation south of Canada more than 12,000 years ago.

Probably the majority, however, now think that a date somewhere between 30,000 and 15,000 years ago is correct for the first colonization.

The subject has remained controversial partly because very few sites which give convincing evidence for an early date have been located and excavated by modern techniques. In some cases doubts exist about whether the tools found were genuinely man-made. The first occupation of an area may have been by such small numbers of people that archaeologists cannot seriously hope to find traces of them; however, once a substantial population had built up, evidence of it should be found.

The key to entry into the New World was the Bering land-bridge. Siberia and the west of Alaska are today separated by as little as 80 km. At times when the sea-level was 100 m lower, the land uncovered was more than a mere bridge: it was a plain hundreds of kilometres wide. It has been suggested that the land-bridge was 'open' only for short periods, but now that we have much better knowledge of ancient sea-levels, it can be seen that it would have been open for long stretches of time before being finally cut 14,000 years ago. Although glaciers covered much of the north, the land-bridge area itself was ice-free in the last glaciation, but very dry and very cold.

In any attempt to trace the origins of the colonization, the obvious place to start is Siberia itself. There is little to suggest that the north-east parts of Asia were inhabited in the last interglacial or earlier, but Soviet archaeologists have been able to trace a definite record back to at least 30,000 years ago. These earliest sites, belonging to the Dyuktai culture, have yielded fine bifacially-flaked points (somewhat like those of the Solutrean). This is an important feature, because bifacial projectile points later became widespread in early American sites, and there is the possibility of a cultural connection.

Thirty to forty thousand years ago, conditions were somewhat milder than during most of the Wisconsin glaciation (as the last glaciation is known in America). This better climate may have encouraged both the occupation of Siberia, and an advance eastwards.

This background presents major difficulties for the acceptance of very early dates claimed for sites in parts of the Yukon. Here, human presence at up to 100,000 years ago has been alleged on the basis of bone tools, and distinctive bone-fractures, which it is claimed could only have been made by man. There are, however, no traces of stone tools, even though raw materials for these were available, and it is very unlikely that this area was the only part of the world

Map labels

Siberia
Ushki
Beringia
Old Crow
Dry Creek
Bluefish Cave

Maximum extent of ice sheets

Smith Creek Cave
Rancho La Brea
Los Angeles
Laguna Del Mar
Meadowcroft
Clovis

El Cedral
Calico Hills
Tlapacoya
Valsequillo
El Bosque
Shoreline in glacial times

Taima Taima

Guitarrero
Ayacucho

Monte Verde

Los Toldos
Fell's Cave

Line of entry allegedly made possible by opening of ice-free corridor 12,000 years ago. The coast may have allowed free entry at much earlier dates.

Core area of Clovis sites common from 11,000 years ago

● Archaeological site or early human remains

■ Site regarded as especially controversial

The Americas, showing the Bering land-bridge, the maximum extent of ice during the last glaciation and early sites discussed in the text.

A cut log, with cut blocks and chips, found near to domestic architectural structures at Monte Verde, Chile. Several radiocarbon dates place the site in the range 13,000–12,000 years ago.

140

where stone was actually abandoned in favour of bone. Even undoubted bone implements from this area can be suspect evidence, because radiocarbon dates can only tell us the time at which the animal lived, not when the tools were made. Bone was often preserved by freezing for long periods, and would have provided suitable material for tool-making at later or even recent dates.

Actual human remains offer the other main chance of documenting human presence. A jaw from Old Crow Basin, Yukon, has not yet been dated. The other site with remains which promised to be of great antiquity, Taber in western Canada, was recently shown by a radiocarbon-accelerator date to belong to the last few thousand years.

The oldest sites in Alaska and the Yukon with unequivocal archaeological evidence appear to be 14–15,000 years old.

Although no very ancient sites are known in the north-west, there is considerable evidence to show that man did enter the New World more than a few thousand years ago. Sites in South America are clearly important, because some of them are more than 10,000 km removed from Beringia (the Bering plains), and they imply a much earlier entry than their own ages. Two cave sites in Peru are well known. At Flea Cave near Ayacucho, investigated by R. S. MacNeish, the archaeological sequence may extend back 19,000 years. Some archaeologists believe that the stone tools from the oldest layers were produced by 'spalling' (natural flaking of rock) from the cave walls, but there seems less doubt that stone tools have been found in layers at least 15,000 years old. In Guitarrero Cave, excavated by Professor T. F. Lynch (Cornell University), there are as yet few dates from the deepest levels, but the earliest occupation on the site is likely to be 12,000 years old, and there is plentiful evidence by 10,000. Bifacial points, somewhat similar to those on the Siberian sites, were found and appear to be representative of a local Andean tradition.

Further early remains come from the site of Monte Verde in Chile, excavated by Dr T. Dillehay (University of Kentucky), and dated to 12–13,000 years ago. There were few stone tools here, but wooden artefacts are excellently preserved through waterlogging. It appears that small stones were selected and rounded by abrasion, perhaps for use as slingstones. Mastodon tusks were used for tools; they were split and shaped into great gouges, probably for wood-working.

Remains of a mastodon, associated with artefacts, were also found by Dr Alan Bryan (University of Alberta) and colleagues at Taima

Taima in Colombia. Radiocarbon dates on bone and on twigs, which probably represent the animal's stomach contents, consistently give ages of about 13,000 years. Other dates as old, or older, come from further claimed sites in South America, including some in Brazil, but potentially early human remains are few. These include a cranial fragment from Lagoa Santa in Brazil, and a mandible from San Augustin in Colombia, but their age has not been determined.

The presence of several early sites in South America ought to imply a much earlier presence further north, but this is not universally accepted. Some American archaeologists believe that occupation goes back only to about 12,000 years ago, the time when sites become plentiful in the mid-west and south-west of the United States. These are sites of the Clovis tradition, characterized by fine stone points, and often associated with kill-sites of large

Meadowcroft rock-shelter, western Pennsylvania, is best seen in winter, because foliage hides it in summer. This view shows the sandstone of which the walls and roof of the rock-shelter are composed.

Sediments in the east face of the excavations at Meadowcroft. Over 60 small depositional units are labelled. The tags indicate particular cultural features, and places where samples were taken for sediment analysis, or studies of pollen and other features.

Projectile points from Meadowcroft rock-shelter and the immediate area, of the type called 'Miller Points'. The point on the left was found at Meadowcroft in layers dated between 11,000 and 12,000 years ago and is hence the oldest dated projectile point south of the glacial ice in the Americas.

game such as elephant and bison. The Clovis points are distinguished by flaking over the whole surface, followed by the removal of a single flake from each side (called fluting), presumably to aid hafting. Apart from the alleged lack of early sites, the hypothesis of 'late colonization' could be supported by the distribution of ice sheets which covered most of Canada. A narrow corridor between western and eastern ice sheets, near the line of the Rocky Mountains, opened up only about 12,000 years ago.

In recent years, however, the evidence for 'Pre-Clovis' sites has steadily built up. The most important site yet found is Meadowcroft, a rock-shelter in western Pennsylvania, where the sequence, excavated under the direction of Professor J. Adovasio (University of Pittsburgh), dates back 16,000 years. Beneath levels which contain Clovis points are others with points lacking the characteristic Clovis flute. The early date for Meadowcroft seems established beyond most reasonable doubt. Arguments that the radiocarbon dates were contaminated by 'old' carbon from coal are not supported by the evidence.

It seems likely that there are other 'Pre-Clovis' sites, probably including Little Canyon Creek Cave in Wyoming. At Smith Creek Cave in Nevada, artefacts unlike the Clovis points have been found in a site dating to 12–10,000 years ago.

Other evidence suggesting an early occupation is yet more controversial. A number of human remains found along the California coast have been studied by various dating techniques. Unfortunately most of the finds were made long ago, and building development in the area has ruled out most possibilities of further archaeological investigation. In two cases, however, radiocarbon dates could be obtained from collagen preserved in the bones. This is regarded as a highly reliable means of dating. The specimen from Laguna produced an age of about 17,000 years, and 'Los Angeles Man' an age of over 23,000 years. A recent study of these remains suggests that they are less specifically 'Mongoloid' than modern American Indians, which supports the idea that they belong to an archaic population.

Most of the other Californian specimens are too small to allow conventional radiocarbon dating, but it was possible for Professor J. L. Bada to carry out amino-acid determinations (racemization dating). These do not by themselves offer an age, but comparisons of the results with those from the radiocarbon dated specimens allow a figure to be calculated. As some of these calculated ages are over 40,000 years, they have been received with considerable scepticism. The Sunnyvale skeleton, estimated at 70,000 years by racemization, has more recently been dated at 8–9,000 years by uranium series, and 3,500–5,000 years by the radiocarbon-accelerator at Tucson, Arizona. This suggests, but does not prove, that all the other remains – there are about half a dozen in total – are relatively young in date.

Even if the California remains are not very old, the early dates for the South American sites and for Meadowcroft provide a sound basis for assessing the spread of human occupation through the Americas. In the cold periods there were probably human groups well adapted to life in the Bering plains, who exploited the marine resources along the coast. Climatic deteriorations between 30–20,000 years ago

would have encouraged them to move south, perhaps following the coast. Throughout the cold periods of the last glaciation, the tropical and subtropical belt of the continents would have presented the most attractive environment, and we would expect to find remains there. Although it is not accepted by all archaeologists, this view seems to be borne out by evidence from Mexico, such as at Tlapacoya, where a hearth has been dated to 22,000 years by radiocarbon, and the site at El Cedral, which is 30,000 years old according to dates provided by juniper wood.

To the early colonizers the Americas would have been truly a 'New World'. Some idea of the wealth of animal life can be gained from the famous Rancho La Brea tar-pits in Los Angeles. Here, many of the animals became trapped in natural bitumen, and their entire skeletons have been preserved. They include mastodons, sabre-tooth tigers, and hundreds upon hundreds of ferocious giant wolves, the 'dire-wolves'. These were probably enticed into the treacherous tar by the prospect of catching game animals already enmeshed. Deer and horse were also abundant in America, but the horse was hunted to extinction (it was reintroduced by the Spaniards thousands of years later). Many other large animals also became extinct at the end of the Pleistocene.

The date and cause of these extinctions are the subject of as much speculation as the disappearance of the European and Australian 'megafauna'. Remains, such as those of the Taima Taima mastodon, or of mammoths found butchered in Arizona and Mexico, show that man was contemporary with these animals and indeed successfully hunted them.

Our clearest impression of the ancient Indian hunters of the great plains comes from the sites where they hunted bison. A classic example is provided by the Olsen-Chubbock site in Colorado, named after its excavators. Here, about 8,500 years ago, a herd of bison was stampeded across level

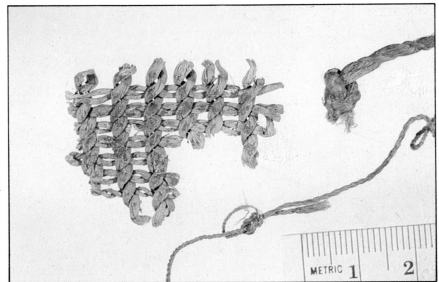

ground, so that they would fall into a deep, hidden gully, where they were easily dispatched. The remains of about 200 beasts were found, accompanied by a few finely-worked stone points, either lance-heads or knives used in the butchery.

The archaeological record favours such discoveries, whereas a camp-site may be recorded by little more than a circle of stones which weighted down the edges of a tepee. The animals provided people with a range of materials: leather, sinews, bone and horn, all of which were important in plains areas, where trees and other resources were scarce.

There were of course other facets to life in early America. Dry caves in the American south-west and the Andes have preserved remains of early basketry and textiles excellently. The development of these crafts can be traced through several thousand years, until eventually fine patterns and complex weaves were widespread. Because of this fine preservation we have a picture of the evolution of craft skills which is lacking in most parts of the world.

Exceptional preservation of organic remains means that early craft skills, up to 10,000 years old, can be seen at Guitarrero Cave. Plant fibres were used for cordage. The only specimens older than those from Guitarrero are from Danger Cave, Utah. Cordage was probably used for hafting, binding, and for making nets and snares, and was present in a highly developed form from an early date.

Africa: later Stone Age and rock art

In the Later Stone Age of Africa, rock art occurs on ten times as many sites as in Europe. Many of the sites are comparatively recent, but the oldest rock engravings are over 20,000 years old. Very small stone implements – microliths – probably originated in Africa.

Inter-group conflict, such as is depicted here, is a rare subject for Later Stone Age painting. Some of the figures have bows and arrows; they are from a site in the south-west of Cape Province, South Africa, and belong to the period between 8,000 and 3,000 years ago.

An eland and a running figure, from the Drakensburg Mountains of south-east Africa. Such bichrome (two-colour) paintings occur relatively late in the local sequence.

A Later Stone Age figure from the Goromonze District in Zimbabwe. It shows a female figure, one of a series of scenes of apparently ritual or mythological significance.

The progression of events in Africa during the later parts of the Stone Age was markedly different from that in Europe, but no less important. The Upper Palaeolithic resembling that of Europe and south-west Asia appears only on the northern fringes of the continent. During most of the same period Middle Stone Age industries continued to be made in other parts of Africa, but they were to be superseded by different kinds of industries belonging to the Later Stone Age.

Much of the wealth of material culture which once existed has perished, since bone as well as wood has little chance of surviving in the tropical and sub-tropical climates. But Africa has at least two major contributions to offer to the cultural record: a new stone-tool technology in the form of 'microliths' and its own rock art.

Microliths are very small stone tools, generally 3 cm long or less, made from small flakes or segments of blades. Usually one side has been blunted by the 'backing' technique, a form of retouching in which tiny flakes are struck off the edge. The final form could be controlled by backing retouch, so that different shapes such as points, triangles, crescents and even trapezes could be made. But the great quantities of flakes which lack retouch are just as likely to have been used as tools. In later parts of the Stone Age microliths commonly occur by the thousand on a single site, so countless millions must have been made in total.

How can these very small tools be explained? There is surprisingly little direct evidence from earlier times, but much more within the last few thousand years. It appears that the microliths were part of composite tools, mounted on handles or shafts. Sometimes they may have been tied on, but

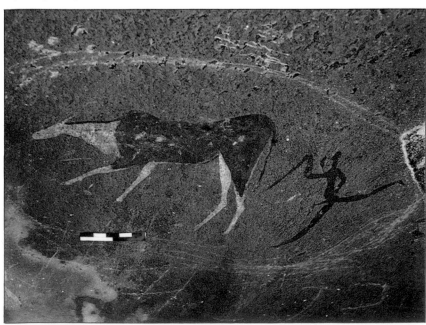

evidence remains from sites, such as Makwe Cave in Zambia, that they were usually fixed by resin or mastic, which would have been obtained from trees. Although the wood does not survive at Makwe, the resin shows how the sharp edges were fitted as projectile points or tangs on arrows at least as early as 3,000 BC. Evidence from the Middle East tells us that microliths were used for other purposes: the tools were sometimes fitted end-to-end, in a row, into a curved wooden or bone handle to give the curved blade desirable in a sickle.

Microliths were first studied in Europe, where they belong mainly to the Mesolithic which follows the Upper Palaeolithic – though some are found in the Solutrean and particularly in the later Magdalenian. But it is now plain that these tools appear at far earlier dates in Africa, in or alongside more traditional Middle Stone Age sites.

The earliest microlithic industries appear more than 40,000 years ago in parts of southern Africa, for example in eastern Lesotho, at Sehonghong. If the Howieson's Poort industries are regarded as microlithic, then they go back even further (see pp 114–115). Although microliths are not continuously present in the sequences, it seems that the idea may well have originated in Africa. Industries where microliths are predominant are classed in the Later Stone Age, but it is now recognized that they can be contemporary with the Middle Stone Age in neighbouring areas.

Between 20,000 and 10,000 years ago, the use of microliths had become almost universal, so that larger stone tools had almost passed out of existence by about 10,000 years ago. Dr David Phillipson of Cambridge University has suggested that the larger Middle Stone Age projectile points were most suitable for spear hunting on open plains, and that climatic changes in the later stages of the glacial period resulted in more wooded vegetation in wide areas, putting a premium on the use of bows and arrows for hunting.

Does this mean that bows and arrows are as old as the oldest microliths? We do not know, but they are occasionally represented in later rock art in southern Africa and there is every likelihood that bows and arrows were an invention of the tropics.

Cave paintings, which provide the other most distinctive feature of the African Later Stone Age, are widely distributed but occur predominantly in the south and east of the continent where suitable rock surfaces in caves and rock-shelters were most common. Many of the paintings are undoubtedly quite recent, as can be determined from the presence of domestic animals, especially cattle, and even the depiction of metal tools. But there is now evidence that some of the art is very much older, as old as some Upper Palaeolithic art in Europe.

As in Europe, some of the African art consists of small objects, which are much more likely to be dated since they can become covered by layers of sediment which incorporate charcoal and bone.

At Apollo II cave in southern Namibia, such art has been dated to about 26,000 years, suggesting a strong possibility that some cave paintings and engravings in the region would be of equal antiquity. In Cape Province, painted stones come from deposits dated up to 7,000 years, but recently remains from Wonderwerk Cave in the north of the province have pushed the proven date for engravings back to at least 10,000 years. The investigators found about half a dozen stones with definite engraved lines. These were not lines caused accidentally by some other activity such as cutting vegetation on a piece of stone, since parts of animal figures could be made out. On one fragment, the hind-quarters of a zebra can be seen. In a much-favoured device, patterns of lines were used for blocking in an area by cross-hatching. Line engraving on rocks has a very wide distribution in Africa, occurring as far north as the Sahara. Surviving paintings are much rarer, but their preservation at Kondoa in Tanzania, for example, and on sites in Kenya indicates how far spread the idea of painting was in the later parts of the Palaeolithic.

Most of the early rock art of Africa has perished, worn away by erosion. Great variety is seen in the later art, but probably it derives from a much older tradition, of which only occasional traces remain. Aesthetically, in its naturalism, colouring, and perspective effects, the art is in no sense inferior to that of Palaeolithic Europe. Its meaning is no easier to determine, but whether it was done for its own sake, or for reasons of ritual and symbolism, it can be appreciated equally.

In this line engraving from the Krugersdorp area, South Africa, a jackal is skilfully portrayed.

Chapter VIII
New directions

Specialization in hunting animals and gathering plant foods carried to its logical conclusion becomes control and manipulation – eventually perhaps domestication. In the Late Pleistocene, 15,000 years ago, we begin to observe specialized collection of plants in the Middle East, and specialized hunting, for example of reindeer in northern Europe.

When the last major ice age phase ended abruptly about 10,000 years ago, all was set for the most far-reaching changes of economy which the human race had ever seen. A mere 5,000 years later, the domestication of animals and plants was widespread and agriculturalists and pastoralists were established almost everywhere throughout the Old World. Similar sequences of development are found in far separated parts of the Old and New Worlds, so that domestication appears to have taken place independently in a number of centres. Agriculture and stock-raising allowed the concentrations of population which eventually provided the economic basis for early civilizations.

Wooden arrows which are over 10,000 years old from Ahrensburg, North Germany. The shafts are made from carefully selected lengths of split pine. The separate lengths were spliced together with great skill.

The Nile in Egypt. Similar sailing craft have been plying the river for more than 5,000 years. The waters are flanked by richly vegetated irrigated fields.

The great thaw

About 15,000 years ago, the last ice age began to draw to a close, as temperatures rose worldwide, and the ice sheets began to retreat. By 10,000 years ago – the beginning of the Holocene – which also heralds the end of the Old Stone Age, the climate was as warm as in the present.

Ice-plucked rocks near Bergen, Norway, are evidence of the former presence of glaciers. The strata of the bedrock slope gently, so that there are occasional outcrops. These were most vulnerable to the effects of the ice, which tore off boulders.

The end of the last ice age 10,000 years ago appears to us as a great milestone in man's history. Most of the spectacular technological achievements of mankind have been made since the start of the subsequent warm period known as the Holocene. But in looking at these exciting phases of human evolution, we cannot really hope to sort out cause and effect, because of the complex mesh of interacting forces. We cannot be sure how far the profound environmental changes of the transition were responsible for the new developments.

We know that there was a sudden increase in economic activity, and a movement towards domestication, pastoralism, farming and village life. Certainly the present-day climate offers a more favourable environment for these things in many areas than ice-age conditions, but it is not the first time such favourable conditions have existed. Although the Holocene changes may have provided a stimulus for human development we may suspect that something similar would have happened anyway. Evolutionary change had been so rapid from 30,000 to 10,000 years ago that a further 10,000 years would probably have brought enormous development whatever the climate.

We can see the beginning of the Holocene as providing changing relationships of climate, plants and animals, and thus new opportunities for human cultural specialization, for instance in hunting methods. Human specialization consistently obtained rewards, and hence was favourable in an evolutionary sense. Because the specialization was cultural rather than genetic, change could be effected quite rapidly when truly necessary.

The climatic changes were sometimes very abrupt, but in other cases it was probably not possible to perceive them within a single lifetime. Rapid unexpected changes are catastrophic for human groups on a local scale, but there are always other areas, where effects are less severe, and where the necessary adaptations can be made successfully. The impact of the changes on human habitations and lifestyles would have been greatest in the temperate regions, more moderate in the lower latitudes, and least in the tropics.

The last ice age came to an end with a series of oscillations. In the late glacial stages of northern Europe, two short warm intervals are recognizable from pollen and stratigraphic records. These are the Bølling, lasting from about 12,400 to 12,000 years ago, and the Allerød, about 11,800 to 11,000 years ago. They are separated by a period of renewed intense cold, the Older Dryas. During the warmer phases, especially the Allerød, hundreds of archaeological sites appear in Europe, extending into southern Scandinavia, but they almost disappear in the colder phases.

At Gönnersdorf in West Germany, the thickness of an ancient soil which formed during the Bølling

tells us that it truly was a temperate interval. Normally the Bølling soil would not be distinguishable from the present soil, but this site was covered by volcanic ash over a metre thick, which thus preserved the separate record.

In the Allerød, coniferous forest became re-established far north in Europe, but the warm interval was not long enough for mixed oak woodland to recolonize the area.

Similar changes would have been apparent in all the present-day temperate regions. If they were not synchronous with the Bølling and Allerød, they were pretty much so. In North America, the Two Creeks interstadial corresponds with the Allerød.

In temperate latitudes, the specialization of many of the larger mammals to the ice-age conditions meant that, as the environment changed, they had to move with the vegetation to which they were accustomed. Reindeer, for instance, are highly specialized to withstand tundra conditions, with a thick coat, hairy muzzle, shortened tail and small ears to avoid loss of body heat, and deeply cleft hooves allowing their weight to be spread on snow. They could not compete when thicker vegetation began to spread north and their cousins the red deer, fallow deer and roe deer began to move with it. Similar specialization is seen in the modern caribou (American reindeer), which exists in two varieties, one adapted to the open tundra and one to the woodland to the south. Each variety depends on particular lichens found in its own habitat, and cannot adjust to different conditions.

The horse, which is by preference an open country animal, would have largely disappeared

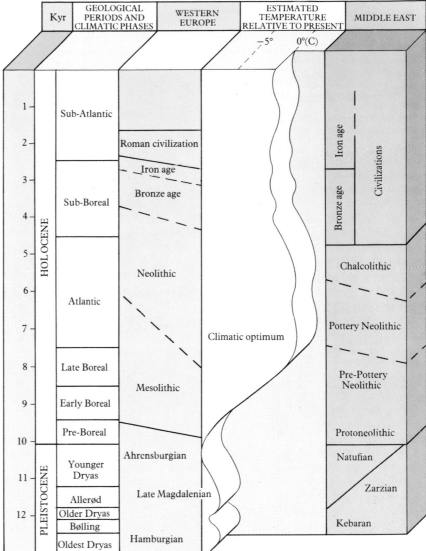

from Europe by the end of the Ice Age. It is much less frequent in sites later than the Magdalenian, whereas the elk, a close relative of the American moose, is increasingly to be found in early postglacial sites.

In the Middle East, which was to become a zone of critical importance, it is more difficult to trace precisely the effects of the transition. We do know, however, that the Sahara, intensely dry through the coldest phases of the Ice Age, became a garden of green with richly vegetated river channels.

These conditions were created at the end of the last glaciation, and persisted for several thousand years. Radiocarbon dates for high lake levels in Ethiopia and East Africa show that there was a period of high rainfall in the early Holocene. Comparable changes in rainfall and vegetation were taking place across Asia, and in the tropical and sub-tropical regions of the world, though they are less well documented.

Probably most of the changes in man's lifestyle from the end of the last glaciation onwards were not consciously formulated, but happened regardless, because there was little alternative but to adapt. But gradually, the facility to weigh up alternatives, to embark on complex courses of action, must also have been strengthened. In those times, as today, there were probably individuals who saw what was necessary before it became imperative, and who could attempt to lead the way.

The Holocene has not been a period of static climate. This chart summarizes the variations in temperature since the end of the Pleistocene, indicating the main climatic periods recognized in western Europe. The archaeological sequence in western Europe is compared with that of the Middle East.

Ice-plucked rocks near Bergen, Norway, are evidence of the former presence of glaciers. The strata of the bedrock slope gently, so that there are occasional outcrops. These were most vulnerable to the effects of the ice, which tore off boulders.

Specialized reindeer hunting

The excellent preservation of organic remains on some late glacial sites in North Germany provides unusual insights into the skills of Late Palaeolithic hunters.

There is good evidence to show that even before the end of the Ice Age, man had developed a specialized way of life, which might depend on intensive exploitation of a single food source. This can be seen most clearly on sites where organic remains are exceptionally well preserved. Such finds are very few indeed, although there are many hundreds of known archaeological sites from the late glacial period throughout Europe.

In the north of Germany, as happened elsewhere, man followed as the ice sheets gradually retreated northwards. This is shown by a scatter of late Magdalenian sites, many of which belong to the Allerød warm phase, though some are earlier and later. Unfortunately, the great majority are surface sites, where little sediment has built up since their occupation by man.

A measure of luck, but more particularly determination, allowed a German archaeologist, Alfred Rust, to remedy this with the discovery in the 1930s of several of the best-preserved Palaeolithic sites ever found. These are at Meiendorf and Stellmoor, a few kilometres from Hamburg. Here, Late Palaeolithic hunters had camped by the side of a small lake, of the kind which forms in a tunnel valley originally created by the melting ice. In each site, there was a sequence of occupations: an earlier phase, resembling the Magdalenian and named the Hamburgian, was followed by a later Ahrensburgian, distinguished by shouldered or tanged points.

At the main Meiendorf site, the Hamburgian hunters had camped on the bank only 2 or 3 m above the water-level. They had flung all the rubbish from their stay into the lake, including the remains of butchered animals. The debris had been sealed in by a rapid accumulation of silts, and had remained waterlogged ever since, and so was exceptionally well preserved. The finds demonstrated that the animals killed were almost exclusively reindeer: bones and antlers from 72 of these were found, whereas other animals, including horses and game birds, were present in much smaller numbers. The bones and antlers had been fully exploited: bones were broken to extract marrow, and the antlers had been cut for tool-making. More, similar, finds were recovered from the Stellmoor site.

Some of the reindeer shoulder-blades at Meiendorf had been pierced through by weapons, which struck the same spot so unerringly as to suggest that these people had control of the reindeer – perhaps herding them in the same way as modern Lapps, and regularly killing them at close quarters. The weapons which best fit the wounds are wooden harpoon heads. There are, however, reasons for doubting this explanation. Wounds apparently caused by arrows are visible on some bones, and in the later Ahrensburgian bows and arrows were certainly in use, for many of them were recovered by Rust. The arrow-shafts, tipped with microliths or shouldered points, were made of split pine. Similar evidence was later found from the Hamburgian also. If bow and arrow, the weapon of the hunter, was

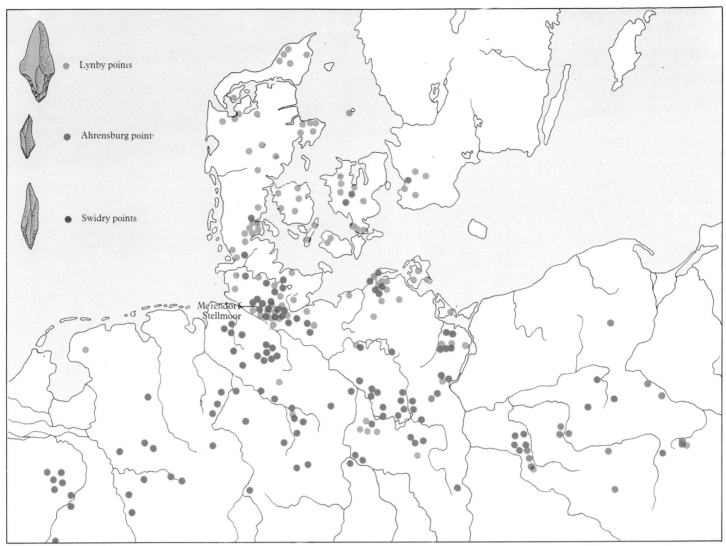

The find-spots of three different kinds of stone point on Late Palaeolithic sites in northern Europe. It is clear that different points were preferred in different areas. This may indicate the existence of distinct cultural groups among the hunters and gatherers, but possible differences in dates of the sites and of activities undertaken may also partly explain the pattern.

Lynby points

Ahrensburg points

Swidry points

Meiendorf
Stellmoor

used to kill these reindeer, it argues against the idea that they were in any sense domesticated. Probably, however, the Magdalenians knew the ways of these animals, and could follow them closely, which helps to account for the success of the hunt.

Similar sites with plentiful reindeer remains occur in the north of France, among them notably Marsangy, Étiolles, Verberie and Pincevent. Pincevent, situated in the valley of the Seine just below the confluence with the river Yonne south-east of Paris, is worthy of special note on many counts. The site was threatened by gravel-working in the early 1960s, and was investigated by a team led by André Leroi-Gourhan and M. Brezillon. The work has shown just how valuable a complete area investigation of a short-term settlement can be, and the techniques employed in the excavation have set a standard for all subsequent work. The finds were not only photographed in position, but also cast, so that the whole occupation surface could be reconstructed for display.

As the positions of all flint fragments were recorded, refitting studies – the reassembly of the pieces – allowed remarkable insights into events on the sites. Some tools, made from flint brought to the site, were abandoned there. Some of the flint used had been brought many kilometres, confirming the mobility of the people. Some cores of local flint, when reconstituted, have pieces missing: these are the new tools which were taken away.

Pincevent 'Habitation I' is typical of the Magdalenian homes which were excavated. Three hearths,

arranged in a row, are surrounded by occupation debris, in a clear pattern which suggests that they nestled between tents. Bones of reindeer are strewn around these camp-fires. There is a tendency, also observed on other sites, for the hearths to be surrounded by tiny flakes of flint, with the bones scattered further away. People tended to do their stone-working by the fire; when eating, they would toss bones over their shoulders. The position of the phalanges or toe bones, which are often found near to the fires, is assumed to give the best evidence of where the butchery took place and the creatures were eaten, since they have little other use. Larger bones are more dispersed. The lack of tidying up at Habitation I suggests that it was a short-term occupation.

Animal bones are preserved on only a few of the late glacial sites, so we do not know that all groups depended mainly on the reindeer. Indeed, at Gönnersdorf, horse was more common among the animal remains, and both horse and reindeer are common in Magdalenian art. But reindeer antler was always preferred to bone as a material for tools and decoration, and there is enough evidence to show the intensity and success of exploitation of this animal, whose meat, fur, sinew, bones and antlers could fulfil many of man's major needs. This great importance is symbolized by a reindeer carcase found at Meiendorf: the animal had been cast out into the lake, weighted down by stones, and surely represents an offering to nature or to the gods for the success of the hunt.

Reindeer are herded by modern Lapps, but the people must follow the animals as they make the seasonal migrations necessary for finding food.

Lengths of reindeer antler were cut at Verberie by stone tools such as borers, in order to produce 'rods' which were then converted into tools such as harpoon heads.

This hearth at Verberie in northern France was found in a Magdalenian site which is interpreted as a seasonal reindeer-hunting camp, because of the large quantity of reindeer bones. The dense distribution of stone tools around the hearth shows that it was a working area.

Specialization along the Nile

Grinding stones suddenly appear and become common in Egyptian late Palaeolithic sites of about 15,000 years ago. They were probably used for preparing plant foods, such as cereal grains and tubers. Recent dating work shows that barley grains found on one site are more recent than was first thought, but the intensive use of plant foods seems certain.

Flint blades (microliths) mounted end to end to form the blade of a wooden sickle, found discarded in a Neolithic grain-pit in the Fayum, Egypt. Similar sickles had been in use from late Palaeolithic times, but handles – which could also be curved – survive only occasionally.

A grindstone and grinder from an Egyptian predynastic site. Such grinding stones first appear on Late Palaeolithic sites about 17,000 years ago.

Photomicrograph of 'sickle gloss' found at the denticulated edge of a sickle from Kahun, Egypt, dated to the twelfth dynasty (63 times actual size).

The specialization that was leading man towards greater control of the environment in the late Pleistocene can be seen very well along the banks of the Nile. Numerous late Palaeolithic sites show the nature of adaptation in this area.

Today, the waters of the river are used to irrigate a corridor of green vegetation, at most a few kilometres wide. But at times in the past, including the early Holocene, the flow of the river was much greater. When the river ran high, fed by the Blue Nile waters from Ethiopia and by the White Nile waters from the equatorial lakes, it kept moist a wide flood plain, which was bordered by luxuriant vegetation. At other times, most recently at about 7-6,000 BC, rainfall was much higher in Egypt itself, and tributaries flowed into the river from areas which are now desert. Even in the present, such watercourses are active for short periods following heavy rainfall.

This riverine environment was of course attractive to people, because of the wealth of animal and plant life which it could support. The river and some oases certainly allowed Late Palaeolithic groups to thrive, even in the coldest period of the last glaciation, when the great aridity of the Saharan belt must have defeated human adaptation everywhere else in that area.

An unusual opportunity to investigate sites along the Nile in northern Sudan and southern Egypt was provided when the Aswan High Dam was being built during the 1960s. On account of this construction the temples at Abu Simbel were dismantled and re-sited above the new water-level, but early sites were threatened as well as later ones. The intensive survey which was carried out by international expeditions before the area was flooded recovered evidence of many sites and, equally important, stimulated further work in other areas of north-east Africa.

A succession of occupation sites was found, scattered along the river in the Wadi Halfa region, revealing many distinctly different traditions of tool-making. The oldest sites which could be dated by radiocarbon are about 30,000 years old. The earlier industries are based on flakes, some of them resembling the Mousterian, others corresponding

with the technology of the African Middle Stone Age (see pp 114–115). But within the last 20,000 years, most of the different phases made use of multitudes of microlithic flakes or blades (see pp 144–145). Some of the excavated collections are dominated by large numbers of tiny backed blades, very similar to those found in Libya and the Maghreb, and these are almost certainly projectile points, perhaps arrow-heads. Some of these bladelets are made in such an idiosyncratic way that they can be linked with others at sites far away on the North African coast. The Afnian and Ballanan phases of the Nile have remarkable similarities with the Eastern Oranian of Libya. This may imply that some of the groups spread out over huge distances, but the similarities are not maintained, suggesting that contact was not kept up.

With these tools are found others which seem to indicate new skills in the gathering and preparation of food. On several sites, large numbers of grinding stones were found, which are reminiscent of those used for preparing grain in much later periods. They were made mainly of the Nubian sandstone which is common in the area and ideal for the purpose. They were first found on the site of Tushka, about 200 km upstream from Aswan, and dated to about 14,500 years ago. Subsequently similar finds were made at slightly later sites near Kom Ombo and Isna to the north. On an older site in southern Egypt, at Wadi Kubbaniya, in excavations directed by Professor F. Wendorf (Southern Methodist University, Dallas), similar grindstones were dated to between 17,000 and 18,000 years ago: they can be divided into mortars, with deep hollows, described as cup-like, and milling stones, with an oval and less deep grinding hollow.

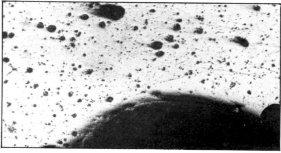

Flint sickle blades were also found on some of these sites. Their use is known because a gloss is found along the cutting edge, acquired through the cutting of many stems of grass or other plants which contain siliceous material. The sickles, too, are reminiscent of finds from later periods, for example in Palestine.

Although other uses of grindstones are possible, for example in the preparation of ochre for colouring, the combination of sickle blades and grindstones on these sites strongly suggests the use of wild cereals. It seems unlikely that cereal grains had not been known as food until this period, but as grindstones are not known at earlier times, we can infer that such food was taking on an increased importance. Probably people had discovered a better way of making a long-known food palatable. There were undoubtedly other plant foods along the Nile, including tubers, but conditions were probably suitable for dense stands of wild cereal grasses with edible grains to form, and this resource was almost certainly exploited.

There is little other firm evidence, but what we have is suggestive. Pond sediments contemporary with the Tushka site included pollen of large grasses, not identified as to species. Similar evidence came from Isna, where some of the pollen was identified, tentatively, as barley.

Whether these beginnings of adaptations to new ways were made from choice or under pressure remains an open question. Even today, we cannot always determine what triggers change. Perhaps adverse conditions away from the river forced use of new foods, and the discovery of new methods of preparation may also have enhanced their attractiveness.

That there was sometimes friction between groups is revealed starkly by the discovery of a Late Palaeolithic cemetery at Jebel Sahaba, north of Wadi Halfa. Jebel Sahaba could not be dated by radiocarbon, but it is probably contemporary with other sites dated to 12–10,000 BC. The cemetery was excavated in haste in the later stages of the Aswan project, but in total 58 skeletons were recovered. These were distributed, individually and in groups across an area. The skeletons were almost all orientated towards the east, and flexed, with the legs drawn up. The finds allow a remarkable conclusion: almost half of these people died by violence. Flint flakes found with the skeletons provide unmistakable proof of this, since in many cases they are actually embedded in the bones, sometimes in a neck vertebra, sometimes the pelvis. Probably other flakes found with the skeletons had caused flesh wounds. In several instances there are savage cut-marks on the bones.

The effectiveness of the weapons used cannot be doubted. Whether the projectiles were spears, or arrows, or both, is not certain, but bows and arrows may already have been in use. The site is approximately contemporary with Ahrensburg, where arrow remains have been found (see pp 150–151). The excavators point out that no population could sustain this level of violence for long, applied indiscriminately to men, women and children. Perhaps it was a special cemetery set aside for victims of violence, or perhaps a time of great tension is represented. A possibility, suggested by Professor Wendorf, one of the excavators, is that climatic conditions were deteriorating at this time, leading to increased conflicts between groups competing for scarce resources.

The excavation of two skeletons interred side by side in the Late Palaeolithic graveyard at Jebel Sahaba in Nubia.

The sea comes up

During the last glacial maximum, the sea was about 120 m lower than now; but as the ice-caps melted, the sea began to rise, by as much as a metre per century. Large areas of continental shelves were flooded, including the land-bridges which connected Siberia and Alaska, New Guinea and Australia, Britain and Europe.

Much of the continental shelf on the eastern coast of the United States was exposed in glacial times. Finds such as mammoth or mastodon teeth demonstrate areas where the sea has risen.

The English Channel west of Dover, showing the positions of ancient cliff lines and river-channels below the sea. The sea has been at low levels on many occasions during glacial periods. High level interglacial cliff lines are also shown.

Nothing seems as timeless and unchanging as the sea, but the tides show us its power to move. Land and sea are in fact in a constantly changing relationship. In the last few thousand years the changes have been relatively minor. The sea nibbles at the soft shores of England, and has destroyed ancient ports such as Dunwich, which is known to us only from records of Saxon and mediaeval times. At Paestum in Italy, coastal movements caused the Greek temples there to be partly submerged in the sea for centuries; the temples are now above sea-level, but the evidence of their past submersion is still to be seen in the form of damage to the columns by marine organisms.

These are just local adjustments, tiny in comparison with the massive changes in sea-level

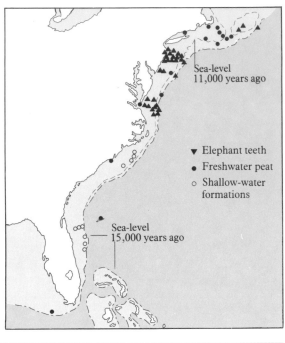

Sea-level 11,000 years ago

▼ Elephant teeth
● Freshwater peat
○ Shallow-water formations

Sea-level 15,000 years ago

Dover
Section
Fosse Dangeard
Southampton
Portsmouth
Hengistbury Head
St Catherine's Deep
Hurd Deep
Cherbourg
Dieppe
Le Havre
La Cotte de St Brelade

＿＿＿ Pronounced and less definite submerged cliff line
＿▲＿ Ancient valley system of large rivers
▬▬ Deeps – greater than 10 m
＿▪▪▪ Ancient high cliff line

which have occurred during the last 2 million years. Raised remnants of old shorelines, in many areas of the world, tell us that on numerous occasions in the past the sea has been at much higher levels. Other kinds of evidence, such as peat, wind-formed sand-dunes or even archaeological sites found under the sea show us that water-levels have also been much lower than they are today.

The main reason for these alterations in sea-level is that during each ice age, the ice sheets which built up on land locked up vast quantities of water, thus depleting the sea. In the coldest phase of the last glaciation, about 18,000 years ago, the sea dropped as far as 130 m below its present level. At other times in the past, sea-levels of warm periods have been even higher than those of the present. Throughout the last 2 million years, there has been a long-term downward trend in sea-level, probably a result of spreading of the ocean floors, which has increased the area of the ocean basins. The shorter-term variations of each glacial cycle are superimposed on this longer trend.

For human settlement, probably the most important cycle was the last one, since in that period of time, human populations have spread to all quarters of the globe. These movements were much aided by the low sea-levels of the glacial maximum, which exposed continental shelves and land-bridges in various parts of the world.

The rise in sea-level towards the end of the last glaciation began about 16,000 years ago, and progressed steadily over a period of 10,000 years, sometimes at a rate of a metre per century. The effects were profound. Gradually, the islands of Indonesia were separated; Australia was sundered from New Guinea and Tasmania; much of the eastern coast of North America was flooded, and so too was the basin of the North Sea in Europe, so that eventually Britain became an island.

How can these events be traced and dated, when the critical areas are all under water? A curious effect of the melting of ice sheets has allowed documentation of the changes in considerable detail. Ice sheets, which are sometimes over a kilometre thick, weigh down the land beneath them, as can be seen in the case of present-day Antarctica. When the ice melts, the land gradually recovers, steadily springing upwards, most of all in areas where the ice was thick, such as Scandinavia and Scotland. This means that the land has sometimes risen more than the sea-level, and consequently old shorelines which formed below the present-day sea-level have been lifted up above it. Very careful measurements of the deformation of the land, of the tilt of the beaches, and dating of the deposits by radiocarbon, allow calculations of the rates of movement and so an estimate of the overall rise in sea-level.

The last rise in sea-level had important consequences for man. Air temperature falls steadily above sea-level, by about 1°C (1.8°F) per 160 m. In temperate regions, the warmest, most sheltered, and best watered regions were those less than 100 m above sea-level. Possibly the bulk of the population in the last ice age inhabited such low-lying areas: for example, the extensive plains of the Bay of Biscay, west of France and south-west Britain.

The effects of the rising sea in Australia are debated. Some authorities believe that the reduction in land area, and hence resources, caused major trauma to the aboriginal peoples. Others believe that the coast could support a dense population, and that people simply moved with it; since the total coastal length did not change much, the population would not have been greatly affected. Nonetheless, people who had occupied the low-lying shelf between Australia and New Guinea would have been displaced, and the population of Tasmania was cut off. Other smaller islands in the area eventually lost

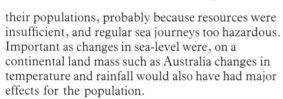

their populations, probably because resources were insufficient, and regular sea journeys too hazardous. Important as changes in sea-level were, on a continental land mass such as Australia changes in temperature and rainfall would also have had major effects for the population.

The Middle East, where profound changes in the way of life were beginning, was also affected. It has been suggested that the rise in sea-level helped to create the pressures which led to domestication. The Mediterranean coastline descends steeply, so not much land was lost there, but two other very important areas were lost: the fringes of the Nile Delta, and the floor of the Arabian Gulf. We have little means of assessing what man was doing there, because the rise of the waters caused rivers to drop their sediment loads earlier, and so to choke up their lower courses – the recent sediments are sometimes 100 m thick. Most of our knowledge of the early stages of the Nile and Mesopotamian civilizations is thus gained from areas further inland, not from the alluvial areas of the lower river valleys.

From about 10,000 years ago, the start of the Holocene period, we suddenly find many coastal archaeological sites. These are commonly middens, where huge numbers of shellfish were consumed,

and their shells thrown into heaps. Remains of other fish are also found. This witnesses the wealth of marine resources in some areas, and we may strongly suspect that these had also appealed to man in earlier times, but that the sites where they were exploited are now covered by the waters. There is some direct evidence to support this: seashells, either for consumption or for use as ornaments, were sometimes carried up to Palaeolithic sites that are still above sea-level.

If most of such coastal sites were lost, is it not possible that domestication, and even the first steps towards civilization, had begun to evolve on low-lying areas now covered by sea or sediments? It is an appealing idea. If, however, these developments had begun much before 10,000 years ago, we would certainly see some reflection of them on sites above modern sea-level.

These two views illustrate the deformation of the earth's surface caused by the Antarctic ice sheet. Left: the top surface of the ice; Right: the extent to which the land surface has been deformed by the ice, which is several kilometres thick in places. If the ice melted, the land surface would 'bounce back' by up to 1,000 metres.

A curve of sea-level during the past 13,000 years. Most curves show the steepest rise in the early Holocene (10,000–8,000 years ago).

A section across the English Channel at Dover, showing approximate dates for the post-glacial rise in sea-level.

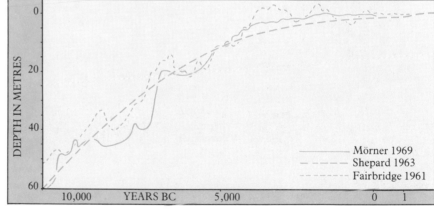

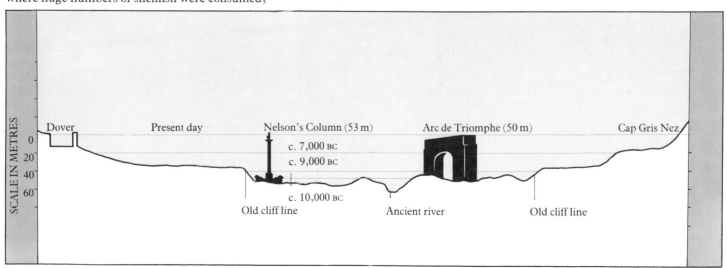

The nature of domestication

First signs of domestication of plants and animals appear only 10,000–12,000 years ago. Because of varying characteristics and behaviour, the word domestication means something different for each animal and plant species. Domestication sometimes leads to changes of form which appear as archaeological evidence.

Wild wheat kernels from Mureybat, Syria, are thin compared with those of a domesticated variety found at Nea Nikomedeia in Greece, 2–3,000 years later.

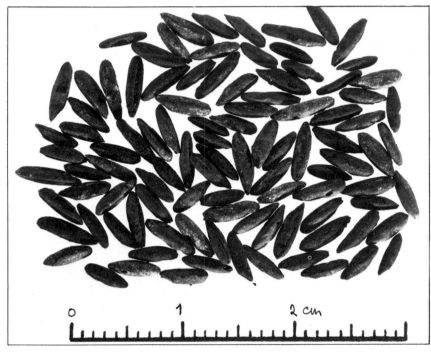

If plants and animals can be controlled, food supplies can be made much greater, and usually more secure. The penalty of the hunting and gathering way of life is that man is dependent on what nature provides. Most of the time this suffices, but in periods of drought, or other climatic hardship, a population can only survive if, by some mechanism, its numbers are kept below what the environment can provide for in the good times. The achievement of domestication meant that expanded populations could survive, and others could expand, and this in turn eventually necessitated higher levels of social organization.

We now usually think of animals and plants as 'wild' or 'domestic', but these concepts are the result of thousands of years of human interference. There is little hard evidence to help us understand the earliest stages of domestication, but it seems that where human groups came to rely heavily on particular animals or plants, they gradually modified their behaviour and environment, little by little, to ensure better control. Such developments begin to become apparent about 10,000 years ago, but their origins may go back twice as far.

The traditional framework of archaeological classification is too outmoded to provide more than a very crude reflection of these developments. According to the nineteenth-century classification, the Palaeolithic, the Old Stone Age, was succeeded by the Neolithic, in which polished stone tools were introduced. This name became linked with the adoption of agriculture and stock-breeding, and the transition from the Palaeolithic was regarded as so momentous that the events came to be labelled the 'Neolithic Revolution'. But as evidence built up, especially from 1950 onwards, it began to appear that the process had been more gradual: an evolution rather than a revolution.

Many archaeologists have attempted to follow this evolution back to its first stages. In recent years, the view has begun to emerge again that the developments were after all relatively sudden: it is difficult to find much firm evidence of domestication 10,000 years ago, but by 7,000 years ago farming villages, cultivated crops and domestic animals had appeared over large areas of the Old World, and similar developments were beginning in the Americas. The changes certainly did not come overnight, but in relation to 2 million years of hunting and gathering, the greatest ever alteration of economy came amazingly suddenly.

There is great variety in the nature and behaviour of animals, and they have therefore been domesticated in different ways. For this reason, Eric Higgs, a prominent exponent of economic archaeology, preferred to talk of man/animal relationships. The relationship between man and dog, for example, is quite different from that between man and pig. Man and dog may co-operate actively in hunting prey; but other animals can be domesticated without even being tame, and are exploited for use as food without achieving any reciprocal benefit.

There are several starting-points for the domestication of animals. One is the keeping of young animals when the mother has been hunted and killed. Another is keeping captured animals for eating at a later date. The advantage of this would have been apparent in any climate where meat decayed rapidly. For the most part, people could only have embarked on keeping animals if they were already sedentary, and had plant foods for the animals. Another possibility is that herd following could have gradually evolved into herd management.

There are three ways in which evidence of animal domestication can be recognized: by changes in the bones, changes in the age pattern of the animal population, and by representations painted or carved by the people themselves. Unfortunately, bone changes do not begin immediately, and may not be apparent for many hundreds of years. Large numbers of near-adult animals among the bones may indicate domestication, but this could simply be the age-group preferred by hunters. All this means that archaeologists are more likely to become aware of domestication in its established stages, and can only suspect it earlier.

The dog is perhaps the earliest of the domestic animals, and was probably first domesticated in the Middle East and in the New World. It begins to be distinguishable from the wolf during the late glacial period. Yet the chief distinctive features are a crowding of the teeth in the jaw and changes in skull size and shape, both of which could conceivably occur naturally in wolves. Many dogs, for instance those of the Asian mountains or Eskimo huskies, are as fierce as the wolves from which they are descended and can still sometimes interbreed successfully with them.

Of the other animals, sheep and goat were of great importance in the Middle East. They were domesticated early, as can be recognized by changes in the shape of the horns of goats. The bones of sheep and goats can be difficult to distinguish from one another in the earlier periods, even for an expert; but gradually they become more common than gazelle (which were hunted). Reliability of meat supply was probably the first prime benefit: milk and wool became important at later stages.

Cattle may have been domesticated independently in areas of south-east Europe and North Africa, and in Asia, where the humped cattle are of separate origin. The pig becomes common on Asian sites from Turkey to China. Other animals, including the camel, were probably domesticated later, when the idea had become well established. Egyptian wall paintings of dynastic times show

gradually, for example, that if too many roots in one area were collected, none would be there next time. In the case of cereals, systematic reaping may have begun long before sowing.

The main early domesticated crops are cereals and legumes in the Middle East, rice, cereals and root crops in the Far East, and a range of peppers, squashes, beans and maize in the New World. These have become different from their natural progenitors in a number of ways. Corn cobs have greatly increased in size since cultivation began. Cereals now usually have larger grains, and a tougher rachis, which ensures that the ears are not lost before threshing. Such morphological changes appear from 10,000 years ago at the earliest, and only a very small number of sites preserve any older plant remains.

Surprisingly, domestication appeared in several widely separated parts of the world at the same time. Independent invention has seemed so unlikely to some people that theories of diffusion were put forward, but these seem to have little substance. Most archaeologists now believe that modern man – the basic raw material necessary for the change – gradually accumulated similar levels of cultural

Paintings at Çatal Hüyük, Turkey, show man and dog working together in the hunt, at around 6,000 BC.

Egyptian dynastic tomb paintings from Beni Hassan show the importance of the dog in hunting, and the use of the ass; the paintings showing antelope being held are most interesting. These pictures are much later than the main phases of domestication, but suggest that experiments were being made into historic times.

clearly that experiments were made even with gazelle and the oryx antelope. In the Americas, fewer animals were domesticated. These included the llama, the alpaca and the guinea-pig.

With plants even more than animals, it is hard to draw the line between straightforward exploitation and true management. People had been gathering plants for millions of years, and probably learnt

experience, encountered similar problems, and arrived at similar adaptations in different parts of the world. Within any one continent, there was no doubt exchange of information about the new practices. All this is reasonable, because it holds true for later ideas and inventions, but there is still a great deal to learn about the way in which the control of plants and animals began.

The Fertile Crescent

The relatively well-watered band of land stretching from Palestine to Iraq is regarded as one of the primary zones of domestication. Numerous early sites testify to this, together with the surviving presence of wild forms of well-known cereal such as wheat and barley.

Nahal Oren, Israel – a view of the site from across the valley, showing the sloping land (talus) in front of the cave, where substantial house foundations were discovered. Archaeologists are interested in the movements of modern herds, because they can give insights into ancient land-use.

Abu Hureyra, Syria – part of the Mesolithic settlement, of c. 9,000 BC, which consists of groups of dwelling pits, surrounded by post-holes, which carried the posts for walls and roofs. The two large querns were probably used for grinding grain, other plant foods, and perhaps red ochre (the scale is 20 cm long).

The Fertile Crescent of the Middle East has long been regarded as one of the most important areas of early domestication. It merits its name, representing a continuous zone of higher rainfall, or well-watered land, stretching from the south of Jordan in the west, round to southern Iraq and Iran in the east. By about 7,000 BC, established farming villages were becoming widespread through this area. It is a varied zone, where stark mountains contrast with large and small plains. The pronounced vertical relief means that there was always a variety of vegetation types adjusted to local microclimates, ranging from great cedar forests to open grasslands. Climatic fluctuations towards the end of the last glaciation brought both drier and much wetter periods, but probably most of the main vegetation types have survived through many glacial cycles.

Archaeologists have sought early traces of domestication in several different parts of the Fertile Crescent: in Jordan, Israel, and hundreds of kilometres to the east, in the Zagros mountains of Iran. In the past few years much work has been done in Syria. Remarkably similar sequences have been traced in these different areas, from the first signs of substantial settlements 10,000 years ago, to the appearance of stock-rearing, cereal growing, use of pottery, and eventually the development of towns and cities. In spite of these similarities very distinct regional traditions in the cultures persist right through the period.

On many sites in Israel, a late Palaeolithic tradition known as the Kebaran is succeeded by the Natufian, named after the site of Wadi-al-Natuf in the Judaean hills. Natufian tools include many finely formed crescent-shaped microliths, sometimes called lunates. Sickle blades are also found, indicating the reaping of plant stalks, probably for obtaining food.

On sites such as Nahal Oren gazelle is still preponderant among the animal bones, so it seems certain that the Natufians were still hunting for their meat. But outside the cave of Nahal Oren, and at Ain Mallaha or Eynan in the Jordan Valley, substantial house foundations have been found. At Ain Mallaha, there is an entire village of large round huts. The economy practised on this site is far from fully understood. The site overlooked the ancient Huleh Lake, which was certainly fished. One or two grains were preserved from the site, but it is not certain whether agricultural activity was going on. Our main conclusion from such a site is that already, by about 9,000–8,000 BC, people had learned to live in one place, exploiting one reliable source, probably supplementing it with others, for their food. It is possible, even so, that such a site was seasonally occupied, and that hunting gazelle in the upland grassland formed part of the way of life.

In recent years, many more Natufian sites have been found, some of them covering great areas. By 7,000 BC, they are succeeded by sites which preserve early evidence of agriculture and animal domestication. Such a sequence is seen well at Beidha, near Petra in Jordan, and can be inferred at Jericho (see pp 160–161).

Developments broadly parallel to those in the Levant have been traced in the foothills of the Zagros mountains in north-east Iraq by a project led by R. Braidwood from the 1950s onwards. The Palaeolithic record there finishes with phases known as the Baradostian and finally the Zarzian, which is

approximately contemporary with the Natufian. At Zawi Chemi Shanidar, a site of this phase seems to document a sudden transition from hunting to sheep herding at c. 8,000 BC. Similar very early evidence of sheep has been claimed from certain other Asian sites, but the evidence is not yet conclusive.

One of the most famous sites in the region is a slightly later settled village named Jarmo, which has many phases of occupation. In the earlier levels, fine stone bowls were found. Pottery does not appear until later levels, from about 6,000 BC. On this site sheep and goats appear as domestic stock, and pigs are also found. Work in recent years has shown that even earlier than the settlement of Jarmo, villages were beginning to appear in Syria along the Euphrates and in the plains to the north: examples are Tell Abu Hureyra, Mureybat and Çayönü Tepesi. In the earliest phases at Abu Hureyra and Mureybat, grain had not yet achieved fully domestic form, so the extent to which it was sown as well as reaped is not fully understood.

Cultivated cereals have not changed fundamentally from the wild forms, to which they are very closely related. The three major cereals in early use, barley, emmer wheat and einkorn wheat, can all be crossed with their wild forms, and such hybridization occurs easily. Sheep and goats may have been domesticated almost anywhere in the Fertile Crescent, perhaps across a wide area, but there is more knowledge about cereal grain because information about modern distribution of plants supplements that available from archaeological sites, where cereal remains amount to a few grains at most. In an important paper, Jack Harlan and Daniel Zohary mapped the present-day distribution of wild wheats and barley, which were probably the progenitors of cultivated varieties, believing that it would offer some clue as to the areas where cereals were first domesticated.

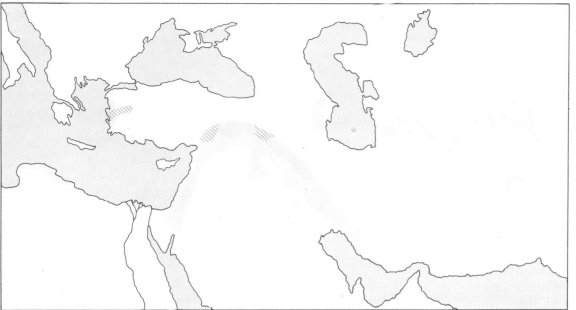

The present-day distribution of wild grain species in the Middle East. Barley is, and almost certainly was, the most widespread.

Barley

Einkorn wheat

Emmer wheat

Both wheats

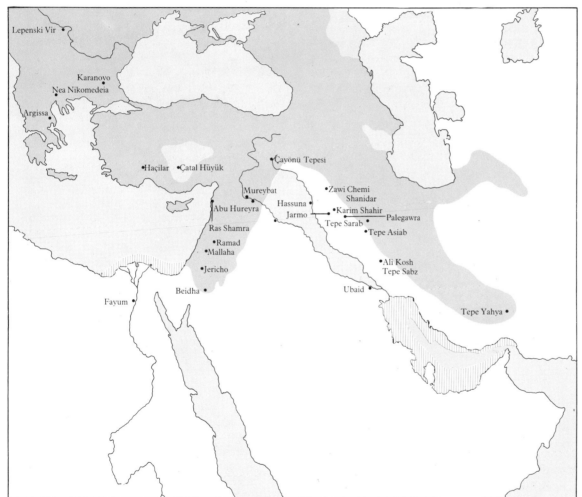

Lepenski Vir

Karanovo
Nea Nikomedeia
Argissa

Haçilar • Çatal Hüyük
Çayönü Tepesi
Mureybat
Zawi Chemi Shanidar
Hassuna
Abu Hureyra
Jarmo • Karim Shahir
Tepe Sarab • Palegawra
Ras Shamra
Tepe Asiab
Ramad
Mallaha
Ali Kosh
Jericho
Tepe Sabz
Beidha
Ubaid
Fayum
Tepe Yahya

The Fertile Crescent, showing some important early sites, and the area where rainfall is over 300 mm today.

Over 300 mm

Areas flooded by postglacial sea rise

The distribution indicates that emmer wheat was probably first domesticated along the Jordan valley, east of Galilee, where there are still large stands of the wild form. Einkorn was probably first cultivated in south-east Turkey. Barley, which was probably the most important crop in ancient times, is so widespread that it could have been cultivated anywhere in the Fertile Crescent. It seems likely that such grain was being collected systematically long before it could actually be called domesticated.

Although the Fertile Crescent was an important centre for these developments, they were not restricted to this area. In comparable landscapes, contemporary people were making similar advances in agriculture and husbandry – to the west in Turkey and south-east Europe, to the south-west in North Africa, and to the east in south and east Asia.

It seems that, in many parts of the world, the specialization that is traceable in earlier times was paying dividends, and also that the consequences of change included the need for further change. Regions like the Fertile Crescent, where relatively few species of plants and animals were found in large numbers, encouraged farming practices to develop; people came to rely on particular species, and this led to manipulation and control.

Jericho

In the PPNB levels at Jericho, skulls were found on which features had been modelled in plaster. Eyes were depicted with shell, and other features painted, providing a realistic impression. These remains seem to indicate an ancestor-cult.

Today, the great majority of people in developed countries live in towns and cities, but before 10,000 years ago there is no record of any settlement approaching the size of a town. Throughout the last 2 million years, people were accustomed to living in temporary camps, or permanent settlements amounting to a few huts at most. Urban life is thus a new phenomenon, not even as yet fully tried out, as the problems of inner-city decay and third world slums show us. The creation of a town implies a major change in economy from the hunting and gathering of earlier times.

Towns are found much earlier in some areas than in others. They seem to have appeared especially early in the Middle East, where substantial villages were already present at about 8,000 BC and where building in mud brick was a common practice. Building and rebuilding time and again on the same site led to the emergence of 'tells' or mounds, some of which are enormous. The Middle East and parts of Asia are dotted with such mounds, of which only a tiny fraction has been excavated, or even recorded.

The archaeologist can be pleased that so much valuable information is preserved, layer by layer, in any tell, but there is a corresponding drawback – it is difficult for any but the vastest excavation to cut through to the base of a sequence, and to tell anything like a complete story. The picture is complicated the more, since the buildings of a settlement frequently occupy only part of a tell at any one time; rebuilding frequently cuts through the old layers, and the oldest settlements are often the smallest, locatable only by luck and good judgement.

One of the clearest and best-excavated examples we have of an early town is at Jericho, a well-watered oasis near the southern end of the Fertile Crescent. The town lies a few kilometres to the north-west of the Dead Sea, 250 m below sea-level. There, excavations directed by Kathleen Kenyon during the 1950s were able to reach the lowest level of the mound, revealing a town older than any other which is known.

On virgin soil at the bottom of the mound, Kenyon found signs of a settlement belonging to the Natufians, the last hunting and gathering populations in the Palestine area. An oval clay platform, bounded by stones at the edges, has been interpreted as a shrine because it was carefully kept clean, and retains stone sockets, in which Kenyon believed totem poles had been erected. This has been dated by radiocarbon to over 9,000 BC. It is not possible to be sure whether there was a widespread Natufian settlement, because the area of excavation at such great depth was limited. From then onwards, however, occupation at the site continued, and a mound began to be built up from the debris of mud-brick houses, which had only a limited lifespan. In this phase at least 4 m of deposit accumulated, in which individual houses and floors are now difficult to pick out.

The location was doubtless attractive for settlement because of nearby freshwater springs, but it is not known whether the early occupation was permanent or merely seasonal. There is no definite evidence for domestication of plants or animals in this early phase, so some archaeologists have questioned whether all-year-round occupation was possible. Nevertheless, the stability and long duration of the settlement is probably good enough justification for the label 'proto-Neolithic' which was applied by Kenyon. Although no certain evidence has been preserved at Jericho, early indications of plant and animal domestication are already found on contemporary sites elsewhere, for example in Iraq, and in any case sure traces of domestication will not be found on every site where it existed. Evidence against the idea of animal domestication in these early levels at Jericho is the high proportion of gazelle, boar and fox, but the proportion of sheep and goat on the site increased steadily through time.

In the next phase, Jericho became a definite town, the earliest known anywhere. There was no formal street plan. The houses, which were round, were packed densely over an area of about 5 hectares. The total population has been estimated at about 2,000 people. Why do we term this a town rather than a village? Perhaps the deciding factor was the discovery of a strong defensive wall which had been built round the settlement at some time during this period.

The wall was located by excavation in two places, and almost certainly surrounded the whole town. The most striking feature is a massive, almost totally solid tower. This construction is 10 m in diameter, and still stands to a height of 8.5 m. A

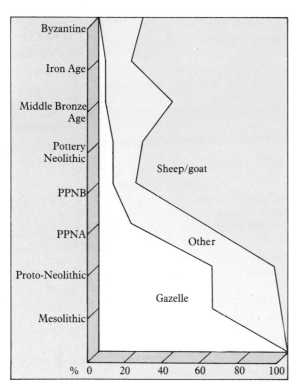

making polished stone tools. In this phase at Jericho the new food-producing economy is present, but pottery – normally a key criterion of the full Neolithic – was not yet in use, hence the term Pre-Pottery Neolithic was coined.

At about 7,000 BC there was a major upheaval at Jericho, and the settlement appears to have been destroyed. When occupation resumed, it was of a very different character. The houses were now square instead of round, and they had finely finished plaster floors. Similar features are found elsewhere in the Levant, and at Beidha there was a gradual change of preference, from round to square houses. The implication is that the walls of Jericho had fallen to invaders who brought with them a new lifestyle.

In this phase, the Pre-Pottery Neolithic B (PPNB), bodies were frequently buried under the floors, and separate skulls have been found on which features had been delicately modelled in plaster and painted. Pottery was still unknown, but it appeared by about 6,000 BC, as on other sites in the area. Jericho, and its defences, which were rebuilt numerous times, were to survive for thousands more years, through biblical times and even into the Christian era.

A graph of the proportions of animals remains found in the Jericho succession. Sheep and goat became steadily more important, as the hunting of gazelle declined.

An impression of the town of Jericho in late PPNA times. The round huts probably resembled those still built in parts of northern Africa. It is difficult to resist the impression that people went to and fro, to cultivate their fields and herd their stock, though these activities would have been in their earliest stages.

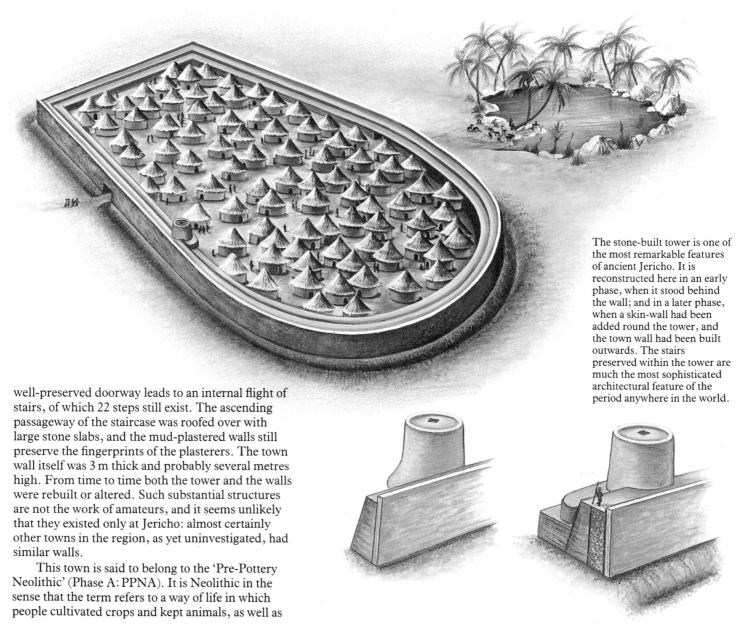

The stone-built tower is one of the most remarkable features of ancient Jericho. It is reconstructed here in an early phase, when it stood behind the wall; and in a later phase, when a skin-wall had been added round the tower, and the town wall had been built outwards. The stairs preserved within the tower are much the most sophisticated architectural feature of the period anywhere in the world.

well-preserved doorway leads to an internal flight of stairs, of which 22 steps still exist. The ascending passageway of the staircase was roofed over with large stone slabs, and the mud-plastered walls still preserve the fingerprints of the plasterers. The town wall itself was 3 m thick and probably several metres high. From time to time both the tower and the walls were rebuilt or altered. Such substantial structures are not the work of amateurs, and it seems unlikely that they existed only at Jericho: almost certainly other towns in the region, as yet uninvestigated, had similar walls.

This town is said to belong to the 'Pre-Pottery Neolithic' (Phase A: PPNA). It is Neolithic in the sense that the term refers to a way of life in which people cultivated crops and kept animals, as well as

Excavating a large site

Large sites, such as towns, can scarcely ever be completely excavated, so archaeologists concentrate on certain aspects of the excavation. Sometimes trenches explore the stratigraphy, attempting to trace sequences of development; sometimes the emphasis is on total excavation of particular areas.

The archaeologist who ventures to investigate a site as large as a town or city needs to plan the exercise on an appropriate scale.

The techniques used for excavating an Old Stone Age site (see pp 36–37) apply in principle to every later period, but they are designed to squeeze the maximum of information from very limited data. Each stone tool found on an early site may provide useful information. In contrast, the wealth of evidence found on city sites is frequently overpowering, and some finds may lack significance – nobody normally wants to know what happened to every piece of an ordinary earthenware jar when it was thrown on the rubbish heap. It is important, therefore, to concentrate on essentials – the key information. At the same time, apparently superfluous material may be worth a great deal to the right specialist. As an example, on some sites excavators used to throw away animal bones, but when studied by specialists in osteology these provide invaluable information concerning the early economy practised.

Only sometimes are resources available, as at Jericho, to allow excavation down to the earliest levels of a major site, and often archaeologists who are attempting to build up a sequence will need to turn to the sites of less successful settlements, which were later abandoned, in order to gain access to the early stages of a local sequence.

As always, survey is an essential first step before operations begin. Perhaps the earliest levels, which may be of the greatest interest, will be visible on one side of a later site, in the bank of a stream-channel which has eroded the mound. Studies of a number of sites may be necessary before it becomes apparent that one has greater potential.

In almost all their excavations archaeologists face a dilemma: should they put more emphasis on recovering a vertical sequence, or should they aim to open up a large area horizontally?

In earlier stages of the work it seems essential to aim for the vertical sequence, otherwise the full history of a site may never become known. But chance clearly plays a large part in what falls within a deep trench of limited area. It may cut through the courtyard of an important building, without touching the building itself. Walls will be encountered here and there, but not in sufficient length to work out a plan of the whole building.

For a full social understanding of a site, large area excavations are needed, including both richer and poorer quarters of the city. Naturally enough, many excavations have tended to concentrate on unearthing major public buildings. This is not only a matter of concern with prestige, past or present, for within the last few thousand years, these are the areas most likely to produce written records. But excavations of ordinary domestic areas take us nearest to the everyday life of people who lived thousands of years ago. Houses, doorways, steps, sleeping platforms, all may be preserved astonishingly well. Contents too may survive, such as traces of a rush mat on the floor.

As well as taking these various needs into account, and deciding on priorities, archaeologists working on a large site need to be well organized. The excavation crew may number hundreds; supplies and possibly living-quarters must be arranged for them and morale must be kept high. Perhaps it is not surprising that some of the most effective archaeologists of the past were also successful in military service.

A great deal still depends on luck. Anyone can decide to put a trench down the steepest side of a tell or mound in the hope that it will section the defences, or to put a trench where the centre of the town might be. It is nevertheless a combination of luck with good judgement and perseverance which results in major discoveries such as the tower at Jericho, or the royal cemetery at Ur. In recent years, many archaeologists have begun to use random-choice techniques of placing trenches, to gain a less biased record, but it is yet to be seen whether this offers a major advantage in practice.

Large excavations produce deep sections which can cut through many layers. This trench dug under the direction of Sir Mortimer Wheeler in 1946, cuts through the main defences of Harappa, a citadel of the Indus civilization. In the photograph the truncated mud-bricks are visible. The steps on the right were cut by the archaeologists to allow the removal of spoil. Wheeler's drawn sections are scientifically measured, but elegantly and stylishly drawn. The man in the base of the trench in the photograph is in much the same position as the lower figure in the drawn section. He is standing by a darker layer, which represents the old land surface, before the defences were built. Long-lasting occupations of the city led to the creation of many layers inside the walls (upper right, drawing and photograph).

On large sites, the procedures for laying out trenches are quite similar to those on smaller sites. The sides of the trenches again act as sections, witnessing the sequence of ancient events. There is less need for each excavator to take a small unit such as a metre square, and generally several people can work together in an area, putting minor finds such as pottery shards in a finds tray labelled with the name of the layer. All is transferred to a bag when the digging of that level has been completed. More important finds are usually marked and lifted individually. As with older sites, samples of soil are taken. These may provide evidence of seeds, vital for studies of early domestication.

Stone features, such as walls, are usually noticed easily enough, but the recognition of ancient decayed mud brick is an art. It is hardly distinguishable from the surrounding fill, which is often made up of similar fallen bricks. Such features – floors, houses, rooms – are the essence of this kind of excavation. Within a trench, they, and the layers within them, are what the archaeologist must observe, record and interpret. The process of interpretation is a continuous one, and cannot be left to the end. In practice an excavation can only be carried out well, and the right areas of the trench excavated in the right order, if the excavator has a feel for the stratigraphy and its meaning during the course of the work on the site.

Drawing plans of the site and of the vertical sections is a crucial task, especially in the latter part of the excavation. Work is often held up so that an important feature can be drawn and photographed before it is dismantled to give access to lower layers.

The sheer quantity of finds can present problems. Often it is difficult to find adequate storage space for all the pottery from a site. The cost of cloth bags and other packaging for finds can be a major item in the budget.

Conservation of finds is also important, since objects which have remained intact for many centuries may begin to deteriorate once they are

brought into the open air. Often wooden objects or metal-work are so delicate that they can only be lifted after careful preparation and strengthening.

The scale of post-excavation work can be as great as that of the excavation. Many specialists may be involved in writing reports; each area of the site must be written up separately, each main category of finds studied and described, and the whole integrated and interpreted.

The scale of some ancient sites is quite amazing. They represent the lasting remains of whole past worlds, and dwarf the prospects of investigation. Nonetheless a great deal has been achieved towards understanding large sites, quite often with only modest resources.

Neolithic houses excavated at Abu Hureyra in Syria are preserved in remarkable detail. In the background, a doorway opens into the street, where the build-up of layers can be seen in a section. In the far corner of the main house, there are the collapsed remains of an oven; in the foreground, the plastered floor has been raised to form a sleeping platform. A second doorway opens to an inner room on the right.

The invention of pottery

Baked clay was known in the Palaeolithic; sometimes it was even shaped to make models. But pottery vessels appear suddenly, 9–8,000 years ago, in wide areas of the Old World from North Africa to Japan, rapidly replacing carved stone bowls in the Middle East.

Pottery was shaped by hand before the potter's wheel was in use. The technique still survives today, especially for making large vessels, where turning by wheel would have little advantage for the craftsman.

The great importance of pottery to the archaeologist is that it endures, often when all else perishes, and that it usually has distinctive characteristics which tell us something about the people who made it.

For the user, pottery has the great advantage of providing useful, durable and clean storage for food and drink. But the earliest convincingly dated pottery is no more than 10,000 years old. How had mankind survived without it for so long? It does have major disadvantages, principally its weight and fragility. Even in recent times pottery has not found favour with hunting and gathering peoples who must move regularly. They have retained their gourds, bags, and baskets, which were in much earlier use.

Palaeolithic dates of about 12,000–10,000 years ago, but the Late Palaeolithic layers were very close to the surface of cave deposits, and it is well known that later material can be introduced into older deposits in such cases. Only a date on the pottery itself can answer this question, and so far pottery is not usually datable by radiocarbon, since it contains so little organic matter. A single TL date seems to support the early dates, but the question must remain open.

In the Far East, other early pottery comes from Spirit Cave in Thailand, at about 6,800 BC, and in Hsienjentung in China it has a similar date. We cannot be sure whether it was separately invented in the Far East and Middle East: early villages in

In a relatively settled community, pottery is extremely useful: as well as providing efficient storage, it does not decay, and it can be used to prepare food over a fire. It can also be aesthetically pleasing, and has become one of the most decorated aspects of material culture.

We do not know when or where pottery first appeared, but sites such as Jarmo and Jericho show clearly that it was not introduced in the Middle East until after 7,000 BC. This seems curious, as baked clay figures had been made on Upper Palaeolithic sites such as Pavlov about 20,000 years earlier, but as so often, the separate strands of an idea were in existence long before they became linked together. Clay often became baked accidentally. Perhaps when cooking food in baskets over a fire, people experimented by lining or coating the baskets with clay in order to seal in liquids. Or perhaps someone, in a flash of inspiration, saw that baked clay could be used to mimic the forms of other containers, such as stone bowls.

Pottery from Japan is claimed to be the earliest yet found, but its antiquity is not universally accepted. Two Japanese pottery sites have Late

Pakistan and India are hardly yet investigated, but sequences such as that at Mehrgarh in Baluchistan have very fine pottery before 4,000 BC.

In North Africa, pottery appears surprisingly early in the Khartoum area, at about 6,000 BC. This suggests that the idea spread within 1,000 years throughout the Middle East, though no pottery of such an early date is known from Egypt itself.

There seems little doubt that pottery was invented entirely independently in the New World, where it first appears at about 2,000 BC, and where it was used extensively in many forms, including statuettes and figures.

The earliest pottery was all hand-made, but in the Middle East and South Asia, the wheel method was introduced very early, certainly before the fourth millennium, and perhaps before the wheel was used in transport. The results of skilful hand-forming can be equally good, and even today the method still survives, especially for the manufacture of very large vessels.

Good quality in a pot derives from careful selection and preparation of the clay, the addition of suitable tempering, careful forming, and then firing to the correct temperature for the right length of time. These skills seem to have been acquired remarkably quickly. Materials for tempering have varied: animal dung, grass, and even sponge spicules have all been used.

The potential of pottery as a medium of art was very quickly realized. Plain wares have always existed, but from earliest times, incised and impressed designs were executed. Cord was often used to impress a pattern, because of the pleasing effect which it created.

Very early on, the discovery was made that painted designs could survive the firing, and remained indelibly marked. Early Hassuna and

Early ships are frequently portrayed on pottery of the Naqada II or Gerzean phase in Egypt, dating from the second half of the fourth millennium BC. On this example the deck cabin and a mast are visible. Such paintings demonstrate the importance of river transport from an early date.

Samarra pottery first appears at around 5,000 BC in the site of Hassuna, northern Iraq. It was a luxury ware imported from the area of Tell es Saawan on the Tigris. Designs were painted on top of a pale slip. The shallow bowl is decorated with stylized paintings of ibexes. 'Face urns' are also common among Samarran wares; the geometric designs are typical of Samarran decoration.

Samarra wares from Mesopotamia have many painted representations of animals, as well as geometric designs. Some vessels from the Egyptian predynastic were specially fired, so that the lower part remained red, but the rim became black.

Pottery can be fired in simple open fires at temperatures of less than 800°C (1,472°F), but harder, finer wares require higher temperatures. Improvements in pyrotechnology – the design of kilns and control of firing – eventually allowed remarkable developments of ceramics in the areas of Egypt, Mesopotamia, the Indus valley and China. As skills accumulated, colour slips were applied, surfaces were burnished, and at length glazes were perfected. Eventually, new types of ceramics appeared which strictly speaking are not 'pottery' (this refers only to earthenware vessels).

Faience objects and vessels, made of sand, lime and alkali, glazed with glass, were developed in Egypt and Mesopotamia during dynastic times. In Syria and Iraq, experiments with firing materials led to the appearance of glass vessels by about 1,600 BC. Baked brick architecture became very popular in the Middle East, especially for important buildings,

where bricks were often glazed. In China, stonewares were known from Shang times, and porcelain, which requires firing temperatures of up to 1,450°C (2,642°F), finally appeared in the 8th–9th centuries AD. Altogether a great variety of fired wares was produced.

Pottery is a valuable marker for the archaeologist, much as stone tools are for earlier dates. Decorated or finely shaped wares are much more diagnostic of a particular culture than stone tools, so we can learn a great deal from the distribution of a particular style of pottery.

In recent years much evidence
has emerged to support the
idea that the East was a
separate centre of
domestication. In South-East
Asia yams were domesticated
as early as 7,000 BC, and in
China the use of rice goes back
at least to 5,000 BC.

Identification of plants from
fragmentary ancient seeds can
be difficult. Six 'peas' from
Spirit Cave (centre) are
compared with local sugar
peas (bottom left and right),
and with two species of palm
kernel (top). The Spirit Cave
'peas' may be palm kernels.

Canarium seed fragments
from Spirit Cave (centre). The
other specimens are from
modern varieties from
Indonesia (top left), Santa
Cruz (top right) and Thailand
(below). These large seeds
were probably crushed to
obtain the fleshy kernels.

Early pottery with cord
impressions, from Spirit Cave
in Thailand.

The origins of plant domestication may be at least as
early in southern and eastern Asia as in the Middle
East, where there is a much fuller archaeological
record. The potential importance of South-East Asia
as a centre of cultivation was postulated by
Carl Sauer in 1952, but only from the 1960s
did archaeological evidence begin to emerge to
support his view. The most compelling evidence has
always been the existence of the major domesticates
themselves, for example rice and yams.

By South-East Asia, Sauer meant Sunda, the
great peninsula which included most of Indonesia,
until the post-glacial rise in sea-level broke it up into
islands. But China to the north and India to the west
are potentially equally important in this story. For
the moment, we must pick our way using a very
small number of sites, but this is steadily increasing.

These areas provided a range of natural plant
foods which must have been staples for a long
period, perhaps hundreds of thousands of years.
They included yams, cucumbers, beans and wild
rice-like plants. As elsewhere, these plants were
eventually given special attention, and some of them
gradually became morphologically distinct from
their wild progenitors.

A starting-place for looking at the food-
producing developments is provided by the final
recognizable phase of the Stone Age, named the
Hoabinhien after a site in Vietnam. This is
widespread in South-East Asia, and characterized by
simple pebble tools, almost Oldowan-like in
character, together with the use of stone axes,
grinding stones, and red ochre. The 'crudity' of
these tools probably reflects their relative
unimportance to their makers. The Hoabinhien has
been linked in its general character with some stone
industries of New Guinea and Australia.

At Spirit Cave in northern Thailand, excavated
by Chester Gorman, phases of the Hoabinhien were
found dating back to 12,000 years, much earlier than
expected. Above these early levels was a later phase
with pottery and slate knives, both of which have
also been found on other sites. The date for this
phase with early pottery is about 6,800 BC, at least as
early as any date for pottery in the Middle East.

It has been debated whether the many
associated plant remains from the earlier phase at
Spirit Cave are wild or domesticated. They include,
in particular, rice-like grains, together with many
other species including water chestnuts and beans or
peas. It seems likely that the rice grains are a wild
form, or at least domestication was so recent that
their form had not yet been influenced. Even today
wild rice is collected in some areas close to the site.

Unlike cereals, rice has the great advantage in
the tropics of thriving in humid and waterlogged
conditions. For that reason it is the major food crop
in China up to a latitude of about 33°, north of which
wheat and millet are more common.

Although the rice-like plants found at Spirit
Cave may have been wild, this seems much less
probable in the case of remains found at Homutu, a
Neolithic site near the Chinese coast, on the south
side of the Hangzhou Bay, and dated to over 4,000
BC by radiocarbon.

Extensive evidence of cultivation was recovered,
demonstrating a heavy dependence on rice, remains
of which were found almost everywhere, sometimes
in layers of husks and other debris over half a metre

thick. The surviving rice grains have been identified
as belonging to the domesticated variety *Oryza
sativa*. House remains, made of wood, suggest a
permanent occupation in one area. It is thought that

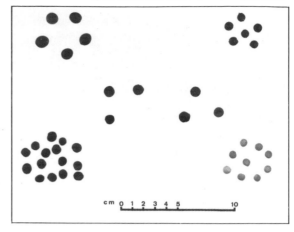

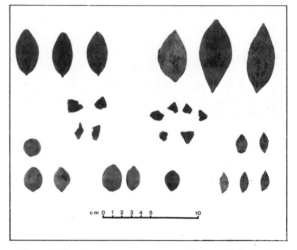

a 'short fallow' system was operated, in which land
was reclaimed for cultivation after it had been rested.
An irrigation system was probably used.

Large numbers of cultivating tools found at
Homutu, made from the shoulder-blades of large
mammals, show the importance of tilling the land.
Altogether a remarkable variety of wooden and bone
tools were preserved. There was also evidence of
animal domestication, certainly of dog, and probably
also of pig and water-buffalo.

Although the certain history of its domestication
cannot be traced back further, there is every
likelihood that the cultivation of rice developed from
about 7,000 BC onwards. The progenitors of rice
extend from eastern India across to China, and rice
may have been domesticated across the entire region.
It was established by the fourth millenium BC at
Non Nok Tha in Thailand, where there is also early
evidence for the humped Indian cattle *Bos indicus*.

Until recently, the Chinese Neolithic has given
the impression of appearing fully fledged at about
5,000 BC, but earlier stages of the story are now
becoming apparent. Hsienjentung, a site in Kiangsi,
appears to be older than 6,800 BC, and has cord-
marked pottery with incised decorations. Similar
pottery is now known from other sites in south
China. As agriculture is well established on sites
such as Homutu, it may be that the earlier stages of
domestication go back to these dates.

The full Neolithic of China, in the period of
5,000 to 2,000 BC, marked by settled villages,
pottery, a range of crops and domestic animals, can

now be divided into at least four regional traditions – those of Yangshao, Tapenkeng, Chinglienkang and Homutu. Some sites, such as Panpotsun (Yangshao), have been very fully excavated, yielding house plans,

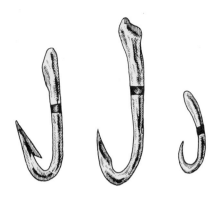

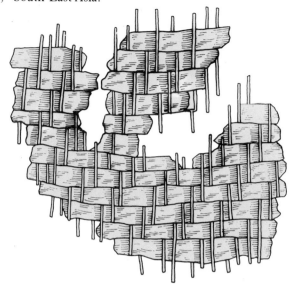

irrigation at such an early date, and we may be fairly sure that if agriculture existed so early in an outlying area, it was also being practised on the mainland of South-East Asia.

Evidence for crafts and skills: bone fish-hooks preserved at Panpotsun; and basketry, reconstructed from impressions on pottery.

A reconstruction of a house in the Yangshao village of Panpotsun, China.

A reconstructed section through one of the pottery kilns excavated at Panpotsun.

A late Neolithic painted Panshan urn, with looped handles, indicates the early refinement of Chinese ceramics.

pottery kilns, cemeteries, and many artefacts. An especially interesting feature is the 'social stratification' evident from the range of grave goods found in cemeteries. This distinction according to wealth and power becomes evident in many societies across the Old World, once settled villages have appeared.

Work in recent years has demonstrated that horticulture was also developing in New Guinea as early as 7,000 BC, strengthening the impression that this was part of a widespread adjustment. We cannot yet be absolutely certain which plants were used in the early stages: yams came from the mainland, possibly in the first phases, but native New Guinea plants may have been cultivated first. In this case, the definite evidence for horticulture resides in irrigation ditches. It was a major archaeological achievement to demonstrate the presence of

Developments in North-East Africa

Along the Nile, traces of early village life are less clear than in south-west Asia. Silting up of the river's lower course makes it impossible to investigate many areas, but settlements to the south in Sudan show intensive fishing, the early use of pottery, and early cattle pastoralism. In the Fayum, farming appears suddenly between 4,000 BC and 3,800 BC.

Egyptian wall paintings in tombs cast light on the appearance of early cattle. The paintings are relatively late, dating to c. 1,500 BC, but they show us that by 3,500 years ago cattle already had the form and variety found in Africa today – raising the possibility that the pattern has a much greater antiquity.

Cattle were widespread in Africa from about 5,000 BC. This specimen from Adrar Bous in the Ténéré Desert of Niger, excavated by Professor J.D. Clark and colleagues, has the most complete skeletal remains and dates to about 3,000 BC. The area where it was found it now too dry for cattle pastoralism.

Did domestication, and the great changes that accompanied it, develop indigenously in Egypt and North-East Africa, or was it brought in by newcomers? It is important to know something about the continuity of development, because this is the area in which Egyptian civilization was to emerge.

In spite of the existence of well-preserved Late Palaeolithic sites, it is very difficult to answer this question, because of the dearth of information from the lower Nile Valley, where the accumulation of silts has buried most of the evidence from later periods. Upstream, the high, fast-flowing Nile of the early Holocene (about 7,000 BC) actually built up a higher flood plain, and then cut down through it, so again much of the evidence has been lost.

Careful studies over a long period in Sudan, to the south, in suitable areas of Egypt itself, and elsewhere in North Africa, have helped us to build up a picture. It is, however, even in the present, an area of strongly contrasting environments, which demand quite different adaptations for subsistence. Thus we would not expect the same way of life to be practised everywhere in the past any more than it is now. Today, there are cultivators and fishermen who remain close to the river, and pastoralists who travel far afield; whereas other peoples manage to grow crops in difficult conditions far from water.

In the early part of the postglacial period, the whole of this area enjoyed a period of good climate with high rainfall. The geologists M. A. J. Williams and D. Adamson (Macquarie University, New South Wales) have been able to reconstruct much of the history of the Blue and White Niles near their confluence. At this time, the White Nile contributed much more water, and ran higher, forming a lake up to 15 km across, and hundreds of kilometres long. This attracted fishing peoples, whose settlements have been excavated by A. J. Arkell at Early Khartoum, and by Professor J. D. Clark at a similar site at Shabona, further south.

The importance of fishing is certain enough, for in addition to bone harpoons, many fish-bones and even fish-hooks were found on the sites. These people lived on low knolls overlooking the river, and caught the plentiful Nile perch, tilapia and catfish.

They found interesting uses for the spines of the catfish, which have serrated edges. These were used for combing patterns into the local 'wavy line' pottery, which is the earliest pottery known along the Nile. First found at 6,000 BC, it is as early as pottery in the Middle East, and suggests the possibility that pottery came into use even earlier further north in Egypt.

In the period of wetter climate, fishing camps were widespread across North Africa; similar harpoons and pottery have been found far to the west and south, for example at Lake Turkana.

There are no signs of domesticated animals on these Early Khartoum sites, but it is questionable whether they would have been brought so close to the river. Further south, present-day Nilotic peoples divide their lives between pastoralism and fishing, and it is quite conceivable that the Early Khartoum people were their direct ancestors. The pattern of cattle herding does seem to have been established by about 3,000 BC, when it is represented by sites such as Shaheinab and Kadero in the Khartoum region.

Cattle were almost certainly domesticated in Africa earlier than this: at Uan Muhuggiag in the Tassili, domestic cattle remains may date back as early as 5,500 BC, and certainly are found by 4,000; from Kenya there are sugestions that they were domesticated even earlier, at 17,000 years ago, but this evidence is highly controversial. Excavations by Professor J. D. Clark and colleagues at Adrar Bous in the Ténéré desert revealed a complete cow skeleton, with finds of the local Neolithic, dated to about 3,000 BC, showing that pastoralist adaptation was widespread in areas which are now desert.

If the idea of domestication was brought to Africa from south-west Asia, we would expect to find earlier dates along the Nile than further west, but this does not appear to be the case. Expeditions led by Professors Wendorf and Schild showed that there were final Palaeolithic hunters and gatherers at least as late as 6,000 years ago along the Nile north of Early Khartoum. There is no pottery in these sites,

been 'deflated' – decapitated by wind erosion. Thus the main structural features preserved were the deep ones: fire pits and grain silos. The latter were circular pits which had been lined with coiled matting of corn straw, stuck with mud and plaster to the wall of the pit. They had been used for storing emmer wheat and barley, which remained in some of them, but there were other finds: two wooden sticks, probably threshing implements; two wooden sickles, one with the actual flint blades remaining in position, bedded in resin; and even a fine boat-shaped basket, which, the finders speculate, may have been used to carry grain for sowing.

Yet there are no signs of animals which are definitely domestic, and no signs of sheep or goat dung, which would be preserved. That these cultivators were still part-time hunters is suggested by the discovery of two of their finely shaped arrow-heads with an elephant and a hippopotamus carcase in the area. Although they practised bifacial stone-working, in these arrow-heads and in knives, their tools bear no relation to the tool-kit of the Late Palaeolithic, only 1,000 years earlier. It seems reasonable to speculate that a new people, already

Egyptian tomb models also show us the activities of everyday life, such as brewing and baking. The main emphasis is on food-preparation, an essential part of obtaining the benefits from domesticated crops such as cereals.

but large numbers of the traditional backed blade microliths.

The earliest certain evidence of an agricultural way of life, accompanied by pottery manufacture, comes from the Fayum depression, about 40 km west of the Nile. The 'Fayum A' main site, investigated in the 1920s by Gertrude Caton-Thompson, has revealed a way of life and cultural style quite different from that of the Late Palaeolithic, and has now been dated to about 3,800–4,000 BC by radiocarbon. Herodotus records that there was a lake here in about 480 BC (Lake Moeris), on about the same level as the Nile, since water flowed to and from it at different times of the year. Its level has since dropped steeply.

The importance of the site is augmented by the excellent preservation of wood, grain and even cloth. But as with many other desert sites, the area has

acquainted with agriculture, had moved in, perhaps from south-west Asia, but perhaps from a lower region of the Nile Valley.

Our lack of knowledge on this point underlines the fact that the main evidence for the final lead-up towards Egyptian civilization along the Nile is surprisingly limited, and apart from the Fayum comes exclusively from Upper Egypt.

The sites of el-Badari and Naqada in Upper Egypt are important, but even these are restricted to a late period, from about 4,500 to 3,000 BC, and most of the groups are known only from their cemeteries. The calibration of radiocarbon dates should add several hundred years to these dates (see pp 198–199), providing a longer record. The appearance of copper tools and painted pottery is evidence which offers only a dim reflection of the origins of one of the world's great civilizations.

New World domestication

Plants domesticated in the New World are now important worldwide, including chilli peppers and maize. More plants were domesticated in Mesoamerica and the Andes than anywhere else, but there were fewer opportunities for animal domestication.

The development of maize cobs, as demonstrated by the Tehuacàn sequence. Over a period of thousands of years, intensive selection led to the development of plants with very much larger cobs.

Domestication of plants and animals probably began at a slightly later date in the New World than in the Old, but it is no less important a phenomenon: plants first domesticated in the New World are now vital staples and cash crops throughout the world.

By the time that the Bering land-bridge was sundered, there was already human occupation from north to south of the great double continent. There was as much diversity of climate and vegetation here as in the Old World, but the different nature of the fauna and flora led to different adaptations.

Altogether more than 100 species of plants were cultivated, including maize (corn), peppers, beans, squashes, tomatoes, potatoes, manioc, and avocadoes. The essential contrast with the Middle East lies in the great range of plants which were brought into cultivation, but in this there were similarities with South-East Asia, where many different kinds of plant were also exploited.

Plant domestication was limited to certain areas. Mesoamerica – Mexico and the isthmus zone to the south – was an important centre, and the area where

early maize cobs to be preserved. The oldest examples, from the Tehuacán valley in Mexico, dating to about 7,000 BP, are still primitive and small. The cobs are generally 2–3 cm long, compared with the 15–20 cm which is typical of modern corn. In later levels at Tehuacán, the size of the cobs increases steadily. Finds from Bat Cave in New Mexico document its spread northwards, and it is also found in the Andes from an early date.

In spite of the early finds, the true origins of maize are still disputed. Some authorities believe that it was cultivated from *teosinte*, a wild plant which still exists, but another view, perhaps less strongly supported, is that *teosinte* itself is a 'renegade' of the cultivated plant. It is accepted that the finds from Tehuacán do not represent the earliest stages of cultivation, which may have taken place elsewhere in Mexico.

Early stages in the domestication of maize in Peru are preserved on two highland cave sites, Guitarrero and Ayacucho. At Guitarrero, some cobs may be more than 6,000 years old. The excavator,

Professor T. F. Lynch, believes that corn had been introduced from Mesoamerica at an early stage, but subsequently went through a long period of local development, in which varieties suited to the cool humid Andean conditions were evolved.

Recently, Dr A. Roosevelt and Professor N. van der Merwe have been able to document the spread of maize into the Orinoco Valley north of the Amazon, between 600 BC and AD 400, even though no cobs are preserved. The usual ratio between carbon-13 and carbon-12 (about 1:100) is slightly altered by the processes of photosynthesis when they are incorporated in plants. Two major groups of plants (known as C_3 and C_4) alter the ratios differently, and since maize is the only C_4 plant entering the diet, its presence can be traced: we are what we eat, and the isotopic ratios in the plants are incorporated in human bones. The measurements obtained indicate that maize formed about 80 per cent of the diet of this area by AD 400.

Apart from the introduction of maize, there appears to have been little exchange of varieties between Mesoamerica and South America, and sometimes different species of the same group were cultivated in the two areas. As dramatic changes in morphology occurred in only a few species, it is often difficult to know the date of domestication, and some workers think that it is more important to emphasize the use of plants, rather than the changes.

It is evident that tubers and roots were already being relied on some 10,000 years ago at Guitarrero

Land over 1,000 m
Early spread of maize

The principal areas of plant domestication in the New World. Although maize spread rapidly after 4,000 BC, there was little transfer of plant strains subsequently. Different species of the same plant group were sometimes domesticated independently in Meso- and South America.

maize was first cultivated. The Andes region in Ecuador, Peru and Bolivia may have been the primary zone for domestication in South America, but parallel developments probably took place in the Amazonian lowlands from early times.

Maize, the best known of the New World crops, was already cultivated 7,000 years ago. Dry conditions in some caves have fortunately allowed

Cave. Beans may have been cultivated there from about 8,000 years ago, and one pepper has been found in levels of the same age range.

On the Peruvian coast, the earliest cultivated peppers are found about 4,500 years ago, but this is a lowland area where irrigation was necessary, and it is probable that the plants had been introduced from elsewhere. By about 2,000 years ago, an Amazonian variety of pepper, *Capsicum chinense*, had reached Peru. Another species is found at Tehuacán about 8,500 years ago, but it may be a wild variety. Within the last 3,000 years at Tehuacán the seed size is large enough to suggest strongly that it was domesticated.

Beans appear at Tehuacán from an early date, as does amaranth, a plant used like spinach. Of the root crops, potatoes were not found north of Colombia before the Spanish Conquest (1519 onwards). Sweet potato was known in lowland Peru by 4,000 years ago, but it is not certain whether its origins were in Mesoamerica or South America.

The scope for animal domestication was very much less, because of a shortage of suitable species.

Large animals were extensively hunted in the late Pleistocene, and mammoth kills are found as late as about 7,000 BC in Mexico. Eventually mammoth, mastodon, horse and other large animals became extinct, and the remaining large herbivores were not suitable for domestication, with the exception of the camelids in South America. This group includes the llama, alpaca and vicuña, which were exploited for their meat, coats, and abilities as pack animals. Their use began several thousand years ago, but the exact date is not known, since there are few morphological changes in the animals, and the main indicator of domestication is their increased presence on archaeological sites.

The only other animals domesticated were the guinea-pig (used for meat, and found on early sites in the Andes) and the dog. Dogs were probably kept mainly for protection, and all those found are the domestic form. Such dogs appear at a very early date: according to Dr Elizabeth Wing, 'so early, in fact, that dogs may have accompanied the first human migration into South America'.

In the last 500 years, New World plant domesticates have been adopted throughout the world. Pineapple, avocado and peanut are commonly grown in Africa; potato and tomato have become staples almost everywhere.

1 Pineapple
2 Pumpkin
3 Sweet potato
4 Marrow
5 Green and red peppers
6 Tomato
7 Potato
8 Chilli pepper
9 Tobacco
10 Peanuts (unshelled)
11 Maize cob
12 Runner beans
13 Pawpaw
14 Avocado

Chapter IX
The final steps to civilization

Civilization arose, not once, but time and again in very different circumstances. The two essential elements in any civilization were modern man with the brain to organize, and food production, the economic base that made it possible. Food production made high population density inevitable – but that could only work if the human society was organized. Not all civilizations have cities, but all have food production and complex social organization. Higher technology is helpful but not essential in every respect – the wheel was unknown in the New World. Local factors influenced the transport, trade and economy, giving each civilization its own distinctive character, customs, arts and religion.

Were all these strange and wonderful developments inevitable? Although things might have happened differently, nature shows a general trend towards complex forms of life, of which mankind is only one.

A mace-head from the Egyptian late proto-dynastic period. It shows the pharaoh 'Scorpion' opening a new irrigation canal. The event was important enough to be depicted on this artefact, which was a symbol of authority.

Post-and-lintel architecture seen at Teotihuacán in Mexico.

The move towards civilization

In the last steps to civilization, concentrations of population, social organization, and social hierarchy all play a part. Irrigation, sometimes involving the construction of canals by large groups of people – was an important aspect.

In the Old World, by 5,000 BC, the foundations had been laid on which developed civilization was to rise; in the New World, also, parallel developments were beginning.

The chains of events which culminated in organized food production did not happen all over the world, but certainly occurred in large parts of it. In contrast, the final steps which led up to civilization were initially restricted to much smaller areas.

In the Middle East, Anatolia, Iran, the Indian subcontinent and China, there was a gradual trend from early village life towards full civilization. It took just about 5,000 years to develop from the time of the earliest settled villages – from about 8,000 BC to 3,000 BC. (The dating of this period, which depends almost entirely on radiocarbon, needs some special explanation. See pp 198–199 for a discussion of radiocarbon calibration.)

It may seem to us as if civilization was brand new when the early Mesopotamian kings gave out the first recorded law codes – before 2,000 BC; but of course to the people of those days the world would have seemed as old as it does to us and society as well established. There may have been an air of challenge, or a feeling of change, but no more so than in a rapidly developing part of today's world.

Can we pick out any particular developments which mark the move towards civilization? We are looking for changes which happened in some areas, but not in others, where illiterate village life persisted even through to the present day.

A mere 7,000 years later, it is very difficult for us to arrive at a real comprehension of what was happening in those times. It is easy enough to provide a descriptive outline, but much more difficult to grasp at the causes underlying the patterns of change. Certainly, food surpluses allowed further specialization, for example the evolution of skilled trades practised by individuals who did not farm; and they encouraged the longstanding human desire for fine things and stimulated a rise in arts and crafts. But other causes also seem to have been at work.

Among the most important changes were the occupation of different geographic areas and an increase of economic scale. Most of the earlier agricultural settlements known to us were in foothill regions, but the great early civilizations all developed in major river valleys, and involved settlements of much greater size with much higher population density. The Nile, Euphrates, Tigris, Indus and Yellow River were truly cradles of civilization.

A new factor often singled out as especially significant is irrigation, which extends the range of farming in areas where rainfall is insufficient, untimely or unreliable. The oldest preserved traces of irrigation have tended to be found in areas outside the major river valleys, where floods and sediments usually destroy or mask the evidence.

In upland valleys and small plains, irrigation can be practised on a small scale: the main ditches may be just a metre or so wide, and individual trees and vegetable plots receive water for short periods from smaller channels which are little more than runnels. At Catal Hüyük in Anatolia, irrigation of this kind was probably beginning before 5,000 BC. In the Deh Luran plain of Iran it began at about the same time; and it was probably in use in China, too, by 4,000 BC if not earlier.

The ancient irrigation system of Geoksyur in Turkmenia, as mapped by G. N. Lisitsina. The distance from the ancient river to Geoksyur is about 1 km. Eventually the altering course of the river made irrigation impossible, and the settlement was abandoned.

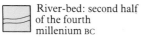

River-bed: second half of the fourth millenium BC

River-bed: second half of the fourth millenium BC (uncertain)

River-bed: first half of the third millenium BC

Small stream-beds belonging to the final period of irrigation

Canal-bed

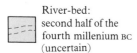

Sand ridges

Settlement

Dried mud

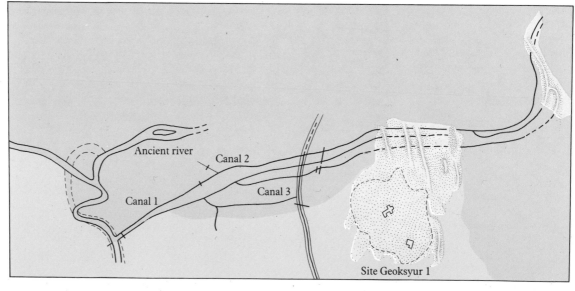

Dried mud crust

Spoil-heaps from the canals

Buried land surface

Alluvial deposits of the outer channels of the ancient delta

Wind-blown sand

Alluvial deposits in the canal

Specific details of early irrigation canals have been unearthed by Soviet archaeologists in the south of Turkmenia, a land which lies east of the Caspian Sea, north of Iran. There, irrigation began in at least the fourth millennium BC, and excavations across the canals show how wide and deep they were. It seems that 1.0–1.5 m was a standard depth, but width varied according to local water-flow and gradient. The soil from the ditch was banked up into levées, traces of which were preserved under later wind-blown sediments.

Although we have very limited archaeological information about early phases of irrigation along the Nile, because of the deposition of later sediments, there is evidence of its importance. When the protodynastic pharaoh 'Scorpion' opened an early canal (perhaps c. 3,100 BC), the act was significant enough to be commemorated on a mace-head (see p 173), itself a notable symbol of authority.

In the Middle East, irrigation was particularly common in Mesopotamia, where there is much evidence of massive irrigation works in dynastic times after 3,000 BC. R. M. Adams, who has carried out studies of irrigation over a long period, suggests that the first cities had already appeared before the large irrigation systems, which involved the canalization of rivers, and reduced the risk of floods. Such canalization greatly increased the scope and effectiveness of small-scale irrigation, which had probably existed much earlier in the area.

The presence of large-scale irrigation implies communal effort, since canals can only be dug by large numbers of people. Defence, also, was an important need requiring large numbers of people and encouraging social organization. The town-dwellers and agriculturalists had a common resource, the wealth of the valleys and plains, and had to guard it against raiders. This is not fanciful, because we know of the importance of armies and warfare right through the period of early civilization. We have records too of the lawless tribesmen who swept in from outlying areas to gain easy pickings.

We can list many forces which would have moulded society 'deterministically' towards civilization. But it is worth stressing that the human raw material was just as important. In those days, there were already people who took pride in their skills; there were those who loved to plan and take action; and those who sought power, at whatever risk. The formalization of behaviour, which is characteristic of man, allowed much greater extension of authority. When the authority amounted to kingly power over a wide domain, the human overview was required: an awareness of space and time, of events, and the creation of effective chains of command. Complex societies were organized and functioned as a direct result of the human capabilities which had emerged.

Ancient representations help us to see advances in agricultural technology. Here are two illustrations of a seed drill, which could be drawn by two oxen, while seed was poured into a funnel. The photograph is of a Babylonian boundary stone, and the drawing is of the carving on a small seal of c. seventh century BC; but working the soil with beasts of burden undoubtedly had a longer history.

Modern irrigation in the Euphrates valley. The contrast between irrigated land and the adjacent desert is very striking.

175

The beginnings of trade

The surplus from agriculture could be translated into other goods, including fine tools. The first signs of long-distance trade of select materials, such as obsidian, occur in early Neolithic times.

The origins of trade are probably to be found in late Palaeolithic times. It is a commonplace to say that in a simple society, each person or family can provide for their own needs; but at a certain level of social complexity, this becomes impracticable. The basis for trade lies in intelligent arrangements between two – or more – parties, from which all benefit.

The early traded objects most recognizable to archaeologists are those made of stone or shell, for which the source can often be established. Shells were often pierced and used as beads in necklaces, or as pendants. On late Palaeolithic sites, such materials have been found hundreds of kilometres from their source: for example, in the Upper Palaeolithic of south-west Europe, marine shells appear far inland, both in the Dordogne and in the Pyrenees. At the Pyrenean site of Isturitz, shells from both the Atlantic and the Mediterranean were found. As it is quite possible that Palaeolithic people travelled over such distances in their normal seasonal movements, we cannot be certain that trade was involved, though exchange of fine objects was very probably taking place.

Once village settlements had appeared, and farming was evolving, most people travelled much less. It is therefore safer to interpret long-distance movements of goods as trade, although two materials which became important early trade goods, shells

This necklace, made of obsidian and cowrie shells, was found at Arpachiyah, Turkey and is dated at c. 5,000 BC. Shells and semi-precious stones were very popular for use in necklaces. They form a high proportion of the traded goods which have survived and can be certainly identified.

An obsidian bowl from Tepe Gawra in northern Iraq. Obsidian, a natural glass, is translucent.

Two obsidian projectile points from Çatal Hüyük in Anatolia. The scale is in centimetres.

and obsidian, had also been transported over long distances in the Palaeolithic.

On early Holocene sites, it is often evident that shells were being traded. The shell *Dentalium* was widely distributed in sites in Israel, for example appearing in ornaments at Beidha, but curiously it was almost absent at Jericho, and at Abou Gosh, a site 30 km further west. At Abou Gosh, over two-thirds of the shells were of marine origin, mainly from the Mediterranean, though some had come from the Red Sea. By contrast, Beisamoun, a contemporary Pre-Pottery Neolithic B site further north by Lake Huleh, yielded scarcely any marine shells. Local freshwater mussels were used for decoration here, even though they are brittle. This may imply a lack of trading with the coast, for economic or political reasons.

Further signs of trade in shells come from Mehrgarh in Pakistan, where in the oldest levels, believed to date back to 6,000 BC, shells are found which had come at least 500 km from the Arabian Sea. The finds included an elaborate shell waistband.

Obsidian, another important trading material, has been particularly well studied. It is a volcanic glass, occurring in various parts of the world, and always prized for its lustrous appearance and usefulness. It can be flaked, like flint, to make tools such as projectile points. Eventually it was found that obsidian could also be ground or turned, to produce other useful objects, for example bowls.

Obsidian can be traced more accurately than shells, because it can be 'fingerprinted' to an exact source. It contains small quantities of various elements, such as iron, sodium, caesium and tantalum, which can be measured by the techniques of neutron activation analysis or optical spectrography. This allows identification since each volcanic source of obsidian has its own characteristic spectrum of values.

As long as 30,000 years ago, obsidian was transported some 300 km to Shanidar from the Lake

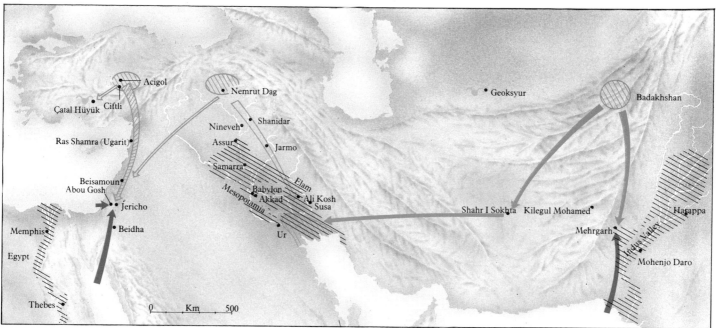

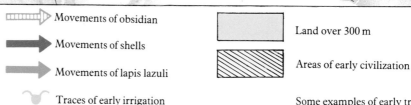

⊏⊐⊏⊐⊏⊐▷ Movements of obsidian	▭ Land over 300 m
➡ Movements of shells	▨ Areas of early civilization
➡ Movements of lapis lazuli	
∿ Traces of early irrigation	

Van area of Turkey, but as this does not greatly exceed the transport distances found for flint elsewhere, it need not amount to trade. In the period from 7,000 to 5,000 BC, however, the obsidian trade was clearly developing throughout the Middle East, and considerable quantities have been found over 500 km from the Anatolian sources.

Obsidian forms only a small proportion of the stone tools on the distant sites, and the total quantities recovered might be regarded as just a few donkey-loads. Nonetheless, much more must remain undiscovered, and the material found is a very definite and precise indicator of trading contacts.

Other goods were also traded over long distances, especially precious stones. At Mehrgarh, these included turquoise and lapis lazuli from further north in central Asia or Afghanistan. Eventually other 'precious stones', in the form of metals, were transported along the same routes. As the normal means of land transport by pack animals – usually donkeys and mules – made the cost of transporting larger objects prohibitive, the emphasis of long-distance trade was on small, precious materials and objects. In this, there is a connection between trade and the eventual development of money (coinage first appeared in Asia Minor in the seventh century BC, but metal ingots of known weight had been in use much earlier).

Trade on a large scale could only be financed by economic surpluses, which became available after the introduction of farming. In a simple society, based mainly on subsistence farming, the surplus does not go far enough to make everybody wealthy, and it is not surprising that in these times we begin to see the emergence of élites, whose power allowed them to amass fine goods not available to others.

The exchange of surpluses allowed the specialization of crafts which is part and parcel of trading. For example, both at Beidha and at Çatal Hüyük, craft specialization is very noticeable in early Neolithic times. The craftsmen included workers of stone, horn and textiles. At Beidha, individual workshops were found, and a butcher's shop. At Çatal Hüyük there is plentiful evidence of trade goods, though the workshops were not found. There was clearly a great deal of local trade within a few kilometres of such settlements, which probably served some of the same functions as modern small market towns. Trade over short distances certainly accounted for the great bulk of transactions in ancient times.

It is no accident that so many of the early civilizations were riverine, since travel by water greatly lowered the cost of transport, and allowed the economic movement of bulk goods. Pottery could be moved by the boat-load over considerable distances; timber, in short supply in Egypt, could be brought in by sea from Lebanon. In the past, as now, trade was vital to the achievement of prosperity.

Some examples of early trade which are particularly well-attested by archaeological evidence. Obsidian trading was important throughout the early Holocene.

A small seal from Çatal Hüyük, made from terracotta. Seals became widespread in the Neolithic of the Middle East; they emphasize the concept of ownership and that goods could pass out of the owner's hands.

The first city states

Between 4,000 and 3,000 years BC, we find signs of cities which were states, ruled by kings. Ur provides a classic example; its fortunes fluctuated through more than 2,000 years. Burials of early kings show their power and prestige which was secular as well as religious.

In a baker's shop at Ur the brick arches of the stoke-holes are still standing after nearly 4,000 years. The tiled tray in the foreground was probably used for kneading dough.

Gradually, during the Neolithic period, the plains of Mesopotamia became covered with small settlements, among which some grew to exceptional size. From 5,000 to 3,000 BC, some settlements began to cover a few hectares, and can be regarded as towns rather than villages. This phenomenon was not restricted to Mesopotamia – it had happened much earlier at Jericho – but here it is apparent across a wide area.

In Egypt, the course of the Nile gave a unity to the country, but in Mesopotamia, the rivers flowed in a network of channels, frequently changing their courses, and fertile zones were separated by areas of marshes, encouraging the growth of politically separate settlements, some of which grew to become city states. The great rivers Tigris and Euphrates today run across extensive plains, but large parts of these have been built up by sediments only within the last few thousand years: formerly, the sea extended much further inland, so that Ur, now 200 km from the sea, was by the side of a lagoon.

Five or six thousand years ago, the southern part of the plains belonged to a people named the Sumerians, who were probably the original inhabitants; the Akkadians, to the north, who eventually became dominant, spoke a Semitic language and perhaps had their origins in Arabia.

The Sumerians may have been the first people anywhere in the world to achieve a full civilization. Our record of the early stages of civilization in this area comes mainly from the great city mounds, but smaller sites have sometimes allowed better access to the archaeology of the early phases.

The stage which presages the emergence of major cities is known as the Al 'Ubaid phase, named after a small site about 6 km to the west of Ur. Here in the 1920s Leonard Woolley found remains of reed houses, along with pottery of a distinctive decorated kind. Subsequently a German expedition discovered similar pottery in deep levels at Ur and at Uruk (Warka). In later work at Eridu, believed by the ancient Sumerians themselves to be the oldest of all cities, pottery of the same kind was found associated with a late Ubaid temple. In a remarkable sequence of development, it overlay a whole series of earlier temple buildings. Beneath eighteen later rebuildings was a very simple chapel, founded on virgin dune sand. The habit of rebuilding temples in this way witnesses the importance and conservatism of religion: similar patterns of rebuilding are found elsewhere, even in the New World. The continuity of occupation at Eridu gives evidence of the key stages in the emergence of Sumerian civilization.

Ur provides a very famous example of a Sumerian city state, such as became numerous in Mesopotamia. Ur was one of the more important, though we need not assume that it was typical: the early phases of the Jemdet Nasr period (c. 3,200–2,600 BC) are in fact better represented at Uruk (Warka), where there is a complex of great religious buildings. But at Ur in 1926, Woolley dug a deep sounding which located a most remarkable royal cemetery estimated to date to about 2,600 BC. There were many simple predynastic burials, in wattle or clay coffins, accompanied by simple goods, but among these, and astonishing in their richness, are the royal burials.

One prince, Meskalamdug, was buried in a straightforward shaft dug in the earth, and the grave offerings were placed at the side of his wooden coffin. We know his name, because it was inscribed on two bowls and a lamp, all of gold. The prince still wore an exquisitely worked gold helmet, beaten from a sheet, and representing the wearer's hair, and even ears. In addition to an array of personal weapons, including axes of electrum (an alloy of silver and gold) and a dagger of gold, there were a great many gold, silver and copper bowls, and even lamps. A set of arrows had flint heads, showing the enduring use of stone for purposes to which it was well-suited.

Similar ornate finds came in even greater numbers from several other royal burials, which were found in underground masonry tomb chambers, approached by descending ramps. The contents of these interments are horrific, as they include not only the monarchs themselves, but also large groups of retainers: soldiers, charioteers, and ladies-in-waiting, who had been put to death at the time of the burial. In the tomb of Queen Puabi there were 59 bodies, including six oxen which had drawn two chariots: with Akalamdug there were 40 attendants; and in another tomb there were 74 bodies, including 68 women, gloriously dressed.

As the burials of these important people were the exception, should the archaeologist lay much emphasis upon them? The answer must be yes, because they tell of the great status which individuals could now achieve. For the previous 2 million years of human cultural evolution, there is hardly anything to point out prominent social status, but in the last few thousand, it suddenly becomes apparent.

Akalamdug is described as 'King of Ur' on a cylinder seal. Though the importance of religion and of temples is apparent in early Sumer, the power of these rulers was clearly secular, and in some sense they provide early examples of a personality cult. The chill strength of that power is brought home to us by the sacrifices, executed no doubt under the authority of the new ruler. There is no means of

telling whether these were the actual retainers, or prisoners or slaves fulfilling that role for the after-life, but the *Epic of Gilgamesh* (a work of Sumerian and Akkadian mythology) also records retainers accompanying a hero in death.

These rulers were monarchs, but are not known in the formal king-lists, which were made out much later, towards 2,000 BC. Although we know their names, which were written on the grave goods (writing appeared in the area at about 3,100 BC), their context is effectively prehistoric, because there are no other written records to provide a framework. The first King of Ur who stands out clearly as a historical figure is Ur-Nammu, founder of the Third Dynasty and the giver of laws. He was responsible for the great ziggurat at Ur, which was restored by later kings and still survives; a complex of fine temples includes his own tomb, which had corbelled brick vaults, illustrating Sumerian skill in architecture. Ur-Nammu was also responsible for massive fortifications, which surrounded the city. These were later dismantled by Elamites from the east, who captured the city around 2,000 BC. The walls are known to have been many metres thick and high, and had a circuit of over 2 kilometres. This emphasizes that Ur was not a small town like Jericho, but an imposing city.

Although there was an emphasis on investigating public buildings, Woolley's excavations of a domestic quarter of the Larsa phase at Ur (c. 1,900 BC), uncovered a revealing picture of ordinary people's lives. The dwellings seemed so similar to recent houses in the Middle East as 'scarcely to merit description', but they provide us with a wealth of detailed information. Passageways, steps, rooms were all measured, and are well preserved. In one house, a dog kennel had stood against a wall, and the outline of its roof is still preserved in the wall plaster. Small shrines, and a bakery with ovens, including the tray for kneading dough, were also excavated.

The ziggurat of Ur, as it is preserved today.

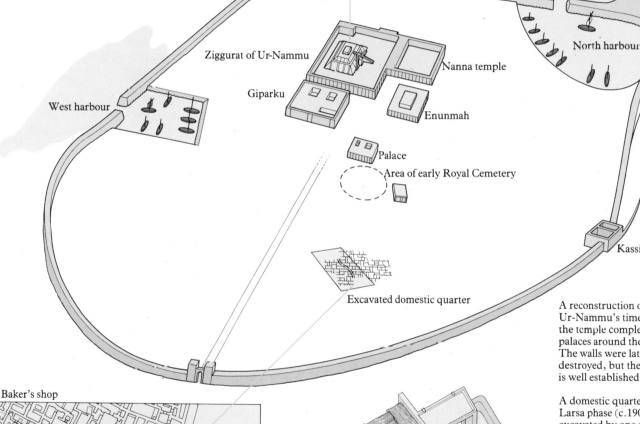

West harbour

Ziggurat of Ur-Nammu

Giparku

Nanna temple

Enunmah

North harbour

Palace

Area of early Royal Cemetery

Kassite fort

Excavated domestic quarter

Baker's shop

Reconstructed house

A reconstruction of the city in Ur-Nammu's time showing the temple complex and palaces around the ziggurat. The walls were later destroyed, but their position is well established.

A domestic quarter of the Larsa phase (c.1900 BC) was excavated by one of Leonard Woolley's expeditions. It is probably typical of private housing during a period of thousands of years.

An architect's reconstruction of a typical large town house of the Larsa phase, showing the central patio. Bases for posts indicate that it was galleried, and steps show that there were upper floors.

179

The origins of metal-working

An intrinsic part of the progress towards civilization was the evolution of technology based on working with fire. Between 7,000 and 3,000 BC a variety of metal-working techniques was mastered, and a range of new tools emerged.

Skills in metal-working developed astonishingly quickly. Gold jewellery from the Royal Cemetery at Ur (c.2,500 BC) includes necklaces, pins and earrings, all made with sophisticated techniques.

A single copper pendant from Shanidar in Iraq may date from the Proto-Neolithic, and be as old as the finds from Çayönü Tepesi, but there is a possibility that this small find is intrusive from a later level.

In the last few thousand years, mankind has acquired a great diversity of skills, and discovered how to work new materials. A mere 10,000 years ago, nobody knew how to use metals; but by 5,000 years ago, exquisite objects were being wrought. Progress must have been very slow, for knowledge was transmitted from master craftsman to apprentice, with the expectation that instructions would be followed exactly; but in total the small steps added up to immense achievements.

Metal is all around us, but only rarely visible and accessible. In some areas, however, rocks are exposed in which native copper occurs in a pure form. This is the case in northern Canada, where ancestors of the Eskimos shaped it into harpoon heads and ornaments. But the main area where the earliest metal-working appears is the Old World, extending from Bulgaria in the west, through Anatolia, and into western Iran. Metals also existed in rich concentrations in the deserts of Egypt, and there are indications that metal-working started at an early date in South-East Asia.

The earliest use of metal yet known is at the site of Çayönü Tepesi, in southern Turkey to the north of the Syrian plains. Here a few copper objects were found in levels dated to about 7,000 BC. The site is only 20 km from a source of native copper, and it is evident that the objects were hammered into shape.

Hammering does not amount to metallurgy. If too prolonged, it causes the metal to harden and become brittle, with a risk of cracking. But if the copper is heated (annealed) in a fire, it becomes malleable again, and it is evident that this metallurgical process was mastered very early.

At first, copper was traded as a luxury good, probably regarded as another remarkable 'stone', and dispersed on the same trade routes as obsidian. A vital step in the development of true metallurgy was the discovery of smelting, the high-temperature process by which pure metal can be produced from ore. We do not know when this first happened, but it seems that progress was rapid. It greatly facilitated the production of metal goods, because ores have a much wider distribution than native copper.

By about 4,000 BC, copper objects were widespread in the Middle East, occurring for example in the Ubaid levels in Mesopotamia, and on predynastic sites in Egypt. Most of the finds are small, simple objects, such as pins and bracelets. At Al'Ubaid, copper was still a luxury, and sickle blades were made of baked clay. Raw materials other than clay were so utterly lacking on the Mesopotamian plains that almost everything needed to be imported.

In the Balkan area, elaborate copper mines already existed by the fourth millenium BC at Rudna Glava in Yugoslavia and Aibunar in Bulgaria. Professor Colin Renfrew (University of Cambridge) believes that this indicates a largely autonomous regional tradition of metal-working in the Balkans from an early date.

Flint had been mined in an organized fashion even earlier, so once it was appreciated that ore existed in veins which could be followed, the technology for exploiting them already existed.

In the initial period of the Middle Eastern civilizations, from about 3,000 BC, there was a truly remarkable development of metallurgy. This is seen in the beginning of the Bronze Age, when alloys of arsenic and copper, or tin and copper (in both cases known as bronze), came into common use, and greatly extended the use of metals. Initially, perhaps, some of the alloys occurred naturally because more than one metallic element was found in the ores, but records show that much of the alloying was deliberate, and its purpose well understood. In Egypt, where no tin was available, arsenic bronze came into common use. It had the attraction of forming a lustrous 'plating' on the surface of a cast object.

One of the great advantages of bronze was not so much that it was harder, but that the metal flowed more easily than copper at a similar temperature, and so could be used more easily for casting. In this, as in many other facets of technology, we can see how an idea useful in one field is taken up in another: seals (generally made of stone in ancient times) and moulds both harness the idea of a positive and negative. Seals first appear at about the time of the first metal at Çayönü, but casting was invented considerably later. The earliest moulds were

carved in stone, so as to form shaped depressions which were then filled with molten metal. A copper axe cast from such a mould was found at Arpachiyah in northern Mesopotamia, dating to before 3,000 BC.

From about 3,000 BC, other metals came into wider use. Gold was appreciated because of its fine appearance, and by 2,500 BC is commonly associated with royal burials, as at Ur. Its earliest use, however, is in a remarkable cemetery at Varna in Bulgaria, which appears to date before 3,000 BC.

By about 2,500 BC, goldsmiths had achieved a variety of delicate skills, hardly surpassed since, even though they had to conquer limitations in the technology available to them. Moulds were sometimes made in two or three pieces, and the hammering of sheet metal had achieved a high standard. In Egypt, gold was panned, and later mined in the deserts east of the Nile. Its importance from early times is suggested by the late predynastic site now known as Naqada: it was named 'Nubt',

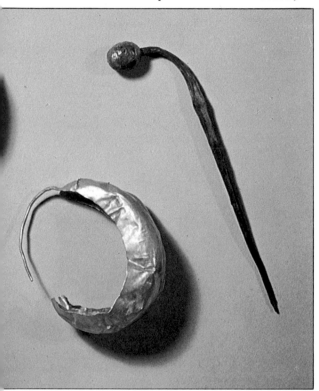

probably after *nub*, the word for gold, which was mined nearby.

Similar developments were taking place in the Far East. At Non Nok Tha in northern Thailand, metal-working seems to go back to about 4,000 BC. Before 2,000 BC, bronze was being cast in two-piece moulds, and some tools were being made with sockets for hafting.

Metal-working in the Far East may have been a totally independent invention, but there were probably always some lines of communication between East and West. In the Andes, however, where metal-working appeared at about 2,000 BC, it does seem to have been developed independently.

The appearance of metal was so important and so apparent in the archaeological record that it has served as one of the foundations of archaeological classification. The formal three-age system of Stone Age, Bronze Age and Iron Age is owed to the Danish archaeologist Christian Thomsen (1788–1865), but it was anticipated far earlier by Lucretius and Homer. Accumulating experience and accurate dating have now shown archaeologists that the changes were not sudden or synchronous. Stone continued in use alongside bronze, and bronze alongside iron. Cost was often a critical factor in what was used.

Iron has a curious history. It appears in a few isolated instances in the third millennium BC, when it had great value because of its rarity. Smelting from iron ore had not yet been mastered, and many of the earliest specimens are made of meteoric iron. Ancient trading accounts show that it was initially valued more highly than silver, and as late as 1,323 BC, of two ceremonial daggers found in Tutankhamun's tomb, one had a blade of gold, the other of iron, showing its special significance.

Regional economic pressures, as well as advances in smelting knowledge, may have led to the increased use of iron. In the Greek late Bronze Age, for example, records from Pylos show a shortage of bronze, perhaps caused by political factors – such as a monopoly on tin, held by an unknown enemy.

From about 1,200 BC, the problems of working iron were conquered, and its use spread rapidly. Iron ores are much more widely distributed than those of copper, and the need for tin is avoided, so ultimately the metal which had been more valuable than gold crashed in value and became plentiful.

Once metal was smelted, the need for casting became apparent. Early moulds consisted of carved depressions in stones. The metal was poured until it was flush with the top, but two-piece moulds were soon introduced.

The origins of writing

Writing is a key feature in developed civilization, greatly extending chains of communication and allowing the records necessary for an organized society. Some symbols date back to the Palaeolithic, but developed systems for use in accounting appear just before 3,000 BC in the Middle East. Many separate types of writing then evolved.

A major trend in human evolution has been towards extended chains of actions, reaching further and further through time and space. We can see this from earliest times, but in spite of the benefits achieved in manipulating the environment, the net effect is to put greater and greater burdens on memory. Well-tried routines can be coped with, provided that they are identical, but problems are caused when repetitive tasks are complicated by small but important variations in content.

Thus writing, when it first appears, is concerned not with penning mighty epics or fine poems, but invariably with the keeping of accounts. It reflects the needs of trade, and the importance of the state and its dealings: princely rulers, priests and merchants were the first to benefit from it.

Writing represents one extension of the symbolic activity which is fundamental to the human way of thinking. Already, in Upper Palaeolithic art, one thing could represent another: many of the signs show this, particularly the female symbols, which resemble those found in later pictographic writing.

The earliest true writing probably has a long ancestry of such signs, but their emergence into a full system appears quite suddenly during the Jemdet Nasr phase in Mesopotamia. This is generally recognized to happen at around 3,100–3,000 BC. Similar systems appear at the same time or very shortly afterwards in Elam (south-west Iran) and in Egypt. Writing was so useful that it must have spread very rapidly. We cannot be sure, however, that it originally started from a single centre, because the ideas underlying it may have been common to international trading systems. Its decidedly later appearance – by several hundred years – in the Indus civilization and China does suggest that the idea had been transmitted from the Middle East.

The earliest writing is pictographic: that is, each sign is a small picture representing an object – a horse's head signifying a horse, an ox's head for an ox, and so on. In Mesopotamia such writing is preserved for us because the most convenient material for writing was raw clay, in the form of small tablets. The nature of the material helped to influence the future course of writing in the area. The earliest signs from Sumeria were scratched diagrammatically, but this tended to tear the clay. It was easier to impress the clay with the stylus (writing implement). This left a distinctive wedge-shaped impression, the origin of the term 'cuneiform' (from the Latin *cuneus*, a wedge). Gradually the signs became so transformed, into clusters of wedges, that they could not possibly be read except by a trained scribe. Both the Sumerian and Akkadian languages were written in cuneiform, which eventually became widely used in the Middle East.

In Elam, at Susa, and elsewhere in the plateau of Iran, a different pictographic system was in use. The counting system used in early tablets has recently been studied in detail. It appears that tokens of clay, in different shapes, were originally used in accounting. It was found that these could be represented more easily on the tablets: there are subtle distinctions between circles, solid discs, and bars. Although it is generally thought that writing began in Mesopotamia, since the tablets are rather earlier than those of Elam, this is not proven, and in both areas a developmental process is apparent.

The signs on this simple tablet (c.3,100 BC) from Godin Tepe, Iran, are interpreted as representing a number. It is believed that actual shaped objects of clay were used before it was appreciated that they could be indicated by impressions on a tablet.

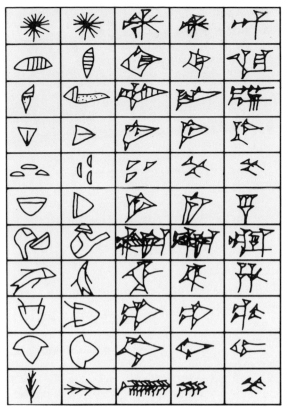

Writing also appears in Egypt at about 3,000 BC, but without any signs of a gradual development, suggesting to some authors that the concept may have been imported from Mesopotamia.

Hieroglyphics, the 'sacred writings', adorn many Egyptian temples, but several forms of script evolved for different uses. Cursive hieroglyphics were used for religious texts; a form named 'hieratic' was in everyday use, until it was replaced by demotic after 700 BC. The hieroglyphic representations kept a pictorial form unlike that of cuneiform, partly because of the different materials on which they were used. They were carved in stone, or written on papyrus, a paper formed from reeds. Reed pens and ink were used, stored in wooden boxes astonishingly like those used by present-day school-children.

A great step forward in the flexibility of writing came with the invention of an alphabetic system. Already, pictographs – which need give little clue to language, as the values are not phonetic – had taken on syllabic meaning, but separate letters were not represented.

The earliest alphabetic system recorded comes from Ugarit in Syria, dating to about 1,400 or 1,300 BC. From early times this area was a trading crossroads, subject to many influences. Among several scripts at Ugarit is the Ugaritic, which has a 32-letter alphabet, preserved on special tablets.

This, or a related version, is probably the ancestor of all later alphabetic scripts. Preserved now only in a cuneiform version used on clay, it was probably also used on other materials. Eventually there emerged from it the Phoenician script, which was passed in modified form to the Greeks, and to the Romans. Hebrew, Arabic, and Russian alphabets all stem ultimately from the early script of this area. As much of this early writing was carried out on perishable materials such as parchment, the archaeological record is strongly biased towards the archives of civilizations which used clay tablets.

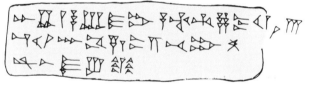

Many years of patient scholarly study have gone into the decipherment and interpretation of early writings. Sometimes, as in the case of the Rosetta stone, different scripts are laid out side by side. Sometimes, as in the Linear B of Crete and the Greek mainland, a recognition of the language involved allows transcription. In other cases, there are few clues as to the language, and progress in interpretation proceeds very slowly: Meroitic, the script from the civilization lying south of Egypt, and the Indus script are still poorly understood.

The appearance of writing does not immediately transform prehistory into history, because the early texts are too fragmentary, and their contents too prosaic, to provide much help in building a chronological framework. But within a few centuries, king-lists emerged, astronomical knowledge was written down, chronicles and epics appeared, and history had begun.

With the coming of writing, we begin to hear from people's own mouths and learn something of their beliefs and view of the world. This evidence is still selective, picked out by the practices of the time as well as by the vagaries of preservation. Yet the richness of such written evidence, when it exists, makes us aware that social behaviour of a kind which does not appear in the ordinary archaeological record must have played a large part in earlier events.

The development of cuneiform writing, shown through the gradual alterations of several signs from their original pictographic forms. The signs represented are as follows: Heaven/god, earth, man, woman, mountain, food, to eat, fish, ox, cow, barley/grain.

An early clay tablet from Iran illustrates the importance of reckoning in trading. By each horse's head are symbols which represent a count.

The earliest preserved alphabet dating to about 1,400 or 1,500 BC, written on a tablet found at Ugarit (Ras Shamra). It has over 30 letters. These are written in cuneiform style, but the alphabet was probably also written in cursive form on other materials.

When the King of Mitanni sent a letter to the Pharaoh of Egypt, Amenophis III who reigned from 1,391–1,353 BC, it was natural to do so on a clay tablet, written in cuneiform. It was equally natural for the Egyptian filing clerk to label it in ink, the usual medium for writing on papyrus.

The ship and the wheel

Water transport has a long history, and before 3,000 BC real ships had appeared in Egypt and Mesopotamia, as we know from paintings and models. On land, the wheel also appeared in Mesopotamia and south Russia at about the same time.

Effective transport was a basic need once states became larger, and trade more common. 'As old as the wheel' is a common phrase implying great antiquity, but the wheel is actually a late invention. For a long time there was no transport on land other than pack animals. Developments in water transport were, however, more rapid.

We can infer the early existence of water-craft, since they must have been used by Palaeolithic people to cross to Australia, and elsewhere. No ship or boat is preserved from times earlier than writing, so we can only refer to other evidence. Predynastic pottery in Egypt commonly bears paintings of boats, which already have sails and deck cabins. As they had appeared in Egypt by 4,000–3,000 BC, we might expect them to have been in use in Mesopotamia at least as early, and this is confirmed by the discovery of boat models made of pitch in graves of the Ubaid period.

Such boats probably contributed greatly to local trade, as they have done until recently. For example, a cargo of fragile pots could easily be transported many kilometres by boat, whereas carrying them even a short distance by land could hardly be contemplated.

Representations from early dynastic times show us that sea-going vessels had been developed in Egypt before 2,500 BC. They would have been in use for trading along the Syrian coast, and would also have been used in the Red Sea, for trading with the unidentified 'land of Punt', which lay somewhere to the south.

The ships in use were probably not exclusively Egyptian; forerunners of the later Phoenician craft, and of the dhows of the Arabian gulf, may already have been sailing. The Indus civilization certainly had major ports on the coast of what is now Pakistan, and contacts with the Arabian Gulf area. In Mesopotamia the city of Ur actually had two harbours within its walls.

Yet Egypt has preserved unrivalled evidence of ancient boat-building skills, in the form of a complete ship of about 2,530 BC, many hundreds of years older than any other preserved. This is a large river craft, buried ceremonially in a pit on the south side of the pyramid of Cheops (Khufu). The pit had remained hidden under rubble until the early 1950s, when the covering slabs were lifted. The ship was complete, but dismantled, the wood still tied in bundles. Many years' patient work were needed to reassemble it in its original form. The craft was buried for the pharaoh's journey down-river in the after-life: it has no mast, but there is speculation that a remaining boat pit may contain a comparable masted ship for use on his voyage upstream. If this sounds lavish, it must be remembered that the purpose of the Cheops ship or ships was ceremonial and symbolic. Wear-marks on the wood show that the ship had been assembled and used.

Details of Egyptian sailing vessels are preserved in boat models found in many tombs. This one dates from about 1,900 BC.

The great funeral ship of King Cheops, reassembled after it was found dismantled in a boat-pit beside the Great Pyramid. It is larger than most sea-going vessels of mediaeval times.

A painted frieze from a house on Thera (Santorini) portrays the fleet coming home, in about 1,500 BC.

This find tells us a great deal about how the early ships were built. The wooden versions were descended from the reed type and were built with a great deal of rope, which was used for tying the planks together. There was as yet no keel, so sea-going ships had a rope tie stretched from stem to stern, to prevent the ship breaking its back. The Cheops ship has a number of oars, which are also present on boat models found in Egyptian tombs.

At Thera (Santorini), the Greek island where an early town has been preserved by deposits from a volcanic eruption, beautiful wall frescoes show ships dating to about 1,500 BC. A whole fleet cruises into port, perhaps in a ceremonial procession, showing that by this time ships had a form of hull more like that known in the classical era. Ships had already been adapted for war, as historical records also reveal – the 'sea people' (probably including the ancestral Greeks) became the scourge of Egypt.

monuments of Europe were built at about the time when the wheel appears, and it seems more than likely that rollers were used for moving the stones. If they were also used for helping to free sledges which were stuck, someone may suddenly have been struck by the full potential of the device.

All very early wheels were solid, made of up to three planks. This kind of wheel, which has survived in use up to the present day among some rural communities of Asia, spread very rapidly. Specimens in Holland have radiocarbon dates of about 2,000 BC, which implies a real calendar date of about 2,500 BC.

Military needs probably stimulated the development of lighter, stronger wheels. Chariots were important to the Hyksos, who invaded Egypt at c. 1,640 BC. Chariots portrayed in a battle between Ramses II and Hittite opponents in Syria in 1,285 BC are shown as light vehicles with spoked wheels.

Carts with solid wooden wheels are shown on the Standard of Ur, dating from the 3rd millennium BC. Similar solid wheels which are almost as old have been found in bogs in the Netherlands.

The magnificence of royal power radiates from this illustration of the Assyrian King Assurbanipal in his chariot, surmounted by a sun-shade (c.650 BC). The spoked wheel was used in chariots for many hundreds of years.

The wheel was more of an innovation than the ship. It was never invented in the New World, where it would have been less helpful on the narrow mountain paths of the Incas. It appeared considerably later than the use of beasts for drawing equipment such as sledges and ploughs. Indeed, regardless of other evidence, we have a hint that the wheel was very new when Mesopotamian writing began, since the early sign for a wheeled vehicle is that of a sledge with a dot beneath it.

This does not necessarily mean that the wheel was invented within the classic civilizations of Mesopotamia and southern Iran, although much of the early evidence comes from that area. Early wheeled vehicles are found, especially in burials, further north across the Caucasus, in the plains area between the Black Sea and the Caspian. Both there and in Mesopotamia, the earliest evidence appears to go back to the fourth millennium BC.

We do not know how the wheel was invented, but logs must often have been used as rollers for moving heavy objects. Many of the great megalithic

Developing civilizations

Through the third and second millennia BC, civilizations became established in many areas of the Middle East, south Asia and the Far East. Extended conquests led to the formation of empires, which rose and frequently fell. But the idea of civilization flourished, together with the growth of literature, arts and technology.

Civilization in its full sense emerged in Mespotamia, as we have seen, at about 3,000 BC, although the presence of writing does not imply that we have reliable king-lists, a continuous history, or even a firm chronology from that earliest period.

In Egypt, we do have a reasonably accurate king-list – albeit in a version compiled after 2,000 BC – and apart from brief turbulent interludes, Egyptian history can be followed as a continuous record from c. 3,100 BC onwards. It thus provides the backbone of our historical dating system.

The historical chronologies of Egypt and Mesopotamia are not, however, absolutely fixed in calendar years in the period c. 3,000–2,000 BC. In Egypt the early king-lists may incorporate errors, but numbers of calibrated radiocarbon dates for the earliest dynastic period correspond well with the historical dates, so the maximum error is not likely to exceed a century. A recorded astronomical event very precisely pins down the 12th dynasty in Egypt,

whose first king, Amenemhet I, came to the throne in 1,991 BC. Another less certain period follows, but from the time of the New Kingdom (about 1,550 BC) errors are constrained within about 10 years, and from 664 BC dates are precisely determined.

In Mesopotamia, the early dynastic times are much less securely dated, but material evidence of trading with Egypt, and a few radiocarbon dates, support dates of c. 3,100–3,000 BC for the first dynastic kings. King-lists do exist for these times, and inscriptions found in excavations have confirmed that many of the kings were real rather than mythical figures (including Gilgamesh) but they are often listed consecutively, even when they actually ruled concurrently in separate cities. Around 2,000 BC, astronomical observations provide a choice of several precise dates for certain events. From these the most likely dates for the accession of Hammurabi are 1,792 or 1,848 BC. The preferred reckoning of 1,792 would give 2,112 BC for the Third Dynasty of Ur, started by Ur-Nammu.

The written records of these early civilizations mean that we now pass – in these limited parts of the world – from prehistory to history. Even so, prehistory can creep back in: in Mesopotamia, written records disappear for over a century after Samsuditana, the last ruler in Hammurabi's dynasty, was overthrown c. 1,595 BC. The term 'proto-historic' is sometimes used to refer to societies contemporary with, and mentioned in, historical records but not possessing them.

The advent of historical evidence does not imply any lesser need for archaeology and archaeological methods. The records of those early times were not intended to help us make up a history; nor is it the purpose of archaeology to provide a substitute narrative 'history'. Archaeology attempts to extract as much information as possible about a society from the material evidence, before or after the beginnings of history.

Nonetheless, where the two approaches operate hand in hand, they give us a much fuller picture of the past. In investigations of early civilizations, it often falls to archaeology to uncover written records. Once interpreted, these may cast more light on past events, and so lead to further archaeological research on more specific questions.

By the second millennium BC, domains of power had become larger, and the transition from city state to nation to empire was well under way. This kind of expansion took place in most areas of early civilization, and must result from a variety of factors, including insecurity among hostile neighbours, and desire for power and wealth. Expansion was based on the skilful use of military power, depending on and promoted by the requirements of trading.

To follow Middle Eastern civilization through the second millennium in historical and political terms would be a herculean task, since there were many minor kingdoms – including client states – for every large empire. The small states acknowledged suzerainty as the need pressed, and the boundaries of the empires were continually advancing and retreating.

In this period the list of civilized peoples grows: major powers included the Hurrians and the Mitanni in the Levant; further west in Anatolia, the Hittites; in Crete, the Minoans; and in mainland Greece, the

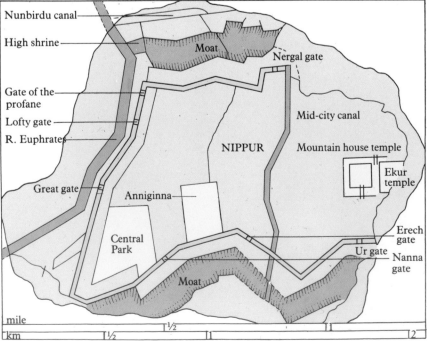

Nunbirdu canal
High shrine
Moat
Nergal gate
Gate of the profane
Lofty gate
R. Euphrates
Great gate
Mid-city canal
NIPPUR
Mountain house temple
Ekur temple
Anniginna
Central Park
Moat
Erech gate
Ur gate
Nanna gate

mile   ½   ½   1
km   1½   ½   1   1   2

Myceneans. The Hittites and Myceneans were the earliest known speakers of Indo-European languages to acquire writing. In the Middle East, many other people were close to civilization, if not formally civilized, such as the Canaanites and the Israelites.

In the course of time, empire after empire flourished and fell. Several of the major powers were largely enduring, notably Egypt, Assyria, Babylon and Elam. Through the second millennium, the pharaohs vied for superiority with first the Mitanni, then the Hittites, their front lines moving backwards and forwards across the area which is now Lebanon and Syria. Later, however, Hittite power fell, and that of Assyria began to rise, often eclipsing that of Babylon, with which it had an uneasy relationship.

When the Babylonians allied with Elam, they could hope to keep the Assyrians in check, but after 750 BC, the Assyrians swept across the whole Middle East, even into Egypt. Eventually Assyrian power crumbled in the face of the Medes, and by 600 BC Babylon was restored to power under Nebuchadnezzar. Elam maintained its independent character – though sometimes allying with Babylon – until it was finally incorporated within the Persian empire, itself overthrown by the Macedonian Alexander the Great in 323 BC.

His rise illustrates a commonly occurring event – that peoples from the fringe of civilization frequently crowded in and made their mark. In the Middle East there were the desert nomads such as the Amorites, and further north, the Cimmerians and the Scythians, who destroyed the Urartian empire to the north of Assyria in the seventh century BC, and even reached Palestine. Across northern Asia, wild horse-riding nomads threatened civilizations until the Christian era.

In the area of modern Pakistan and western India, another and separate early civilization flourished. This Indus civilization, named after the river valley along which it extended, is now known to have had long Neolithic antecedents, as has been demonstrated by investigations at Mehrgarh and other sites. As the Indus script remains undeciphered, less is known in historical terms about the mature civilization, which suddenly appeared across a wide area at about 2,400 BC, according to calibrated radiocarbon dates. It seems likely that civilization in the area received a sudden impetus in the third millennium, perhaps as a result of the diffusion of writing and other ideas from Mesopotamia, and that a particular group or élite was able to extend its power over a wide area. At about 1,700 BC, the civilization came to a violent end, recorded by skeletons of massacre victims found in the streets of Mohenjo-daro, a major site.

Whereas the civilizations of western Asia came and went in a restless changing tradition, those of the Far East, which became established just a little later, have endured in a much more stable and continuous fashion. This is especially true for China, not the only civilization of the area, but through the ages the largest, the most powerful and culturally the richest. Symbolic of the continuity – which was cultural rather than political – is Chinese writing, which is still pictographic, having remained so since its first conception; the details of the pictograms have changed and their numbers have vastly increased, but throughout almost 4,000 years some of the same forms have persisted.

The importance of Chinese civilization is obvious, since it provides the cultural heritage of a quarter of mankind. A point to emphasize is the great diversity of China, ancient and modern: the country as we know it is about 2,500 by 2,500 km in extent, reaching from the tropics into temperate latitudes. Its many peoples are reflected in many languages, but this gives a strength to the pictographic script; clumsy as it seems to have a script with thousands of separate signs, it is able to transcend local differences of spoken language.

The first full civilization to be recognizable in China is that of the Shang, beginning at about 1,750 BC. The Shang belongs to the north part of China, along the middle course of the Huang Ho (Yellow River). This is still the most highly cultivated area, on account of the good loess soils, a region of wheat rather than rice.

In a masterly review of Chinese archaeology K.C. Chang lists the following features as

The first preserved map, is of the city of Nippur, on the River Euphrates, and dates to c.1,500 BC. It was found with other curiosities in a pot belonging to a later period, and had evidently become part of a small 'museum' collection. Distances are marked on the original, showing that in most dimensions it was an accurately surveyed map.

Although the exact sounds of ancient music are beyond reconstruction, paintings, such as these from an Egyptian tomb of c.1,500 BC, show the developed form of musical instruments. The charm of these girl musicians is captured with an informality lacking in most Egyptian art.

distinguishing the Shang from earlier times: urbanism; palatial, as well as domestic, architecture; human sacrifice; sharp contrast of social classes; ceremonial and artistic activities of the aristocracy, marked by burials with rich ornaments of stone (including jade); bronze metallurgy; use of chariots, and the taking of prisoners; and an elaborate writing system. Remarkably enough, all bear a close similarity to the features which we have been distinguishing in other civilizations of the Old World. Many, too, probably pass further back into early Chinese culture than can yet be followed. For example, social stratification had already appeared in cemeteries of the earlier Neolithic period at Homutu, Panpotsun and other sites. Metal-working too certainly began before Shang – in the previous

features may, however, have been introduced from western Asia, including chariots, which appeared there considerably earlier than in China.

In spite of the substratum of social organization and technology shared with other Old World civilizations, Chinese civilization has always had its own flavour, and it has contributed substantially to technological improvement. Early Chinese writing, we know, was painted upon wood or bamboo, though it has only survived on animal shoulder-blades and turtle shells, and when cast on bronze vessels. But in the last centuries BC, in the Han dynasty, the Chinese invented real paper. From Shang times, hemp and silk were cultivated to make fabrics. Beautiful silk paintings have been found in Chu period tombs (about 500 BC) in southern China.

Chinese bronze-smiths were able to cast vessels with elaborate raised surface designs. This one, of the type named *Ting*, belongs to the Shang dynasty.

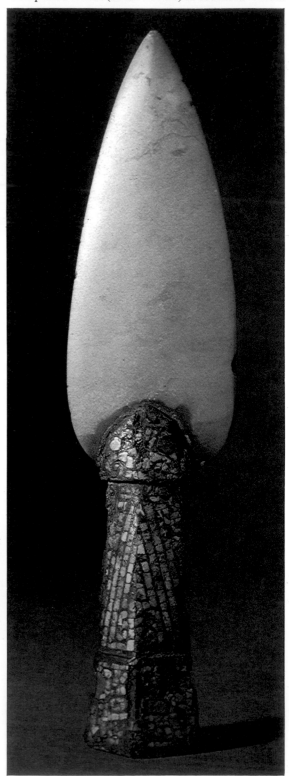

A Shang dynasty spearhead shows the originality of Chinese art. The white jade blade is mounted in a hafting-stem of bronze, inlaid with turquoise mosaic.

Lungshan culture at Shantung, small bronze plates have been found, and in the Chichia phase of Kansu, copper objects were recovered.

Metal-working also began at an early stage elsewhere in South-East Asia, so the predominant impression is that it evolved entirely separately in the East. For Chang, 'the question is no longer *whether* bronze metallurgy began indigenously in North China: it is, rather, *where* and *how*.' Other cultural

In the Chou period, which followed Shang from about 1,100 BC, the state of Chou was the most advanced and most powerful in south China. Some of the cities were large and impressive: the wall of Icheng in Hupei enclosed an area of about 2 by 1.5 km. The range of material culture included jade, lacquer-work, wood-carving and iron-work.

The construction of the great wall, over 4,000 km in length, was completed by Shih Huang Ti, whose reign (246–210 BC) marks the end of internal feuding, and the foundation of a united empire. The building of the wall emphasizes that the threat of invading horsemen from the north was as real here as in the Middle East. The Huns had invaded Honan as early as 660 BC (at the same time as the Scythian invasion of Urartu).

Chinese civilization was the predominant cultural influence in Korea, and then in the first millennium AD in Japan, whose script is derived from the Chinese.

This short outline is sufficient to show that by the end of the 3rd millennium BC, or soon afterwards, all those major features which we regard as characteristic of civilization (see pp 8–9), including urbanization and writing, were widely established across the Old World, from the eastern Mediterranean to China. In any attempt to interpret the pattern and course of events many questions spring to mind. What determined the geographic and social pattern of the developing civilizations? Did they have to be urban and sedentary? Did they have to rise and fall? What was the relationship between them and the surrounding uncivilized peoples? Once established, did civilization maintain its impetus – did accumulated experience lead people to be better at being civilized?

There is no doubt that the early civilizations faced problems, but the apparently endless round of warfare was broken by long periods of stability, sometimes lasting for hundreds of years, and comparing well with Europe in the last 300 years.

Two of the major problems, environment and outsiders, sometimes went together. The Holocene is not climatically unchanging, and cycles of poorer climate have sometimes lasted for several hundred years. The cyclical nature of the incursions by nomads, from Arabia or from further north, suggests an environmental influence. Drought or excessive cold would certainly have induced some of them to migrate, but it seems equally possible that success in their way of life led to increased population, and to warrior groups moving further afield to seek their fortunes.

The relationship between the civilizations and surrounding peoples is a curious one. In spite of many wars, the outsiders could not be subdued. They had numbers, mobility and the advantage of initiative. Their material culture was not necessarily primitive – as Scythian metal-working shows – and trade with them may often have been important. Sometimes, too, the nomads had an appreciation of the civilized states which they overcame – and they furnished some of the most vigorous rulers of civilized states. The relationships were turbulent, violent, but perhaps essentially symbiotic.

A quite separate environmental problem which affected early civilizations, especially in Mesopotamia, was that of salinity. The productivity of the river valleys depended on irrigation, but the waters were saline. Prolonged intensive farming could lead to excessive salt being deposited in the soil or brought up from deeper levels. This encouraged the growing of the more tolerant barley rather than wheat, but in some areas agricultural productivity was severely affected. Some authorities believe that salinization was the major source of crises checking second-millennium civilization in the Middle East.

These recurring problems need not hide the general, steadily broadening rise in cultural sophistication which is amply depicted in art and written records. Perhaps it can be argued that metal-working and engineering technology were on a plateau throughout the 2nd millennium, but literature, philosophy, religious concepts and astronomy were all advancing.

A silk manuscript, found in a tomb in southern China, dating from the later first millennium BC, and illustrating early Chinese writing.

A horse model found in the passageway of a tomb of the Tang period, and dating to the ninth century AD. About 40 cm high, it was originally one of a cavalcade, and would have had a rider or groom. Such horses were put in graves as an act of ritual to escort the dead, a tradition which extends back to the last centuries BC.

New World civilization

In the Americas organized societies, which can be described as civilizations, emerged in the Andes and Mesoamerica. They developed later than in the Old World, but appear to be entirely independent in inspiration.

The principal areas of the New World civilizations. They did not evolve in lowland forest regions, except in some parts of Mesoamerica.

Original area of the Olmecs

Oaxaca

The extent of lowland tropical evergreen rain forest

Core area of early Peruvian civilization

Extent of Inca Empire after 1500 AD

New World civilizations had a distinctive character; they were very different from those of the Old World in social organization, cultural style, and technology.

As in the Old World, only certain favoured areas were able to develop and sustain civilization in the full sense. Two distinct regions stand out: Mesoamerica, including much of modern Mexico and the area to the south; and much further south, the central Andes and adjacent coastal zone in Peru. By the time the Spaniards arrived (1519 in Mexico, 1532 in Peru) the area of civilization was more extensive than this, reaching along the Andes more or less continuously from a latitude of about 35° south to 35° north.

Civilization certainly came later in the New World than in the Old, but the length of time in which it developed from the beginnings of food production was very similar, in the order of 4 or 5,000 years. The areas which attained civilization were those where the greatest variety of crops was domesticated, and where the most reliable surpluses could be obtained.

Although the temperate climate of the highlands is one factor sometimes invoked as stimulating civilization, organized societies were also found in hot lowlands such as the Yucatan peninsula, where greater emphasis was on root crops rather than maize.

The terms applied to New World prehistory were coined to fit the local progression, and labels such as Neolithic and Bronze Age do not appear. American archaeologists named Formative Classic and Post-Classic periods, which originally implied particular levels of development. But it was found that these varied very much from area to area, and the period names are now used mainly chronologically. Nonetheless, the Formative period in Mesoamerica was thus named to mark the emergence of civilization, and broadly it does so.

In Mesoamerica, settled farming life becomes widely apparent in the few hundred years following 2,000 BC. During the Formative period pottery and

villages appeared in the plateau area, in southern Mexico, and in coastal lowlands. A growth in population density throughout the period is very marked, and the widespread cultivation of maize is probably the main cause.

Throughout the first millennium BC, the size of settlements increased, and monumental buildings, such as temple complexes, appear in a number of areas. They came first in the Olmec lowlands, where it was necessary to practise a shifting agriculture. Similar developments are noted in the Oaxaca Valley of southern Mexico, and in the highlands in the area of the present Mexico City. The cultures are all regionally distinct, but already there is evidence of their influence on each other, and trade of fine materials, which came to include goods similar to those in the Old World – obsidian, shells and pottery.

From 500 BC onwards, it is likely that hieroglyphic writing systems were developing, though these achieve their full form only with the beginning of classic Maya civilization before c. AD 300 in Guatemala and Yucatan. Only a proportion of the Mayan glyphs or symbols can be read, but their calendar system can be interpreted. The Maya did not comprehend the movements of celestial bodies, but recorded them with great accuracy, and had mathematical notation adequate for their calculations. Their year was based on 18 months of 20 days, with an extra five days regarded as unlucky; but there was also a 260-day cycle which had ritual significance. This form of calendar was widespread in Mesoamerica, but differs from the reckoning of the Egyptians, Babylonians and Chinese, who all used variants of the lunar month, in some cases making adjustments to keep in time with the solar calendar.

As the Maya achieved prominence through the first millennium AD, so did the civilization of Teotihuacán in the valley of Mexico. This great metropolis, dominated by the pyramids of the Sun and the Moon, is estimated to have had a population

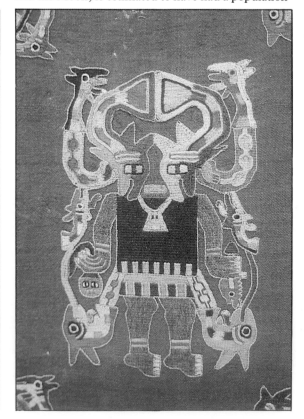

of 200,000. The pyramids rival those of Egypt in base area, but have a less steep incline. Their function was different, since they were built to raise a temple towards the sky, not to bury a dead king.

Similar temples, to a comparable pantheon of gods, were built by the Toltecs, the Aztecs, and other peoples. In Mexico City, the Aztec pyramids have been relocated in recent years alongside the Spanish cathedral built to replace them. The foundations show that one pyramid was built over another, as the old one began to sink in the lake mud and royal prestige and religious reasons demanded a grander successor.

These civilizations are distinguished by the magnificence of their art, the fearsome symbolism of some of the carved stone figures, and the apparent cruelty of their religious rites, which regularly included human sacrifice to the gods.

In Peru, agriculture was also leading to larger settlements from about 2,000 BC onwards, especially along the coast, where maize had been introduced. From about 1,800 BC pottery begins to appear, and here, too, temples and large ceremonial centres were built. These buildings and those in Mesoamerica show that, as in the Old World, religion was a powerful cohesive force in the growth of civilization. People were utterly dependent upon their crops and the good weather conditions which would allow them to grow. Their needs and faith appear to have strengthened the religious hierarchy.

Following the same pattern as in Mesoamerica, a number of local sophisticated cultures, such as the Chavin, developed and passed in Peru before the Inca civilization emerged. By the 1500s AD, the Incan empire embraced a sea-coast length of at least 4,000 km and extended 800 km inland in places. This great territory was evidently ruled by a well-organized system of government with a minimum of military force, though the remarkable Inca roads would have allowed the rapid movement of troops. In this mountainous country, where the wheel was unknown, the suspension bridge had been invented, built from ropes and wood, and bridges are recorded as crossing gaps of over 60 m.

The ancient Peruvians, who were skilled in working bronze, copper and gold, had also mastered many advanced techniques of pottery manufacture. Their arts, crafts and agricultural knowledge compared well with those of upland Mexico.

Questions raised by the evolution of civilization in the New World have often been the subject of debate. In the 1920s, theories of diffusion reigned: if civilization appeared in the New World, it must have been brought from the Old. Thor Heyerdahl sailed from the Mediterranean to South America in a papyrus boat, to show that it could be done. But of course, the demonstration that a determined person can cross the Atlantic – knowing that there is a place to aim for – does nothing to prove that anybody did this in the past.

Now the pendulum of views has swung the other way, and almost everybody believes that all American civilization was entirely indigenous. Strong arguments in favour of this belief are that American cultures are distinctive, and that there is appearance of continuous development from the first signs of cultivation several thousand years ago.

Yet from about 2,500 BC boats were sailing in the Mediterranean, which were as large as or larger than the mediaeval ships used by the European discoverers of the New World (few of which had keels more than 30 m long). These ancient ships were not made of papyrus, which would become waterlogged, but of wood. As the earliest Neolithic of north-west Europe is found on the coast, it too implies developed maritime communications at an early date.

If just three ships per day were leaving or returning to the Mediterranean, then over the course of a thousand years (from, say, 2,500 to 1,500 BC) there would have been over a million opportunities for a ship to go adrift in the Atlantic.

Textiles were highly developed in South America, and were a vehicle of artistic representation. This is a Paracas mantle from Peru. Some ancient Peruvian textiles are exceptionally well preserved because of the dry climate.

Offerings to the gods were important in all early Mesoamerican civilizations. This Toltec figure of a god at Tula, Mexico, resembles many others in its composition, with the tray for offerings mounted on the god's stomach.

The pyramid of the Sun at Teotihuacán was originally surmounted by great figures of gods. The base of the pyramid is almost the size of those in Egypt, but this building had quite a different function, serving as the base for a temple, not a tomb.

Although there is a considerable chance that this happened, it is likely that for the survivors of a shipwreck death by massacre or disease would have been the normal outcome. If low-level contact did take place, conspicuous cultural change would not be expected. Egypt and Mesopotamia, for example, had little effect upon one another's cultural style, even though artefacts and history prove that there was contact between them.

It is not, therefore, sensible to expect an archaeological answer to these speculations, but they are not trivial. The New World civilizations are certainly indigenous in style and character, but their appearance, so close in time to the emergence of civilization in the Old World, after so many thousands of years of separate development, makes the question of their origins one of enduring interest.

The Maya calendar stone. The Maya possessed a developed system of writing, and a sophisticated calendrical notation.

The growth
of architecture

Building has been important for human comfort from the earliest times. The development of formal architecture in the last few thousand years reflects new economic and social needs. Raw materials and technology have always influenced architectural style.

Among all the arts and sciences, architecture – one of the most fundamental and practically based – can be selected to offer an example of the persistence of ideas through thousands of years. By its very scale, it demands planning abilities more than almost any other human activity.

One of the most fundamental needs of human beings is a 'special' environment, constructed by human hands: enclosed space for living, ceremonial space to impress, domestic space for cooking.

In the history of architectural theories, it is especially interesting to trace the major ideas for enclosing and roofing over space. The first step, of enclosing space, was present in the Palaeolithic. The principle of pillar and lintel, or bridging, is seen in the mammoth-bone huts of Russia, and was also achieved in wood. In the postglacial world, new techniques accumulated rapidly. Mud bricks allowed imposing structures to be built.

Perhaps 10,000 years ago, in the Middle East, a transition was made from round to rectangular structures. The latter are more suitable for close packing and allow roofing with timbers cut to equal length. At about the same time, stairs appear. By the

An early arch in the ziggurat at Choga Zambil, an Elamite city in Iran.

time of the first writing, baked brick was being used in some areas, making possible more permanent and elaborate buildings. Elsewhere, including western Europe, large stone structures, such as chambered long-barrows, were being built before 3,000 BC. Larger buildings presented greater problems, solved in different ways according to local materials and aspirations.

A sure knowledge of practical geometry is shown in the plans of the major public buildings, from Egypt through to China. The great pyramids were laid out close to perfection around 2,500 BC. So too were the ziggurats and temples of Ur. Early tablets from Mesopotamia even give details of mathematical exercises, which obviously had practical application. Street plans are much less regular; full city planning had to wait for later times in most cases.

The controlling factor in a lintel was the length of timber available, or the length of stone which could be worked and lifted. In Egypt, where stone was plentiful, and used for shorter spans, the length of the date palm was the normal limitation in flat roofing. Only for special purposes would cedar in longer lengths be imported from Lebanon.

In Mesopotamia and Iran, shortages of stone and timber placed a premium on the skilled use of brickwork. The true arch had been invented by about 3,000 BC, and is found in tombs at Ur, where it is even used in simple vaulting. The idea of the arch was conserved in the area for more than 2,000 years before it spread to other regions, presumably because the need for it had not been felt elsewhere. Fine examples of arches are preserved in the ziggurat at the Elamite city of Choga Zambil, built by King Untash-napirisha in the thirteenth century BC; and also in the great gateways to Babylon from the time of Nebuchadnezzar (604–562 BC) which were faced in glazed brick, decorated with figures of animals.

In ancient Greece and in China, as in Egypt, pillar and lintel construction was the most common. Sometimes gaps could be bridged by corbelling. In this technique successive courses of masonry were edged out over a gap, until they met in the middle, providing a triangular span over a door or passage. This method was used in brick for the tomb of Ur-Nammu at Ur: in stone, it is common in the 'cyclopean' masonry (in which very large close-fitting stones are used) of Mycenae and Tiryns in Greece, several hundred years later, c. 1,500 BC.

But simple gabled buildings with lintels supported by columns remained the rule in Greece throughout classical times. There are numerous indications in the architecture of stone temples that they are derived from earlier wooden forms. This is particularly so in the pillows or capitals surmounting the columns, and in the details of the entablature above. Within this simple model, great refinements of proportion and finish were achieved. In the Parthenon, gentle convex curves were employed in the base and columns to counter the optical illusion of sagging given by straight lines.

Use of the arch was greatly extended in Roman architecture, where one of the earliest examples is the 'Cloaca Maxima', the main drain into the Tiber, which still exists. Aqueducts were supported by arches and the triumphal arch had a symbolic significance. Arches were often built out of thin bricks or tiles.

The Romans also built vaults, especially over public buildings such as baths. These are amongst the best preserved buildings at Pompeii, since the vaults survived intact, when wooden-roofed buildings collapsed or burnt.

Roman architecture is often regarded as conservative, but the use of fine vaulting in basilicas provided the ultimate model for later Christian churches. In materials, concrete was the major Roman contribution, and it was extensively used in flooring and roofing. Frequently, Roman masons used skins of fine masonry, overlying a concrete and rubble core, often bonding through with a few courses of brick to give the structure extra strength.

The arch persisted in Romanesque architecture, and was greatly refined in Gothic churches throughout the Middle Ages, when concrete, brick and tile had passed out of use, and all depended upon masonry. Pointed arches allowed their heights to be varied, greatly facilitating vaulting of spaces of varying width. Paradoxically, the finest vaulting of all, Perpendicular fan-vaulting, was rapidly replaced in the Renaissance by a return to classical-style vaulting (seen for example in the Basilica of St Peter's in Rome).

Arches were also used with great effect in Islamic architecture, in direct descent from earlier architecture of the Middle East. The dome was favoured, as in the Dome of the Rock at Jerusalem, and the Blue Mosque in Istanbul. In the Far East and in the New World, pillar and lintel construction remained the norm.

The last revolutions in architecture have come with use of iron and then steel construction within the last 200 years. This, together with the use of reinforced concrete, makes possible the construction of giant office buildings, and once more the arch has been squeezed out, except in some great bridges.

The passage down to the well, in the citadel of Mycenae, c. 1,500 BC. The passage is vaulted by corbelling. The true arch was not in use at Mycenae, and the distant door is bridged with a lintel of stone.

Fan-vaulting of the Perpendicular style at Sherborne Abbey in England (late 15th century AD). This represents the most elaborate development of bridging by means of the arch.

Early high-rise buildings were built with steel frames hidden by a cladding of more traditional style, even including arches which were not structurally necessary. Now that the structural freedom given by steel is more fully and openly exploited, the simple post-and-lintel arrangement in use before the arch was invented has again become predominant.

The course of civilization

Civilizations have risen and fallen, but civilization itself has never seriously faltered, though its focus has constantly shifted.

In the 5,000 years since the first civilizations appeared, many have risen and fallen. Earlier civilizations were enclaves of order, vulnerable to outside peoples who had no cause to respect their stability. The well-ordered society of civilization can easily break down – much more easily than is realized by most of the people who benefit from it. When all went well, societies could survive, but invasion, famine or disease could very soon upset the balance.

When a civilization collapses people are forced to rely upon themselves: they leave the 'cash' economy of surplus and return to subsistence farming. In the ancient world, this was always feasible, as unindustrialized societies are never far from their agricultural base, but the reversion would never have been achieved without great hardship. At such times, basic skills survive, but more refined levels of knowledge, shared by fewer people, are often lost.

Sometimes civilizations were taken over by others, with a transfer of power, but no fundamental change. Although most archaeologists and historians today have a greater interest in social history, administration and the arts than in battles, the key role of force throughout the development of early civilization should not be overlooked. In the very long term, after countless battles and skirmishes, the numbers and powers of the 'civilized' have now grown to the point that former aggressors have been assimilated, and the main dangers reside within the civilized world itself.

The later developments of civilization have been described in many more books than there are pages in this one. What points, then, are worth singling out, in the perspective of the millions of years which have led up to our present position?

First, a great variety has endured. It is 8 or 10,000 years since farming developed, but there are still hunters and gatherers in the world today. They are quite as intelligent as people in 'developed'

societies, but we cannot assume that they would arrive at civilization within another 8,000 years, if left to themselves; their environment may not demand or allow it. This is a purely academic question anyway, because the developments of civilization have been brought to them by others.

Major differences of environment, and hence of cultural adaptation, slowed down the progress of civilization outside its early centres. Although culture allows change, it does not necessarily encourage it, and conservatism is often rightly a strong factor. Hunters and gatherers may find it difficult to adapt to modern civilization, because the gulf between the cultures is so great as to make hybrid strategies impossible. Subsistence farmers of the present day are reluctant to adopt new methods, until they are certain that the disadvantages do not outweigh the advantages, because for them the risks of unsuccessful change are often very high.

A further restriction to the spread of civilization stemmed from the limited ability of early communities to create wealth. Subsistence farming was at the base of their economic pyramid, and although there were surpluses, they were sufficient to raise only small élites to the full benefits of civilization. In tropical Africa, climate, vegetation and animal diseases militated against this, but many of the features of civilization eventually appeared, as at Zimbabwe in the second millenium AD. In ancient Greece and Rome, prosperity became widespread, and cash farming was important, but even there, slaves and illiterate peasants were an important part of the total picture.

The unified scientific framework achieved since the Renaissance in Europe, and the technological advances which followed from it, have made prosperity and the trappings of civilization much more widely available. The rapid rise to prosperity of all the countries which became populated by settlers from Europe has depended partly upon that technology being applied to a farming and industrial

Grinding machinery at a bakery in Pompeii. This shows a simple degree of industrialization, but the grain was actually ground on site and the machines were turned by hand.

The ruins of the great enclosure at Zimbabwe (14th–16th century AD). It was built by a society who possessed several elements of formal civilization, but writing was not in use.

base, and partly upon the fund of developed skills originally transferred from the homelands. It contrasts with the great problems of acculturation in former colonies of the Third World, where choosing an appropriate balance between indigenous and imported ideas is exceptionally difficult.

All this illustrates that the transmission of ideas is not a simple matter. It is very difficult to define progress in the matter of culture. Here we have talked freely of ideas spreading, and of cultural evolution, but these remain controversial areas in archaeological theory.

As Professor Colin Renfrew has noted in his book *Before Civilization*, 'the argument has raged in many areas between those preferring a 'historical' (i.e. diffusionist) explanation and those preferring an evolutionist (i.e. independent invention) explanation for specific inventions' – that is, between diffusionists and those who believe in independent invention.

Professor Renfrew notes that diffusionist views were prevalent in Europe until the development of radiocarbon dating in 1950s, when it was shown that many developments in the later Neolithic in Europe actually appeared *earlier* there than in the civilizations which had supposedly stimulated them. Yet he does not believe that this justifies a reversion to an evolutionist approach, arguing rather that in large measure the debate is outmoded; less important than the source of an idea – inside or outside – is how it came to be accepted and developed in a society.

Thus Renfrew dismisses both diffusion and evolution as offering general explanatory principles. In his view, evolution applied to human culture need imply little more than gradual development. Broad similarities in different parts of the world cannot be explained in this way, 'for to ascribe all progress everywhere to innate properties of the mind of man is to give an explanation so general as to be meaningless'.

Renfrew was sensibly cautious in suggesting how prehistoric archaeology might arrive at a new approach, but using the language of the 'New Archaeology', an approach to archaeological interpretation which has arisen in the last 20 years, he urged the value of a 'systems' approach, a new 'paradigm', with several related 'parameters' 'which we can recognize as determining culture change'. They include the factors of population growth and density, social organization, the subsistence pattern, and contacts with other communities.

These analyses are very helpful in showing the danger of using such terms as diffusion and evolution uncritically, without attention to what is implied by them in a specific context. With much of this it is difficult to disagree, but if we throw the 'old' models out of the window, we seem to be left with just the interrelations of the parameters in the new paradigm, as a kind of endless musical chairs. If we take just the last few thousand years, a certain amount argues in favour of this. In that period there has been no time for significant biological evolution. If man is the same everywhere, a universal factor, then, the argument goes, static equilibrium models are the most appropriate for describing human society. It becomes difficult to argue that there was cultural evolution, rather than mere gradual change, because we find it difficult to say objectively what is 'primitive' and 'advanced'.

Yet a systems model postulating equilibrium does not seem to meet the pattern of long-term parallel trends towards cultural complexity operating over most of the world. We have a record of millions of years, providing a long perspective on mankind, and evolution, cultural as well as biological, is manifestly part of that perspective.

Some solution to the paradox is available from considering the different pace of biological change and cultural change. Culture itself is ultimately a part of biology, depending undeniably upon our genetic constitution for its existence. This genetic basis for the mind of modern man has probably assumed its modern form only within the last 100,000 years, although its foundations were laid much earlier.

Much as each of us has a fixed genetic constitution, but can continue to learn through a lifetime, so similarly it takes many thousands of years before the potential released by genetic changes of long ago is realized in terms of cultural complexity. There must be a relationship between the two levels of evolution, but we do not know whether in thousands or tens of thousands of years.

Archaeologists may feel that cultural evolution is too different from biological evolution to make a comparison, but the view is not shared by all evolutionary biologists. For Julian Huxley the parallels were valid, and for Bernhard Rensch, 'although it springs from a different root, the rise of man's culture has been subject to similar laws and constraints to those that have governed the evolution of other living organisms.' Just as genes are subject to natural selection, favoured in some circumstances, and discriminated against in others, so the same is true for ideas. Archaeologists will continue to seek out explanations, and indeed to debate the nature of explanation itself; but in the emergence of man, and the rise of civilization, transmission of ideas (of which diffusion is one aspect) and evolution are cardinal principles.

An astrolabe of c. AD 1400. Astrolabes were invented by the Arabs, for calculating directions in the desert, using the positions of the stars. They are the first of a series of navigational aids which were to transform travel and communications. In the west they were made with increasing precision and sophistication at the beginning of the Renaissance. Later they were replaced by the sextant.

Does the past foretell the future?

If the past is dead, why do we study it? As the present is but an instant, we are all totally dependent upon past experience for our strategies for coping with the future. An understanding of the distant past, too, can help us to plan intelligently for the future.

The growth in population is probably the greatest problem which faces the world today. The diagram shows world population between 1800 and 1980. Some have felt that a check in the rate of increase will come about only as the result of a disaster. But a check has already appeared, giving the hope that overall population will moderate.

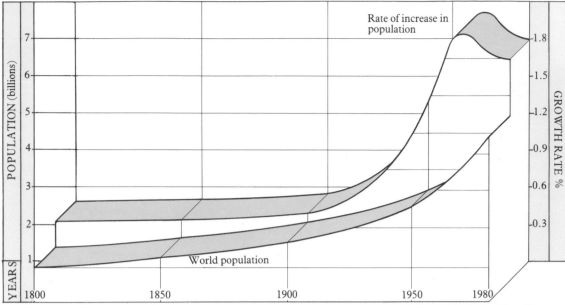

Does the value of archaeology lie only in interpreting the past? Some do not think so, and books about our evolution often finish by looking forwards, drawing lessons from the past. For those who think that the difference between us and the chimpanzees is that we have lived by killing, the message is that we are almost predestined to continue in the same way, and to have a bloody future – unless in some drastic way we collect ourselves, and 'learn' how to behave more sensibly. A similar admonition underlies the opposite theory: that hunters and gatherers had a pacific, well-organized way of life, until the pressures of the last few thousand years made us uncharacteristically brutal.

These are over-simplifications, which have an ideological – though not necessarily political – theme. It seems more realistic and rewarding to see the past as it was, as much as we are able, and to draw what conclusions we can without thinking that a new order can suddenly be obtained.

Undeniably, the present counts for far more to us than most things in the past; consequently, many accounts review early human activity as if the sole point was to lead up to us. The crude and primitive in the more distant past is enhanced, so that this part of the record can be put in its place and effectively minimized. This interpretation is convenient, but essentially wrong, because it adjusts the past to what we want it to be.

If, as we commonly accept, the lives and values of the most 'primitive' people on earth today are worth as much as those of any reader of this book, then surely each moment of the past, each person, had equal value. But to provide a coherent account, facts must be selected which are related to one another; for the purposes of generalizing and understanding, we choose those facts upon which most seems to depend.

Even in a book like this largely devoted to the Old Stone Age we cannot distinguish the difference between say 150,000 and 140,000 years ago. We do not know what the individuals of those two periods thought, felt, enjoyed and suffered, or how different they were. But we can at least appreciate that to those people, their lives were as important as ours are to us.

It is inevitable that we use the past when looking to the future; as the future by definition is not yet here, and the present is but an indefinable rolling instant, all our plans and actions are based on memories and assessments of the past. This is equally true of the smallest child and the most eminent statesman. Our choice lies in the length of past perspective which we select as being relevant. For most aspects of everyday life, we have a perspective of days, months or years.

There are reasons for clinging to a short perspective. It helps us to avoid great and insoluble questions. A long perspective can lessen our importance and make us appear insignificant. People feel comfortable with a historical background of a few thousand years: so it can be daunting to see ourselves as just one more of 50,000 generations of thinking beings. But human beings are able to come to terms with being small specks in the universe – we need only to look up at the stars – and once we adopt the long perspective, its virtue is that the extent of past human time shows us how much future time we must hope to plan for.

It is a problem that we cannot foretell the effects of our actions very far into the future. But in the past, also, change has been cumulative, largely because changes made for the good have always had consequences which have necessitated further change. Admittedly, there have been harmful effects of change, such as over-grazing, irresponsible cultivation, or warfare, but the total impact of these can be over-stressed.

It would be banal to say that because things have always gone well in the past, they always will. But leaving aside comparisons of different ways of life, it is very difficult to say that the human course has been retrograde. Looking back – whether we summarize impersonally 'this is what culture allowed', or whether we say directly 'this is what our ancestors did' – we can be thankful for the inheritance which past generations, surviving in an unbroken chain, have left us. In spite of some reprehensible actions, the people of the past on the whole acquitted themselves well – they not only survived, but steadily added to the cultural heritage. They gradually accumulated all the means which make life easier, longer and more secure. Much of this we may attribute to recent medical advances, but a great deal goes back into prehistory: skills and practices, now often forgotten, helped people to better lives, and the flexibility of culture gave their descendants the opportunity to learn afresh.

In the last 100 years two World Wars and a decreased faith in the goodness of science – which stems largely from developments in military technology – have tended to jade views about our future excessively. But at all stages of human history, social and economic constraints have restricted the use of weapons so that wars are limited in time and geographical extent. Warfare is much less acceptable morally than it was a century ago, whereas the benefits of science have been extended to many more people. If precedent counts for anything, then the long perspective suggests that we shall continue to get by.

Bridges are symbolic of human achievement. The concept of bridge-building is at least as old as the arch, but mastery of new materials – reinforced concrete and steel – has enabled advances of a dramatic kind to be made in the last two centuries. To take advantage of the materials, theory and design must also advance, but even in this century there has been an element of trial and error, and major disasters have sometimes occurred before good practice has been perfected. This process seems characteristic of human progress. The Humber bridge in Britain is one of the world's finest modern suspension bridges, although it is debated whether the great capital cost of the bridge was justified. Mankind is successful enough that it can survive without always making optimum decisions.

Appendix I: Radiocarbon dates

In this book radiocarbon dates have been expressed in the form of 'about 8,500 BC'. This approach has been adopted because a radiometric dating method not give us precise dates.

Although we know the half-life of carbon-14 (C^{14}), that is, the period in which half of a quantity of C^{14} will decay, the actual breakdowns of the radioactive isotope in a sample happen in a random fashion. In conventional radiocarbon dating, the breakdowns must therefore be counted for a long period before a precise estimate of the amount of C^{14} present can be obtained. In dating by radiocarbon-accelerator, the actual atoms of C^{14}, rather than breakdowns, are counted, but the position is somewhat similar, because the C^{14} occurs at random in the sample. There is always some remaining doubt, expressed as an error term attached to the date – normally as a ± figure, e.g. $6,500 \pm 250$ years. This does not mean that the date *must* be between 6,250 and 6,750 years, because the error term is a *standard deviation*. There is a 67 per cent chance that the date falls within one standard deviation of the mean (i.e. between 6,250 and 6,750 years) and a 95 per cent chance that it falls within two standard deviations of the mean (i.e. between 6,000 and 7,000 years). Some laboratories can achieve high precision measurements (e.g. ± 15 years), and precision can also be improved by measuring a number of samples from the same context.

'Raw' radiocarbon dates are expressed in a timescale of years BP (before present, taken as 1950), calculated on the assumption that the half-life of radiocarbon is 5,568 years. 5,730 is now known to be a more accurate estimate, but radiocarbon daters have agreed not to make the alteration (only 3 per cent in any case), because of the confusion which would be caused, and also because the revised dates would not be more 'real'. Even when measured as precisely as possible, radiocarbon years do not correspond absolutely with real calendar years.

This is because rates of C^{14} production in the upper atmosphere have varied at times in the past. Fortunately, the extent of the variations through the last few thousand years has been assessed 'dendrochronology', the construction of chronologies from tree rings. Precise time-scales back to about 7,000 BC can be provided by a continuous record of old trees such as the bristle-cone pine and sequoia of western America, and the oak in Europe. When radiocarbon dates for rings of a certain age are plotted against the real ages, curves can be constructed, which can then be used to correct or 'calibrate' other radiocarbon dates. If radiocarbon ages corresponded exactly with real ages, the curve would be a straight line, but as radiocarbon levels have varied considerably in the past, it is actually an irregular 'wiggly' curve.

As the tree-ring record does not extend beyond the Holocene, Palaeolithic dates have to be taken without correction, and so the dates stand as they are, or 1,950 years are deducted to make them BC. Comparisons with uranium dates suggest that discrepancies are not more than 2,000 years in the past 30,000 years.

For the early Holocene, also, radiocarbon years can be treated approximately as calendar years, but the last few thousand years need special care. Around 3,000 BC, the difference between raw and calibrated dates can be as much as 500 years, so that a radiocarbon date of about 5,000 BP is after calibration not around 3,000 BC, but 3,500 BC in calendar years. (Some archaeologists use small letters – ad, bc – for uncalibrated dates, to emphasize that calibration has not been performed; but ideally, raw radiocarbon dates should be expressed only on the BP scale).

On the time-scale of this book, calibration has not been of major importance, because before 7,000–6,000 BC we do not know how much to add or subtract. At some point, however, we must encounter the dislocation between radiocarbon and historical dates, unless we perform calibration. Where this should be a major issue is in the approach to Egyptian and Mesopotamian civilization, but in practice there are pitifully few radiocarbon dates occupying the thousand years 4,000–3,000 BC.

Thus we can slide from a few calibrated radiocarbon dates to the historical chronology, just noting that the final predynastic periods become a few hundred years longer when calibration is applied, and that calibrated radiocarbon dates coincide very well with the historical chronologies in the period 3,000–2,500 BC. Where it is necessary to compare radiocarbon dates for later prehistory in Europe with historical dates for the Middle Eastern civilizations, calibration is of course a critical factor.

A calibration curve for radiocarbon dates prepared from dating results of tree ring samples of known age. As an example, a value of 4,500 radiocarbon years BP reads off as C. 3,000 BC on the calibrated scale. A real date would be expressed with its statistical uncertainty, which is also reflected in the calibration.

The parameters of the earth's orbit vary in a cyclical way. The effects of the three main factors through the Upper Pleistocene are illustrated here.

RADIOCARBON YEARS BP

UNCALIBRATED EXPRESSED AD/BC

CALIBRATED AGE

| BC | 6,000 | 5.000 | 4,000 | 3,000 | 2,000 | 1,000 | 0 | 1,000 | AD |

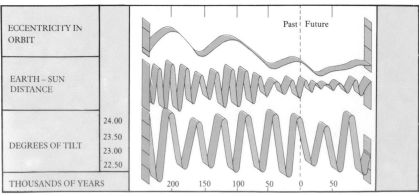

ECCENTRICITY IN ORBIT

EARTH – SUN DISTANCE

DEGREES OF TILT
24.00
23.50
23.00
22.50

THOUSANDS OF YEARS

Past | Future

200   150   100   50   0   50

Recent research has led to astonishing advances in our knowledge of ice-age chronology.

Ice ages have occurred at several stages in the earth's history, notably at about 700 million and 300 million years ago, and then again in the last 3 million years. It has been suggested that the position of the continents relative to the poles, and the distribution of land and sea, have an effect in inducing ice ages, but it is likely that there are also other factors.

The fluctuations which occur within an ice age are much better understood. Their history through the last 2 million years is recorded with extraordinary completeness in the ocean cores, in which some well-dated events can be recognized (see pp 28–29).

The advances in our knowledge have been achieved by the use of precise information about variations in the earth's orbit. The idea that changes in orbital parameters might affect climate in a cyclical way was set forward by the Yugoslav mathematician M. Milankovitch in the 1920s. In the last few years, the theory has become much easier to test, because of the existence of the cores, more sophisticated mathematical methods for analysing their 'periodicities', and more precise calculations of the time period involved in variations in the earth's orbit. Variations in earth-sun distance, in the tilt of the earth's axis, and the eccentricity of its orbit, happen in measurable cycles, which are clearly recognizable in the cores. The main cycle lengths are about 100,000, 40,000 and 20,000 years.

These measurements offer the hope of a master chronology of the Pleistocene, accurate to within a few thousand years. This will not come from a single core, because of interruptions, such as breaks in deposition, but from a compound record of cores.

Appendix II: Ice ages— the orbital chronometer

SOME KEY DATES IN YEARS BP (⋆ = CALIBRATED C¹⁴ DATES WITH 95 PER CENT CONFIDENCE RANGE)			
Iraq, skeleton Meskalamdug (BM-64)	C^{14}	3,920 ± 150 (2,875–2,095 BC)*	YEARS BP
Iraq, skeleton Queen Puabi (BM-76)	C^{14}	3,990 ± 150 (2,905–2,160 BC)*	
Egypt, Tarkhan, reign of King Djet	C^{14}	4,150 ± 110 (3,020–2,420 BC)*	
Egypt, Tarkhan, reign of King Djet	C^{14}	4,160 ± 1,100 (3,030–2,425 BC)*	
Jericho, PPNB (BM-1320)	C^{14}	8,540 ± 65	
Jericho, PPNA (BM-252)	C^{14}	9,582 ± 89	
Jericho, Natufian (BM-1407)	C^{14}	11,090 ± 90	
Stellmoor, Ahrensburgian (Y-159-2)	C^{14}	10,320 ± 250	
Gönnersdorf, Magdalenian (Ly-768)	C^{14}	12,380 ± 230	
Meadowcroft, Palaeo Indian (SI-2354)	C^{14}	16,175 ± 975	
Meadowcroft, lowest occupation (SI-2060)	C^{14}	19,600 ± 2,400	
Laugerie-Haute, Middle Solutrean (GrN-4495)	C^{14}	19,740 ± 140	
Abri Pataud, Perigordian IV (GrN-4477)	C^{14}	26,600 ± 200	
Abri Pataud, early Aurignacian (GrN-4507)	C^{14}	34,250 ± 675	
Lake Mungo 2, NSW (ANU-331)	C^{14}	32,750 ± 1,250	
La Quina, late Mousterian (GrN-2526)	C^{14}	35,250 ± 530	
Border Cave, early LSA (Pta-446)	C^{14}	37,500 ± 1,200	
Istállóskö, early 'Aurignacian'	C^{14}	39,800 ± 900	
Haua Fteah, late Mousterian (GrN-2564)	C^{14}	43,400 ± 1,300	
Nahal Zin, Middle-Upper Palaeolithic transition	C^{14}	45,000 ± 2,400	
	Uranium	46,500 ± 2,900	
Border Cave, MSA (Pta-1274)	C^{14}	47,200 + 4,200 − 2,750	
Shanidar, level D Mousterian (GrN–1495)	C^{14}	50,600 ± 3,000	
Tata, Hungary, Mousterian	Uranium	101 ± 12	KYR (THOUSANDS)
Tata, Hungary, Mousterian	Uranium	109 ± 15	
Pech de l'Azé, France	Uranium	123 ± 15	
Last Interglacial	Uranium (many dates)	c.127 ± 5	
La Chaise, France, Bed 11	Uranium	145 ± 16	
Zuttiyeh Cave, Jabrudian	Uranium	c.148	
Gademotta, Ethiopia, early MSA	K/Ar	149 ± 13	
Gademotta, Ethiopia, early MSA	K/Ar	181 ± 6	
Kapthurin, Kenya, over Acheulean	K/Ar	230 ± 8	
La Cotte, Jersey, basal (OxTL222)	TL	238 ± 35	
Tautavel, Arago	TL	c.350	
Olorgesailie, Acheulean	K/Ar	425 ± 9	
Olorgesailie, Acheulean	K/Ar	c.486	
Brunhes-Matuyama transition	K/Ar	c.0.734 ± 10	MYR (MILLIONS)
Isernia, Italy	K/Ar	0.73 ± 0.04	
Kariandusi, Kenya	K/Ar	c.0.95–1.1	
Karari Tuff, E. Turkana	K/Ar	1.32 ± 0.10	
Okote Tuff, E. Turkana	K/Ar	1.56 ± 0.02	
Chesowanja Basalt	K/Ar	1.42 ± 0.07	
Pliocene-Pleistocene boundary	(K/Ar)	c.1.6	
KBS Tuff (E. Turkana)	K/Ar	1.8 ± 0.1	
Olduvai Bed I (Tuff Ib)	K/Ar	1.79 ± 0.03	
Olduvai Bed I (basalt)	K/Ar	1.96 ± 0.09	
Omo, Shungura, Tuff F	K/Ar	2.06 ± 0.10	

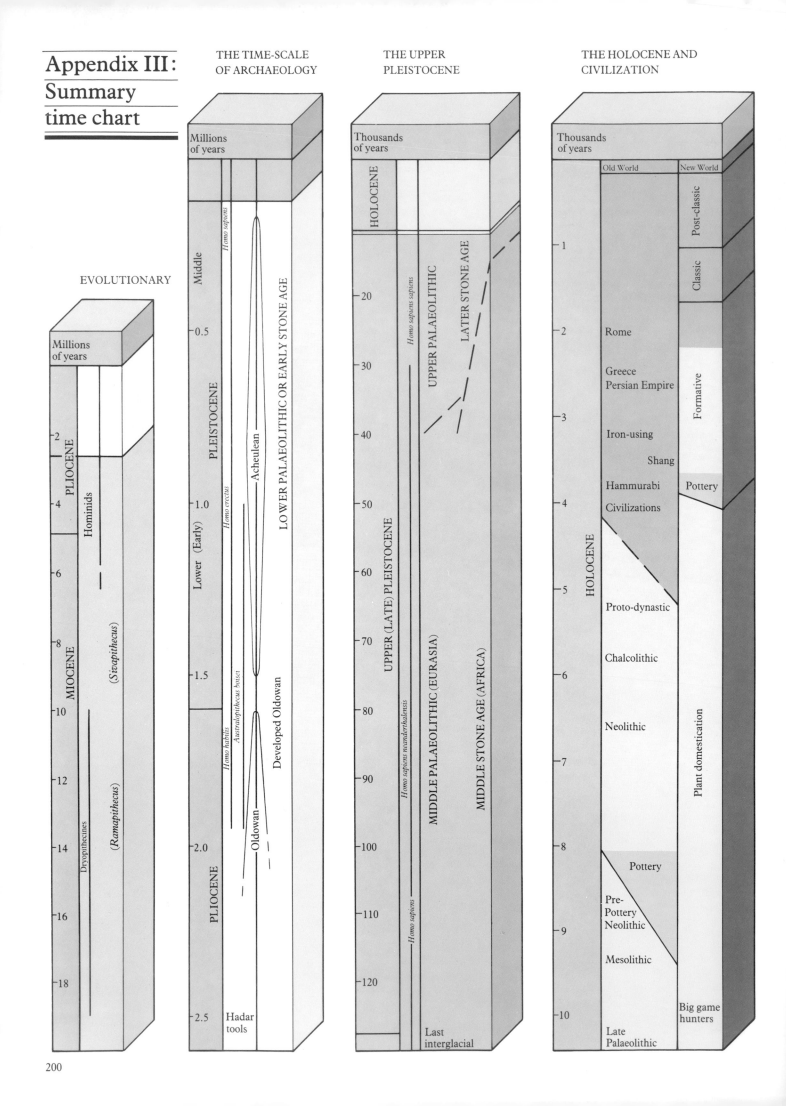

Appendix III: Summary time chart

THE TIME-SCALE OF ARCHAEOLOGY

THE UPPER PLEISTOCENE

THE HOLOCENE AND CIVILIZATION

EVOLUTIONARY

Millions of years

MIOCENE

Dryopithecines

(Ramapithecus)

(Sivapithecus)

PLIOCENE

Hominids

2
4
6
8
10
12
14
16
18

Millions of years

Middle

Homo sapiens

PLEISTOCENE

Lower (Early)

Homo erectus

Homo habilis

Australopithecus boisei

Acheulean

Developed Oldowan

Oldowan

LOWER PALAEOLITHIC OR EARLY STONE AGE

PLIOCENE

Hadar tools

0.5
1.0
1.5
2.0
2.5

Thousands of years

HOLOCENE

Homo sapiens sapiens

UPPER PALAEOLITHIC

LATER STONE AGE

UPPER (LATE) PLEISTOCENE

Homo sapiens neanderthalensis

MIDDLE PALAEOLITHIC (EURASIA)

MIDDLE STONE AGE (AFRICA)

Homo sapiens

Last interglacial

20
30
40
50
60
70
80
90
100
110
120

Thousands of years

Old World | New World

Post-classic

Classic

Rome

Greece
Persian Empire

Iron-using

Shang

Hammurabi

Civilizations

Proto-dynastic

Chalcolithic

Neolithic

Pottery

Pre-Pottery Neolithic

Mesolithic

Late Palaeolithic

HOLOCENE

Formative

Pottery

Plant domestication

Big game hunters

1
2
3
4
5
6
7
8
9
10

ACHEULEAN: the tradition of tool-making characterized by hand-axes; widespread in Africa, Europe and parts of Asia, total duration c. 1.5 million to 150,000 years ago, named after St Acheul in France.

AHRENSBURGIAN: a Late Palaeolithic tradition of northern Germany, characterized by shouldered points, tanged for fitting to arrow shafts (c. 10,000 BP).

ARTEFACT: any man-made object, from a stone flake or pot to a spacecraft.

ATERIAN: a Middle Palaeolithic tradition of north-west Africa characterized by pressure-flaked points and tanged points.

AURIGNACIAN: the first major Upper Palaeolithic tradition of Europe which started c. 34,000 years ago in France; characterized by long retouched blades, steep scrapers and split-base bone points.

AUSTRALOPITHECUS: the earliest defined genus of hominid (almost all specimens occur in the time-range 4.0–1.3 million years ago). The following species have been named:
A. afarensis – early form in Ethiopia
A. africanus – early form in Southern Africa
A. robustus – later robust form in southern Africa
A. boisei – later robust form in East Africa

BADARIAN: a predynastic Egyptian culture, of the early fourth millennium BC.

BIPEDALISM: the habit of walking on two feet; apes can walk bipedally for short distances, but of the mammals, only the hominids became fully adapted to bipedal walking.

BLADE: a long and narrow stone flake; a blade must be at least twice as long as broad. Blades became much favoured in the Upper Palaeolithic, but are found in some earlier phases. In the Upper Palaeolithic they were sometimes struck with punches.

BLADELET: a small blade of the type used in the Upper Palaeolithic.

BP: Before Present. In the radiocarbon time-scale this is measured from AD 1950.

BRONZE AGE: the first major metal age; starts at different times in different parts of the world: c. 3,000 BC in the Middle East, 2,000 BC in western Europe and China. There is no formal Bronze Age in the New World.

BULB OF PERCUSSION: the cone-like shape on the fracture surface of a stone flake, which indicates the place where the hammer struck.

CHALCOLITHIC: the copper age which intervenes between the Neolithic and Bronze Age in areas of early metal-working, c. 5,000–3,000 BC.

CHÂTELPERRONIAN: the earliest Upper Palaeolithic tradition in France beginning c. 34,000 years ago.

CHOPPER: a stone tool with a working edge formed by flakes removed from two directions. Found in the Oldowan, but can also appear in recent industries.

CLACTONIAN: an early flake industry known from several sites in south-east England, probably of Hoxnian age. The name has also been used in other parts of Europe.

CHROMOSOMES: thread-like structures occurring in every cell of an organism and carrying the inherited characteristics of the organism. They are composed of DNA.

CLEAVER: a form of biface found alongside the hand-axe on Acheulean sites especially in Africa. Cleavers have a transverse or oblique cutting edge much like an axe.

COLLAGEN: the major protein of bone constituting about 20 per cent by weight in fresh bone; the organic component of bone used in radiocarbon dating – the inorganic component is largely calcium phosphate.

CONTINENTAL SHELF: area surrounding a continental land mass and largely covered by shallow sea. More of the shelf is exposed in glacial periods, when sea-level is low.

CORE: the piece of stone which a stone-knapper works, so as to produce flakes. Early choppers and polyhedrons can be regarded as core tools; cores occur in specialized forms, e.g. Levallois core, prismatic core.

CUNEIFORM: the term employed to describe early writing in the Middle East in which wedge-shaped impressions are left on a clay tablet.

CURSIVE: rounded forms of script used in everyday informal writing, usually on papyrus, paper or wax.

DNA: Deoxyribonucleic acid; thread-like molecules found in chromosomes (and some viruses), which store the genetic code.

DRYOPITHECINES: a group of fossil apes of the Miocene period.

ELECTRON MICROSCOPE: a microscope in which an electron beam is used to illuminate the object, allowing much greater resolution than in a light microscope. Enlargement of up to 200,000

times has been achieved. Scanning electron microscopes allow a sharp image of three-dimensional detail.

EVENT: a magnetic polarity event is a relatively short period in which magnetic direction is different from that of the general epoch.

FAULT: a fracture in geological strata caused by stress. The movement of the rocks on the two sides of the fault can be horizontal or vertical, and varies from centimetres to many kilometres.

FLAKE: a piece struck from a core. It usually shows characteristics of conchoidal fracture, such as a bulb of percussion and concentric rings.

FLINT: a rock highly suitable for stone-working, and found as nodules or tablets in chalk and limestone, or re-deposited as pebbles in clay and gravels. A black, grey or brown coloured material, with conchoidal fracture.

FOSSIL: a preserved organism of Pleistocene or earlier age; the original material may have been replaced by mineral matter, but this need not be so. Holocene remains are sometimes called 'sub-fossil'.

GENE: a unit based on a chromosome, controlling an individual inherited characteristic. A sequence of three nucleic acids in the chromosome controls the coding of a particular protein.

GEOMAGNETIC REVERSAL: a reversal of the earth's magnetic field, in which the magnetic poles switch positions, moving from north to south and vice versa. This has happened several times within the past 2 million years.

GLACIAL PERIOD OR GLACIATION: ice age cold periods, in which ice-caps and glaciers expanded. Strictly speaking, glaciation refers to the action rather than period. Even in the glacial periods large parts of the land surface were ice-free.

GRAVETTIAN: the second major Upper Palaeolithic tradition of Europe, extending from Russia to Spain, and lasting from c. 27,000 BC to 19,000 BC. Known as the Upper Perigordian in France.

GÜNZ: the early glaciation in the Alpine sequence preceding the Mindel.

HAND-AXE: the most characteristic tool of the Acheulean, also known as *biface*, on account of the two worked surfaces. Normally 8–30 cm long.

HIEROGLYPHICS: literally 'sacred signs' (from the Greek), a formal style of

ancient Egyptian writing. Also applied broadly to other scripts, e.g. the Mayan.

HOLOCENE: the last 10,000 post-glacial years.

HOLSTEIN: an interglacial of north-west Europe, preceding the Saale.

HOMINIDS: the family of man, including all species of *Australopithecus* and *Homo*.

HOMINOIDEA: the superfamily including the hominids and pongids.

HOMO: the genus of man. Species commonly recognized are as follows:
Homo habilis – late Pliocene/early Pleistocene
Homo erectus – early/middle Pleistocene
Homo sapiens, consisting of the two subspecies:
Homo sapiens neanderthalensis – late middle/late Pleistocene
Homo sapiens sapiens – late Pleistocene/Holocene

HOXNIAN: an interglacial recognized at Hoxne in eastern England, and probably corresponding to the Holstein of northern Europe. Probably c. 330,000 years BP.

INDUS CIVILIZATION: an early civilization of the Indus Valley in Pakistan, from c. 2,400 to 1,700 BC.

INTERGLACIAL: a warm period intervening between glacial periods; usually lasting for 10,000 years or more, and as warm as or warmer than the present.

INTERSTADIAL: a short relatively warm period in a glacial period.

IRON AGE: the third major epoch of traditional archaeological classification. Iron became common from c. 1,200 BC.

JABRUDIAN: a stone industry of the Lower/Middle Palaeolithic transition in the Middle East, c. 150,000 BP.

KARARI INDUSTRY: an early stone industry (c. 1.5 Myr) found on sites of the Karari escarpment at East Turkana. It can be classified within the Developed Oldowan.

KNAPPER: a person who works stone tools, using the principles of percussion and conchoidal fracture.

LATE STONE AGE (LSA): the later stages of the Palaeolithic in Africa and parts of Asia characterized by the use of microlithic tools.

LEVALLOIS TECHNIQUE: a sophisticated technique of stone-working in which artefacts are pre-shaped on the core by flaking and then 'released' with a single blow.

MAGDALENIAN: the principal Upper Palaeolithic tradition of western Europe from about 16,000 to about 10,000 BC.

MESOLITHIC: the Stone Age epoch which succeeds the

Palaeolithic in Europe, about 10,000 years ago. Characterized by use of microliths, and adaptations to post-glacial environment. Also occasionally used for contemporary phases in Middle East and North Africa, which are otherwise known as final Palaeolithic or Epipalaeolithic.

MICROLITH: a small stone artefact, normally under 3 cm long, used in composite tools, e.g. arrow-tips, sickle-blades. Predominant in Mesolithic and African and Indian Later Stone Age.

MIDDLE STONE AGE (MSA): part of the Palaeolithic, in Africa, and some areas of Asia, occupying a period from c. 180,000 years ago at earliest to c. 10,000 at latest, and loosely corresponding with the Middle Palaeolithic of other areas.

MINDEL: a glaciation in the classic Alpine sequence, named after the River Mindel, and now taken to represent a long and complex cold period, over 300,000 years old.

MIOCENE: (23–5 million years ago) the geological period of the Tertiary, in which apes evolved towards modern forms, and which encompasses hominid origins.

NEOLITHIC: the New Stone Age. Originally classified by the presence of polished stone tools, now usually used for societies with food production and pottery, after c. 7,000 BC. Only used in Old World, often poorly defined.

OLDOWAN: the oldest widely-recognized tradition of tool-making, found at Olduvai and other sites in Africa. Early sites at Hadar and Omo can be set within this tradition.

OLIGOCENE: the period of the Tertiary in which the first apes appear, c. 130 million years ago.

PALAEOLITHIC: the Old Stone Age; on current estimates it begins 2.6 million years ago and finishes 10,000 years ago or later.

PAPYRUS: a reed-like plant formerly found along the Nile in Egypt from which the Egyptians made a form of paper.

PERIGORDIAN: an Upper Palaeolithic tradition divided into Lower Perigordian (Châtelperronian) and Upper Perigordian (Gravettian); many French archaeologists do not postulate a close connection between the two.

PHOTOMICROGRAPH: a photograph taken through a microscope (optical or electron).

PLEISTOCENE: a geological period (1.6 million–10,000 years ago) coinciding approximately with the appearance and development of *Homo*.

PLIOCENE: (5.0–1.6 Myr) the final period of the Tertiary, immediately preceding the Pleistocene and having the earliest hominids and archaeological sites.

POTASSIUM-ARGON: an important dating method for Middle Pleistocene and older periods applicable only to volcanic rocks, in which radioactive potassium (K) breaks down yielding radiogenic argon (Ar).

PRE-AURIGNACIAN: a late Lower Palaeolithic/Middle Palaeolithic industry in the Middle East and North Africa distinguished by long flake-blades.

PRIMATES: the order of mammals including man, the apes, Old and New World monkeys, lemurs, lorises and tarsiers. Probably originally aboreal (tree-living), but many species have become adapted to terrestrial life.

PROTEINS: important nitrogenous organic compounds composed of chains of amino-acids in specific sequences; e.g. collagen, the structural protein of bone and cartilage.

QUATERNARY: nominally, the fourth and most recent major system of geological time, comprising the Pleistocene and Holocene. The term is widely used for convenience, but the Quaternary is not heralded by major geological changes, and is effectively part of the Tertiary.

RADIOCARBON DATING: a dating method important for the last 50,000 years. Measurements are made of the surviving proportion of radioactive carbon in organic substances.

RAMAPITHECUS: a genus of Miocene apes found in Africa, Europe and Asia, believed by some authors to be an ancestral hominid.

RISS: the penultimate Alpine glaciation; a long and complex period starting c. 300,000 years ago, and finishing c. 130,000 years ago.

SAALE: the equivalent of the Riss glaciation, as named further north in Europe.

SANGOAN: a late variant of the Acheulean in parts of southern Africa, coeval with some Middle Stone Age industries.

SCRAPER: a class of stone tools, having retouch along one or more edges. Not necessarily used for scraping.

SIVAPITHECUS: a genus of Miocene ape found in Asia and Africa, some species having affinities with the orang-utan. A skull found in Pakistan dates to 8 million years.

SOLUTREAN: a tradition of the Upper Palaeolithic, found in south-west Europe, about 20,000 years ago. Important in Spain as well as southern France. Characterized by very finely worked laurel-leaf points.

STADIAL: the colder stages of any ice age.

STILLBAY: a name applied to some Middle Stone Age industries in eastern Africa, characterized by small lance-like points.

TANGED POINT: a projectile point with a shaped projection at the base to assist in hafting.

TERTIARY: the geological system lasting from about 65 million years ago to the beginning of the Pleistocene (or to present: see Quaternary).

TILL: boulder clay or drift. Material deposited by glaciers or rivers running from glaciers, ranging through from clay to sand, gravel and boulders.

TRADITION: the name given to a grouping of Palaeolithic industries of similar character; often known as an industrial tradition, or even cultural tradition.

TRAVERTINE: a form of freshwater limestone or tufa deposited by hot springs in volcanic regions. Sometimes synonymous with tufa.

TUFA: a name for deposits largely composed of calcium carbonate and formed by deposition from solution, usually in limestone regions, in caves and around springs.

TUFF: a rock formed by the hardening of volcanic ash or dust. Tuffs may be composed of volcanic glass fragments, crystal chips or the debris of older rocks.

URANIUM SERIES DATING: a dating method based on the radioactive decay of uranium (U) and its daughter elements. Limited to shells, corals and limestone deposits, useful up to c. 300,000 years.

WÜRM: the last ice age, occupying most of the last 100,000 years. Known as the Wisconsin in North America, the Devensian in Britain.

Chinese Transliteration
As some site names have been well-known for many years, an abbreviated version of the Wade-Giles system has been used. The following equivalents may be useful:

WADE-GILES	PINYIN
Hsi-hou-tu	Xihoudu
Yüan-mou	Yuanmou
Yang Yüan	Yang Yuan
Chou-k'ou-tien	Zhoukoudian
Ting-ts'un	Dingcun
Ma-pa	Maba
Hsin-tung	Xindong
Shui-yen	Shuiyan
Ho-mu-tu	Hemudu
Ta-p'en-k'eng	Dapenkeng
Pan-p'o	Banpo
Yang-shao	Yangshao
Pan-shan	Banshan
Lung-shan	Longshan

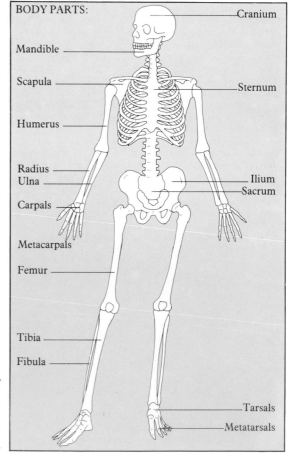

BODY PARTS:
Cranium
Mandible
Scapula
Sternum
Humerus
Radius
Ulna
Ilium
Sacrum
Carpals
Metacarpals
Femur
Tibia
Fibula
Tarsals
Metatarsals

GENERAL BOOKS ON PREHISTORY AND THE PALAEOLITHIC

Bordes, F. *The Old Stone Age*. McGraw Hill. New York. 1968.

Braidwood, R. *Prehistoric Men*. Chicago Natural History Museum. Chicago. 1957 (3rd edn.).

Clark, J.G.D. *World Prehistory in New Perspective*. Cambridge University Press. Cambridge. 1974 (3rd edn.).

Coles, J.M. & Higgs, E.S. *The Archaeology of Early Man*. Faber and Faber. London. 1968.

Hodges, H. *Artifacts*. John Baker. London. 1964.

Howell, F.C. *Early Man*. Time-Life International. 1971.

Sherratt, A. (ed.) *The Cambridge Encyclopaedia of Archaeology*. Cambridge University Press. Cambridge. 1980.

Wymer, J. *The Palaeolithic Age*. Croom Helm. London. 1982.

SOME BOOKS OF HISTORICAL IMPORTANCE

Breasted, J.H. *The Conquest of Civilization*. Harpers. New York. 1926.

Bronowski, J. *The Ascent of Man*. BBC. London. 1973.

Childe, V.G. *The Dawn of European Civilization*. Routledge and Kegan Paul. London. 1925.

Childe, V.G. *Social Evolution*. Watts. London 1951.

Darwin, C. *The Descent of Man*. John Murray. London. 1874 (2nd edn.).

Drummond, H. *The Ascent of Man*. Hodder and Stoughton. London. 1901.

Flint, R.F. *Glacial and Pleistocene Geology*. Wiley. New York. 1957.

Huxley, T.H. *Man's Place in Nature*. Macmillan. London. 1863.

Oakley, K.P. *Frameworks for Dating Fossil Man*. Weidenfeld and Nicholson. London. 1966.

Read, C. *The Origin of Man*. Cambridge University Press. Cambridge. 1920.

MANKIND AND EVOLUTIONARY BIOLOGY

Hamburg, D.A. & McCown, E.R. (eds.) *The Great Apes*. Benjamin. Menlo Park, California. 1979.

Huxley, J. *Evolution: the Modern Synthesis*. George Allen and Unwin. London. 1974 (3rd edn.)

Rensch, B. *Homo sapiens: vom Tier zum Halbgott*. Vandenhoek and Ruprecht. Gottingen. 1972.

Young, J.Z. *An Introduction to the Study of Man*. Oxford University Press. 1974.

PHYSICAL ANTHROPOLOGY AND HUMAN EVOLUTION

Ardrey, R. *African Genesis*. Collins. London. 1961.

Ardrey, R. *The Hunting Hypothesis*. Collins. London. 1976.

Boyce, A.J. (ed.) *Chromosome Variations in Human Evolution*. Taylor and Francis. London. 1975.

Buettner-Janusch, J. *The Origins of Man*. Wiley. New York. 1966.

Day, M. *Guide to Fossil Man*. Cassell. London. 1977 (3rd edn.).

Isaac, G.Ll. & McCown, E.R. (eds.) *Human Origins*. Benjamin. Menlo Park, California. 1976.

Johanson, D.C. & Edey, M.A. *Lucy*. Granada. London. 1981.

Katz, S.H. (ed.) *Biological Anthropology*. Readings from Scientific American. 1975.

Leakey, R.E. & Lewin, R. *Origins*. Macdonald and Jane's. London. 1977.

Pfeiffer, J.E. *The Emergence of Man*. Harper and Row. New York. 1972 (2nd edn.).

Reader, J. *Missing Links: the Hunt for Earliest Man*. Collins, London; Little, Brown, Boston. 1981.

Washburn, S.L. *The Study of Human Evolution*. University of Oregon Press. Oregon. 1968.

Wood, B.A. *Human Evolution*. Chapman and Hall. London. 1978.

HUNTERS AND GATHERERS

Lee, R.B. & DeVore, I. (**eds.**) *Man the Hunter*. Aldine. Chicago. 1968.

Thomas, E.M. *The Harmless People*. Secker and Warburg. London. 1959.

Turnbull, C. *The Forest People*. Pan. London. 1961.

ETHNOARCHAEOLOGY AND TAPHONOMY

Binford, L.R. *Bones: Ancient Men and Modern Myths*. Academic Press. New York. 1981.

Brain, C.K. *The Hunters or the Hunted? An Introduction to African Cave Taphonomy*. University of Chicago Press. Chicago. 1981.

Behrensmeyer, A.K. & Hill, A.P. (eds.) *Fossils in the Making: Vertebrate Taphonomy and Paleoecology*. University of Chicago Press. Chicago. 1980.

Yellen, J.E. *Archaeological Approaches to the Present: Models for Reconstructing the Past*. Academic Press. New York. 1977.

PLEISTOCENE GEOLOGY, ENVIRONMENTAL CHANGE AND

ARCHAEOLOGICAL SCIENCE

Aitken, M.J. *Physics and Archaeology*. Clarendon Press. Oxford. 1974 (2nd edn.).

Baillie, M.G.L. *Tree-ring Dating and Archaeology*. Croom Helm. London. 1982.

Bowen, D.O. *Quaternary Geology*. Pergamon Press. Oxford. 1978.

Butzer, K.W. *Environment and Archaeology: an Ecological Approach to Prehistory*. Aldine. Chicago. 1971.

Goudie, A.S. *Environmental Change*. Clarendon Press. Oxford. 1977.

Hedges, R.E.M. Radiocarbon dating with an accelerator: review and preview. *Archaeometry* 23, 1, 3–18. 1981.

Imbrie, J. & Imbrie, K.P. *Ice Ages: Solving the Mystery*. Macmillan. London. 1979.

Keeley, L.H. *Experimental Determination of Stone Tool Uses*. University of Chicago Press. Chicago. 1978.

Klein, J., Lerman, J.C., Damon, P.E. & Ralph, E.K. Calibration of radiocarbon dates. *Radiocarbon* 24, 103–150. 1982.

Tooley, M.J. *Sea-level Changes: North-West England during the Flandrian Stage*. Clarendon Press. Oxford. 1978.

West, R.G. *Pleistocene Geology and Biology*. Longman. London. 1977 (3rd edn.).

ARCHAEOLOGY OF THE EARLY SITES

Bishop, W.W. (ed.) *Geological Background to Fossil Man*. Scottish Academic Press. Edinburgh. 1978.

Butzer, K.W. & Isaac, G.Ll. (eds.) *After the Australopithecines*. Mouton. The Hague. 1975.

Chinese Academy of Sciences. *Atlas of Primitive Man in China*. Science Press. Peking. 1980.

Clark, J.D. (ed.) *The Cambridge History of Africa. Volume I: From the Earliest Times to c. 500 BC*. Cambridge University Press. Cambridge. 1982.

Gowlett, J.A.J. Mental abilities of early man. In Foley, R.A. (ed.) *Community Ecology and Human Adaptation in the Pleistocene*. Academic Press. London. 1984.

Holloway, R.L. The casts of fossil hominid brains. In Isaac and Leakey (eds.), *Human Ancestors*, 74–83.

Isaac, G.Ll. & Leakey, R.E.F. (eds.) *Human Ancestors*. Readings from Scientific American.

Freeman. San Francisco. 1979.

Perlès, C. L'homme préhistorique et le feu. *La Recherche* 60, 6, 829–839. 1975.

Roche, H. *Premiers outils taillés d'Afrique*. Société d'Ethnographie. Paris. 1981.

Young, J.Z., Jope, E.M. & Oakley, K.P. (eds.) *The Emergence of Man*. Royal Society of London. 1981.

Olduvai

Hay, R.L. *Geology of the Olduvai Gorge*. California University Press. California. 1976.

Leakey, M.D. *Olduvai Gorge, Volume III*. Cambridge University Press. Cambridge. 1971.

Leakey, M. *Olduvai Gorge: My Search for Early Man*. Collins. London. 1979.

Lake Turkana

Coppens, Y., Howell, F.C., Isaac, G.Ll. & Leakey, R.E.F. (eds.) *Earliest Man and Environments in the East Rudolf Basin*. University of Chicago Press. Chicago. 1976.

Leakey, M.G. & Leakey, R.E. (eds.) *Koobi Fora Research Project*, Volume I: *The Fossil Hominids and an Introduction to their Context*. Clarendon Press. Oxford. 1978.

Chesowanja

Bishop, W., Hill, A. & Pickford, M. Chesowanja: a revised geological interpretation. In Bishop, W.W. (ed.), *Geological Background to Fossil Man*, 309-328. 1978.

Gowlett, J.A.J., Harris, J.W.K., Walton, D. & Wood, B.A. Early archaeological sites, hominid remains and traces of fire from Chesowanja, Kenya. *Nature* 294, 125–129.

Kilombe

Gowlett, J.A.J. Kilombe – an Acheulian site complex in Kenya. In Bishop, W.W. (ed.), *Geological Background to Fossil Man*, 337–360. 1978.

Gowlett, J.A.J. Procedure and form in a Lower Palaeolithic industry: stoneworking at Kilombe, Kenya. *Studia Praehistorica Belgica* 2, 101–109. 1982.

Olorgesailie

Isaac, G.Ll. *Olorgesailie*. University of Chicago Press. Chicago. 1977.

Shipman, P., Bosler, W. & Davis, K.L. Butchering of giant geladas at an Acheulian site. *Current Anthropology* 22, 257–264. 1981.

MIDDLE PALAEOLITHIC AND MIDDLE STONE AGE

Allchin, F.R. & Hammond,

N. (eds.) *The Archaeology of Afghanistan*. Academic Press. New York. 1978.

Bordes, F. *A Tale of Two Caves*. Harper and Row. New York. 1972

Callow, P. & Cornford, J. (eds.) *La Cotte de St Brelade: the Charles McBurney Excavations*. (In press)

Cauvin, J. (ed.) *Préhistoire du Levant*. CNRS. Paris. 1981.

Coon, C.S. *Seven Caves*. Jonathan Cape. London. 1957.

De Lumley, H. (ed.) *La Préhistoire Francaise*. CNRS. Paris. 1976.

Gábori, M. *Les Civilisations du Paléolithique moyen entre les Alpes et l'Oural*. Akademiai Kiado. Budapest. 1976.

Klein, R.G. *Ice Age Hunters of the Ukraine*. University of Chicago Press. Chicago. 1973.

McBurney, C.B.M. *The Haua Fteah*. Cambridge University Press. Cambridge. 1967.

Marks, A.E. (ed.) *Prehistory and Paleoenvironments in the Negev, Israel*, Volume I. Southern Methodist University Press. Dallas. 1976.

Laville, H., Rigaud, J.-P. & Sackett, J. *Rock Shelters of the Périgord*. Academic Press. New York. 1980.

Roe, D.A. *The Lower and Middle Palaeolithic Periods in Britain*. Routledge and Kegan Paul. London. 1981.

Ronen, A. (ed.) *The Transition from Lower to Middle Palaeolithic and the Origin of Modern Man*. BAR International Series 151. Oxford. 1982.

Singer, R. & Wymer, J. *The Middle Stone Age at Klasies River Mouth in South Africa*. University of Chicago Press. Chicago. 1982.

Trinkaus, E. & Howells, W.W. The Neanderthals. *Scientific American* 241, 94–105. 1979.

Wendorf, F. & Schild, R. *A Middle Stone Age Sequence from the Central Rift Valley, Ethiopia*. Polska Akademia Nauk. Wroclaw. 1974.

ECONOMIC APPROACHES

Bailey, G. (ed.) *Hunter-Gatherer Economy in Prehistory*. Cambridge University Press. Cambridge. 1983.

Dennell, R. *European Economic Prehistory: a New Approach*. London. 1983.

Higgs, E. S. *Papers in Economic Prehistory*. Cambridge University Press. Cambridge. 1972.

Clutton-Brock, J. & Grigson, C. (eds.) *Animals and Archaeology I: Hunters and Their Prey*. BAR

International Series 163. Oxford. 1983.

UPPER PALAEOLITHIC AND LATER STONE AGE

Breuil, H. *Four Hundred Centuries of Cave Art*. F. Windels. Montignac. 1952.

Capitain, L., Breuil, H.& Peyrony, D. *La Caverne de Font de Gaume, aux Eyzies*. Monaco. 1910.

Leroi-Gourhan, A. *Préhistoire de l'art occidental*. Paris. Mazenod. 1965.

Leroi-Gourhan, A. *The Dawn of European Art: an Introduction to Palaeolithic Cave Paintings*. Cambridge University Press. Cambridge. 1982.

Marshack, A. *The Roots of Civilization*. Weidenfeld and Nicholson. London. 1972.

Martin, P.S. & Wright, H.E. *Pleistocene Extinctions: the Search for a Cause*. Yale University Press. Yale. 1967.

Rust, A. *Vor 20,000 Jahren: Rentierjäger der Eiszeit*. Karl Wachholtz. Neumünster. 1972.

Taute, W. *Die Stielspitzen-Gruppen im Nördlichen Mitteleuropa*. Bohlau. Cologne. 1968.

Ucko, P.J. & Rosenfeld, A. *Palaeolithic Cave Art*. Weidenfeld and Nicholson. London. 1967.

THE AMERICAS

Bray, W., Swanson, E. & Farrington, I.S. *The New World*. Elsevier. Oxford. 1977.

Browman, D.L. (ed.) *The Earliest Americans*. Mouton. The Hague. 1978.

Browman, D.L. (ed.) *Advances in Andean Archaeology*. Mouton. The Hague. 1978.

Browman, D.L. (ed.) *Cultural Continuity in Mesoamerica*. Mouton. The Hague. 1978.

Bryan, A.L. (ed.) *Early Man in America from a Circum-Pacific Perspective*. Archaeological Researches International. Edmonton. 1978.

Carlisle, R.C. & Adovasio, J.M. (eds.) *Meadowcroft: collected papers*. Pittsburgh. 1982.

Flannery, K.V. (ed.) *The Early Mesoamerican Village*. Academic Press. New York. 1976.

Lynch, T.F. (ed.) *Guitarrero Cave: Early Man in the Andes*. Academic Press. New York. 1980.

AUSTRALIA

Jones, R. Emerging picture of Pleistocene Australians. *Nature* 246, 278–281. 1973.

Keast, A. (ed.) *Ecological Biogeography of Australia*, Volume III. W. Junk. The Hague. 1981.

Mulvaney, D.J. *The Prehistory of Australia*.

Pelican. Harmondsworth. 1975 (revised edn.).

AFRICA

Clark, J.D. *The Prehistory of Africa*. Thames and Hudson, London; Crown, New York. 1970.

Inskeep, R.R. *The Peopling of Southern Africa*. David Philip. Capetown and London. 1978.

Phillipson, D. *The Later Prehistory of Eastern and Southern Africa*. Heinemann Educational. London. 1977.

Sampson, C.G. *The Stone Age Archaeology of Southern Africa*. Academic Press. New York. 1974.

Wendorf, F. (ed.) *The Prehistory of Nubia*. Fort Burgwin, Taos. 1968.

Wendorf, F. & Schild, R. *Prehistory of the Nile Valley*. Academic Press. New York. 1976.

LATER PREHISTORY AND AGRICULTURAL ORIGINS

Clutton-Brock, J. *Domesticated Animals from Early Times*. Heinemann and BMNH. London. 1981.

Harlan, J.R., de Wet, J.M.J. & Stemler, A.B.L. *Origins of African Plant Domestication*. Mouton. The Hague. 1976.

Harris, D.R. Breaking ground: agricultural origins and archaeological explanations. *Institute of Archaeology Bulletin* 18, 1–20.

Jarman, M.R., Bailey, G.N. & Jarman, H.N. (eds.) *Early European Agriculture: its Foundations and Development*. Cambridge University Press. Cambridge. 1982.

Lechevallier, M. *Abou Gosh et Beisamoun*. Association Paléorient. Paris. 1978.

Mellaart, J. *The Neolithic of the Near East*. Thames and Hudson. London. 1975.

Reed, C.A. (ed.) *Origins of Agriculture*. Mouton. The Hague. 1977.

Ucko, P.J. & Dimbleby, G.W. (eds.) *The Domestication and Exploitation of Plants and Animals*. Duckworth. London. 1969.

CIVILIZATIONS

Adams, R. McC. & Nissen, H.J. *The Uruk Countryside*. University of Chicago Press. Chicago. 1972.

Baines, J. & Malek, J. *Atlas of Ancient Egypt*. Phaidon. Oxford. 1980.

Boethius, A. *Etruscan and Early Roman Architecture*. Pelican History of Art. Harmondsworth. 1978.

Braidwood, R.J. & Willey, G.R. (eds.) *Courses Towards Urban Life*. Edinburgh University

Press. Edinburgh. 1977.

Chang, K.C. *The Archaeology of Ancient China*. Yale University Press. Yale. 1977.

Diringer, D. *Writing*. Thames and Hudson. London. 1962.

Fagan, B.M. (ed.) *Avenues to Antiquity*. Readings from Scientific American. Freeman. San Francisco. 1976.

Hammond, N. (ed.) *South Asian Archaeology*. Noyes Books. New Jersey. 1973.

Hinz, W. *The Lost World of Elam*. New York University Press. New York. 1973.

Levi, P. *Atlas of the Greek World*. Phaidon. Oxford. 1980.

Lloyd, S. *The Art of the Ancient Near East*. Thames and Hudson. London. 1961.

Lloyd, S. *The Archaeology of Mesopotamia*. Thames and Hudson. London. 1978.

Moorey, P.R.S. (ed.) *The Origins of Civilization*. Clarendon Press. Oxford. 1979.

Piggott, S. *The Earliest Wheeled Transport, from the Atlantic Coast to the Caspian Sea*. Thames and Hudson. London. 1983.

Postgate, N. *The First Empires*. Elsevier. Oxford. 1977.

Renfrew, A.C. *Before Civilization*. Cape. London. 1973.

Speiser, W. *China, Spirit and Society*. Methuen. London. 1960.

Tylecote, R.F. *A History of Metallurgy*. The Metals Society. London. 1976.

Wheeler, Sir Mortimer *The Indus Civilization*. Cambridge University Press. Cambridge. 1968 (3rd edn.).

Woolley, C.L. *The Sumerians*. Clarendon Press. Oxford. 1928.

JOURNALS

There is not sufficient space to refer to all specialist papers, but the following journals are major sources of up-to-date information: *African Archaeological Review; American Antiquity; American Journal of Physical Anthropology; Antiquity; Archaeometry; Azania* (Journal of the British Institute in Eastern Africa); *Bulletin de la Société Préhistorique Française; Current Anthropology; Gallia Préhistoire; Iraq; Journal of Field Archaeology; Journal of Human Evolution; L'Anthropologie; La Recherche; Man; Nature* (London); *Oceania; Paléorient; Proceedings of the Prehistoric Society; Quaternary Research; Scientific American; South African Archaeological Bulletin; World Archaeology; Wen Wu; Yearbook of Physical Anthropology*.

I am especially grateful to Dr. Mark Newcomer, whose skills in reproducing early technology have made possible many of the photographs in this book; also to Mrs Evelyn Hendy, who found extra time to type the manuscript. I thank all my colleagues in the radiocarbon unit for their interest and support, especially Dr. R.E.M. Hedges and Dr. R. Gillespie. The Oxford radiocarbon unit is supported by S.E.R.C. Several of my colleagues in the Research Laboratory for Archaeology provided photographs or advice: I thank Dr. M.J. Aitken FRS, Dr. N. Debenham, Gillian Spencer and Dr. M. Pollard. I should emphasize that my colleagues are in no way responsible for any scientific misinterpretations which may have crept into the text. My other personal acknowledgements are to those who have made my fieldwork possible: the late Prof. W.W. Bishop and Prof. C.B.M. McBurney; to Prof. Glynn Isaac, and Mr. Richard Leakey; to my colleagues Dr. J.W.K. Harris and Prof. B.A. Wood; to the Government and people of Kenya, and particularly to all of the excavation crews. (*The author directed excavations at Kilombe and was Co-Director with J.W.K. Harris of excavations at Chesowanja*). In writing the book, I have come to hold a strengthened regard for my fellow archaeologists for all that they have achieved in a century and more. This must be very much a book about other people's work, and I am most grateful for the help which I have received, especially for the use of photographs.

J.A.J. Gowlett

Credits

ARTWORK
Ted Hammond, David Johnston, Elaine Keenan, Aziz Khan, Steve Kyte, Simon Roulstone, Tudor Art Studios, John Woodcock. After the following authors: 10–11, R.B. Lee & I. DeVore (1968) (modified); 12, H. Seuanez, *Phylogeny of Human Chromosomes*, Springer, Berlin (1979); 15, J. Napier, *Scientific American* (1967); J. Biegert, *Primatologia* (1961); 26, T.D. White in D.C. Johanson & M.A. Edey (1981); 28–29, V. Maglio, *Nature* 225 (1970); G.J. Kukla in K.W. Butzer and G.Ll. Isaac (eds.) (1975); N.J. Shackleton & N.D. Opdyke, *Quaternary Research* 3 (1973), *Nature* 270 (1977); J.M. Harris & T.D. White, *Transactions of the American Philosophical Society* 69, 2 (1979); 38–39, 54–55, 66–67, 68–69, 71, 81, J.A.J. Gowlett; 48–49, J.A.J. Gowlett & J.W.K. Harris (1981); B. King in Bishop, W.W. (ed.) (1978); 50, M.D. Leakey (1972); 65, C.R. Peters & E.M. O'Brien, *Current Anthropology* 22, 2 (1981); 64–65, J.E. Yellen (1977); 72–73, P. Shipman et al. (1981); 74–75, R.L. Holloway (1974); 86–87, N.J. Shackleton & D.W. Parkin, *Nature* 245 (1973); J. Chappell & H.H. Veeh (1978); 96, J. Mangerud el al. *Nature* 277 (1979); 103, J. Chappell & H.H. Veeh, *Geological Society of America Bulletin*, 89 (1978); G.M. Woillard & W.G. Mook, *Science* 215 (1981); E. van Campo et al., *Nature* 296 (1982); S.J. Johnsen et al., *Nature* 235 (1972); 105, E. Trinkaus & W.W. Howells, *Scientific American* 241 (1979); A.R. Santa Luca, *J. Human Evolution* 7 (1978); 106, J.L. Heim, *Archives de L'Institut de Paléontologie Humaine*, 35; 114, C.B.M. McBurney (1967); 116–117, E. Mironescu in A. Paunescu, *Dacia* IX (1965); 124, M. Gábori (1976); 125, E.S. Higgs & C. Vita-Finzi in Higgs, E.S. (ed.) (1972); 127, (in part) H. Laville et al. (1980); 139, drawing by Joan Goodrum, courtesy of J. Mulvaney; 151, W. Taute (1968); 154–155, K.O. Emery, *Scientific American* 221 (1969); G.L. Kellaway et al., *Philosophical Transactions of the Royal Society* A, 279 (1975); M.J. Tooley (1978); 161, K.M. Kenyon, *Palestine Exploration Quarterly* (1960); 159, J. Harlan & D. Zohary, *Science* 153 (1966); 161, graph after data in J. Clutton-Brock, *Proceedings of the Prehistoric Society* 45 (1979); 167, K.C. Chang (1967), after *Wen Wu*; 174, G.N. Lisitsina, *Antiquity* 43 (1969); 177, (in part) A.C. Renfrew et al., *Proc. Prehist. Soc.* 32 (1966); I. Perlman & J. Yellin in Lechevallier, M. (ed.) (1978); 178, C.L. Woolley, *Ur Excavations*, London and Philadelphia (1934); 183, D. Diringer (1962); after Frau G. Ulbrich in W. Hinz (1964); 196, K.K.S. Dadzie, *Scientific American* 243 (1980); 198, J. Klein et al. (1982); 199, J. Imbrie & K.P. Imbrie (1979)

PHOTOGRAPHS
T *top* B *bottom* C *centre* L *left* R *right*
AAA Photo 10; Prof. J.M. Adovasio 141T; Dr. Martin Aitken 78, 86; Bryan & Cherry Alexander 133, © 1981 Time Life Books B.V. from *People of the World* Series, 150T; Antiquités Préhistoriques d'Aquitaine 128T, 129T & B; Arctic Camera 102; Ashmolean Museum 152C, 172, 184T, 189B; Barnaby's Picture Library 56L; Prof. G. Bosinski 130, 131B; Braunschweigisches Landesmuseum 98B, 112L; British Antarctic Survey 155; British Museum 112R (Michael Holford), 120B (Michael Holford), 123C, 152L, 160, 167, 169 (Michael Holford), 175T, 176T, 180–181, 183, 185L (Michael Holford), 188R (Michael Holford); British Museum (Natural History) 91B, 94–95, 104B; Daniel Cahen 91TL; J. Allan Cash 197; Prof. Desmond Clark 60T, 168B; Bruce Coleman Ltd. 13; Colorphoto Hans Hinz 121, 125; Prof. R.S. Davis 93; Prof. Michael Day 41TL, 101; Prof. Tom Dillehay 140; Dr. Charlie Dortch (Western Australian Museum) 138 T & C, 139; John Dumont 52B, 152T; Explorer Agency 14; Dr. Bernard Fielden 184C; Werner Forman Archive 191B; Friedrich-Schiller Universität, Jena 186; Dr. Diane Gifford (from *Origins* © Rainbird) 34, 35T & B; Richard Gillespie 108, 195; J.A.J. Gowlett 7, 22, 30T (showing Bw. Kimolo Kimeu), 31 (showing Bw. Bernard Kanunga), 32, 33, 45T & B, 47, 68, 69, 70, 72, 73, 81, 92, 106T, 109R (showing Dr. Robert Hedges), 110, 111, 113, 119T, 126, 131T, 148–149, 173, 191TL & TR, 192 TR, 193; Walther Hinz 192L; Hirmer Verlag 165C & B, 179, 187; Michael Holford 165T, 168T, 192BR; courtesy Hungarian National Museum 98T; R.R. Inskeep 144T & BR; Istanbul Museum 9; Dr. Don Johanson (courtesy Dr. J.W.K. Harris) 27B, (courtesy Prof. Bernard Wood) 27T & C, 44; Peter Kain (© Richard Leakey) 41TR, 60B, 66, 67; A. J. Legge 158T; Henri de Lumley 90TR; Prof. Thomas Lynch 142, 143; Dr. W.C. McGrew 12–13, 16; James Mellaart 157T, 176BR, 177; Harry Merrick 30B; Dr. Andrew Moore (© Tell Abu Hureyra Excavation) 158B, 163T; Marion & Tony Morrison 190; Prof. D.J. Mulvaney 137 T & B, 138; Musée d'Antiquités Nationales, St. Germain-en-Laye 120T, 131C, 132, 132–133 (all photos Jean Vertut); Musée Ceruschi 188L (Michael Holford); Musée de l'Homme 106B; National Archaeological Museum, Athens 184B; From P.E. Newberry, *Beni Hassan 1893* (courtesy Egypt Exploration Society) 157B; Dr. Mark Newcomer 52T & C, 56R; Robert S. Peabody Foundation for Archaeology 170; Picturepoint Ltd. 11; Pitt Rivers Museum 144BL, 145; M. Pollard 164; © John Reader 1983: 18, 19, 24, 25, 41B, 119B; Dr. Neil Roberts 175BL & BR; © Roxby Archaeology Ltd (Peter Rauter): 38, 39, 53, 57, 61, 63, 80, 91TR, 95, 115, 122, 123T; Royal Ontario Museum 182; Arthur M. Sackler Foundation 189T; Scala 185R, 194L; Schleswig-Holsteinisches Landes-museum 146; G. Sieveking 90B; Society of Antiquaries (courtesy of Michael Wheeler, Q.C.) 164B; Prof. Ralph Solecki 99, 107, 180B; Gillian Spencer 194R; Dr. Chris Stringer 84; Prof. Erik Trinkhaus 104T, 105, 118; Dr. Charles Turner 90TL, 97; University Museum, University of Pennsylvannia 8, 166B, 176BL; Jean Vertut 128–129, 134; Prof. Fred Wendorf 153; Sir Mortimer Wheeler, from *The Indus Civilisations* (courtesy Michael Wheeler, Q.C.) 162–163; Dr. Ruth Whitehouse 6; Prof. Bernard Wood 59; Roger Wood 147; Prof. D. Yen with permission from *Sunda and Sahul: Prehistoric Studies in South East Asia, Melanesia & Australia*, edited by Allen, Golsen & Jones, 1977 © Academic Press Inc. (London) Ltd. 166T; Dr W. van Zeist 156.

Front Cover Knopf Edition: Acheulean hand-axe, courtesy Dr. Mark Newcomer. © Roxby Archaeology Limited (photographer Peter Rauter) Back Cover: cave painting from Lascaux (colorphoto Hans Hinz)

EDITORS: Louisa McDonnell, Emma Fisher; ART DIRECTION: David Pearce; DESIGN: Karen Blincoe; PICTURE RESEARCH: Caroline Lucas; TYPESETTING Tradespools Limited; REPRODUCTION by F.E. Burman Limited

Index

206